Schaum's Quick Guide to Business Formulas

Schaum's Quick Guide to Business Formulas

201 Decision-Making Tools for Business, Finance, and Accounting Students

Joel G. Siegel, Ph.D., CPA
Financial Consultant
Professor of Finance and Accounting
Queens College

Jae K. Shim, Ph.D.
Financial Consultant
Professor of Finance and Accounting
California State University, Long Beach

Stephen W. Hartman, Ph.D.
Managerial Consultant
Professor of Management
New York Institute of Technology

McGraw-Hill
New York   San Francisco   Washington, D.C.   Auckland   Bogotá
Caracas   Lisbon   London   Madrid   Mexico City   Milan
Montreal   New Delhi   San Juan   Singapore
Sydney   Tokyo   Toronto

Library of Congress Cataloging-in-Publication Data

Siegel, Joel G.
    Schaum's quick guide to business formulas : 201 decision-making tools for business, finance, and accounting students /
Joel G. Siegel, Jae K. Shim, Stephen W. Hartman.
        p.   cm.
    Includes index.
    ISBN 0-07-058031-6
    1. Business enterprises—Finance—Handbooks, manuals, etc.
    2. Corporations—Finance—Handbooks, manuals, etc.   I. Shim, Jae K.
II. Hartman, Stephen.   III. Title.
HG4027.3.S54   1992
    658.15—dc20   97-40332
                                                             CIP

McGraw-Hill

A Division of The McGraw-Hill Companies

15 16 17 DOC/DOC 1 4 3

ISBN 0-07-058031-6

The sponsoring editor for this book was Theodore C. Nardin, the editing supervisor was Jane Palmieri, and the production supervisor was Susan W. Babeuf. It was set in Century Schoolbook by McGraw-Hill's Professional Book Group composition unit.

Printed and bound by R. R. Donnelley & Sons Company.

This book was originally published under the title *The McGraw-Hill Pocket Guide to Business Finance.*

Roberta M. Siegel
Loving Wife and Colleague

Chung Shim
Dedicated Wife

Stephanie R. Hartman
Beautiful Daughter

Alan G. Hartman
Unbelievable Son

ABOUT THE AUTHORS

Joel G. Siegel, Ph.D., CPA, is a financial consultant to companies and professor of finance and accounting at Queens College of the City University of New York. He was previously employed by Coopers and Lybrand, CPAs, and Arthur Andersen, CPAs. Dr. Siegel has acted as a consultant in finance and accounting to such organizations as Citicorp, International Telephone and Telegraph, United Technologies, American Institute of CPAs, and Person-Wolinsky Associates.

Dr. Siegel is the author of 32 books and about 200 articles on financial and accounting topics. His books have been published by McGraw-Hill, Prentice Hall, Harper and Row, Macmillan, John Wiley, Barron's, and the American Institute of CPAs. He has been published in many financial journals, including *The Financial Analysts Journal, Financial Executive,* and *The CPA Journal.*

In 1972, he was the recipient of the Outstanding Educator of America Award. Dr. Siegel is listed in *Who's Where Among Writers* and *Who's Who in the World.*

Jae K. Shim, Ph.D., is professor of finance and accounting at California State University, Long Beach, and president of the National Business Review Foundation, a financial consulting firm. Dr. Shim has many financial consulting responsibilities. He earned his Ph.D. from the University of California at Berkeley.

Dr. Shim has authored 23 professional books and has published many articles in professional journals. He is a recipient of the 1982 Credit Research Foundation Award.

Stephen W. Hartman, Ph.D., is professor in the School of Management at the New York Institute of Technology. He earned his Ph.D. from Syracuse University. Dr. Hartman's experience includes being a registered representative with a major brokerage firm, acting as a financial advisor, authoring a weekly investing column, acting on financial advisory boards, being nominated as the comptroller candidate for Suffolk County, New York, and holding public office as a finance director for the town of Babylon, New York.

In addition to authoring several books, Dr. Hartman has written numerous articles, a Harvard Case Study, and research reports on many areas in finance. He has extensive experience acting as a consultant to business in financial matters.

Contents

Preface

To make life easier for undergraduate and graduate studentms taking accounting, finance, or statistics courses, especially financial statement analysis, this study guide assembles 201 of the most common financial tools—formulas, tables, models—used in business today. A quick scan of the table of contents will show you that the tools range from A (No. 1, Accounts Payable Ratios) to Z (No. 201, Z-Score Model). Each tool is alphabetized, cross-referenced, and numbered to provide you with a handy study reference.

For students broadly familiar with many of the financial analysis concepts described here, this book will supply a reference guide to practical computation for problem solving and decision making. All of the business community's most useful, up-to-date financial problem-solving tools are now available in a single, easy-to-find place that explains what signals to watch out for, when to take action, and how others are interpreting the same business signals. It prepares students for the business world upon graduation.

Leafing through this study guide will provide you with an appreciation of the wide range of analytical tools available to examine how a specific company is performing under current market conditions. The practical applications described for each tool are designed to encourage students to improve the ways through which they measure business activity performance, spot problem areas in advance, and take preventive actions that will keep business activities on the right track.

All of the tools included here are packaged in a format that is intended to be easy-to-read and easy-to-apply. It will help students comprehend better and improve grades on exams and term papers. For each of the 201 tools, you will find:

- A concise definition of the tool and the broad business issue addressed. Tools include ratios, models, statistical methodologies, strategic decision-making processes, and basic rules of thumb.

■ A brief statement of the computational method used to analyse a business problem. In some cases, a series of useful computations are provided (as No. 25, Breakeven Formulas; No. 31, Cash Ratios; and No. 199, Working Capital); in other cases, the computation description provides alternative methods that suit different business situations (as in No. 52, Depreciation Formulas and No. 148, Present Value of an Annuity).

■ Examples of how these tools are used in a practical way, with one or more illustrations based either on company data or situations in which individuals need to analyze a financial problem (as in No. 180, Simple Interest).

■ Identification of the types of individuals that are most likely to rely upon a specific tool, including financial managers, individual and institutional investors, business managers, marketing directors, sales personnel, accountants, creditors, tax analysts, bankers, production supervisors, and plant managers.

The tools range from listings of basic, simple ratios to descriptions of more complex regression analysis and other forms of high-level statistical modeling. This college study guide and reference book describes both simple and complex tools in a way that is understandable and to the point for students seeking a fresh approach to looking at business issues. Whenever possible, students are told which popular computer spreadsheet programs and other computation tools on the market can perform complex analyses in the quickest time, so as to make high-level analyses accessible to the broadest range of students regardless of major.

We hope that you will find this guide helpful, comprehensive, and useful, keeping it within arm's reach when doing homework and studying for tests.

All important accounting and finance topics are presented in a manner to significantly enhance student knowledge of the subject. The study guide is also recommended for students in private study, those seeking college credit by examination, and students preparing for professional examinations such as the Certified Public Accountant (CPA), Certificate in Management Accounting (CMA), and Chartered Financial Analyst (CFA) examinations.

1 Accounts Payable Ratios

DEFINITION. Accounts payable ratios reveal how long it takes a company to pay its suppliers and whether a company is in a good position to obtain short-term credit in the form of cost-free funds.

HOW IS IT COMPUTED? Two accounts payable ratios are commonly used:

1. Sales to accounts payable:

$$\frac{\text{Sales}}{\text{Accounts payable}}$$

2. Accounts payable to average daily purchases (also called "days purchases in accounts payable"):

$$\frac{\text{Accounts payable}}{\text{Purchases/360 days}}$$

Example Assume the following data for two time periods:

	Year 1	Year 2
Accounts payable	$ 50,000	$ 40,000
Purchases	800,000	750,000
Sales	2,000,000	1,300,000

The relevant ratios for each of the years are:

	Year 1	Year 2
Sales to accounts payable	$\dfrac{\$2,000,000}{\$50,000} = 40$	$\dfrac{\$1,300,000}{\$40,000} = 32.5$
Days purchases in accounts payable	$\dfrac{\$50,000}{\$800,000/360} = 22.50$	$\dfrac{\$40,000}{\$750,000/360} = 19.20$

The lower of the two sales-to-accounts payable ratios indicates the company's improved ability in year 2 to obtain short-term credit in the form of cost-free funds.

The decrease in the days purchases in accounts payable has a positive sign, because it indicates that the company is able to repay creditors more quickly in year 2 than in year 1.

HOW IS IT USED AND BY WHOM?

Short-Term Creditors and Financial Management.
Short-term creditors use accounts payable ratios as indicators of a company's financial strength. For example, if trade credit declines, as indicated by an increase

in the ratio of sales to accounts payable, creditors may have less faith in a company's financial health.

The days purchases in accounts payable determines the average number of days that it takes for the company to pay short-term creditors. This ratio is used by creditors and financial management to measure the extent to which accounts payable represents current rather than overdue obligations. These analysts typically make a comparison to the terms of purchase.

A decline in the payment period may indicate that the company is taking advantage of prompt payment discounts or is using shorter purchase terms as leverage in negotiating with suppliers for lower prices. An increase in the payment period may indicate that the company is having financial problems, requiring it to stretch out its payables; on the other hand, this situation could also indicate that the business is managing its payables properly, taking greater advantage of interest-free financing by delaying payments to creditors.

2 Accounts Receivable Management

DEFINITION. Accounts receivable management assists financial credit managers in determining the opportunity cost associated with holding receivable balances. Key components of this type of analysis are a determination of a company's investment in accounts receivable, its discount policy, and relaxation of credit standards—all aspects of receivable management that have an impact on a company's bottom line. Each is discussed below.

1 INVESTMENT IN ACCOUNTS RECEIVABLE

How Is It Computed?

a. Investment in accounts receivable:

$$\frac{\text{Days held}}{360} \times \text{annual credit sales}$$

b. Investment in accounts receivable:

$$\text{Average accounts receivable} \times \text{cost}$$

Example 1 Assume that a company sells on terms of net 30 days, with accounts that are on average 20 days past due. Annual credit sales are $600,000. The company's investment in accounts receivable is:

$$\frac{50}{360} \times \$600,000 = \$83,333.28$$

Example 2 Assume that the cost of a product is 30 percent of its selling price, and that the cost of capital is 10 percent of its selling price. On average, sales are $70,000 per month and accounts are paid 4 months after sale. The investment in accounts receivable from this product is calculated as follows:

Accounts receivable: 4 months × $70,000	$280,000
Investment in accounts receivable: $280,000 × (0.30 + 0.10)	112,000

2 DISCOUNT POLICY.
To determine whether the company should offer a discount for the early payment of accounts receivable, management has to compare the return on freed cash from faster collection versus the cost of the discount, where

Return on freed cash = reduction in average accounts receivable balance

$$\times \text{ rate of return}$$

Example 3 This example illustrates the outcome in one company's situation:

Current annual credit sales	$14,000,000
Collection period	3 months
Terms	net 30
Minimum rate of return	15%

Management is considering offering a 3/10, net 30 discount. Management expects 25 percent of the company's customers to take advantage of this discount. The collection period is expected to decline to 2 months.

The discount should be offered, as indicated by the following analysis.

Advantage of a discount

Increased profitability:

Average accounts receivable balance before a

change in policy: $\dfrac{\text{Credit sales}}{\text{Accounts receivable turnover}} = \dfrac{\$14,000,000}{4} = \$3,500,000$

Average accounts receivable balance after change in policy   2,333,333

Reduction in average accounts receivable balance	$1,166,667
Rate of return	× 0.15
Return	$ 175,000

Disadvantage of a discount

Cost of the discount: 0.03 × 0.25 × $14,000,000	$ 105,000
Net advantage of discount	$ 70,000

3 RELAXATION OF CREDIT STANDARDS.
Management may find it useful to evaluate whether to give credit to marginal customers.

How Is It Computed?

a. Compare the earnings on sales obtained and the added cost of the receivables. In a case where a company has idle capacity, the additional earnings equal the contribution margin on the incremental sales because fixed costs are constant. The additional cost on the additional receivables is derived from the greater number of bad debts and the opportunity cost associated with tying up funds in receivables for a longer time period.

b. New average unit cost = Total cost/units.

c. Additional profitability = additional units × contribution margin per unit.

d. Additional bad debts = additional receivables × bad debt percentage.

e. Opportunity cost in accounts receivable = additional investment in accounts receivable × minimum return.

Example 4 The following illustrates one company's analysis of whether it should relax credit standards.

Sales price per unit	$120
Variable cost per unit	$80
Fixed cost per unit	$15
Annual credit sales	$600,000
Collection period	1 month
Minimum return	16%

If management liberalized the credit policy, the company projected that the following would occur:

- Sales would increase by 40 percent.
- The collection period on total accounts would be 2 months.
- Bad debts on the increased sales would be 5 percent.

Preliminary calculations:

Current units ($600,000/$120)	5,000
Additional units (5,000 × 0.4)	2,000

The new average unit cost was calculated as follows:

	Units ×	Unit cost =	Total cost
Current units	5,000 ×	$95	$475,000
Additional units	2,000 ×	$80	160,000
Total	7,000		$635,000

$$\text{New average unit cost} = \frac{\text{Total cost}}{\text{units}} = \frac{\$635,000}{7,000} = \$90.71 \quad \text{(rounded)}$$

Note that, at idle capacity, fixed cost remained constant. Thus, the incremental cost is just the variable cost of $80 per unit, which would cause the new average unit cost to drop.

Advantage of relaxing credit standards

Additional profitability:

Incremental sales volume	2,000 units
× Contribution margin per unit	
(selling price − variable cost): $120 − $80	× $40
Incremental profitability	$ 80,000

Disadvantage of relaxing credit standards

Incremental bad debts:

Incremental units × selling price:	$240,000
2,000 × $120	
Bad debt percentage	× .05
Additional bad debts	$ 12,000

Opportunity Cost of Funds Tied up in Accounts Receivable

Average investment in accounts receivable after change in policy:

$$\frac{\text{Credit sales}}{\text{Accounts receivable turnover}} \times \frac{\text{Unit cost}}{\text{Selling price}} = \qquad \$105,828$$

$$\frac{\$840,000\text{(a)}}{6} \times \frac{\$90.71}{\$120}$$

(a) 7,000 units × $120 = $840,000

Current average investment in accounts receivable:

$$\frac{\$600,000}{12} \times \frac{\$ 95}{\$120} \qquad 39,583$$

Additional investment in accounts receivable	$ 66,245
× Minimum return	× 0.16
Opportunity cost of funds tied up	$ 10,599

Net Advantage of Relaxation in Credit Standards

Additional earnings		$ 80,000
Less: Additional bad debts	$12,000	
Opportunity cost	10,599	22,599
Net savings		$ 57,401

HOW IS IT USED AND BY WHOM?

Financial and Credit Management. Managers need to monitor their investment in receivables and analyze whether offering a discount would speed up collections, resulting in improved earnings. If excessive funds are tied up in accounts receivable, companies risk draining corporate resources and lowering profitability. Managers must also weigh the risks involved in extending credit to marginal customers against the rewards of increased sales. The management analysis described above reveals whether these moves improve overall profitability despite the fact that receivable balances are outstanding longer.

3 Accounts Receivable Ratios

DEFINITION. Five important accounts receivable ratios indicate how effectively a company is managing its investment in receivables. Accounts receivable turnover—one of the key accounts receivable ratios—indicates how fast the company is collecting from customers. The average collection period is another useful ratio, which indicates the average number of days that receivables are outstanding.

HOW IS IT COMPUTED? The five most useful ratios are listed below.

1. Accounts receivable turnover:

$$\frac{\text{Annual credit sales}}{\text{Average accounts receivable}}$$

Average accounts receivable:

$$\frac{\text{Beginning accounts receivable} + \text{ending accounts receivable}}{2}$$

In determining the turnover ratio, notes receivable generated by normal sales and discounted notes receivable should be included within accounts receivable. If sales vary greatly during the year, monthly or quarterly sales figures should be used to achieve proper averaging so that the ratio is not distorted.

2. Average collection period:

$$\frac{365}{\text{Accounts receivable turnover}}$$

3. Trend in accounts receivable:

Accounts receivable (last year) − accounts receivable (this year)

4. Accounts receivable by total assets:

$$\frac{\text{Accounts receivable}}{\text{Total assets}}$$

5. Accounts receivable by sales:

$$\frac{\text{Accounts receivable}}{\text{sales}}$$

To judge the appropriateness of a company's collection and credit policy, a company's ratios must be compared with industry norms or ratios of major competitors within the same industry.

Example A company reports the following data for the years ended December 31, 19X1, and December 31, 19X2.

	19X1	19X2
Sales	$400,000	$500,000
Total assets	600,000	650,000
Accounts receivable	50,000	90,000

On January 1, 19X1, accounts receivable was $45,000.

For this company, three ratios are used to analyze accounts receivables:

	19X1	19X2
a. Accounts receivable turnover (sales/average accounts receivable)	$\dfrac{\$400,000}{\$47,500} = 8.42$	$\dfrac{\$500,000}{\$70,000} = 7.14$
b. Collection period (365/turnover)	$\dfrac{365}{8.42} = 43.3$ days	$\dfrac{365}{7.14} = 51.1$ days
c. Accounts receivable to total assets	$\dfrac{\$50,000}{\$600,000} = 8.3\%$	$\dfrac{\$90,000}{\$650,000} = 13.8\%$

In this example, the realization risk in accounts receivable is higher in 19X2. This is shown by a lower turnover rate, a longer collection period, and a higher ratio of accounts receivable to total assets in that year.

HOW IS IT USED AND BY WHOM?

Management. Accounts receivable ratios are determined to appraise the degree of realization risk in accounts receivable. In general, higher accounts receivable turnovers are good indicators of successful companies, since they show that these companies collect quickly from customers and are thus in a better position to invest funds. An excessively high ratio, however, may indicate that the company's credit policy is too stringent, and the company is not tapping its profit potential through sales to higher-risk customers. Before changing its credit policy, a company should weigh the profit potential against the risk inherent in selling to more marginal customers. (See No. 2, Accounts Receivable Management, for a discussion of reward analysis.)

In terms of the collection period, the longer receivables are outstanding beyond the expected payment date relative to industry norms, the lower is the probability of collection. Management should analyze separate collection periods by type of customer, major product line, and market territory. Use of an aging schedule is helpful. Note that in some cases, however, a longer collection period may be justified for example, in a company that has extended its credit terms in connection with the introduction of a new product or to meet heightened competition within the industry.

A sharp rise in accounts receivable relative to the previous year may infer higher realization risk. This could suggest that the company is selling to more marginal-credit customers. Management must examine the trends in accounts receivable to total assets and in accounts receivable to sales to identify unusual increases in receivables.

Short-Term Creditors. Accounts receivable ratios are examined by short-term creditors as an indication of corporate *liquidity*. A high turnover ratio and short collection period—indications that a company is able to collect quickly from customers—is looked upon favorably by creditors.

4 Acid-Test (Quick) Ratio

DEFINITION. The acid-test or quick ratio is a stringent test of liquidity that compares the most liquid current (quick) assets to current debt.

HOW IS IT COMPUTED?

$$\frac{\text{Cash} + \text{market securities} + \text{accounts receivable}}{\text{Current liabilities}}$$

Inventory is not included in the acid-test ratio calculation because of the length of time needed to convert inventory into cash. (Note that certain types of inventory can actually be more liquid than slow-paying receivables.) Additionally, prepaid expenses are not included in this analysis because they cannot be converted into cash and thus are not capable of covering current liabilities.

In general, the acid-test ratio must at least be.1:1, but determination of an adequate ratio depends on the characteristics of the particular industry under examination. Comparisons to competing companies must also be made.

Example The following balance sheet information for a company is available for 19X1 and 19X2:

	19X1	19X2
Quick assets	$160,000	$150,000
Current liabilities	140,000	155,000

The acid-test ratios are 1.14 for 19X1 and 0.97 for 19X2. The decrease in the ratio from 19X1 to 19X2 indicates a decline in company liquidity—for example, in 19X2, for every $1 in current debt, only $0.97 in quick assets existed to cover it.

HOW IS IT USED AND BY WHOM?

Short-Term Creditors. A significant decline in the quick ratio indicates deterioration in the company's liquidity, which could indicate the company's inability to satisfy its maturing debt immediately, if it had to do so.

Financial Management. A lower quick ratio may mean that the company will have greater difficulty borrowing short-term funds. A very low ratio may indicate that the company will be unable to meet its short-term debt payments.

5 Actual Cash Value

DEFINITION. In insurance policies, actual cash value (ACV) refers to the original cost of property minus depreciation over years of use.

HOW IS IT COMPUTED?

$$ACV = P - \left[CA \times \left(\frac{P}{n} \right) \right]$$

where P = purchase price of the item
  CA = current age in years
  n = expected life in years.

Example Suppose that your 6-year-old VCR was stolen. A new VCR costs $400 and has an expected life of 8 years. ACV is

$$\$400 - \left[6 \times \left(\frac{\$400}{8} \right) \right] = \$100$$

HOW IS IT USED AND BY WHOM?

Individuals and Insurance Agents. ACV may be the basis for reimbursement when a claim is made for loss under an insurance policy.

6 Adjusted Gross Income

DEFINITION. For tax purposes, adjusted gross income (AGI) is the difference between a taxpayer's gross income and any adjustments to that income.

HOW IS IT COMPUTED?

Gross income
Less: Individual retirement account (IRA) deduction
    One-half of self-employment tax
    Self-employed health insurance deduction
    Keogh retirement deduction
    Penalty on early withdrawal of savings
    Alimony payment
Equals adjusted gross income

Example Suppose that a taxpayer's gross income is $130,000. Adjustments to gross income include $10,000 in alimony paid, $200 penalty on early withdrawal of savings, and a $5,000 Keogh pension contribution. The calculation of the adjusted gross income is:

$$\$130,000 - \$10,000 - \$200 - \$5,000 = \$114,800$$

HOW IS IT USED AND APPLIED? AGI is the basis for determining the eligibility of and limitations for other components of the taxpayer's tax—for example, to calculate medical expenses (7.5 percent of AGI) or miscellaneous expenses (2 percent of AGI).

7 Alpha Value

DEFINITION. The alpha value of a security, also called the *average differential return*, is the excess return that would be expected on the security if the excess return on the market portfolio were zero. In the context of a mutual fund, the alpha value represents the difference between the return on a fund and a point on the market line that corresponds to a beta (see No. 19, Beta) equal to the fund, where the market line describes the relationship between excess returns and the portfolio beta.

HOW IS IT COMPUTED?

$$\text{Alpha} = \text{beta} \times (r_m - r_f)$$

where r_m = market return and r_f is the risk-free rate.

Example 1 If the market return (r_m) is 8 percent and the risk-free rate (r_f) is 5 percent, the market excess return ($r_m - r_f$) equals 3 percent. A portfolio with a beta of 1 should expect to earn a market rate of excess return ($r_m - r_f$) equal to 3 percent (1 × 3%).
  A fund with a beta of 1.5 should provide excess returns of 4.5 (1.5 × 3%).

HOW IS IT USED AND APPLIED? Alpha value has been used to evaluate the performance of mutual funds. Generally, a positive alpha (excess return) indicates superior performance, while a negative alpha leads to the opposite conclusion.

Example 2 The fund in Example 1 has a beta of 1.5, which indicates an expected excess return of 4.5 percent along the market line, but actual excess return was only 4.1 percent. This means that the fund has a negative alpha of 0.4 percent (4.1% - 4.5%). The fund's performance is therefore inferior to that of the market.

WHO USES IT AND WHEN?

Investors and Fund Managers. "Keep your alpha high and your beta low" is a basic strategy for those who wish to generate good investment performance. Key questions for fund managers are:

1. Can the company perform consistently at positive alpha levels?
2. Can the company generate returns better than those that are available along the market line?

8 Amortized Loan

DEFINITION.   An amortized loan is one that is paid off in equal periodic installments and includes varying portions of principal and interest during its term. Examples include auto loans, mortgage loans, and most commercial loans.

HOW IS IT COMPUTED?   There are two ways to find the periodic amortized amount:

1. Divide the principal loan amount (A) by PVIFA, which is a factor shown in Table 4 of the Appendix (Present Value Interest Factor of an Annuity of $1); that is,

$$\text{Amount of loan} = A = \frac{P}{\text{PVIFA}}$$

2. Use a table such as Table 5 in the Appendix (a table of monthly installment loan payments), which provides the monthly payment required to retire a $1000 installment loan for a selected annual interest rate and term.

Example 1   Assume that a firm borrows $2000 to be repaid in three equal installments at the end of each of the next three years. The bank charges 12 percent interest. The amount of each payment is

$$P = \$2000$$

$$\text{PVIFA}(12\%, 3 \text{ years}) = 2.402$$

Therefore,

$$A = \frac{\$2000}{2.402} = \$832.64$$

Example 2   Jerry takes out a $15,000, 48-month loan at 12 percent interest. He wants to determine the monthly installment loan payment.
  Using Table 5, he completes the following three steps.

Step 1. Divide the loan amount by $1,000:

$$\frac{\$15,000}{\$1,000} = 15$$

Step 2. Find the payment factor from Table 5 for the specific interest rate and loan maturity. In this case, the Table 5 payment factor for 12 percent and 48 months is $26.34.

Step 3. Multiply the factor obtained in step 2 by the amount from step 1:

$$\$26.34 \times 15 = \$395.10$$

Jerry's monthly installment loan payment is $395.10.

HOW IS IT USED AND APPLIED?   Once the periodic loan amount has been computed, a *loan amortization schedule* can be developed. Each loan payment consists partly of interest and partly of principal. The interest component of the payment is largest in the first period (because the principal balance is the highest) and subsequently declines, whereas the principal portion is smallest in the first period (because of the high interest) and increases thereafter.

Example 3 Using the same data as in Example 1, the following amortization schedule is established:

Year	Payment	Interest	Repayment of principal	Remaining balance
0				$2,000.00
1	$832.64	$240.00[a]	$592.64[b]	1,407.36
2	832.64	168.88	663.76	743.60
3	832.64	89.23	743.41[c]	

[a]Interest is computed by multiplying the loan balance at the beginning of the year by the interest rate. Therefore, interest in year 1 is $2,000(0.12) = $240; interest in year 2 is $1,407.36(0.12) = $168.88; and interest in year 3 is $743.60(0.12) = $89.23. (All figures are rounded.)

[b]The reduction in principal equals the payment less the interest portion ($832.64 − $240.00 = $592.64).

[c]Not exact because of accumulated rounding errors.

WHO USES IT AND WHEN?

Lenders. Lenders working for banks and finance companies must be able to calculate the periodic payment amount, and break it down into principal-reduction and interest portions, and apply the payment properly to separate loan accounts for each borrower.

Consumers and Borrowers. Borrowers need to know the amount of the periodic payment and, perhaps more important, how to determine how much they can save in total interest if they prepay before maturity.

9 Annual Percentage Rate

DEFINITION. Annual percentage rate (APR) is a true measure of the effective cost of credit—the ratio of the finance charge to the average amount of credit in use during the life of the loan, expressed as a percentage rate per year.

HOW IS IT COMPUTED? The following discussion explains how the effective APR is calculated for various types of loans, including single-payment and installment loans.

Single-Payment Loans. A single-payment loan is paid in full on a given date. There are two ways of calculating APR on single-payment loans: the simple interest method and the discount method. The difference between the two is in the amount the borrower actually receives.

1 Simple interest method. Under the simple interest method, interest is calculated only on the amount borrowed (proceeds). The formulas for the simple interest method are

$$\text{Interest} = \text{Principal} \times \text{rate} \times \text{time} = p \times r \times t$$

$$\text{APR} = \frac{\text{average annual finance charge}}{\text{Amount borrowed or proceeds}}$$

Under the simple interest method, the stated simple interest rate and the APR are always the same for single-payment loans.

Example 1 Kim took out a single-payment loan of $1000 for 2 years at a simple interest rate of 15 percent. The interest charge will be ($1000 × 15% × 2 years) = $300. Hence the APR is

$$\text{APR} = \frac{\$150}{\$1000} = 15\%$$

2 Discount method. Under the discount method, the borrower prepays the finance charges. The interest is determined and then deducted from the amount of the loan.

The discount method always gives a higher APR than the simple interest method for single-payment loans at the same interest rate.

Example 2 Using the same figures as in Example 1, the amount actually received is $1000 − $300 = $700—not $1000. Thus, the APR is

$$\text{APR} = \frac{\$150}{\$700} = 21.43\%$$

Therefore, the rate the lender must quote on the loan is 21.43 percent, not 15 percent.

Installment Loans. Most consumer loans use the add-on method. The methods for calculating the APR on add-on loans are: (1) the actuarial method, (2) the constant-ratio method, (3) the direct-ratio method, and (4) the N-ratio method.

The *actuarial method* is the most accurate in calculating the APR and the one lenders use most. It can be defined as interest computed on unpaid balances of principal at a fixed rate, with each payment applied first to interest and the remainder to principal. Since calculation by this method involves complicated formulas, annuity tables or computer programs are commonly used.

The *constant-ratio method* is used to approximate the APR on an installment loan by the use of a simple formula, but this method overstates the rate substantially. The higher the quoted rate, the greater is the inaccuracy of the method. The constant-ratio formula is

$$\text{APR} = \frac{2MC}{P(N + 1)}$$

where M = number of payment periods in one year
$\quad\;\; N$ = number of scheduled payments
$\quad\;\; C$ = finance charges in dollars (dollar cost of credit)
$\quad\;\; P$ = original proceeds

The *direct-ratio method* has a more complex formula than the above but is easier than the actuarial method. Compared to the actuarial method, the direct-ratio method understates the APR slightly. The direct-ratio formula is

$$\text{APR} = \frac{6MC}{3P(N + 1) + C(N + 1)}$$

For most loans, the *N-ratio method* gives a much more accurate approximation to the APR than either the constant-ratio or the direct-ratio method. The results of the *N*-ratio method may be either slightly higher or lower than the true rate, depending on the maturity of the loan and the stated rate itself. The *N*-ratio formula is

$$\text{APR} = \frac{M(95N + 9)C}{12N(N + 1)(4P + C)}$$

Example 3 Assume that Kim borrows $1000 to be repaid in 12 equal monthly installments of $93.00 each with a finance charge of $116.00. Assuming that an annuity table or computer program gives an APR of 20.76 percent, the APR under each of the four methods is computed as follows.

Actuarial method: The APR under this method is 20.76 percent, obtained from an annuity table or computer program.

Constant-ratio method:

$$\text{APR} = \frac{2MC}{P(N + 1)}$$

$$= \frac{2 \times 12 \times 116}{1,000(12 + 1)} = \frac{2,784}{13,000} = 21.42\%$$

Direct-ratio method:

$$\text{APR} = \frac{6MC}{3P(N + 1) + C(N + 1)}$$

$$= \frac{6 \times 12 \times 116}{3 \times 1,000(12+1) + 116(12 + 1)} = \frac{8,352}{40,508} = 20.62\%$$

N-ratio method:

$$\text{APR} = \frac{M(95N + 9)C}{12N(N + 1)(4P + C)}$$

$$= \frac{12(95 \times 12 + 9) \times 116}{12 \times 12 \times 13 \times [4(1,000) + 116]} = \frac{1,599,408}{7,705,152} = 20.76\%$$

These approximation formulas should not be used if any variation exists in the amounts of payments or in the time periods between payments—for example, balloon payments or extended-first-payment loans.

Note that some lenders charge fees for a credit investigation, a loan application, or life insurance. When these fees are required, the lender must include them in addition to the finance charge in dollars as part of the APR calculations.

HOW IS IT USED AND APPLIED?   The lender is required by the Truth in Lending Act (Consumer Credit Protection Act) to disclose to a borrower the effective *annual percentage rate (APR)* as well as the finance charge in dollars.

Banks often quote their interest rates in terms of dollars of interest per hundred dollars. Other lenders quote in terms of dollars per payment. These different practices often lead to confusion among borrowers, but fortunately APR can eliminate this confusion.

WHO USES IT AND WHEN?

Borrowers.   By comparing the APRs of different loans, the borrower is able to compare the costs of the loans and to shop for the best deal.

Example 4   Which of the two quotes below offers Kim the best deal on her auto loan?

Bank A offers a 7 percent car loan if Kim puts 25 percent down. If she buys a $4000 auto, therefore, she will finance $3000 over a 3-year period with carrying charges amounting to $630 (7% × $3000 × 3 years = $630). She will make equal monthly payments of $100.83 for 36 months.

Bank B will lend Kim $3500 on the same car. Use of the constant-ratio formula shows that Kim must pay $90 per month for 48 months.

The APR calculations (using the constant-ratio formula) follow:

$$\text{Bank A:} \quad \text{APR} = \frac{2 \times 12 \times 630}{3,000(36 + 1)} = \frac{15,120}{111,000} = 13.62\%$$

$$\text{Bank B:} \quad \text{APR} = \frac{2 \times 12 \times 820}{3,500(48 + 1)} = \frac{19,680}{171,500} = 11.48\%$$

For Bank B, it was necessary to multiply $90 × 48 months to arrive at a total cost of $4320. Therefore, the total cost of credit is $4320 − $3500 = $820. Based on the APR, Kim should choose Bank B over Bank A.

10 Applied (Predetermined) Overhead Rate

DEFINITION.   An applied overhead rate is a rate determined at the beginning of a period to apply overhead based on actual production for the same period. This rate is commonly used to apply factory overhead to a given job, product, or production department.

HOW IS IT COMPUTED?

$$\text{Applied overhead rate} = \frac{\text{budgeted annual overhead}}{\substack{\text{budgeted annual activity units} \\ \text{(direct labor hours, machine hours, etc.)}}}$$

Example   Assume a case in which the predetermined overhead rate is based on machine hours. Budgeted overhead is $200,000 and budgeted machine hours are 100,000. The applied overhead rate is calculated as

$$\frac{\$200,000}{100,000} = \$2 \text{ per machine hour}$$

During the year, actual machine hours were 96,000. Actual overhead was $198,000. The variance is calculated as follows:

Actual overhead	$198,000
Applied overhead (96,000 hours × $2)	192,000
Underapplied overhead	$ 6,000

HOW IS IT USED AND BY WHOM?

Cost Accountants, Management, and Marketing Managers. Applied overhead is used to determine uniform unit cost figures for each period in a seasonal business. These cost figures are more representative than actual cost figures which are distorted because of seasonal activity.

Predetermined overhead rates also provide for more rapid product costing, which gives management more rapid cost information. Since individual jobs or products are priced once they are completed, immediate pricing data is available.

11 Arbitrage

DEFINITION.   The process of simultaneously buying and selling the same or complementary securities or commodities in different markets is called arbitrage. True arbitrage is a riskless transaction. Arbitrage takes advantage of market inefficiencies while eliminating them in the process. Those engaging in arbitrage are known as arbitragers.

HOW IS IT COMPUTED?

Stock or Commodities.   Arbitrage takes advantage of the price differential between the same or comparable securities or commodities trading simultaneously on two different exchanges. An arbitrager purchases the security on the exchange with the lower price and simultaneously sells it on the exchange with the higher price:

$$\pi = (Y_b - X_a) \times Q$$

where π = arbitrage profit
  Y_b = price of higher-priced comparable security or commodity on Exchange B
  X_a = price of lower-priced comparable security or commodity on Exchange A
  Q = quantity

Currencies.   Arbitrage can also be applied to foreign currency trading. Here the computation is relatively straightforward:

Arbitrage profits = investment receipts − loan payments

When arbitraging currencies, hedging practices consist of buying forward contracts. The cost of the forward contract is a discount on the future value of the investment. This results in an adjusted currency exchange ratio:

Adjusted exchange ratio = exchange ratio +

discount rate of currency forward contract

Example 1: Stock   Stock XYZ is trading on the New York Stock Exchange for $5 per share and trading simultaneously on the London Exchange for $5.50 per share. A member broker buys 5000 shares of the stock on the New York Stock Exchange and simultaneously sells 5000 shares on the London Exchange. The profit is:

$$P = (Y_b - X_a) \times Q$$

$$= (\$5.50 - \$5.00) \times 5000$$

$$= \$0.50 \times 5000$$

$$= \$2500$$

The arbitrage profit is $2500. Note that this and similar transactions increase the demand and therefore the price of the New York Stock Exchange security and simultaneously lower the price of the security traded on the London Exchange. This impact continues until the prices of the two securities are in parity.

Example 2: Currencies   Arbitrage can also be applied to currency trading. Suppose that a company borrows $500,000 in New York for 90 days at 7 percent and converts it, at the current market rate of 1.5 marks to the dollar, into 750,000 German marks. The German marks are then invested at 9 percent interest for 90 days.

Arbitrage profit = investment receipts − loan payments

$$= \frac{(DM750,000 \times 0.09)/4}{1.5} - \frac{(\$500,000 \times 0.07)}{4}$$

$$= \$11,250.00 - \$8,750.00$$

In this case a covering transaction is also made to protect the transaction against currency fluctuations. To this end, a forward contract is sold for the proceeds of the investment at a 1 percent discount. Thus, adjusting for the 1 percent discount of the forward contract, the adjusted exchange rate is 1.5 + 0.01 = 1.51.

The adjusted arbitrage profit is now

$$\text{Arbitrage profit} = \frac{(DM750,000 \times 0.09)/4}{1.51} - \frac{(\$500,000 \times 0.07)}{4}$$

$$= \$11,175.50 - \$8,750.00$$

$$= \$2,425.50$$

The arbitrage transaction increases the demand for funds in New York while increasing the supply of funds in Germany. This raises the interest rate in New York while lowering it in Germany, so that eventually no further arbitrage profits are possible.

HOW IS IT USED AND APPLIED? The arbitrage method is used to attempt a riskless transaction between two identical or comparable securities or commodities. It takes advantage of price differentials between the same security or commodity trading on two different exchanges or in arbitraging two different international currency interest rates.

WHO USES IT AND WHEN?

Commodities and Securities Traders. Arbitrage is used when seeking to exploit the price differences between the same or comparable securities on two different exchanges. These opportunities exist for very fleeting periods of time, requiring traders to act quickly in order to take advantage of the differences.

Financial Managers. Managers often seek to take advantage of international interest-rate differentials for various currencies. These transactions are hedged by using forward contracts and currency options in order to guard against fluctuations in currency exchange ratios.

12 Arithmetic Average Return

DEFINITION. Arithmetic average (mean) is a measure of return over a single holding period or over multiple periods. An alternative measure of multiperiod average (mean) returns is the *geometric average return*.

HOW IS IT COMPUTED? The arithmetic average return is simply the arithmetic average of successive one-period rates of return. It is defined as

$$\text{Arithmetic return} = \frac{1}{n} \cdot \sum r_i$$

where n is the number of time periods and r_i is the single-holding-period return (HPR) in time t.

Example Consider the following data, where the price of a stock doubles in one period and then depreciates back to the original price. Assume no dividends.

	Time period		
	$t = 0$	$t = 1$	$t = 2$
Price (end of period)	$50	$100	$50

The holding-period return (HPR) for periods 1 and 2 is computed as follows:

$$\text{Period 1 } (t = 1): \quad \text{HPR} = \frac{\$0 + (\$100 - \$50)}{\$50} = \frac{\$50}{\$50} = 100\%$$

$$\text{Period 2 } (t = 2) \quad \text{HPR} = \frac{\$0 + (\$50 - \$100)}{\$100} = \frac{-\$50}{\$100} = -50\%$$

Therefore, the arithmetic average return is the average of 100 percent and −50 percent, which is 25 percent, as shown below:

$$\frac{100\% + (-50\%)}{2} = 25\%$$

WHO USES IT AND WHEN?

Investors. When an investor holds an investment for more than one period, it is important to understand how to compute the average of the successive rates of return. The arithmetic average return, however, can be quite misleading in multiperiod return calculations. (See No. 80, Geometric Average Return.)

13 Asset Utilization (Turnover)

DEFINITION. Asset utilization, or turnover, indicates the efficiency with which corporate assets generate revenue.

HOW IS IT COMPUTED? Several types of calculations are commonly used to analyze asset utilization. Each involves an examination of the ratio of sales to some other aspect of a company's assets.

1. Total asset turnover:

$$\frac{\text{Sales}}{\text{Total assets}}$$

2. Sales to specific assets:

  a. Sales to cash:

$$\frac{\text{Sales}}{\text{Cash}}$$

  b. Accounts receivable ratio:

$$\frac{\text{Sales}}{\text{Accounts Receivable}}$$

  c. Inventory ratio:

$$\frac{\text{Sales}}{\text{Inventory}}$$

  d. Sales to working capital:

$$\frac{\text{Sales}}{\text{Working capital}}$$

  e. Fixed asset turnover:

$$\frac{\text{Sales}}{\text{Fixed assets}}$$

f. Sales to other assets:

$$\frac{\text{Sales}}{\text{Other assets}}$$

Higher ratios reflect favorably on the company's ability to employ assets effectively.

Example Implications of the use of the total asset turnover ratio are illustrated by comparing the performance of two companies:

	Company A	Company B
Sales	$ 1,000,000	$20,000,000
Total assets	10,000,000	10,000,000
Turnover of assets	0.1 times	2 times

This analysis shows that for Company A, each dollar invested in assets supports only $0.10 in sales, whereas Company B obtains $2 of sales for each dollar invested in assets. The appropriate question that should be prompted by this analysis is to ask why Company A's turnover is so low. Are there excess assets that generate little or no return? Are there idle assets that Company A should dispose of? Are the assets inefficiently or uneconomically utilized?

The conclusion of this analysis is that Company A can achieve more immediate and significant improvements by concentrating on improving turnover—by either increasing sales, reducing its investment, or both.

HOW IS IT USED AND BY WHOM?

Management and Financial Analysts. Managers and financial analysts understand that assets should not be held by an enterprise unless they contribute to sales or profitability; thus, utilization of many of these turnover ratios is critical to understanding the productivity of assets. Higher ratios of asset utilization are better because they indicate that assets are more productive in obtaining a return. A high ratio for one industry, however, may be considered a low ratio for another.

In certain special situations, such as developmental companies, the meaning of asset turnover may have to be modified because most assets are committed to the development of future potential. Similarly, if abnormal supply situations exist or if strikes occur, these factors affect capital utilization and require separate evaluation and interpretation.

The following provides some guidance to interpreting high and low ratios:

- A high ratio of sales to cash may be caused by a cash shortage that could eventually result in a liquidity crisis if the company has no other ready sources of funds. A low turnover may also indicate the holding of idle cash balances, resulting in less return being earned. Cash accumulated for specific purposes or contingencies may result in a temporary drop in the turnover ratio.

- A low ratio of sales to receivables may indicate overextension of credit, and collection problems. A high ratio may point to an overly stringent credit policy.

- A low ratio of sales to inventory may indicate overstocking, slow-moving goods, overestimation of sales, or a lack of balance in inventory. A temporary problem, such as a strike at a major customer, may also be responsible. A high turnover may represent underinvestment in inventory, which can cause deficient customer service and lost sales.

- A low ratio of sales to fixed assets may signal inefficient or obsolete equipment, excess capacity, or interruptions in the supply of raw materials.

14 Audit Fees to Sales

DEFINITION. The ratio of audit fees to sales reveals the fee charged by the accounting firm in auditing the company's financial records relative to sales.

HOW IS IT COMPUTED?

$$\frac{\text{Audit fees}}{\text{Sales}}$$

Example Suppose that a company reports the following:

	19X1	19X2
Professional accounting fees	$ 80,000	$ 200,000
Sales	3,000,000	3,500,000

The ratio of audit fees to sales is $80,000/$3,000,000 = 0.03 for 19X1 and $200,000/$3,500,000 = 0.06 for 19X2.

Why the sudden increase in audit fees? Was it because more audit time was required because of problems with the company's financial records or internal control structure? Was the audit report date delayed? The sharp increase in audit fees raises many questions and concerns. However, an explanation might be that the company switched from a small CPA firm to a "Big 6" CPA firm, or that the company merged with another.

HOW IS IT USED AND BY WHOM?

Management, Investors, and Creditors. A significant increase in accounting fees may imply that accounting errors were found or that other irregularities exist.

15 Average (Arithmetic Mean)

DEFINITION. The average, or arithmetic mean, is the sum of a set of numbers divided by the number of values in the set. The average is a measure of central tendency.

HOW IS IT COMPUTED? The formula for calculating an average is:

$$\bar{x} = \frac{\sum x}{n}$$

The average (mean) equals the sum of the data divided by the quantity of data observations.

Example Suppose that an investor buys 100 shares of XYZ stock at its perceived lowest price in a given trading week every week for 10 weeks. At the end of the 10 weeks, the investor wishes to know the average per-share purchase price for the stock over the 10-week trading period. The calculation of the average per-share price follows:

Week	Price per share
1	$15.00
2	12.00
3	13.25
4	11.00
5	10.50
6	14.00
7	12.50
8	15.50
9	12.75
10	10.00

$$\text{Average} = \frac{15 + 12 + 13.25 + 11 + 10.5 + 14 + 12.5 + 15.5 + 12.75 + 10}{10}$$

$$= \frac{126.50}{10} = \$12.65$$

HOW IS IT USED AND APPLIED? Average analysis is necessary in almost all aspects of financial analysis. Averaging is essential in detecting trends within a period of time. For example, it may be essential for a company to know its average daily sales within a particular period of time in order to adjust inventory levels. Average daily sales would be calculated by dividing total sales by the total number of days.

Note that an extreme value in the set of numbers can have a disproportionate influence on the computation of the average. Thus, in the example of trading the XYZ stock, if in Week 6 the lowest price was $25 per share rather than $14 per share, the total of XYZ stock would be $141 and the average would be $14.10 rather than $12.65.

The average can assume a value that is not present in the set of numbers being calculated. For example, the average of 1, 3, 5, is 4.5, even though the value of each observation is an integer. This can lead to an impractical conclusion regarding generalization of the discrete data.

WHO USES IT AND WHEN?

Managers and Financial Analysts. Averaging is an essential statistic for understanding the general trend of a given group of data. An average allows the analyst to focus on the central tendency of a data set without being distracted by unique differences. If there are extreme deviations in a few of the data observations, however, use of median analysis may be more appropriate. (See No. 118, Median.)

16 Bad-Debt Ratios

DEFINITION. Bad-debt ratios measure expected uncollectibility on credit sales. An increase in bad debts is a negative sign, since it indicates greater realization risk in accounts receivable and possible future write-offs.

HOW IS IT COMPUTED?

1. Bad debts to sales:

$$\frac{\text{Bad debts}}{\text{Sales}}$$

2. Bad debts to accounts receivable:

$$\frac{\text{Bad debts}}{\text{Accounts receivable}}$$

Example Suppose, for example, that a company reports the following financial data:

	19X1	19X2
Sales	$100,000	$130,000
Accounts receivable	30,000	40,000
Bad Debts	2,000	2,200

The financial analyst concludes that the company is selling to more risky customers in 19X2 relative to 19X1.

The results of the relevant ratios follow:

	19X1	19X2
Bad debts to sales	2.0%	1.7%
Bad debts to accounts receivable	6.7%	5.5%

Since the firm is selling to more risky customers, its bad debt provision should rise in 19X2; however, the ratios of (1) bad debts to sales and (2) bad debts to accounts receivable actually went down. The effect of understanding the bad-debt provision is to overstate net income and accounts receivable. Hence, net income should be reduced for the incremental earnings arising from the unrealistic lowering of bad debts. If the financial analyst decides that a realistic bad-debt percentage-to-accounts receivable ratio is 6.5 percent, then the bad-debt expense should be $40,000 × 6.5% = $2,600. Net income should thus be reduced by $400 ($2,600 less $2,200).

HOW IS IT USED AND BY WHOM?

Financial Analysts. Investment and credit analysts examine trends in bad-debt ratios. Unwarranted reductions in bad-debt provisions lower the quality of earnings. This can occur when there is a reduction in bad debts even though the company is selling to less creditworthy customers and/or actual bad-debt losses are on the rise.

Firms that intentionally overstate bad-debt provisions to establish accounting cushions will report understated earnings. A company may attempt to manage its earnings by first increasing and then lowering its bad-debt provision.

Firms that provide substantial bad-debt allowances in the current year because inadequate provisions for bad debts were made in previous years distort their earnings trends. Firms that take sudden, substantial accounts receivable write-offs may have previously understated their bad-debt expense provisions.

17 Bank Reconciliation

DEFINITION. Preparation of a bank reconciliation is based on information contained in a bank statement—deposits made, checks cleared, and charges or credits (deductions or additions) to the account. For example, a bank charge is a deduction from a company's account, whereas the amount collected on a customer's note is an addition. Canceled checks, debit memoranda for charges, and credit memoranda for credits are typically enclosed with the bank statement.

The ending balance in the bank statement rarely agrees with the ending balance in the cash account according to the books; thus, a bank reconciliation is required to reflect the reconciling items. Once completed, the adjusted bank balance must match the adjusted book balance. When this occurs, both records are correct.

HOW IS IT COMPUTED? The cash balance per the books must be the same as the balance in the bank account at the end of the period. Reconciling differences relate to (1) items shown on the company's books but not on the bank statement and (2) items shown on the bank statement but not on the depositor's books. Examples and explanations of each follow.

Reconciling Items for the Bank Statement. The bank balance is adjusted for several types of items that are reflected on the company's books but not on the bank statement.

Outstanding checks: Checks that have been issued by the company but have not yet cleared the bank. The total of the outstanding checks is deducted from the bank balance. (An exception is an uncleared certified check—a check for which the bank immediately sets aside funds for payment. A certified check is not considered outstanding, since both parties—the company and the bank—know about it.)

Deposits in transit: Cash that has been received at the end of the period but is either not yet deposited or was deposited after the bank prepared its statement. Deposits in transit are added to the bank balance.

Errors in recording checks: Mistakes, such as transposition errors, made in the recording of checks. An item should be added to the bank balance, for example, if it was previously overstated on the books.

Bank errors in charging or crediting the company's account: If a company's account is charged in error for another firm's cleared check, the company's bank balance is understated, so the company should add the amount of this check to its own bank balance. On the other hand, if a deposit made by a firm was incorrectly credited to the account of another company, the other company should make the adjustment and reduce its bank balance.

Reconciling Items for the Books. The book balance (cash account) is adjusted for items that are shown on the bank statement but are not reflected on the books. Such items include the following.

Bank charges: Bank service fees reduce the book balance, but these amounts are not known until the bank statement is received. Examples include monthly service charges, cost per check, check printing costs, and stop-payment fees.

NSF "not sufficient funds" checks: Checks that have "bounced" because of insufficient funds in the customer's checking account. In such a case, the company's bank issues a debit memorandum for the dishonored amount and the book balance is reduced.

Collections: Notes and other items collected by the bank for a nominal fee. The proceeds received less the charge (in the form of a credit memorandum) are credited to the corporate account. The net amount acts as an addition to the book balance.

Interest earned: Interest income credited by the bank on the checking account increases the book balance.

Errors on the books: Various types of mistakes may be made on the books. Two examples of mistakes and corrections follow (assume that the amount of the check is correct).

1. A $50 check is written, which is more than the $45 amount entered as a cash disbursement. In this case, cash disbursements are understated by $5; thus, the balance per books should be reduced by this amount.

2. A $100 check is written, which is less than the $120 amount shown as a cash disbursement. Here, cash disbursements are overstated, and the book balance should be increased by $20 to correct the error.

After the bank reconciliation has been prepared, journal entries are made for the reconciling items that affect the book balance. Journal entry is necessary because the amounts on the books must be updated to reflect any items on the bank statement of which the firm was unaware during the period. Reconciling items entered as an adjustment to the bank balance are not journalized, however, since they are already on the books. Such reconciling items will probably be shown on the next bank statement.

Example ABC Corporation provides the following data in connection with the preparation of its bank reconciliation at June 30, 19XX:

Balance per bank	$4889
Balance per books	4400
Outstanding checks:	
Check 410	500
Check 423	200
Deposit in transit	300
Collection on note:	
Principal	200
Interest	16
Collection fee on note	12
NSF check	100
Monthly service charge	15

The following shows the proper form for the bank reconciliation:

ABC Corporation

Bank Reconciliation
June 30, 19XX

Balance per bank		$4889
Add: Deposits in transit		300
		$5189
Less: Outstanding checks		
410	$500	
423	200	700
Adjusted bank balance		$4489
Balance per books		$4400
Add: Proceeds on note		216
		$4616
Less:		
NSF check	$100	
Collection fee	12	
Service charge	15	127
Adjusted book balance		$4489

HOW IS IT USED AND BY WHOM?

Depositors. A bank reconciliation is prepared and used by a depositor, whether an individual or business entity, to assure that the balance per the depositor's records agrees with the balance per the bank's records after accounting for all reconciling items. If a discrepancy exists after the bank reconciliation has been prepared, an investigation should be made to uncover any errors or irregularities, such as a fraud perpetrated by a book-keeper.

18 Barron's Confidence Index

DEFINITION. Barron's confidence index looks at the trading pattern of bond investors to determine the timing of buying or selling stocks. The value of the index is published weekly in *Barron's*. The index is based on the belief that bond traders are more sophisticated than stock traders and identify stock market trends sooner. The index is used in *technical* investment analysis.

HOW IS IT COMPUTED?

$$\text{Barron's confidence index} = \frac{\text{yield on Barron's 10 top-grade corporate bonds}}{\text{yield on Dow Jones 40 bond average}}$$

The numerator will have a lower yield than the denominator because it consists of higher-quality bonds. With bonds, as with any investment, a lower risk means a lower return. Hence, since top-grade bonds have lower yields than lower-grade bonds, the index will always be below 100. Normally, the trading range is between 80 and 95. When bond investors are bullish, yield differences between the high-grade and low-grade bonds will be small; in these instances the index may be near 95.

Example If the Dow Jones yield is 13 percent while the Barron's yield is 12 percent, the confidence index will be:

$$\frac{12\%}{13\%} = 92.3$$

HOW IS IT USED AND BY WHOM?

Investment Analysts. If actions of bond traders today are known, a prediction can be made regarding what stock traders will do next. Many analysts believe that a lead time of several months exists between Barron's confidence index and stock market performance.

If Wall Street conditions are bearish, bond-market investors will want to hold top-quality issues. Some investors who continue to put their money in average or lower-quality bonds will want a high yield for the increased risk. Under these conditions, Barron's confidence index will decline, since the denominator will become larger. If confidence is high, investors are apt to purchase lower-grade bonds. As a result, the yield on high-grade bonds will decrease as the yield on low-grade bonds increases.

19 Beta

DEFINITION. Many investors hold more than one financial asset. A portion of a security's risk (called *unsystematic risk*) can be controlled through diversification. This type of risk is unique to a given security. Non-diversifiable risk, more commonly referred to as *systematic risk*, results from forces outside the firm's control and is therefore not unique to a given security. Purchasing power, interest rates, and market risks fall into this category. This type of risk is measured by *beta*.

Characteristics associated with use of beta are as follows:

1. There is a relationship between a stock's expected (or required return) and its beta.

2. The following formula, known as the capital-asset pricing model (CAPM) (see No. 26) is helpful in determining a stock's expected return:

$$r_j = r_f + b(r_m - r_f)$$

where r_f = risk-free rate (the rate on a security such as a T-bill)
b = beta, the index of systematic risk
r_m = expected market return (such as Standard & Poor's 500 Stock Composite Index)
$(r_m - r_f)$ = the market risk premium, the risk-free rate minus expected market return

3. In words,

Expected return = risk-free rate + (beta × market risk premium)

4. The relevant measure of risk is the risk of the individual security, or its beta. The higher the beta of a security, the greater the return expected (or demanded) by the investor.

HOW IS IT COMPUTED? In measuring an asset's beta, an indication is needed of the relationship between the asset's return and the market return (such as the return on the Standard & Poor's 500 Stock Composite Index or the Dow Jones 30 Industrials). This relationship can be computed statistically by determining the regression coefficient between asset and market returns. The method is presented below.

$$b = \frac{\mathrm{Cov}(r_j, r_m)}{\sigma_m{}^2}$$

where $\mathrm{Cov}(r_j, r_m)$ is the covariance of the returns of the assets with the market returns, and $\sigma_m{}^2$ is the variance (standard deviation squared) of the market return.

An easier way to compute beta is to determine the slope of the least-squares linear regression line $(r_j - r_f)$, where the excess return of the asset $(r_j - r_f)$ is regressed against the excess return of the market portfolio $(r_m - r_f)$.

The formula for b is:

$$b = \frac{\sum MK - n\overline{M}\,\overline{K}}{\sum M^2 - n\overline{M}^2}$$

where $M = (r_m - r_f)$
$K = (r_j - r_f)$
n = number of years
$\overline{M}$ = average of M
$\overline{K}$ = average of K

Example Compute the beta coefficient, b, using the following data for stock x and the market portfolio:

Year	Historic rates of return	
	$r_j(\%)$	$r_m(\%)$
19X5	-5	10
19X6	4	8
19X7	7	12
19X8	10	20
19X9	12	15

Assume that the risk-free rate is 6 percent. For easy computation, it is convenient to set up the following table:

Year	r_j	r_m	r_f	$(r_j - r_f) = K$	$(r_m - r_f) = M$	M^2	MK
19X5	-0.05	0.10	0.06	-0.11	0.04	0.0016	-0.0044
19X6	0.04	0.08	0.06	-0.02	0.02	0.0004	-0.0004
19X7	0.07	0.12	0.06	0.01	0.06	0.0036	0.0006
19X8	0.10	0.20	0.06	0.04	0.14	0.0196	0.0056
19X9	0.12	0.15	0.06	0.06	0.09	0.0081	0.0054
				-0.02	0.35	0.0333	0.0068

$$\overline{K} = -0.004 \qquad \overline{M} = 0.07$$

Therefore, beta is:

$$b = \frac{\sum MK - n\overline{M}\,\overline{K}}{\sum M - n\,\overline{M}^2} = \frac{0.0068 - (5)(-0.004)(0.07)}{0.0333 - (5)(0.07)^2} = \frac{0.0082}{0.0088} = 0.93$$

HOW IS IT USED AND APPLIED? Beta measures a security's volatility relative to an average security. Put another way, beta is a measure of a security's return over time to that of the overall market.

For example, if ABC's beta is 2.0, it means that if the stock market goes up 10 percent, ABC's common stock goes up 20 percent; if the market goes down 10 percent, ABC goes down 20 percent.

Following is a guide on how to read betas:

Beta	What it means
0	The security's return is independent of the market. An example is a risk-free security such as a T-bill.
0.5	The security is only half as responsive as the market.
1.0	The security has the same responsiveness or risk as the market (i.e., average risk). This is the beta value of a market portfolio such as Standard & Poor's 500 or the Dow Jones 30 Industrials.
2.0	The security is twice as responsive, or risky, as the market.

Beta is widely used in assessing the risk or instability of a mutual fund. Beta shows how volatile a mutual fund is compared with the market as a whole, as measured by the Standard & Poor's 500 index of the most widely held stocks.

For example, if the S&P goes up 10 percent and your fund goes up 10 percent in the same period, the fund has a beta of 1. But if the fund goes up 20 percent, it has a beta of 2, meaning that it is twice as volatile as the market. The higher the beta, the greater is the risk.

Beta	What it means
1.0	The fund moves up and down just as much as the market.
> 1.0	The fund tends to climb higher in bull markets and dip lower in bear markets than the S&P index.
< 1.0	The fund is less volatile (risky) than the market.

Betas for stock and mutual funds are widely available in many investment newsletters and directories. An example is *Value Line Investment Survey*. Following is a list of some selected betas:

Company	Beta
Apple Computer	1.25
Bristol-Meyers	1.00
IBM	.95
Neiman-Marcus	1.65
Mead Corporation	1.45
Mobil Corporation	.85

SOURCE: *Value Line Investment Survey,* March 8, 1991.

WHO USES IT AND WHEN?

Financial Managers. Financial managers use beta to determine the approximate cost of equity capital. (See also No. 41, Cost of Capital.)

Investors and Professional Fund Managers. Beta of a particular stock or mutual fund is useful in predicting how much the security or mutual fund will go up or down, provided that financial analysts and investors know which way the market will go. Beta helps in determining risk and expected return.

20 Black-Scholes Option-Pricing Model

DEFINITION. The Black-Scholes option-pricing model is used to determine the equilibrium value of an option. It provides insight into the valuation of debt relative to equity.

HOW IS IT COMPUTED?

$$\text{Present value of call option} = PN(d_1) - \text{EX}e^{-r_f t}N(d_2)$$

where P = price of stock now
$N(d)$ = cumulative normal probability density function
EX = exercise price of option
t = time to exercise date
r_f = (continuously compounded) risk-free rate of interest
e = 2.71828

$$d_1 = \frac{\log(P/\text{EX}) + r_f t + \sigma^2 t/2}{\sigma\sqrt{t}}$$

σ^2 = variance per period of (continuously computed) rate of return on the stock

The formula, while somewhat imposing, actually uses readily available input data, with the exception of σ, or volatility. P, EX, r_f, and t are easily obtained.

IMPLICATIONS OF THE OPTION MODEL. The value of the option increases with the level of stock price relative to the exercise price (P/EX), the time to expiration times the interest rate ($r_f t$), and the time to expiration times the stock's variability ($\sigma^2 t$).

Some important points regarding the model are:

* The option price is always less than the stock price.
* The option price never falls below the payoff to immediate exercise ($P - \text{EX}$ or zero, whichever is larger).
* If the stock is worthless, the option is worthless.
* As the stock price becomes very large, the option price approaches the stock price less the present value of the exercise price.

HOW IS IT USED AND BY WHOM?

Investors and Portfolio Managers. The model indicates what an option is worth.

21 Bond Valuation

DEFINITION. The process of determining bond valuation is based on finding the present value of an asset's expected future cash flows using the investor's required rate of return.

HOW IS IT COMPUTED? The basic bond valuation model can be defined mathematically as

$$V = \sum_{t=1}^{n} \frac{C_t}{(1 + r)^t}$$

where V = intrinsic value or present value of an asset,
C_t = expected future cash flows in period $t = 1, \ldots, n$
r = investor's required rate of return

The valuation process for a bond requires knowledge of three basic elements:

1. The amount of the cash flow to be received by the investor, which is equal to the periodic interest to be received and the face value to be paid at maturity
2. The maturity date of the bond
3. The investor's required rate of return

The periodic interest can be received annually or semiannually. If the interest payments are made annually, then

$$V = \sum_{t=1}^{n} \frac{I}{(1 + r)^t} + \frac{M}{(1 + r)^n} = I(\text{PVIFA}_{r,n}) + M(\text{PVIF}_{r,n})$$

where I = interest payment each year = coupon interest rate × par value
M = par value, or maturity value, typically $1000
r = investor's required rate of return
n = number of years to maturity
PVIFA = present-value interest factor of an annuity of $1 (Appendix Table 4)
PVIF = present-value interest factor of $1 (Appendix Table 3)

Example A bond maturing in 10 years has a coupon rate of 8 percent. The par value is $1000. Investors consider 10 percent to be an appropriate required rate of return considering the risk level associated with the bond. The annual interest payment is 8% × $1000 = $80. The present value of this bond is:

$$V = \sum_{t=1}^{n} \frac{I}{(1 + r)^t} + \frac{M}{(1 + r)^n} = I(\text{PVIFA}_{r,n}) + M(\text{PVIF}_{r,n})$$

$$= \sum_{t=1}^{10} \frac{\$80}{(1 + 0.1)^t} + \frac{\$1000}{(1 + 0.1)^{10}}$$

$$= \$80(\text{PVIFA}_{10\%,10}) + \$1000(\text{PVIF}_{10\%,10})$$

$$= \$80(6.145) + \$1000(0.386)$$

$$= \$491.60 + \$386.00 = \$877.60$$

If the interest is paid semiannually, then

$$V = \sum_{t=1}^{2n} \frac{I/2}{(1 + 2/r)^t} + \frac{M}{(1 + r/2)^{2n}}$$

$$= \frac{I}{2}(\text{PVIFA}_{r/2,2n}) + M(\text{PVIF}_{r/2,2n})$$

HOW IS IT USED AND BY WHOM?

Investors. The bond valuation model is used to determine how much a bond is worth as an input to making an investment decision. If the current market price of the bond (say, $900) is less than its theoretical value (say, $930), the bond should be purchased.

22 Bond Yield

DEFINITION. Bond yield is the return a bond investor receives as a percentage of the original bond investment. Bond yields are determined by the stated coupon interest rate, the face value of the bond, the maturity date, and the market valuation, each of which is discussed below. Generally, the greater the investment risk associated with a bond, the higher will be the bond yield.

Face Value. The stated redemption value of the bond is also known as par value. Normally, most bonds are stated in $1000 denominations.

Coupon Interest Rate. An issuer states that a bond will pay a designated number of dollars of interest annually. Bond issuers typically pay one-half the annual interest semiannually. When this interest payment is divided by the face value of the bond, the result is the coupon interest rate. Thus, a bond that pays $120 annually has a coupon interest rate of $120/$1000 or 12 percent.

Market Value. The market value of a bond is determined by several factors, the first of which is whether a specific bond is a new issue or an outstanding bond.

The most important factors determining a new issue's coupon interest rate are the current market rate of interest, the credit rating of the issuer, the quality of the revenues securing the bond, market timing, call features, and other related factors.

For outstanding bonds, the coupon interest rate is an exceedingly important determinant of the market value of the bond. The higher the general market interest rates, the lower will be the market value of an outstanding bond. Other issues that factor into the market value of an outstanding bond include whether or not it can be redeemed by the issuer prior to the stated redemption date (call date), the time left prior to redemption, the financial ability of the issuer, the quality of the revenues backing the bond, and general market conditions.

HOW IS IT COMPUTED?

Current Yield (Simple Yield). Current yield, or simple yield, considers only the market price of a bond and the coupon interest payment. Therefore, the current yield of a bond will fluctuate according to the market price:

$$\text{Current yield} = \frac{\text{coupon interest payment}}{\text{market price of bond}} \times 100$$

Perpetual Bond.   A perpetual bond is one that has no maturity date. The formula for computing the yield on a perpetual bond is:

$$\frac{I}{P}$$

where P = market value of bond
I = interest

Yield to Maturity (YTM).   There are several ways to calculate yield to maturity, r. One method is to use yield-to-maturity tables, where the YTM can be referenced quickly. Another method is found on many financial calculators, where r can be easily computed.
   The formula for calculating yield to maturity is:

$$P = \sum_{t=1}^{n} \frac{I}{(1 + r)^t} + \frac{M}{(1 + r)^n} = I \times \text{PVIFA}(r,t) + M \times \text{PVIF}(r,n)$$

where PVIFA = present value of an annuity interest factor (Appendix Table 4)
   PVIF = present value interest factor (Appendix Table 3)
   P = current price of the bond
   I = annual interest payments
   M = maturity value or principal of the bond
   r = yield to maturity of the bond
   t = time period payment
   n = number of years until the bond matures

The formula for computing an approximate yield to maturity is:

$$\text{Approximate yield to maturity} = \frac{I + (M - P)/n}{(P + M)/2}$$

Example 1: Current Yield   The following calculates the current yield on a bond selling at \$940 with a coupon interest payment of \$80.00 per bond:

$$\text{Current yield} = \left(\frac{\text{coupon interest payment}}{\text{market price of the bond}} \right) \times 100 = \frac{80}{940} = 8.51\%$$

Example 2: Perpetual Bond   Assume a \$1000 face value perpetual bond with a market price of \$950 paying \$120 in annual interest. What is the yield of the bond?

$$\frac{I}{P} = \frac{120}{950} = 0.1263 = 12.63\%$$

Example 3: Yield to Maturity Suppose that the current market price of a 15-year bond having a coupon interest payment of $120 with 14 years remaining before maturity is $870. What is the yield to maturity?

$$P = \sum_{t=1}^{n} \frac{I}{(1 + r)^t} + \frac{M}{(1 + r)^n} = I \times \text{PVIFA}(r,t) + M \times \text{PVIF}(r,n)$$

In this example, the price of the bond, P, is $870; the number of years to maturity, n, is 14; the maturity value, M, is $1000; and the annual interest payment is $120. However, the equation must be solved for r, the yield to maturity.

Here a trial-and-error approach must be used to approximate the yield to maturity using the following steps:

1. Develop an approximate estimate of the yield to maturity.
2. Use the approximate yield to calculate the present value of the bond's cash flows including the purchase price, interest payments, and principal payment.
3. If a positive present value is found, try a higher rate. Conversely, if a negative present value is found, try a lower rate.
4. Continue the procedure until a rate is achieved that allows the present value of the cash flows to be zero.

An approximate yield to maturity is calculated as follows:

$$\text{Approximate yield to maturity} = \frac{I + (M - P)/n}{(P + M)/2}$$

$$= 120 + \frac{(1000 - 950)/14}{950}$$

$$= \frac{120 + 50/14}{950}$$

$$= \frac{120 + 3.57}{950} = 13.01\%$$

Having approximated the yield to maturity, the calculation continues:

$$\$870 = \sum_{t=1}^{14} \frac{120}{(1 + 13.01)^t} + \frac{\$1000}{(1 + 13.01)^{14}}$$

Since bonds call for the payment of a designated amount of interest for a given number of years and for the repayment of the par value on the bond's maturity date, the formula for the present value of an annuity interest factor (PVIFA) plus the present value interest factor (PVIF) can be used for the income stream:

$$\$870 = 120(\text{PVIFA}_{14.187\%,14}) + \$1000(\text{PVIF}_{14.187\%,14})$$

$$= 120(5.950) + 1000(0.156)$$

Using the present value of an annuity interest factor and present value interest factor tables, the rounded yield to maturity for the bonds is 14.187 percent, which is more than a percentage point higher than that found using the approximation method.

SEMIANNUAL COMPOUNDING. Although some bonds do pay interest annually, the majority pay interest semiannually. In order to compute the yield to maturity of a semiannually compounding bond, the formula must be modified:

1. Divide the annual coupon interest payment by 2 to determine the amount of interest paid each 6 months.
2. Multiply the years to maturity, n, by 2 to determine the number of interest periods.
3. Divide the annual interest rate, r, by 2 to determine the semiannual interest rate.

The modified semiannual formula for computing yield to maturity is:

$$P = \sum_{t=1}^{2n} \frac{I}{2}\left[\frac{1}{(1 + r/2)^t}\right] + M\left[\frac{1}{(1 + r/2)^{2n}}\right]$$

$$= \frac{I}{2}(\text{PVIFA}_{r/2,2n}) + M(\text{PVIF}_{r/2,2n})$$

Example 4 Using the original example of a 15-year bond having a coupon interest payment of $120 with 14 years remaining before maturity and selling at a market price of $870, there are two semiannual interest payments of $60 rather than the $120 annual payment. Once again, the calculation must solve for r by interpolating the PVIFA and PVIF tables using the previously solved 14.2%/2 = 7.1% yield to maturity as the starting point:

$870 = $60(\text{PVIFA}_{,7.0924\%, 28\text{ periods}}) + $1,000(\text{PVIF}_{,7.0924\%, 28\text{ periods}})

$= $60(12.0467) + $1000(0.1472)$

Using the present value of an annuity interest factor and present value interest factor tables, the rounded semiannual yield to maturity for the bonds is 7.0924 percent.

HOW IS IT USED AND APPLIED? The determination of bond yield is essential to make bond investments consistent with investment objectives. The current yield is, however, substantially lower than the yield to maturity, since it does not include the compounding effect of a bond and the retirement of its principal.

WHO USES IT AND WHEN?

Investors and Financial Analysts. Yield is an important determinant of a bond rating, but it must be compared with the risk of a bond. The yield on a bond is the effective cost to the issuing corporation and the real rate of return earned by the investor. It is essential for the investor to perform bond yield analyses before committing to a particular bond investment.

Corporate Financial Officers and Financial Managers. An issuing company must consider the cost of bond financing as well as the terms of the bond issue.

23 Book Value per Share

DEFINITION. Book value per share is the net assets available to common stockholders divided by the shares outstanding, where net assets represent stockholders' equity less preferred stock. Book value per share tells what each share is worth per the books based on historical cost.

HOW IS IT COMPUTED?

1. Book value per share of preferred stock:

$$\frac{\text{Liquidation value of preferred stock + preferred dividends in arrears}}{\text{Preferred shares outstanding}}$$

2. Book value per share of common stock:

$$\frac{\text{Total stockholders' equity} - \text{(liquidation value of preferred stocks + preferred dividends in arrears)}}{\text{Common shares outstanding}}$$

Care must be taken in computing the liquidation value of preferred stock. Some companies have preferred stock issues outstanding that give the right to significant liquidation premiums, which may substantially exceed the par value of such shares. The effect of such liquidation premiums on the book value of common stock can be quite material.

Example The following illustrates how book value per share is calculated from the different components of a company's financial information.

Total stockholders' equity	$4,000,000
Preferred stock, 6% dividend rate, 100,000 shares, $10 par value, $12 liquidation value	
Common stock, 200,000 shares, $20 par value	
Preferred dividends in arrears for 3 years	
Liquidation value of preferred stock, 100,000 shares × $12	$1,200,000
Preferred dividends in arrears:	
Par value of preferred stock, 100,000 × $10	$1,000,000
Preferred dividend rate	× 6%
Preferred dividend per year	$ 60,000
Number of years	× 3
Preferred dividend in arrears	$ 180,000

Book value per share for preferred stock:
$$\frac{\$1,200,000 + \$180,000}{100,000 \text{ shares}} = \frac{\$1,380,000}{100,000} = \$13.80$$

Book value per share for common stock:
$$\frac{\$4,000,000 - \$1,380,000}{200,000 \text{ shares}} = \frac{\$2,620,000}{200,000} = \$13.10$$

HOW IS IT USED AND BY WHOM?

Investors.   A comparison of book value per share with market price per share gives an indication of how the stock market views the company. Generally, market price per share should be higher than book value per share, because the former is based on current prices. For example, if a company's market price per share of stock is currently $20 and the book value per share is $26, the stock is probably not favored by investors.

An acquiring company may pay a market price less than the liquidation value (breakup value) for an acquired company in order to obtain a profit by liquidating the acquired business.

24 Breadth Index

DEFINITION.   The *breadth index,* used in technical analyses, computes the net advances or declines in stocks on the New York Stock Exchange from each trading day. When there are net advances, a strong market exists. The magnitude of strength depends on the spread between the numbers of advancing and declining issues.

HOW IS IT COMPUTED?

$$\text{Breadth index} = \frac{\text{number of net advances or declines in securities}}{\text{number of securities traded}}$$

Example On a particular day, suppose that net declining issues are 58. Securities traded are 1,475. The breadth index is:

$$\frac{\text{Declining issues}}{\text{Number of issues traded}} = \frac{58}{1475} = -3.9$$

HOW IS IT USED AND BY WHOM?

Investment Analysts.   Securities analysts are interested in the direction of the market in order to identify strength or weakness. Advances and declines typically follow the same direction as a standard market average (e.g., the Dow Jones Industrial Average), but they may go in the opposite direction at a peak market or bottom.

Breadth analysis emphasizes change instead of level. The computed breadth index is compared to popular market averages. Usually, consistency exists in the related index and market movements. In a bull market, however, securities analysts should watch out for an extended disparity between the two—for example, when the breadth index moves gradually downward to new lows while the Dow Jones Industrial Average climbs to new highs.

A comparison may also be made of the breadth index over a number of years. The breadth index may also be compared to a base year or included in a 150-day moving average.

Market strength is indicated when both the breadth index and the Dow Jones Industrial Average are increasing; market weakness is evidenced when both decline.

25 Breakeven Formulas

DEFINITION. Breakeven formulas are useful to all businesses in determining the point at which a business can begin to turn a profit. The three most common breakeven formulas, described below, determine the breakeven point, the margin of safety, and the cash breakeven point.

1 BREAKEVEN POINT

Definition. The breakeven point is the sales volume at which total revenue equals total costs, resulting in zero profit—that is, the minimum sales necessary to avoid a loss.

How Is It Computed?

$$\text{Sales} = \text{variable costs} + \text{fixed costs}$$

Fixed costs are those that remain constant regardless of activity (such as rent), whereas variable costs are those that vary with activity (such as materials).

If sales are necessary to make a desired before-tax profit, the formula becomes:

$$\text{Sales} = \text{variable costs} + \text{fixed costs} + \text{desired profit}$$

Example 1 If the selling price is $25, variable cost per unit is $10, and fixed costs are $15,000, the breakeven units are:

$$S = \text{VC} + \text{FC}$$
$$\$25U = \$10U + \$15,000$$
$$\$15U = \$15,000$$
$$U = 1,000$$

$$\text{Total sales} = 1,000 \text{ units} \times \$25 = \$25,000$$

If the desired profit is $3000, the unit sales needed are:

$$S = \text{VC} + \text{FC} + P$$
$$\$25U = \$10U + \$15,000 + \$3,000$$
$$\$15U = \$18,000$$
$$U = 1,200$$

2 MARGIN OF SAFETY

Definition. The margin of safety is the amount by which sales revenue may drop before losses begin.

How Is It Computed?

$$\text{Margin of safety} = \frac{\text{expected sales} - \text{breakeven sales}}{\text{expected sales}}$$

Example 2 If projected sales are $30,000 with a breakeven sales of $25,000, the projected margin of safety is:

$$\frac{\$30,000 - \$25,000}{\$25,000} = 20\%$$

3 CASH BREAKEVEN POINT

Definition. The cash breakeven point is the sales volume that will cover all cash expenses during a period. Not all fixed operating costs involve cash payment (e.g., depreciation expense).

How Is It Computed?

Cash breakeven point = sales = variable costs + fixed cash costs

The cash breakeven point is lower than the usual breakeven point because noncash charges are subtracted from fixed costs.

Example 3 Assume the same facts as in Example 1, except that the fixed costs of $15,000 include depreciation of $1,500. The cash breakeven point units are:

$$S = VC + FCC$$
$$\$25U = \$10U + \$13,500$$
$$\$15U = \$13,500$$
$$U = 900$$

HOW IS IT USED AND APPLIED? Breakeven analysis is used for many purposes, including to determine:

- The sales volume required to break even
- The sales volume necessary to earn a desired profit
- The effect that changes in selling price, variable cost, fixed cost, and output have on profit
- The selling price that should be charged
- The desired variable cost per unit or fixed costs

Breakeven analysis is used to organize thinking on important broad aspects of any business—for example, determining the breakeven occupancy rate for a hotel or the breakeven passenger load rate for an airline flight.

The margin of safety is a measure of operating risk. The larger the ratio, the safer is the situation due to the reduction in risk in reaching the breakeven point.

The cash breakeven point is used when a company has a minimum of available cash, or the opportunity cost of holding excess cash is too high.

Financial Managers, Management Executives, Marketing Managers, and Production Managers. Different managers within a company use breakeven analysis because it is important when beginning a new activity, such as starting a new line of business, expanding an existing business, or introducing a new product or service.

Examples of questions that are commonly answered by breakeven formulas include the following:

- *Financial managers:* What is the financial feasibility of a proposed investment?

- *Management executives:* Have the company's breakeven possibilities been improving or deteriorating? What will be the impact of major labor negotiations?

- *Marketing managers:* Will a major marketing campaign generate sufficient sales to justify the cost of the campaign? Would introduction of a new product add or detract from the company's profitability?

- *Production managers:* Would modernization of production facilities pay for itself?

26 Capital-Asset Pricing Model

DEFINITION. The capital-asset pricing model (CAPM) relates the risk measured by the beta value to the level of expected or required rate of return on a security. The model, also called the *security market line (SML),* is a general relationship that shows the risk-return trade-off for an individual security.

HOW IS IT COMPUTED? The model of SML is given as:

$$r_j = r_f + b(r_m - r_f)$$

where r_j = expected (or required) return on security j
r_f = return on a risk-free security (such as a T-bill)
r_m = expected return on the market portfolio (such as Standard & Poor's 500 Stock Composite Index or Dow Jones 30 Industrials)
b = beta, an index of nondiversifiable (noncontrollable, systematic) risk

The whole term $b(r_m - r_f)$ represents the risk premium, the additional return required to compensate investors for assuming a given level of risk.

In words, the CAPM (or SML) equation shows that the required (expected) rate of return on a given security (r_j) is equal to the return required for securities that have no risk (r_f) plus a risk premium required by investors for assuming a given level of risk. The higher the degree of systematic risk (b), the higher the return on a given security demanded by investors.

Example If the market return (r_m) is 8 percent, the risk-free rate (r_f) is 5 percent, and ABC stock's beta is 1.5, then the required return on the stock is:

$$r_j = r_f + b(r_m - r_f)$$
$$= 5\% + 1.5(8\% - 5\%)$$
$$= 9.5\%$$

HOW IS IT USED AND APPLIED?   The model shows that investors in individual securities are assumed to be rewarded only for systematic, uncontrollable, market-related risk, known as the beta (b) risk. All other risk is assumed to be diversified away and thus is not rewarded.

The key component in the CAPM, beta (b), is a measure of the security's volatility relative to that of an average security. For example, $b = 0.5$ means that the security is only half as volatile, or risky, as the average security; $b = 1.0$ means that the security is of average risk; and $b = 2.0$ means that the security is twice as risky as the average risk.

WHO USES IT AND WHEN?

Financial Managers.   Financial managers use beta to determine the approximate cost of equity capital. (See also No. 41, Cost of Capital.)

Professional Money Managers.   The beta of a particular stock or mutual fund is useful in predicting how much the security or mutual fund will go up or down, provided that financial analysts and investors know which way the market will go. Beta helps analysts to determine risk and expected return.

Investors.   Investors can determine the required rate of return on a stock by using the model.

27 Capitalization Rate

DEFINITION.   Capitalization rate, also called *cap rate* or *income yield*, is a widely used method of determining the rate of return on a real estate investment.

HOW IS IT COMPUTED?   The capitalization rate is found by dividing the net operating income (NOI) for the first year by the total investment.

Example   Assume that net operating income = \$18,618 and purchase price = \$219,000. Then the cap rate is

$$\frac{\$18,618}{\$219,000} = 8.5\%$$

If the market rate is 10 percent, the fair market value of similar property is \$18,618/10% = \$186,180. The property may be overpriced.

HOW IS IT USED AND APPLIED?   The capitalization rate, when applied to the earnings of an investment, determines its appraisal or market value. The higher the cap rate, the lower the perceived risk to the investor and the lower the asking price paid. Whether a piece of property is overpriced or not depends on the rate of similar property derived from the marketplace.

There are two limitations to use of the cap rate: (1) It is based on only the first year's NOI; and (2) it ignores return through appreciation in property value.

WHO USES IT AND WHEN?

Real Estate Investors and Agents. The cap rate assists real estate investors who are interested in buying income-producing property in ascertaining the value of that property.

Mortgage Bankers and Brokers. Bankers and brokers may use the cap rate to determine the appraised value of a property to see if it qualifies for the loan under consideration.

28 Cash Flow Ratios

DEFINITION. Cash flow from operations represents the cash earnings of a business. Utilization of cash flow ratios shows the degree to which net income is backed up by a liquid source of funds. Cash reinvestment into a business indicates the ability of a company to position for future corporate growth.

HOW IS IT COMPUTED? The process of analyzing a company's cash flow is as follows.

1. Cash flow from operations is calculated as:

Net income
Add: Noncash expenses (e.g., depreciation, amortization)
Less: Noncash revenue (e.g., amortization of deferred revenue)
Cash flow from operations

---

2. This calculation is followed by analyzing the operational cash flow over net income:

$$\frac{\text{Cash flow from operations}}{\text{Net income}}$$

3. A third calculation is derived by stating the cash flow generated from operations less cash payments required to pay debt principal, dividends, and capital expenditures.

4. Cash reinvestment ratio is determined by identifying cash employed and cash obtained:

Cash employed =

increases in gross plant and equipment + increase in net working capital

Cash obtained = income after tax plus depreciation

5. The cash reinvestment ratio is calculated as follows:

$$\frac{\text{Cash employed}}{\text{Cash obtained}}$$

6. Cash flow coverage ratio =

$$\frac{\text{net operating income} + \text{lease expense} + \text{depreciation}}{\text{interest} + \text{lease expense} + [\text{preferred dividends}/(1 - \text{tax rate})] - [\text{principal payments}/(1 - \text{tax rate})]}$$

Example A condensed income statement for a company and the pertinent cash flow analysis follow:

Sales		$1,000,000
Less: Cost of sales		300,000
Gross margin		$ 700,000
Less: Operating expenses		
Salary	$100,000	
Rent	200,000	
Telephone	50,000	
Depreciation	80,000	
Amortization expense	60,000	
Total operating expenses		490,000
Income before other items		$ 210,000
Other revenue and expense		
Interest expense	$ 70,000	
Amortization of deferred revenue	40,000	
Total revenue and expense		30,000
Net income		$ 180,000

The ratio of cash flow from operations to net income is 1.55, calculated as follows:

Cash flow from operations:		
Net income		$180,000
Add:		
Noncash expenses		
Depreciation	$80,000	
Amortization expense	60,000	140,000
Less: Noncash revenue		
Amortization of deferred revenue		(40,000)
Cash flow from operations		$280,000

$$\frac{\text{Cash flow from operations}}{\text{Net income}} = \frac{\$280,000}{\$180,000} = 1.55$$

Financial Management. Earnings are of higher quality if they are backed up by cash, since cash can be used to meet debt payments, buying fixed assets, and so forth.

A high cash reinvestment ratio indicates that more cash is being used in the business.

Short-Term Creditors. A company with a high percentage of internally generated cash earnings has better liquidity.

29 Cash-Management Models

DEFINITION. Cash-management models are used to determine the optimal cash that a company should have available, considering costs, return rate, and fluctuations in cash flow.

HOW IS IT COMPUTED? Two models are useful in determining the optimal level of cash.

William Baumol's Model. In William Baumol's model, costs are expressed as:

$$F\frac{(T)}{C} + i\frac{(C)}{2}$$

where F = fixed cost of a transaction
T = total cash needed for the time period
i = interest rate on marketable securities
C = cash balance

The optimal level of cash is:

$$C = \sqrt{\frac{2FT}{i}}$$

Miller-Orr Model. In the Miller-Orr model, the optimal cash balance, Z, is computed as

$$Z = \sqrt[3]{\frac{3F\sigma^2}{4i}} + LL$$

where F = fixed cost of a securities transaction, assumed to be the same for buying and selling
i = daily interest rate on marketable securities
σ^2 = variability of daily net cash flows
LL = actual value for the lower limit

LL is set by management.

The upper control limit, UL, can be computed as

$$UL = 3Z - 2LL$$

Example 1 Using William Baumol's model, assume there is an estimated need for $4,000,000 in cash over a 1-month period. The cash account is expected to be disbursed at a constant rate. Assume that the opportunity interest rate is 6 percent per annum, or 0.5 percent for a 1-month period, and that the transaction cost each time borrowing or withdrawing occurs is $100.

The optimal transaction size (the optimal borrowing or withdrawal lot size) and the number of transactions that the company should make during the month is calculated as follows:

$$C^* = \sqrt{\frac{2FT}{i}} = \sqrt{\frac{2(100)(4,000,000)}{0.005}} = \$400,000$$

The optimal transaction size is $400,000.
The average cash balance is:

$$\frac{(C^*)}{2} = \frac{\$400,000}{2} = \$200,000$$

The number of transactions required is:

$$\frac{\$4,000,000}{\$400,000} = 10 \text{ transactions during the month}$$

Example 2 Using the Miller-Orr model, assume the following:

Fixed cost of a securities transaction	$10
Deviation in daily net cash flows	$50
Daily interest rate on securities (10%/360)	0.0003

The optimal cash balance, the upper limit of cash needed, and the average cash balance are determined as follows:

$$Z = \sqrt[3]{\frac{3(10)(50)}{4(0.0003)}} = \sqrt[3]{\frac{3(10)(50)}{0.0012}} = \sqrt[3]{\frac{1,500}{0.0012}} = \sqrt[3]{1,250,000} = \$102$$

The optimal cash balance is $102.
The upper limit is (3 × $102) = $306.
The average cash balance is ($102 + $306)/3 = $136.

A brief elaboration on these findings is needed for clarification. When the upper limit of $306 is reached, ($306 − $102) = $204 of securities will be purchased to achieve the optimal cash balance of $102. When the lower limit of $0 dollars is reached, $102 of securities will be sold to reach the optimal cash balance of $102.

HOW IS IT USED AND BY WHOM?

Financial Management. Financial managers use the cash models to find the optimal amount of cash to have on hand based on needs, costs, rate of return, and other relevant factors.

William Baumol's model is used to determine the optimum amount of transaction cash under known, certain business conditions. The objective is to minimize the sum of fixed costs associated with transactions and the opportunity cost of holding cash balances.

The Miller-Orr model is a stochastic approach used when uncertainty exists regarding cash payments. This model embraces the following features:

- The model places upper and lower limits for cash balances.
- When the upper limit is reached, a transfer of cash is made to marketable securities.
- When the lower limit is reached, a transfer is made from marketable securities to cash.
- A transaction will not take place as long as the cash balance falls within the limits.
- The objective of the model is to meet cash requirements at the lowest possible cost.

30 Cash Plus Cash Equivalents to Working Capital

DEFINITION. This ratio of cash plus cash equivalents to working capital looks at cash plus marketable securities having a maturity of 3 months or less relative to working capital. (The definition of cash equivalents used in this ratio is that defined by the Financial Accounting Standards Board in order to prepare the statement of cash flows.)

HOW IS IT COMPUTED?

$$\frac{\text{Cash plus cash equivalents}}{\text{Working capital}}$$

(See No. 199, Working Capital.)

Example A company reports the following information:

	19X1	19X2
Cash and cash equivalents	$100,000	$ 90,000
Working capital	300,000	350,000

The relevant ratios are cash plus cash equivalents to working capital = 0.33 for 19X1 and 0.26 for 19X2. The ratios indicate that the company's liquidity has deteriorated, since it has less cash and cash equivalents available as a liquid base in 19X2.

HOW IS IT USED AND BY WHOM?

Management, Credit Analysts, and Lenders. The cash and cash equivalents of a company are the most liquid assets of the business. A high balance offers protection to short-term creditors in meeting debt that is coming due in the near future.

31 Cash Ratios

DEFINITION. Cash ratios indicate the adequacy of a company's liquid fund base to meet expenses and obligations. Adequate cash flow is needed not only for a company to stay afloat but to achieve capital growth.

HOW IS IT COMPUTED? Several cash ratios are commonly employed:

1. $\dfrac{\text{Cash flow}}{\text{Total debt}}$

2. $\dfrac{\text{Cash flow}}{\text{Long-term debt}}$

3. $\dfrac{\text{Cash + marketable securities}}{\text{Total current assets}}$

4. $\dfrac{\text{Cash + marketable securities}}{\text{Total current liabilities}}$

5. $\dfrac{\text{Cash + marketable securities + receivables}}{\text{Year's cash expenses}}$

6. Cash flow-to-capital expenditures ratio:

$$\frac{\text{Cash flow from operations} - \text{dividends}}{\text{expenditures for plant and equipment}}$$

7. Cash flow adequacy ratio:

$$\frac{\text{Five-year sum of cash flow from operations}}{\substack{\text{Five-year sum of capital expenditures, inventory additions,}\\ \text{and cash dividends}}}$$

Example Two cash flow ratios are calculated based on the following company information:

	19X1	19X2
Cash flow	$ 600,000	$ 300,000
Total debt	2,000,000	2,500,000
Long-term debt	1,000,000	1,300,000

The relevant ratios are:

	19X1	19X2
Cash flow to total debt	30%	12%
Cash flow to long-term debt	60%	23%

From 19X1 to 19X2, the company has experienced a significant deterioration in liquidity. The company may be in a cash squeeze and unable to meet its obligations when they fall due.

HOW IS IT USED AND BY WHOM?

Financial Management.   The cash flow-to-total debt ratio indicates a company's ability to satisfy its debts. It is useful in predicting bankruptcy. Cash flow to long-term debt appraises the adequacy of available funds to meet noncurrent obligations.

The ratio of cash plus marketable securities to current liabilities indicates the immediate amount of cash available to satisfy short-term debt. This ratio is much more conservative than the acid-test ratio (see No. 4, Acid-Test Ratio).

Concern is also directed to how many times a company's immediate liquid resources are sufficient to meet cash expenses.

The cash flow-to-capital expenditures ratio indicates a company's ability to maintain plant and equipment from cash provided from operations, rather than by borrowing or issuing new stock.

The purpose of the cash flow adequacy ratio is to determine the degree to which an enterprise has generated sufficient cash flow from operations to cover capital expenditures, net investment in inventories, and cash dividends. To remove cyclical and other erratic influences, a five-year total is used in the computation. A ratio of 1 reveals that the company has covered its needs based on attained levels of growth without the need for external financing. If the ratio drops below 1, internally generated cash may be inadequate to maintain dividends and current operating growth levels. This ratio may also reflect the impact of inflation on the fund requirements of the company.

32 Certainty-Equivalent Approach

DEFINITION.   The certainty-equivalent approach to capital budgeting is drawn directly from the concept of utility theory. This method forces the decision maker to specify at what point the firm is indifferent to the choice between a certain sum of money and the expected value of a risky sum.

HOW IS IT COMPUTED?   Once certainty-equivalent coefficients are obtained, they are multiplied by the original cash flow to obtain the equivalent certain cash flow. Then, the accept-or-reject decision is made, using the normal capital-budgeting criteria. The risk-free rate of return is used as the discount rate under the net present value (NPV) method and as the cutoff rate under the internal rate of return (IRR) method.

Example   XYZ, Inc., with a 14 percent cost of capital after taxes, is considering a project with an expected life of 4 years. The project requires an initial certain cash outlay of $50,000. The expected cash inflows and certainty-equivalent coefficients are as follows:

Year	After-tax cash flow	Certainty-equivalent coefficient
1	$10,000	0.95
2	15,000	0.80
3	20,000	0.70
4	25,000	0.60

The risk-free rate of return is 5 percent. We compute the NPV and IRR. The equivalent certain cash inflows are obtained as follows:

Year	After-tax cash inflow	Certainty-equivalent coefficient	Equivalent certain cash inflow	PVIF at 5%	PV
1	$10,000	0.95	$ 9,500	0.9524	$ 9,048
2	15,000	0.80	12,000	0.9070	10,884
3	20,000	0.70	14,000	0.8638	12,093
4	25,000	0.60	15,000	0.8227	12,341
					$44,366

$$NPV = \$44,366 - \$50,000 = -\$5,634$$

By trial and error, we obtain 4 percent as the IRR. Therefore, the project should be rejected, since (1) NPV = - $5,634, which is negative, and/or (2) IRR = 4 percent is less than the risk-free rate of 5 percent.

HOW IS IT USED AND APPLIED? This is one of many methods available to deal with variable (uncertain) future cash flows associated with a capital-budgeting project. This method is most effective when the analyst has a clear idea about his or her utility (preference) function. Otherwise, use of other methods such as (No. 165) the Risk-Adjusted Discount Rate or (No. 183) the Simulation Model, are recommended.

HOW IS IT USED AND BY WHOM?

Project Analysts. Project analysts and capital-budget program directors need to be equipped with techniques such as this to be able to handle risky investment projects.

33 χ^2 (Chi-Square) Test

DEFINITION. The χ^2 (chi-square) test is a statistical test for the significance of a difference between classifications or subclassifications. This test is applied to sample data in testing regardless of whether two qualitative population variables are independent.

HOW IS THE TEST PERFORMED? The χ^2 test involves three steps:

Step 1: Calculate the χ^2 statistic, which is defined as:

$$\chi^2 = \sum \frac{(f_o - f_e)^2}{f_e}$$

where f_o = individual observed frequencies of each class
          f_e = individual expected frequencies of each class

Step 2:   Find the table value at a given level of significance. (See the χ^2 table—Table 8 in the Appendix.)

Step 3:   If the calculated value is greater than the table value, the null hypothesis is rejected, which means that the two variables or classifications are associated.

Example   Consider the following survey data regarding the granting of degrees in finance:

	Master's degrees	Doctor's degrees	Total
Men	466	169	635
Women	180	29	209
Total	646	198	844

The null hypothesis is: The sex and the granting of graduate degrees in finance are independent.

In order to calculate χ^2, it is necessary to construct an expected-value table on the basis of the assumption that sex and graduate degrees are independent of one another. If no association exists, it would be expected that the proportion of men and women receiving master's degrees would be the same as that receiving doctor's degrees. First, the expected frequencies based on the premise of independence are computed:

$$\frac{635}{844} = 0.7524 \qquad \frac{209}{844} = 0.2476$$

Then, the expected values from the proportions of totals are computed:

$$0.7524 \times 646 = 486$$
$$0.2476 \times 646 = 160$$
$$0.7524 \times 198 = 149$$
$$0.2476 \times 198 = 49$$

These expected values give the following table:

	Master's degrees	Doctor's degrees	Total
Men	486	149	635
Women	160	49	209
Total	646	198	844

Step 1:   Calculate χ^2 to determine how far the observed table differs from the expected table:

$$\chi^2 = \frac{(466 - 486)^2}{486} + \frac{(180 - 160)^2}{160} + \frac{(169 - 149)^2}{149} + \frac{(29 - 49)^2}{49} = 14.171$$

Step 2: The χ^2 value at the 0.05 level of significance with one degree of freedom (from Table 8 in the Appendix) is 3.841. The degree of freedom is calculated as (no. rows − 1) × (no. of columns − 1) = (2 − 1)(2 − 1) = 1.

Step 3: As shown in exhibit 33.1, since the calculated value is greater than the table value (14.171 > 3.841), the null hypothesis is rejected—that is, sex is associated with the granting of master's degrees and doctor's degrees in finance.

HOW IS IT USED AND APPLIED?

The chi-square test has many applications. It is a statistical test of independence (or association) to determine if membership in categories of one variable is different as a function of membership in the categories of a second variable. It is important to note, however, that there are limitations to this test: (1) The sample must be big enough for the expected frequencies for each cell (the rule of thumb is at least 5); and (2) the test does not say anything about the direction of an association.

WHO USES IT AND WHEN?

Marketing Managers. Managers need to know whether the differences they observe among several sample proportions are significant or due only to chance. For example, marketing managers are concerned that their brand's share may be distributed unevenly across the country. They may conduct a survey in which the country is divided into a specific number of geographic regions and see if the consumers' decisions as to whether or not to purchase the company's brand has anything to do with geographic location.

Financial Managers. A financial consultant might be interested in the differences in capital structure for different firm sizes in a certain industry. To see if firm sizes have the same capital structure (or if firm sizes have nothing to do with the capital structure), the financial consultant must survey a group of firms with assets of different amounts, divide these into groups, and classify each firm according to predetermined debt/equity ratio groups.

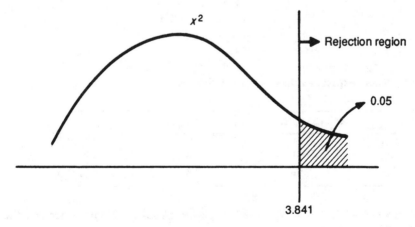

Exhibit 33.1 Rejection region in chi-square test analysis.

34 Coefficient of Variation

DEFINITION. The coefficient of variation is a measure of relative dispersion, or relative risk. It represents the degree of risk per unit of return.

HOW IS IT COMPUTED? The coefficient of variation is computed by dividing the standard deviation (σ) by the expected value $E(x)$, where

$$E(x) = \sum x_i p_i$$

where x_i is the outcome for the ith possible event and p_i is the probability of occurrence of that outcome, and

$$\sigma = \sqrt{\sum [x_i - E(x)]^2 p_i}$$

Example Consider two investment proposals, A and B, with the following probability distribution of cash flows in each of the next five years:

	Cash inflows			
Probability	.2	.3	.4	.1
A	$ 50	$200	$300	$400
B	100	150	250	850

The expected value of the cash inflow for proposal A is:

$$\$50(.2) + \$200(.3) + \$300(.4) + \$400(.1) = \$230$$

The expected value of the cash inflow for proposal B is:

$$\$100(.2) + \$150(.3) + \$250(.4) + \$850(.1) = \$250$$

The standard deviations of proposals A and B are computed as follows:

For A: $\sigma = \sqrt{(\$50 - \$230)(.2) + (\$200 - \$230)(.3) +}$
$$\overline{(\$300 - \$230)(.4) + (\$400 - \$230)(.1)} = \$107.70$$

For B: $\sigma = \sqrt{(\$100 - \$250)(.2) + (\$150 - \$250)(.3) +}$
$$\overline{(\$250 - \$250)(.4) + (\$850 - \$250)(.1)} = \$208.57$$

Proposal B is more risky than proposal A, since its standard deviation is greater.

Note the following:

Proposal	Expected value [$E(x)$]	Standard deviation (σ)
A	$230	$107.7
B	250	208.57

The coefficient of variation for each proposal is:

$$\text{For A:} \quad \frac{\$107.7}{\$230} = .47$$

$$\text{For B:} \quad \frac{\$208.57}{\$250} = .83$$

Therefore, because the coefficient is a relative measure of risk, B is considered more risky than A.

HOW IS IT USED AND APPLIED?   In finance, the standard deviation is used as an indicator of the risk involved in an investment, since it measures the variability of returns around the expected return from an investment. Financial managers can also use expected value and standard deviation to make important inferences from past data. The problem with the standard deviation is that it is a measure of absolute risk. It can only be used to compare investments with the same expected returns.

WHO USES IT AND WHEN?

Investors and Financial Analysts.   The coefficient of variation is used to compare investments with differing expected returns.

35 Common-Stock Valuation

DEFINITION.   The process of valuing common stock involves finding the present value of an asset's expected future cash flows using the investor's required rate of return. Thus, the basic security valuation model can be defined mathematically as:

$$V = \sum_{t=1}^{n} \frac{C_t}{(1 + r)^t}$$

where V = intrinsic value or present value of a security
C_t = expected future cash flows in period $t = 1\ldots, n$
r = investor's required rate of return

The value of a common stock is the present value of all future cash inflows expected to be received by the investor. The cash inflows expected to be received are dividends and the future price at the time of sale of the stock.

HOW IS IT COMPUTED?

Single Holding Period.   For an investor who is holding a common stock for only one year, the value of the stock is the present value of both the expected cash dividend to be received in one year (D_1) and the expected market price per share of the stock at year-end (P_1). If r represents an investor's required rate of return, the value of common stock (P_0) is:

$$P_0 = \frac{D_1}{(1 + r)^1} + \frac{P_1}{(1 + r)^1}$$

Example 1 Assume that an investor is considering the purchase of stock A at the beginning of the year. The dividend at year-end is expected to be \$1.50, and the market price by the end of the year is expected to be \$40. If the investor's required rate of return is 15 percent, the value of the stock is:

$$P_0 = \frac{D_1}{(1 + r)^1} + \frac{P_1}{(1 + r)^1} = \frac{\$1.50}{(1 + 0.15)} + \frac{\$40}{(1 + 0.15)}$$

$$= \$1.50 \times \text{PVIF}(15\%,1) + \$40 \times \text{PVIF}(15\%,1)$$

$$= \$1.50(0.870) + \$40(0.870)$$

$$= \$1.31 + \$34.80 = \$36.11$$

For PVIF, refer to Table 3 in the Appendix.

Multiple Holding Periods. Since common stock has no maturity date and is often held for many years, a more general, multiperiod model is needed. The general common-stock valuation model is defined as:

$$P_0 = \sum_{t = 1} \frac{D_t}{(1 + r)^t}$$

where D_t is the dividend in period t.

Three cases of growth in dividends are explained below: (1) zero growth, (2) constant growth, and (3) nonconstant, or supernormal, growth.

1. Zero growth. In the case of zero growth (i.e., $D_0 = D_1 = \ldots = D$), the valuation model reduces to:

$$P_0 = \frac{D}{r}$$

This is the case with a perpetuity. This model is most applicable to the valuation of preferred stocks, or to the common stocks of very mature companies such as large utilities.

Example 2 Assuming that dividends (D) equals \$2.50 and r equals 10 percent, the value of the stock is:

$$P_0 = \frac{\$2.50}{0.1} = \$25$$

2. Constant growth. In the case of constant growth, if we assume that dividends grow at a constant rate g every year [i.e., $D_t = D_0 (1 + g)^t$], then the general model simplifies to:

$$P_0 = \frac{D_1}{r - g}$$

In words,

$$\text{Common stock value} = \frac{\text{dividend in year 1}}{(\text{required rate of return}) - (\text{growth rate})}$$

This formula is known as Gordon's valuation model and is most applicable to the valuation of the common stocks of very large or broadly diversified firms.

Example 3   Consider a common stock that paid a $3 dividend per share at the end of last year and is expected to pay a cash dividend every year at a growth rate of 10 percent. Assume that the investor's required rate of return is 12 percent. The value of the stock is:

$$D_1 = D_0(1 + g) = \$3(1 + 0.10) = \$3.30$$

$$P_0 = \frac{D_1}{r - g} = \frac{\$3.30}{0.12 - 0.10} = \$165$$

3. Nonconstant, or supernormal, growth.

Firms typically go through life cycles, during part of which their growth is faster than that of the economy and during part of which their rate of growth falls sharply. The value of stock during the supernormal growth period can be found by taking the following steps: (a) Compute the dividends during the period of supernormal growth and find their present value; (b) find the price of the stock at the end of the supernormal growth period and compute its present value; and (c) add these two present value figures to find the value (P_0) of the common stock.

Example 4   Consider a common stock whose dividends are expected to grow at a rate of 25 percent for 2 years, after which the growth rate is expected to fall to 5 percent. The dividend paid last period was $2. The investor desires a 12 percent return. To find the value of this stock, take the following steps.

a. Compute the dividends during the supernormal growth period and find their present value. Assuming that D_0 is $2, g is 15 percent, and r is 12 percent,

$$D_1 = D_0(1 + g) = \$2(1 + 0.25) = \$2.50$$

$$D_2 = D_0(1 + g)^2 = \$2(1.563) = \$3.126$$

or

$$D_2 = D_1(1 + g) = \$2.50(1.25) = \$3.126$$

$$\text{PV of dividends} = \frac{D_1}{(1 + r)^1} + \frac{D_2}{(1 + r)^2} = \frac{\$2.50}{(1 + 0.12)} + \frac{\$3.125}{(1 + 0.12)^2}$$

$$= \$2.50 \times \text{PVIF}(12\%, 1) + \$3.125 \times \text{PVIF}(12\%, 2)$$

$$= \$2.50(0.8929) + \$3.125(0.7972)$$

$$= \$2.23 + \$2.49 = \$4.72$$

b. Find the price of the stock at the end of the supernormal growth period. The dividend for the third year is:

$$D_3 = D_2(1 + g') \qquad \text{where } g' = 5\%$$

$$= \$3.125(1 + 0.05) = \$3.28$$

The price of the stock is therefore:

$$P_2 = \frac{D_3}{r - g'} = \frac{\$3.28}{0.12 - 0.05} = \$46.86$$

PV of stock = $46.86 × PVIF(12%, 2) = $46.86(0.7972) = $37.36

c. Add the two PV figures obtained in steps 1 and 2 to find the value of the stock:

$$P_0 = \$4.72 + \$37.36 = \$42.08$$

THE PRICE-EARNINGS (P/E) RATIO—A PRAGMATIC APPROACH.

The dividend valuation models discussed so far are best suited for those companies that are in the expansion or maturity stage of their life cycle. A more pragmatic approach to valuing a common stock is to use the P/E ratio (or multiple). Many financial managers use the simple formula:

Forecasted price at the end of year =

estimated EPS in year t × estimated P/E ratio

Of course, for this method to be effective in forecasting the future value of a stock, (*a*) earnings need to be projected correctly and (*b*) the appropriate P/E multiple must be applied.

Example 5 XYZ Corporation had earnings per share (EPS) of $5. EPS is expected to grow at a rate of 20 percent. The company's normal P/E ratio is estimated to be 7, which is used as the multiplier. The value of the stock is:

$$\text{Estimated EPS} = \$5(1 + 0.20) = \$6.00$$

Therefore, the expected price of the stock is $6 × 7 = $42.

Forecasting EPS is not an easy task. Many securities analysts use a simple method of forecasting EPS—a sales forecast combined with an after-tax profit margin, as follows:

Estimated earnings in year t =

estimated sales in year t × after-tax profit margin expected in year t

$$\text{Estimated EPS in year } t = \frac{\text{estimated earnings in year } t}{\text{number of common shares outstanding in year } t}$$

Example 6 Assume that in the year just ended, XYZ Corporation reported sales of $60 million and revenues are estimated to grow at a 4 percent annual rate. The after-tax profit margin should amount to about 8 percent, and the number of common shares outstanding is 400,000 shares. Calculate as follows:

$$\text{Estimated earnings in year } t = \$60 \text{ million} \times 0.04 = \$2.4 \text{ million}$$

$$\text{Estimated EPS in year } t = \frac{\$2.4 \text{ million}}{400,000 \text{ shares}} = \$6 \text{ per share}$$

More sophisticated methods of forecasting sales and earnings, such as linear regression, are available.

HOW IS IT USED AND APPLIED?

The valuation of a security is an important factor in the financial manager's decision-making process. Failure to understand the concepts and computational procedures in valuing a security may preclude sound financial decisions. This fact is evident in the company's objective of maximizing the value of its common stock.

Investors and Securities Analysts.   Predicting the future price of a stock is not an easy task. The valuation models described above may be helpful in this endeavor.

36 Contribution Margin

DEFINITION.   Contribution margin is the difference between sales and the variable costs of the product or service—that is, the amount of money available to cover fixed costs and generate profit. Contribution margin is an internal measure that is crucial to management decision making.

HOW IS IT COMPUTED?   There are two ways to calculate the contribution margin. The simplest method assumes that variable costs include both variable manufacturing costs and variable operating expenses. The sample calculation of contribution margin is thus:

Sales
Less: Variable costs
Equals: Contribution margin

Often, the contribution margin computation is shown in more detail as:

Sales
Less: Variable manufacturing costs
Equals: Manufacturing contribution margin
Less: Variable operating expenses
Equals: Contribution margin
Less: Fixed costs
Equals: Net income

Further analysis is provided by determining the contribution margin ratio:

$$\text{Contribution margin ratio} = \frac{\text{Contribution margin}}{\text{sales}}$$

Example 1   Sales are $15,000, variable costs are $6,100, and fixed costs are $4,000. The contribution margin equals:

Sales	$15,000
Less: Variable costs	6,100
Equals: Contribution margin	$ 8,900

The contribution margin of $8,900 is the amount available to cover fixed costs.

Example 2 Ten thousand units have been sold at $30 per unit. Variable cost per unit is $18, and fixed costs total $100,000. Therefore, fixed cost per unit is ($100,000/10,000) = $10. Assume that idle capacity exists. A prospective customer is willing to buy 100 units at a price of only $20 per unit.

The order should be accepted, even though the offering price is below the normal selling price, because it results in additional profit of $200 computed as follows:

Sales (100 × $20)	$2000
Less: Variable costs (100 × $18)	1800
Contribution margin	$ 200
Less: Fixed costs	0
Net income	$ 200

The analytical implication here is that a company can sell an item below the normal selling price when idle capacity exists, as long as there is a contribution margin, because these sales will help to cover fixed costs or add to profits. The contribution-margin calculation requires the segregation of fixed and variable costs, which is needed in breakeven analysis.

HOW IS IT USED AND BY WHOM?

Management Accountants and Cost Analysts. The applications of contribution margin include analysis of whether to:

- Accept or reject a special order in cases where idle capacity exists
- Keep, drop, or add a product line
- Make or buy a certain part

For example, if contribution-margin analysis is employed to determine the optimum utilization of capacity, the alternative with the highest contribution margin per unit would be selected, assuming that interchangeable capacity exists.

This analysis can also be used to appraise proposals and programs. Contribution-margin analysis can be used to determine the bid price on a contract or order based on the desired profit on that contract.

Management accountants and cost analysts find contribution-margin analysis valuable in evaluating the performance of a department as a whole and department management. A high contribution-margin ratio is preferred, since it shows a greater contribution to profits for each sales dollar generated.

37 Controllable (Budget, Spending) Variance

DEFINITION. The overhead controllable variance reveals the occurrence of excess spending, enabling management to determine the reasons for any excess spending and measures that are desirable to control costs.

HOW IS IT COMPUTED?
Controllable variance =

actual overhead versus budgeted adjusted to standard hours

where

Budgeted adjusted to standard hours =

fixed overhead (denominator or budget hours ×

standard fixed overhead rate) +

variable overhead (standard hours × standard variable overhead rate)

Example For a certain firm, the standards for total overhead are:

Variable overhead: 2 hours @ $6 = $12 per unit
Fixed overhead: 2 hours @ $20 = $40 per unit

The actual figures are:

Production	9,500 units	
Denominator activity	10,000 units	
Variable overhead	$115,000	$535,000
Fixed overhead	$420,000	

The controllable variance is found as:

Actual overhead		$535,000
Budgeted adjusted to standard hours		
Fixed overhead, 10,000 × 2 = 20,000 × $20	$400,000	
Variable overhead, 19,000 × $6	114,000	514,000
Variance		$ 21,000 Unfav.

HOW IS IT USED AND BY WHOM?

Cost Accountants. The result of the controllable variance calculation may indicate changes in the amount charged for overhead services or changes in the correlation between overhead items and the variable used to measure output. If such changes are of a permanent nature, management may have to revise output levels.

Management uses the overhead budget variance as a basis for determining the extent to which cost centers are within their budgeted cost levels. Use of such variances is valuable in formulating decisions regarding cost-center operations.

The controllable variance is the responsibility of the foreman, since he or she influences the amount of overhead actually incurred. An unfavorable variance may be due to price increases, to a lack of control over costs, and/or to waste.

38 Conversion Ratio

DEFINITION. The conversion ratio applies to the number of shares of stock the holder of a convertible security receives when the conversion is made.

HOW IS IT COMPUTED?

$$\text{Conversion ratio} = \frac{\text{face value of convertible security}}{\text{conversion price}}$$

The conversion price is the effective price the holder pays for the common stock when the conversion is effected. The conversion price is reduced by the percentage amount of any stock dividend or stock split so that the common stock shareholder maintains his or her proportionate interest.

Example A $100,000 bond is convertible into common stock at a conversion price of $50 per share. The conversion ratio is:

$$\frac{\$100,000}{\$50} = 2,000 \text{ shares}$$

This means that holders of convertible bonds may exchange them for 2000 shares of common stock.

HOW IS IT USED AND BY WHOM?

Management and Investors. The conversion ratio indicates how many common shares will be exchanged for a convertible bond or convertible preferred stock. The conversion value of a security equals the common stock price times the conversion ratio.

39 Corporate Planning Models

DEFINITION. A corporate planning model is an integrated business planning model in which marketing and production models are linked to the financial model. More specifically, a corporate model is a description, explanation, and interrelation of the functional areas of a firm (accounting, finance, marketing, production, and others) expressed in terms of a set of mathematical and logical relationships so as to produce a variety of reports including financial statements. The ultimate goals of a corporate planning model are to improve quality of planning and decision making, reduce the decision risk, and, more important, influence or even shape the future environment favorably.

Today more and more companies are using, developing, or experimenting with some form of corporate planning model. This is due primarily to development of planning and modeling software packages that make it possible to develop the model without much knowledge of computer coding or programming. For the accountant and financial analyst, the attractive features of corporate modeling are the formulation of budgets, budgetary planning and control, and financial analyses that can be used to support management decision making. However, corporate modeling involves much more than the generation of financial statements and budgets. Depending on the structure and breadth of the modeling activity, a variety of capabilities, uses, and analyses are available.

HOW IS IT DEVELOPED? Corporate planning models can be categorized according to two approaches: simulation and optimization. Simulation models are attempts to represent mathematically either the operations of the company or conditions in the external economic environment. By adjusting the values of controllable variables and assumed external conditions, the future implications of present decision making can be estimated. Probabilistic simulation models incorporate probability estimates into the forecast sequence, whereas deterministic models do not. Optimization models are intended to identify the best decision, given specific constraints.

The advent of corporate simulation languages enables analysts with little programming experience to write modeling programs in an English-like programming language—for example, IFPS, SIMPLAN, or XSIM. In addition, a number of spreadsheet programs, such as Lotus 1-2-3 and Excel, are also available for use by corporate planning modelers. Since 1979, nearly every Fortune 1000 company has used corporate simulation models. Increasingly, small- and medium-sized firms are introducing this analytical tool.

Example A majority of corporate models in use are recursive and/or simultaneous models. In *recursive models*, each equation can be solved one at a time by substituting the solution values of the preceding equations into the right-hand side of the next equation. An example of a recursive-type financial model is:

(1)	SALES	= A - B*PRICE + C*ADV
(2)	REVENUE	= SALES*PRICE
(3)	CGS	= 0.70*REVENUE
(4)	GM	= SALES - CGS
(5)	OE	= $10,000 + .2*SALES
(6)	EBT	= GM - OE
(7)	TAX	= 0.46*EBT
(8)	EAT	= EBT - TAX

In this example, the selling price (PRICE) and advertising expenses (ADV) are given. A, B, and C are parameters to be estimated, and

$$SALES = \text{sales volume in units}$$

$$REVENUE = \text{sales revenue}$$

$$CGS = \text{cost of goods sold}$$

$$GM = \text{gross margin}$$

$$OE = \text{operating expenses}$$

$$EBT = \text{earnings before taxes}$$

$$TAX = \text{income taxes}$$

$$EAT = \text{earnings after taxes}$$

Simultaneous models are frequently found in econometric models that require a higher level of computation methods, such as matrix inversion. An example of this type of financial model is presented below:

```
(1) INT    = 0.10*DEBT
(2) EARN   = REVENUE - CGS - OE - INT - TAX - DIV
(3) DEBT   = DEBT(- 1) + BOW
(4) CASH   = CASH(- 1) + CC + BOW + EARN - CD - LP
(5) BOW    = MBAL - CASH
```

Note that earnings (EARN) in Eq. (2) are defined as sales revenue minus CGS, OE, interest expense (INT), TAX, and dividend payment (DIV). Note that INT is a percentage interest rate on total debt in Eq. (1). Total debt in Eq. (3) is equal to the previous period's debt [DEBT(− 1)] plus new borrowings (BOW). New debt is the difference between a minimum cash balance (MBAL) minus cash. Finally, the ending cash balance in Eq. (5) is defined as the sum of the beginning balance [CASH(− 1)], cash collection, new borrowings, and earnings, minus cash disbursements and loan payments on the existing debt (LP). Even though the model presented here is simple, it is still simultaneous—that is, it requires the use of a method capable of solving simultaneous equations.

HOW IS IT USED AND APPLIED?

Generally speaking, a corporate model can be used to:

1. Simulate an alternative strategy by evaluating its impact on profits

2. Help establish corporate and division goals

3. Measure the interactive effect on segments within the firm

4. Help management better understand the business and its functional relationships and help improve decision-making ability

5. Link the firm's goals and strategies to its master budgets

6. Assess critically the assumptions underlying environmental constraints

Types of Analysis.

Management's choice of one type of corporate model over another depends on the types of analysis the company wishes to perform. There are typically three types of model investigations.

The first type of investigation seeks to answer "what is" or "what has been" questions—for example, what is or has been the firm's profit when the price of raw material is $12.50? Thus, the model examines such relationships as the relationship between variables of the firm and external macroeconomic variables such as GNP or inflation. The goal of this type of model investigation is to obtain a specific answer based on the stipulated relationship.

The second type of investigation is based on simulation or sensitivity analysis and focuses on "what if" questions. This analysis often takes the following form: "What happens under a given set of assumptions if the decision variable(s) is (are) changed in a prescribed manner?" For example, "What will happen to the company's cash flow and net income if it initiates a reduction in price of 10 percent and an increase in advertising budget of 25 percent?"

The third type of question that can be addressed with corporate planning modeling takes the following form: "What has to be done in order to achieve a particular objective?" This type of analysis is often called "goal seeking," and usually requires the use of optimization models such as linear programming and goal programming.

Typical Questions Addressed via Corporate Modeling. The following is a list of questions addressed by corporate modeling:

- What are the effects of different pricing policies?

- What is the effect of different interest rates and current exchange rates on the income statement and balance sheet of the firm?

- What will be the demand for the end products of the firm at various locations and at different times?

- What is and will be the unit contribution margin for certain production, transportation, and sales allocations?

- What are the absence and turnover rates of the employees of the firm, and what effects will they have?

- What is the effect of advertising and distribution expenditures on sales?

- What marketing strategies can and should the firm follow?

- What do price–demand or supply relations on the output or input side of the firm look like? What are the effects of price/cost changes on sales?

- How do certain states of the national or world economy influence sales of the firm on the one side and purchase price of production factors on the other?

- What is the nature of the conditions that must be fulfilled if the total sales of the firm at a certain time are supposed to be higher than a certain budget value?

- Should the firm produce and sell a certain product, purchase and sell the product, or not get involved at all?

- In what range will the return on investment on various projects and units lie?

- How will the income statement, the balance sheet, and the cash flow statement develop for several operating divisions? What will their contributions be?

- What effects with respect to the financial position of the firm could an acquisition or merger with another firm have?

Benefits Derived from the Corporate Planning Models. Benefits that can be derived from corporate planning models include the following:

- The ability to explore more alternatives
- Better-quality decision making
- More effective planning
- A better understanding of the business
- Faster decision making
- More timely information
- More accurate forecasts
- Cost savings

WHO USES IT AND WHEN?

Financial Planners and Budget Analysts. Using a corporate planning model, financial managers are able to generate pro-forma financial statements and financial ratios. These are the basic tools for budgeting and profit planning. The model will enable them to perform risk analysis and "what if" experiments.

Corporate Planners and Strategists. In the face of uncertainty about the future, management is particularly interested in determining the best possible course of action under given circumstances. The model is used as a tool to help minimize risk and uncertainty and develop the best course of action for the company. For example, using corporate planning models, a firm can examine the effects of proposed mergers and acquisitions with more certainty and estimate the potential profits from new markets with more confidence.

40 Correlation Analysis

DEFINITION. Correlation analysis measures the extent to which two variables in a data set co-vary in a linear fashion. Variables X and Y can be considered correlated when a change in one is associated with a consistent and equivalent change in the value of the other. A variable can have a positive, negative, or no correlation with another variable.

HOW IS IT COMPUTED?

Method 1. The correlation coefficient is the standardized covariance of the relationship between the two variables X and Y:

$$r = \frac{\text{cov}(X, Y)}{S_x S_y}$$

where r = coefficient of correlation of X and Y
cov = covariance of X and Y
S_x = standard deviation of X

S_y = standard deviation of Y
n = number of observations

The formula for the covariance of X and Y is:

$$\text{cov}(X, Y) = \frac{\sum (X - \overline{X})(Y - \overline{Y})}{n}$$

Example 1   A correlation matrix may be prepared by computer to show the correlation between variables, such as between components of a company's product line as given in Exhibit 40.1. A perfect correlation of 1.0 will exist, of course, between measures of the same variable, as in A and A, B and B, etc. However, the majority of the correlation measures between the products in Exhibit 40.1 are statistically insignificant—that is, there is no significant correlation. The correlation measure of 0.00 between products B and E and between B and F indicates that virtually no correlation exists between these products. For products C and E the correlation of 0.73 is positive and could be statistically significant. This would indicate that products C and E are closely tied to each other, which would require further management analysis of this relationship.

The strong -0.85 relationship between products A and C indicates these products are negatively correlated with each other, resulting in diversification.

Example 2   The management of a firm has launched a new advertising campaign and would like to know the nature of the relationship between the dollars spent on advertising and the sales generated. This is a good example of interval data where a possible relationship can easily be tested with the correlation coefficient.

In order to calculate the correlation coefficient, the covariance first has to be computed between advertising expenditures, X, and sales, Y. The computation is presented in Exhibit 40.2.

The difficulty with covariance as a measure of the degree of the relationship between two variables is that the size of the sample affects the outcome of the measure. The advantage of the coefficient of correlation is that it standardizes the results for the size of the sample by dividing the covariance by the product of the standard deviation of X and Y:

$$r = \frac{\text{cov}(X, Y)}{S_x S_y}$$

The computation of the correlation of X and Y is shown in Exhibit 40.3.

In this example, the correlation between advertising expenditures and sales is $r = +0.87$. This tells management that advertising spending is strongly associated with increased sales.

Exhibit 40.1   Correlation

Product	A	B	C	D	E	F
A	1.00	0.26	-0.85	-0.01	-0.07	0.22
B	0.26	1.00	-0.02	-0.07	0.00	0.00
C	-0.85	-0.02	1.00	0.01	0.73	0.23
D	-0.01	-0.07	0.01	1.00	0.01	-0.02
E	-0.07	0.00	0.73	0.01	1.00	0.45
F	0.22	0.00	0.23	-0.02	0.45	1.00

Exhibit 40.2 Computation of the covariance of X and Y, where $cov(X, Y) = \Sigma(X - \bar{X})(Y - \bar{Y})/n$

Month	X Expen- ditures	X^2	Y Adver- tising Sales	Y^2	$X - \bar{X}$	$Y - \bar{Y}$	$(X - \bar{X})$ $\times$ $(Y - \bar{Y})$
January	24	576	58	3,364	– 13.44	– 10.22	137.43
February	32	1,024	64	4,096	– 5.44	– 4.22	22.99
March	31	961	64	4,096	– 6.44	– 4.22	27.21
April	37	1,369	68	4,624	– 0.44	– 0.22	0.10
May	42	1,764	75	5,625	4.56	6.78	30.88
June	46	2,116	74	5,476	8.56	5.78	49.43
July	48	2,304	70	4,900	10.56	1.78	18.77
August	38	1,444	68	4,624	0.56	– 0.22	– 0.12
September	39	1,521	73	5,329	1.56	4.78	7.43
Sum	337	13,079	614	42,134			294.11
Covariance	$(X, Y) = \dfrac{294.11}{9} = 32.68$						

Exhibit 40.3 Computation of the correlation of X and Y

Month	$(X - \bar{X})^2$	$(\bar{Y} - Y)^2$
January	180.75	104.49
February	29.64	17.83
March	41.53	17.83
April	0.20	0.05
May	20.75	45.94
June	73.20	33.38
July	111.42	3.16
August	0.31	0.05
September	2.42	22.83
Sum	460.22	245.56

$$S_x = \sqrt{\frac{460.22}{9}} = 7.15$$

$$S_y = \sqrt{\frac{245.56}{9}} = 5.22$$

$$S_x \times S_y = 7.15 \times 5.22 = 37.35$$

$$r = \frac{32.68}{37.35} = 0.87$$

Method 2: The Product Moment Method. A second method for the direct computation of the correlation coefficient is called the product moment method:

$$r = \frac{N(\sum XY) - (\sum X)(\sum Y)}{\sqrt{N(\sum X^2) - (\sum X)^2}\sqrt{N(\sum Y^2) - (\sum Y)^2}}$$

Example 3 Using the same data as in Example 2, we can complete the computations for the product moment method:

$$r = \frac{9 \times 23{,}285 - (206{,}918)}{\sqrt{9(13{,}079) - (113{,}569)}\sqrt{9(42{,}134) - 376{,}996}}$$

$$= \frac{209{,}565 - 206{,}918}{\sqrt{117{,}711 - 113{,}569}\sqrt{379{,}206 - 376{,}996}}$$

$$= \frac{2{,}647}{\sqrt{4{,}142}\ \sqrt{2{,}210}}$$

$$= \frac{2{,}647}{\sqrt{9{,}153{,}820}}$$

$$= \frac{2{,}647}{3{,}025.53}$$

$$= 0.87$$

Thus, the product moment correlation produces the same $r = 0.87$ as the covariance method.

Method 3: Graphing. The degree of correlation between Y and X can also be graphed. Such graphs illustrate a perfect positive correlation ($+1$), perfect negative correlation (-1), and no correlation (0) between the variables Y and X. Of course, the correlation between variables may range from -1.0 to $+1.0$.

HOW IS IT USED AND APPLIED? In business and industry, correlation analysis is a very effective tool used to measure the strength and direction of an association between Y and X where interval data are available. Countless applications exist, including the previously illustrated association between products, advertising expenditures and sales, wages and productivity, financial ratios and the market price of stock, various measures of finance and associated corporate outcomes, and any nonfinancial set of interval data. Squaring the correlation coefficient produces the coefficient of determination, which measures the percentage of variation in Y, the dependent variable, associated with the variation in X, the independent (explanatory) variable.

WHO USES IT AND WHEN?

Managers and Financial Analysts. The correlation coefficient is used to measure the strength and direction of an association between Y and X where interval data is used. The correlation coefficient is very effective in determining whether associations exist between a determined set of data, the strength of the association, and the direction of the association, whether it is positive or negative. For example, negative correlation between products or investments reduces overall risk.

41 Cost of Capital

DEFINITION. The cost of capital is defined as the rate of return that is necessary to maintain the market value of the firm (or price of the firm's stock).

HOW IS IT COMPUTED? The cost of capital is computed as a weighted average of the various capital components, which are items on the right-hand side of the balance sheet, such as debt, preferred stock, common stock, and retained earnings. Each element of capital has a component cost that is identified by the following:

k_i = before-tax cost of debt

$k_d = k_i(1 - t)$ = after-tax cost of debt, where t = tax rate

k_p = cost of preferred stock

k_s = cost of retained earnings (or internal equity)

k_e = cost of external equity, or cost of issuing new common stock

k_o = firm's overall cost of capital, or a weighted average cost of capital

Each of these calculations is described below, as well as the determination of historical, target, and marginal weights.

Cost of Debt. The before-tax cost of debt can be found by determining the internal rate of return (or yield to maturity) on bond cash flows. However, the following short-cut formula may be used for approximating the yield to maturity on a bond:

$$k_i = \frac{I + (M - V)/n}{(M + V)/2}$$

where I = annual interest payments
M = par or face value, usually $1000 per bond
V = market value or net proceeds from the sale of a bond
n = term of the bond in n years

Since the interest payments are tax-deductible, the cost of debt must be stated on an after-tax basis.

Example 1 Assume that the Carter Company issues a $1000, 8 percent, 20-year bond whose net proceeds are $940. The tax rate is 40 percent. Then, the before-tax cost of debt, k_i, is:

$$K_i = \frac{I + (M - V)/n}{(M + V)/2}$$

$$= \frac{\$80 + (\$1000 - \$940)/20}{(\$1000 + \$940)/2} = \frac{\$83}{\$970} = 8.56\%$$

Therefore, the after-tax cost of debt is:

$$k_d = k_i(1 - t)$$

$$= 8.56\% \, (1 - 0.4) = 5.14\%$$

Cost of Preferred Stock.

The cost of preferred stock, k_p, is found by dividing the annual preferred stock dividend, d_p, by the net proceeds from the sale of the preferred stock, p, as follows:

$$k_p = \frac{d_p}{p}$$

Since preferred stock dividends are not a tax-deductible expense, these dividends are paid out after taxes. Consequently, no tax adjustment is required.

Example 2 Suppose that the Carter Company has preferred stock that pays a $13 dividend per share and sells for $100 per share in the market. The flotation (or underwriting) cost is 3 percent, or $3 per share. Then the cost of preferred stock is:

$$k_p = \frac{d_p}{p}$$

$$= \frac{\$13}{\$97} = 13.4\%$$

Cost of Equity Capital.

The cost of common stock, k_e, is generally viewed as the rate of return that investors require on a firm's common stock. Two techniques for measuring the cost of common stock equity capital are widely used: (1) Gordon's growth model and (2) the *capital-asset pricing model* (CAPM) approach.

Gordon's growth model.

Gordon's model is:

$$P_0 = \frac{D_1}{r - g}$$

where P_0 = value (or market price) of common stock
D_i = dividend to be received in 1 year
r = investor's required rate of return
g = rate of growth (assumed to be constant over time)

Solving the model for r yields a formula for the cost of common stock:

$$r = \frac{D_1}{P_0} + g \quad \text{or} \quad k_e = \frac{D_1}{P_0} + g$$

Note that r is changed to k_e to show that it is used for the computation of cost of capital.

Example 3 Assume that the market price of the Carter Company's stock is $40. The dividend to be paid at the end of the coming year is $4 per share and is expected to grow at a constant annual rate of 6 percent. Then the cost of this common stock is:

$$k_e = \frac{D_1}{P_0} + g = \frac{\$4}{\$40} + 6\% = 16\%$$

The cost of new common stock, or external equity capital, is higher than the cost of existing common stock because of the *flotation costs* involved in selling the new common stock. Flotation costs, sometimes called *issuance costs,* are the total costs of issuing and selling a security, including printing and engraving, legal fees, and accounting fees.

If f is flotation cost in percent, the formula for the cost of new common stock is:

$$k_e = \frac{D_1}{P_0(1 - f)} + g$$

Example 4 Assume the same data as in Example 3, except that the firm is trying to sell new issues of stock A and its flotation cost is 10 percent. Then:

$$k_e = \frac{D_1}{P_0(1 - f)} + g$$

$$= \frac{\$4}{\$40(1 - 0.1)} + 6\% = \frac{\$4}{\$36} + 6\% = 11.11\% + 6\% = 17.11\%$$

(See also No. 81, Gordon's Dividend Growth Model.)

Capital-asset pricing model (CAPM) approach. An alternative approach to measuring the cost of common stock is to use the CAPM, which involves the following steps:

1. Estimate the risk-free rate, r_f, generally taken to be the U.S. Treasury bill rate.

2. Estimate the stock's beta coefficient, b, which is an index of systematic (or nondiversifiable market) risk.

3. Estimate the rate of return on the market portfolio, r_m, such as the Standard & Poor's 500 Stock Composite Index or Dow Jones 30 Industrials.

4. Estimate the required rate of return on the firm's stock, using the CAPM equation:

$$k_e = r_f + b(r_m - r_f)$$

Again, note that the symbol r_j has been changed to k_e.

Example 5 Assuming that r_f is 7 percent, b is 1.5, and r_m is 13 percent, then:

$$k_e = r_f + b(r_m - r_f) = 7\% + 1.5(13\% - 7\%) = 16\%$$

This 16 percent cost of common stock can be viewed as consisting of a 7 percent risk-free rate plus a 9 percent risk premium, which reflects that the firm's stock price is 1.5 times more volatile than the market portfolio to the factors affecting nondiversifiable, or systematic, risk. (See also No. 26, Capital-Asset Pricing Model.)

Cost of Retained Earnings. The cost of retained earnings, k_s, is closely related to the cost of existing common stock, since the cost of equity obtained by retained earnings is the same as the rate of return that investors require on the firm's common stock. Therefore,

$$k_e = k_s$$

Measuring the Overall Cost of Capital. A firm's overall cost of capital is the weighted average of the individual capital costs, with the weights being the proportions of each type of capital used. Let k_o be the overall cost of capital:

$$k_o = \sum(\text{percentage of total capital structure}$$

supplied by each source of capital × cost of capital for each source)

$$= \sum w_d k_d + w_p k_p + w_e k_e + w_s k_s$$

where w_d = percent of total capital supplied by debts

w_p = percent of total capital supplied by preferred stock

w_e = percent of total capital supplied by external equity

w_s = percent of total capital supplied by retained earnings (or internal equity)

Weights. The weights used in this analysis can be *historical, target,* or *marginal.*

Historical weights. Historical weights are based on a firm's existing capital structure. The use of these weights is based on the assumption that the firm's existing capital structure is optimal and therefore should be maintained in the future. Two types of historical weights can be used: book-value weights and market-value weights.

Book-value weights. The use of book-value weights in calculating the firm's weighted cost of capital assumes that new financing will be raised using the same method the firm used for its present capital structure. The weights are determined by dividing the book value of each capital component by the sum of the book values of all the long-term capital sources. The computation of overall cost of capital is illustrated in the following example.

Example 6 Assume the following capital structure and cost of each source of financing for the Carter Company:

Capital asset		Cost
Mortgage bonds ($1000 par)	$20,000,000	5.14% (from Example 1)
Preferred stock ($100 par)	5,000,000	13.40% (from Example 2)
Common stock ($40 par)	20,000,000	17.11% (from Example 4)
Retained earnings	5,000,000	16.00% (from Example 3)
Total	$50,000,000	

The book-value weights and the overall cost of capital are computed as follows:

Source	Book value	Weight	Cost	Weighted cost
Debt	$20,000,000	40%[a]	5.14%	2.06%[b]
Preferred stock	5,000,000	10	13.40%	1.34
Common stock	20,000,000	40	17.11%	6.84
Retained earnings	5,000,000	10	16.00%	1.60
Total	$50,000,000	100%		11.84%

Overall cost of capital = k_o = 11.84%

[a]$20,000,000/$50,000,000 = 0.40 = 40%.
[b]5.14% × 40% = 2.06%.

Market-value weights. Market-value weights are determined by dividing the market value of each source by the sum of the market values of all sources. The use of market-value weights for computing a firm's weighted-average cost of capital is theoretically more appealing than the use of book-value weights, because the market values of the securities closely approximate the actual dollars to be received from their sale.

Example 7 In addition to the data from Example 6, assume that the security market prices are as follows:

Mortgage bonds = $1100 per bond.
Preferred stock = $90 per share.
Common stock = $80 per share.

The firm's number of securities in each category is:

$$\text{Mortgage bonds} = \frac{\$20,000,000}{\$1,000} = 20,000$$

$$\text{Preferred stock} = \frac{\$5,000,000}{\$100} = 50,000$$

$$\text{Common stock} = \frac{\$20,000,000}{\$40} = 500,000$$

Therefore, the market value weights are:

Source	Number of securities	Price	Market value
Debt	20,000	$1,100	$22,000,000
Preferred stock	50,000	$ 90	4,500,000
Common stock	500,000	$ 80	40,000,000
Total			$66,500,000

The $40 million common-stock value must be split in the ratio of 4 to 1 (the $20 million common stock versus the $5 million retained earnings in the original capital structure), since the market value of the retained earnings has been impounded into the common stock.

The firm's cost of capital is as follows:

Source	Market value	Weight	Cost	Weighted average
Debt	$22,000,000	33.08%	5.14%	1.70%
Preferred stock	4,500,000	6.77	13.40%	0.91
Common stock	32,000,000	48.12	17.11%	8.23
Retained earnings	8,000,000	12.03	16.00%	1.92
Total		100.00%		12.76%
	$66,500,000			

Overall cost of capital = k_o = 12.76%

Target weights. If the firm has a target capital structure (desired debt–equity mix) that is maintained over the long term, then the use of that capital structure and associated weights can be used in calculating the firm's weighted cost of capital.

Marginal weights. Marginal weights involve the use of the *actual* financial mix used in financing the proposed investments. In using target weights, the firm is concerned with what it believes to be the optimal capital structure or target percentage. In using marginal weights, the firm is concerned with the actual dollar amounts of each type of financing needed for a given investment project. This approach, while attractive, presents a problem: The cost of capital for the individual sources depends on the firm's financial risk, which is affected by the firm's financial mix. If the company alters its present capital structure, the individual costs will change, which makes it more difficult to compute the weighted cost of capital. The important assumption needed is that the firm's financial mix is relatively stable and that these weights will closely approximate future financing practice.

Example 8 The Carter Company is considering raising $8 million for plant expansion. Management estimates using the following mix to finance this project:

Debt	$4,000,000	50%
Common stock	2,000,000	25
Retained earnings	2,000,000	25
Total	$8,000,000	100%

The company's cost of capital is computed as follows:

Source	Marginal Weights	Cost	Weighted Cost
Debt	50%	5.14%	2.57%
Common stock	25	17.11%	4.28
Retained earnings	25	16.00%	4.00
	100%		10.85%

Overall cost of capital = k_o = 10.85%

HOW IS IT USED AND APPLIED? Financial managers must know the cost of capital (the minimum required rate of return) in (1) making capital budgeting decisions, (2) helping to establish the optimal capital structure, and (3) making decisions such as leasing, bond refunding, and working capital management. The cost of capital has been used either as a discount rate under the NPV method or as a hurdle (cutoff) rate under the IRR method.

WHO USES IT AND WHEN?

Financial Managers. Cost of capital is a very important concept within financial management, because it is the rate of return that must be achieved in order for the price of the stock to remain unchanged. Therefore, the cost of capital is the minimum acceptable rate of return for the company's new investments. Financial officers should be thoroughly familiar with the ways to compute the costs of various sources of financing for financial, capital budgeting, and capital structure decisions. A comparison should be made of the cost of capital rates under alternative financing strategies (e.g., mix of debt, preferred stock, and common stock). The financial manager should typically issue the financing instrument that results in the lowest overall cost of capital.

Top Management and Corporate Strategists. Top managers must have a good understanding of the cost of capital before making important strategic decisions such as mergers, acquisitions, and buyouts.

Investment and Credit Analysts. An increase in a company's cost of capital relative to competing companies in the industry means that it is viewed as being more risky in the eyes of the investment and credit community.

42 Cost of Credit

DEFINITION. The cost of credit is the cost of not taking credit terms extended for a business transaction. Credit terms usually express the amount of the cash discount, the date of its expiration, and the due date. A typical credit term is 2/10, net/30. If payment is made within 10 days, a 2 percent cash discount is allowed; otherwise, the entire amount is due in 30 days. The cost of not taking the cash discount can be substantial.

HOW IS IT COMPUTED? The formula for computing the cost of credit if a cash discount is not taken is:

$$\text{Credit cost} = \frac{\% \text{ discount}}{100 - \% \text{ discount}} \times \frac{360}{\text{credit period} - \text{discount period}}$$

Example Suppose that Alan Steel Works has extended $900 of trade credit to a customer on terms of "2/10, net/30." The customer can either pay $900 × 98% = $882 at the end of the 10-day discount period, or wait for the full 30 days and pay the full $900. By waiting the full 30 days, the customer effectively borrows $882 for an additional 20 days, paying $900 − $882 or $18 in interest.

This information can be used to compute the credit cost of borrowing this money:

$$\text{Credit cost} = \frac{\% \text{ discount}}{100 - \% \text{ discount}} \times \frac{360}{\text{credit period} - \text{discount period}}$$

$$= \frac{2}{100 - 2} \times \frac{360}{30 - 10}$$

$$= \frac{2}{98} \times \frac{360}{20}$$

$$= 36.73\%$$

As this example illustrates, the annual percentage cost of offering a 2/10, net/30 trade discount is almost 37%.

The 20-day discount period occurs 18 times per year. Using this information, it is possible to compute the effective annual rate of interest on a 360-day year:

$$\text{Effective annual credit cost} = \left(1 + \frac{\text{credit cost}}{\text{times compounded per year}}\right)^{\text{times compounded per year}} - 1$$

$$= \left(1 + \frac{36.73}{18}\right)^{18} - 1$$

$$= 43.85\%$$

Annualized, the 36.73 percent cost of interest amounts to a substantial 43.85 percent.

Some examples of additional credit costs are illustrated in Exhibit 42.1.

HOW IS IT USED AND APPLIED? The acceptance of trade credit is a normal part of doing business and is considered a spontaneous source of financing since it normally expands as the volume of business increases. It is not unusual for a manufacturer to ship merchandise and wait a specified period of time for payment. Often trade credit is extended to a business that is not qualified to obtain bank financing.

The cost of trade credit may be of secondary importance to some buyers when no other form of credit is available; however, when other credit is

Exhibit 42.1   Cost of additional credit if cash discount is not taken

	Credit terms			
Discount	Days	Net	Percent	Annualized
1	10	20	36.36%	43.59%
1	10	30	18.18%	19.88%
2	10	20	73.47%	106.95%
2	10	30	36.73%	44.12%
3	10	20	111.34%	199.38%
3	10	30	55.67%	73.75%
3	15	30	74.23%	107.72%
3	15	45	37.11%	44.53%

available, it may be worth doing some comparison shopping. Often, the buyer may be paying a hidden financing charge in terms of higher merchandise prices. At other times, trade credit may represent a virtual subsidy by a seller to a customer, e.g., by a manufacturer to a distributor, and it should be utilized.

Trade credit can serve the dual purpose of financing purchases while using the funds to finance credit sales to customers.

WHO USES IT AND WHEN?

Managers, Comptrollers, and Sales Managers. The computation of the cost of credit is an essential part of doing business. The cost of not taking trade credit usually increases during relatively good economic periods, with more generous discounts being offered; in periods of economic downturn, however, the cost of not taking trade credit usually declines as the discount terms are reduced.

Management must examine trade credit terms carefully.

43 Cost of Prediction Errors

DEFINITION. There is always a cost involved with a failure to predict a certain variable accurately. The cost of the prediction error can be substantial, depending on the circumstances. For example, failure to make an accurate projection of sales could result in poor production planning, too much or too little purchase of labor, and so on, thereby causing potentially huge financial losses.

HOW IS IT COMPUTED? The cost of the prediction error is basically the contribution or profit lost because of an inaccurate prediction. It can be measured in terms of lost sales, disgruntled customers, and idle machines.

> **Example** Assume that a company has been selling, for $1.00 each, a toy doll that has a cost of $0.60. The fixed cost is $300. The company cannot return any unsold dolls. It has predicted sales of 2000 units. However, unforeseen competition has reduced sales to 1500 units. The cost of its prediction error—that is, its failure to predict demand accurately, is calculated as follows:
>
> 1. Initial predicted sales = 2000 units.
>   Optimal decision: purchase 2000 units.
>   Expected net income = (2000 units × $0.40 contribution) − $300 fixed costs = $500.
> 2. Alternative parameter value = 1500 units.
>   Optimal decision: purchase 1500 units.
>   Expected net income = (1500 units × $0.40 contribution) − $300 fixed costs = $300
> 3. Results of original decision under alternative parameter value:
>   Expected net income:
>   Revenue (1500 units × $1.00) − cost of dolls (2000 units × $0.60) − $300 fixed costs = $1500 − $1200 − $300 = $0.
> 4. Cost of prediction error: (2) − (3) = $300.

HOW IS IT USED AND APPLIED? It is important to be able to determine the cost of the prediction error in order to minimize the potential detrimental effect on future profitability of the company. Prediction relates to sales, expenses, and purchases.

WHO USES IT AND WHEN?

Sales Managers, Budget Analysts, and Financial Analysts. Business people need to keep track of past prediction records to ensure that (1) future costs can be minimized and (2) better forecasting methods can be developed.

44 Credit Cost on Installment Purchase

DEFINITION. The cost associated with buying on the installment basis, credit cost on installment purchases is the amount paid for the privilege of distributing the original unpaid balance over a period of time.

HOW IS IT COMPUTED?

Credit cost = total cost on the installment plan – actual cash price

Example An item priced at $5000 is being offered at a 10 percent discount. The down payment is $300 and the carrying charge is $400. The remainder of $4700 is to be paid in 10 equal monthly installments. Calculate the credit cost as follows:

$$\text{Total cost on the installment plan} = \$5000 + \$400 = \$5400$$
$$\text{Actual cash price} = \$5000 \times 90\% = \$4500$$
$$\text{Cost of credit} = \$5400 - \$4500 = \$900$$

HOW IS IT USED AND BY WHOM?

Purchasers and Sellers. The cost of credit is computed by those buying or selling on the installment plan.

45 Current-Liability Ratios

DEFINITION. Current-liability ratios indicate the degree to which current debt payments will be required within the year. Understanding a company's liability is critical, since if it is unable to meet current debt, a liquidity crisis looms.

HOW IS IT COMPUTED?

1. Current liabilities to noncurrent liabilities.

$$\frac{\text{Current liabilities}}{\text{Noncurrent liabilities}}$$

2. Current liabilities to total liabilities.

$$\frac{\text{Current liabilities}}{\text{Total liabilities}}$$

These ratios are compared to industry norms.

Example Assume the following financial data for a company:

Current liabilities	$ 500,000
Noncurrent liabilities	600,000
Total liabilities	1,100,000

The relevant ratios are:

Current liabilities to noncurrent liabilities	83.3%
Current liabilities to total liabilities	45.5

These are compared to industry norms:

Current liabilities to noncurrent liabilities	45.0%
Current liabilities to total liabilities	24.0

The company's liquidity is unfavorable relative to the industry norm, as indicated by the company's high level of current debt.

HOW IS IT USED AND BY WHOM?

Short-Term Creditors and Financial Management. A high ratio of current liabilities to total liabilities indicates less corporate liquidity, since there is a greater portion of current debt. If a high ratio exists, the company must take steps to reduce its excessive short-term debt—steps such as financing on a long-term basis with bonds or stock issuances, or selling assets to obtain funds.

46 Current Ratio

DEFINITION. The current ratio, which is subject to seasonal fluctuations, is used to measure the ability of an enterprise to meet its current liabilities out of current assets. Because it shows the margin of safety available to cover any possible shrinkage in the value of current assets, it is an indicator of liquidity. The current ratio conveys the degree to which current assets are available to cover every $1 of short-term debt.

HOW IS IT COMPUTED?

$$\text{Current ratio} = \frac{\text{current assets}}{\text{current liabilities}}$$

Note: Current assets that are pledged to secure long-term liabilities are not available to meet current debt. If these current assets are included in the calculation of the ratio, a distortion results.

In general, the current ratio must be at least 2:1. The adequacy of the current ratio depends on the particular industry under examination. For a complete understanding of the implications, a comparison must be made to competing companies.

Example A company reports the following balance sheet information for 19X1 and 19X2:

	19X1	19X2
Current assets	$110,000	$120,000
Current liabilities	70,000	55,400
Current ratio	1.57	2.17

The trend in the ratio has improved during the year, indicating better liquidity in 19X2 than in 19X1. For example, in 19X2, for every $1 in current debt, the company has $2.17 in current assets to cover it.

ANALYTICAL IMPLICATIONS AND WARNINGS. If the current ratio increases substantially while the quick ratio remains basically constant, a buildup in inventory is indicated.

A high current ratio is needed when a company has difficulty borrowing on short notice. A limitation of the use of this ratio is that it may rise just before financial distress, due to the company's desire to improve its cash position by, for example, selling fixed assets. Such dispositions have a detrimental effect on productive capacity.

Another limitation peculiar to the current ratio is that it is excessively high when inventory is carried on a LIFO (last-in, first-out) basis.

HOW IS IT USED AND BY WHOM?

Short-Term Creditors. A sharp decline in the current ratio indicates a deterioration in a company's liquidity, which may mean that the company will be unable to meet its current debt when that debt is due. Liquidity means the readiness and speed with which current assets can be converted to cash.

Financial Management. A lower current ratio may mean that a company will have greater difficulty borrowing short-term funds. A very low ratio may indicate that the company will be unable to meet its payments.

The current ratio measures the reserve of liquid funds in excess of current obligations that is available as a margin of safety against uncertainty and against the random shocks to which the flow of funds within an enterprise are subject. Random shocks, such as strikes, extraordinary losses, and other uncertainties, can temporarily and unexpectedly stop or reduce the inflow of funds.

47 Decision Matrix

DEFINITION. Decisions are made under either certainty or uncertainty. Decision making under certainty means that for each decision there is only one event and therefore only one outcome for each action. Decision making under uncertainty, which is more common in reality, involves several events for each action together with its probability of occurrence.

When decisions are made in a world of uncertainty, it is often helpful to make computations of (1) *expected value,* (2) *standard deviation,* and (3) *coefficient of variation.*

Although statistics such as expected value and standard deviation are essential for choosing the best course of action under uncertainty, the decision problem can best be approached using what is called *decision theory.* Decision theory and use of a decision matrix is a systematic approach to making decisions, particularly in making decisions under uncertainty.

HOW IS IT FORMULATED AND COMPUTED? Decision theory utilizes an organized approach such as a *decision matrix* (or *payoff table*), which is characterized by:

1. The *row* representing a set of alternative courses of action available to the decision maker

2. The *column* representing the state of nature or conditions that are likely to occur and over which the decision maker has no control

3. The *entries* in the body of the table representing the outcome of the decision, known as payoffs, which may be in the form of costs, revenues, profits, or cash flows.

By computing the expected value of each action, the best one can be selected.

Example 1   Assume the following probability distribution of daily demand for a product:

Daily demand	0	1	2	3
Probability	.2	.3	.3	.2

Also assume that unit cost = $3, selling price = $5 (i.e., profit on each unit sold = $2), and salvage value on unsold units = $2 (i.e., loss on each unsold unit = $1). Either 0, 1, 2, or 3 units can be stocked. The question is: How many units should be stocked each day? Assume that units from one day cannot be sold the next day. Then the payoff table can be constructed as follows:

		State of nature				
Demand		0	1	2	3	Expected value
Stock (probability)		(.2)	(.3)	(.3)	(.2)	
	0	$0	0	0	0	$0
Actions	1	− 1	2	2	2	1.40
	2	− 2	1[a]	4	4	1.90[b]
	3	− 3	0	3	6	1.50

[a]Profit for (stock 2, demand 1) equals (number of units sold)(profit per unit) − (number of units unsold)(loss per unit) = (1)($5 − 3) − (1)($3 − 2) = $1.
[b]Expected value for (stock 2) is: − 2(.2) + 1(.3) + 4(.3) + 4 (.2) = $1.90.

The optimal stock action is the one with the highest expected monetary value—i.e., stock 2 units.

EXPECTED VALUE OF PERFECT INFORMATION. Suppose the decision maker can obtain a perfect prediction of which event (state of nature) will occur. The expected value with perfect information is the total expected value of actions selected on the assumption of a perfect forecast. The expected value of perfect information can then be computed as:

Expected value with perfect information −

expected value with existing information

Example 2 From the payoff table in Example 1, the following analysis yields the expected value with perfect information:

		State of nature				
Demand		0	1	2	3	Expected value
Stock (probability)		(.2)	(.3)	(.3)	(.2)	
	0	$0				$0
Actions	1		2			0.60
	2			4		1.20
	3				6	1.20
						$3.00

Alternatively,

$$\$0(.2) + 2(.3) + 4(.3) + 6(.2) = \$3.00$$

With existing information, the best the decision maker can obtain is to select stock 2 and obtain $1.90. With perfect information (forecast), the decision maker could make as much as $3. Therefore, the expected value of perfect information is $3.00 − $1.90 = $1.10. This is the maximum price the decision maker is willing to pay for additional information.

HOW IS IT USED AND APPLIED? Whenever decisions are made under conditions of uncertainty, which is common in reality, it means that they involve several events for each action together with its probability of occurrence. The decision situation can best be approached using a decision matrix. This approach is unique in that it answers a critical question such as "How much am I willing to pay for additional information?"

The additional information can be costly, however, particularly if it involves use of a computer and research staff. Therefore, the cost of the additional information must be weighed against the benefit to be derived from it.

WHO USES IT AND WHEN?

Sales Managers. Salespeople use a decision matrix to determine the optimal stock size in the face of uncertain demands in the market.

48 Decision Tree

DEFINITION. Use of a decision tree is another approach to decision making under uncertainty. It is a pictorial representation of a decision situation.

HOW IS IT FORMULATED AND COMPUTED? As in the case of the *decision matrix* approach (See No. 47, Decision Matrix), the decision tree shows decision alternatives, states of nature, probabilities attached to the state of nature, and conditional benefits and losses. The decision tree approach is most useful in a sequential decision situation.

Example Assume that XYZ Corporation wishes to introduce one of two products to the market this year. The probabilities and present values (PV) of projected cash inflows are given below.

Product	Initial investment	PV of cash inflows	Probability
A	$225,000		1.00
		$ 450,000	0.40
		200,000	0.50
		– 100,000	0.10
B	80,000		1.00
		320,000	0.20
		100,000	0.60
		– 150,000	0.20

A decision tree analyzing the two products is shown in Exhibit 48.1. Based on the expected net present value, the company should choose product A over product B.

HOW IS IT USED AND APPLIED? Whenever decisions are made under conditions of uncertainty, which is common in reality, it means that they involve several events for each action together with its probability of occurrence.

The decision situation can best be approached using a decision matrix or decision tree. Unique to this approach is the ability to handle sequential decisions from a long-term perspective in a systematic and pictorial manner.

WHO USES IT AND WHEN?

Sales Managers, Product Managers, and Project Analysts. Salespeople use the decision tree to determine the optimal stock size in the face of

Exhibit 48.1   A decision tree analyzing two products

		Initial investment (1)	Probability (2)	PV of cash inflow (3)	PV of cash inflow (2 × 3) = (4)
			0.40	$450,000	$ 180,000
		$225,000	0.50	$200,000	100,000
	Product A		0.10	– $100,000	– 10,000
			Expected PV of cash inflows		$ 270,000
Choice A or B					
	Product B		0.20	$320,000	$ 64,000
		$ 80,000	0.60	$100,000	60,000
			0.20	– $150,000	– 30,000
			Expected PV of cash inflows		$ 94,000

For Product A:

Expected NPV = expected PV – I = $270,000 – $225,000 = $45,000

For Product B:

Expected NPV = $94,000 – $80,000 = $14,000

uncertain demands in the market. Product managers use it to determine whether to develop a new product. Project managers use it to decide whether to keep an old plant, renovate it, or build a new plant.

49 Decomposition of Time Series

DEFINITION.   When sales exhibit seasonal or cyclical fluctuation, a forecasting method called classical decomposition is used to deal with seasonal, trend, and cyclical components together. Assume that a time series is combined into a model that consists of the four components—trend (T), cyclical (C), seasonal (S), and random (R). This model is of a multiplicative type, i.e.,

$$Y_t = T \times C \times S \times R$$

where Y_t is the time series data (for example, sales, earnings, cash flow).

HOW IS IT COMPUTED? The classical decomposition method is illustrated step by step, by working with the quarterly sales data. The approach basically requires the following four steps:

1. Determine seasonal indices, using a four-quarter moving average.

2. Deseasonalize the data.

3. Develop the linear least-squares equation in order to identify the trend component of the forecast.

4. Forecast the sales for each of the four quarters of the coming year.

The data to be used are the quarterly sales data for a video set over the past 4 years (see Exhibit 49.1). The analysis begins by showing how to identify the seasonal component of the time series.

Step 1: Use moving average to measure the combined trend-cyclical (*TC*) components of the time series. This eliminates the seasonal and random components, *S* and *R*. More specifically, step 1 involves the following sequences of steps:

a. Calculate the four-quarter moving average for the time series, which was discussed above. However, the moving average values computed do not correspond directly to the original quarters of the time series.

b. Resolve this difficulty by using the midpoints between successive moving-average values. For example, since 6.35 corresponds to the first half of quarter 3 and 6.6 corresponds to the last half of quarter 3, (6.35 + 6.6)/2 = 6.475 is used as the moving average value of quarter 3. Similarly, (6.6 + 6.875)/2 = 6.7375 is associated with quarter 4. A complete summary of the moving-average calculation is shown in Exhibit 49.2.

c. Next, calculate the ratio of the actual value to the moving average

Exhibit 49.1   Quarterly sales data for video sets over the past 4 years

Year	Quarter	Sales
1	1	5.8
	2	5.1
	3	7.0
	4	7.5
2	1	6.8
	2	6.2
	3	7.8
	4	8.4
3	1	7.0
	2	6.6
	3	8.5
	4	8.8
4	1	7.3
	2	6.9
	3	9.0
	4	9.4

Exhibit 49.2 Moving-average calculation for video set sales time series

Year	Quarter	Sales	Four-quarter moving average	Centered moving average
1	1	5.8		
	2	5.1		
			6.35	
	3	7		6.475
			6.6	
	4	7.5		6.7375
			6.875	
2	1	6.8		6.975
			7.075	
	2	6.2		7.1875
			7.3	
	3	7.8		7.325
			7.35	
	4	8.4		7.4
			7.45	
3	1	7		7.5375
			7.625	
	2	6.6		7.675
			7.725	
	3	8.5		7.7625
			7.8	
	4	8.8		7.8375
			7.875	
4	1	7.3		7.9375
			8	
	2	6.9		8.075
			8.15	
	3	9	0	
	4	9.4		

value for each quarter in the time series having a four-quarter moving average entry. This ratio in effect represents the seasonal-random component, $SR = Y/TC$. Y represents the time series data. The ratios calculated this way appear in Exhibit 49.3.

d. Arrange the ratios by quarter and then calculate the average ratio by quarter in order to eliminate the random influence. For example, for quarter 1, $(0.975 + 0.929 + 0.920)/3 = 0.941$.

e. The final step adjusts the average ratio slightly (e.g., for quarter 1, 0.941 becomes 0.939), which will be the seasonal index. See Exhibit 49.4.

Step 2: After obtaining the seasonal index, remove the effect of season from the original time series. This process is referred to as *deseasonalizing* the time series. For this, the original series must be divided by the seasonal index for that quarter. This is shown graphically in Exhibit 49.5 and in tabular form in Exhibit 49.6.

Step 3: On the graph, the time series seems to have an upward linear trend. To identify this trend, a least-squares trend equation is developed, as shown in Exhibit 49.6.

Exhibit 49.3   Seasonal random factors for the video set time series

Year	Quarter	Sales	Four-quarter moving average	Centered moving average (*TC*)	Seasonal random component (*SR* = *Y/TC*)
1	1	5.8			
	2	5.1			
			6.35		
	3	7		6.475	1.081
			6.6		
	4	7.5		6.738	1.113
			6.875		
2	1	6.8		6.975	0.975
			7.075		
	2	6.2		7.188	0.863
			7.3		
	3	7.8		7.325	1.065
			7.35		
	4	8.4		7.400	1.135
			7.45		
3	1	7		7.538	0.929
			7.625		
	2	6.6		7.675	0.860
			7.725		
	3	8.5		7.763	1.095
			7.8		
	4	8.8		7.838	1.123
			7.875		
4	1	7.3		7.938	0.920
			8		
	2	6.9		7.950	0.868
			7.9		
	3	9			
	4	8.4			

Step 4:   Develop the forecast using the trend equation and adjust the forecast to account for the effect of season. The quarterly forecast, as shown in Exhibit 49.7, can be obtained by multiplying the forecast based on trend times the seasonal factor.

HOW IS IT USED AND APPLIED?   The classical decomposition model is a time-series model used for forecasting. This means that the method can be used only to fit the time-series data, whether it is monthly, quarterly, or annual. The types of time-series data the company deals with include sales, earnings, cash flows, market share, and costs.

As long as the time series displays the patterns of seasonality and cyclicality, the model constructed should be very effective in projecting the future variable.

Exhibit 49.4   Seasonal component calculations for the video set time series

Quarter	Seasonal random factor (SR)	Seasonal factor (S)	Adjusted S
1	0.975		
	0.929		
	0.920	0.941	0.939
2	0.863		
	0.860		
	0.868	0.863	0.862
3	1.081		
	1.065		
	1.095	1.080	1.078
4	1.113		
	1.135		
	1.123	1.124	1.121
		4.009	4.000

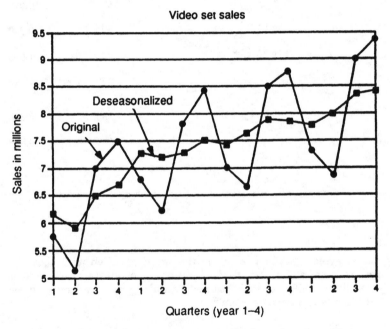

Exhibit 49.5   Actual versus deseasonalized data for the video set time series.

Exhibit 49.6   Deseasonalized data for the video set time series

Year	Quarter	Sales	Seasonal factor (S)	Deseasonalized data	t	tY	t²
1	1	5.8	0.939	6.18	1	6.18	1
	2	5.1	0.862	5.92	2	11.84	4
	3	7	1.078	6.49	3	19.48	9
	4	7.5	1.121	6.69	4	26.75	16
2	1	6.8	0.939	7.24	5	36.21	25
	2	6.2	0.862	7.20	6	43.17	36
	3	7.8	1.078	7.24	7	50.65	49
	4	8.4	1.121	7.49	8	59.93	64
3	1	7	0.939	7.45	9	67.09	81
	2	6.6	0.862	7.66	10	76.60	100
	3	8.5	1.078	7.89	11	86.74	121
	4	8.8	1.121	7.85	12	94.18	144
4	1	7.3	0.939	7.77	13	101.06	169
	2	6.9	0.862	8.01	14	112.11	196
	3	9	1.078	8.35	15	125.23	225
	4	9.4	1.121	8.38	16	134.13	256
				117.81	136	1051.34	1496

Using least-squares formulas, yield
$b = 0.14693$
$a = 6.1143$
   which means that $y = 6.1143 + 0.14693t$ for the forecast periods
$t = 17$
   18
   19
   20

Exhibit 49.7   Sales forecasts for year 5

Year	Quarter	Trend forecast	Seasonal factor	Quarterly forecast
5	1	8.6120[a]	0.939	8.0873
	2	8.7589	0.862	7.5470
	3	8.9058	1.078	9.6004
	4	9.0528	1.121	10.1508

[a] $y = 6.1143 + 0.14693t = 6.1143 + 0.141693(17) = 8.6120$.

WHO USES IT AND WHEN?

Business Economists and Forecasters.   Forecasters use various prediction methods. The classical decomposition model must be used in conjunction with other sophisticated models such as regression methods and the Box-Jenkin model. The method(s) used should be the one(s) that forecast best based on the particular circumstances of the company.

50 Defensive Interval Ratio

DEFINITION. The defensive interval ratio is a liquidity ratio that reveals the ability of the business to meet its current debts.

HOW IS IT COMPUTED?

Defensive interval ratio =

$$\frac{\text{Defensive assets}}{\text{Projected daily operational expenditures} - \text{noncash charges}}$$

where

Defensive assets = cash + marketable securities + receivables

and

Projected daily operational expenditures =

$$\frac{\text{Cost of sales} + \text{operating expenses} + \text{other ordinary cash expenses}}{360}$$

Example A company has cash of $30,000, marketable securities of $38,000, receivables of $46,000, projected daily expenditures of $450,000, and noncash charges of $20,000. The defensive interval ratio is:

$$\frac{\$114,000}{(\$450,000 - \$20,000)/360} = \frac{\$114,000.00}{\$1,194.44} = 95 \text{ days} \quad \text{(rounded)}$$

This analysis shows that defensive assets can cover projected daily expenditures by 95 days.

HOW IS IT USED AND BY WHOM?

Financial Management and Short-Term Creditors. The defensive interval ratio indicates the period of time the entity can operate on its liquid assets without needing revenues from the next period's sources. It reveals corporate near-term liquidity as a basis for meeting expenditures.

51 Deposits Times Capital Ratio

DEFINITION. The deposits times capital ratio is a type of debt/equity ratio for banks. It expresses a relationship between stockholders' equity and the size of a bank's deposits. The larger a bank's deposits are, the greater is its potential investment return as the deposits are converted into investments. Also, a greater deposit base affords more protection to stockholders.

HOW IS IT COMPUTED?

$$\text{Deposits times capital} = \frac{\text{Total average deposits}}{\text{Average stockholders' equity}}$$

Example The following information is available for a bank:

	19X1	19X2
Total average deposits	$9268	$8329
Average stockholders' equity	$ 428	$ 375
Deposits times capital	21.65	22.21

The deposits times capital ratio for the bank actually increased from 21.65 in 19X1 to 22.21 in 19X2, even though both deposits and stockholders' equity declined. However, stockholders' equity declined more rapidly in 19X2 than total average deposits, which increases the deposits times capital ratio. The higher ratio in 19X2 is more favorable because it means more protection for stockholders. Also, a larger deposit base provides greater investment return opportunities for the bank.

HOW IS IT USED AND BY WHOM?

Depositors and Stockholders. The deposits times capital ratio provides a comparative indicator for depositors when considering the safety of a bank and for stockholders looking for security indicators.

52 Depreciation Formulas

DEFINITION. Depreciation is a means of reducing accounting income by spreading out the deductible cost of a fixed asset (e.g., plant, equipment, vehicles) over its estimated life. Two causes of depreciation are physical use and obsolescence. Among the commonly used depreciation methods are the straight-line and the units-of-production methods. The latter method results in a variable depreciation charge based on units produced. Accelerated depreciation methods provide for a more rapid rate of expensing the cost of the asset in early years. The two major accelerated methods are sum of the years' digits (SYD) and double declining balance (DDB). These four methods of depreciation are explained below.

Straight-Line Method. The straight-line method is the easiest and most popular method of calculating depreciation. It results in equal periodic depreciation charges. The method is most appropriate when an asset's usage is uniform from period to period, as is the case with furniture. The annual depreciation expense is calculated as:

$$\text{Depreciation} = \frac{\text{cost} - \text{salvage value}}{\text{number of years of useful life}}$$

Example 1 An automobile is purchased for $20,000 and has an expected salvage value of $2,000. The auto's estimated life is 8 years. Its annual depreciation is calculated as follows:

$$\text{Depreciation} = \frac{\text{cost} - \text{salvage value}}{\text{number of years of useful life}}$$

$$= \frac{\$20,000 - \$2,000}{8 \text{ years}} = \$2,250 \text{ per year}$$

An alternative means of computation is to multiply the *depreciable* cost ($18,000) by the annual depreciation rate, which is 12.5 percent in this example. The annual rate is calculated by dividing the number of years of useful life into 1 (1/8 = 12.5 percent). The result is the same: $18,000 × 12.5 percent = $2,250.

Units-of-Production Method.

Under the units-of-production method, depreciation varies with output.

$$\text{Depreciation per unit} = \frac{\text{Cost} - \text{salvage value}}{\text{Estimated total units}}$$

Total depreciation = units of output for year × depreciation per unit

Example 2 The cost of a machine is $11,000, and it has a salvage value of $1,000. The estimated total of units to be produced is 5,000. Four hundred units are produced in the first year.

$$\text{Depreciation per unit} = \frac{\$11,000 - \$1,000}{5,000} = \$2 \text{ per unit}$$

Depreciation in year 1 = 400 units × $2 = $800

Sum-of-the-Years'-Digits (SYD) Method.

Under the SYD method, depreciation decreases over time. The number of years of life expectancy is enumerated in reverse order in the numerator, and the denominator is the sum of the digits. For example, if the life expectancy of a machine is 8 years, write the numbers in reverse order: 8, 7, 6, 5, 4, 3, 2, 1. The sum of these digits is (8 + 7 + 6 + 5 + 4 + 3 + 2 + 1), or 36. Thus, the fraction for the first year is 8/36, while the fraction for the last year is 1/36. The sum of the eight fractions equals 36/36, or 1. Therefore, at the end of 8 years, the machine is completely written down to its salvage value.

The following formula may be used to find the sum of the years' digits (*S*) quickly:

$$S = \frac{(N)(N + 1)}{2}$$

where N represents the number of years of expected life.

Example 3 In Example 1, the *depreciable* cost of the automobile is $18,000 ($20,000 − $2,000). Using the SYD method, the computation for each year's depreciation expense is

$$S = \frac{(N)(N + 1)}{2} = \frac{8(9)}{2} = \frac{72}{2} = 36$$

The computation is as follows:

Year	Fraction ×	Depreciable base ($) =	Depreciation expense
1	8/36	$18,000	$ 4,000
2	7/36	18,000	3,500
3	6/36	18,000	3,000
4	5/36	18,000	2,500
5	4/36	18,000	2,000
6	3/36	18,000	1,500
7	2/36	18,000	1,000
8	1/36	18,000	500
Total			$18,000

Double-Declining-Balance (DDB) Method. Under the DDB method, depreciation expense is highest in the earlier years and lower in the later years. First, a depreciation rate is determined by doubling the straight-line rate. For example, if an asset has a life of 10 years, the straight-line rate is 1/10 or 10 percent, and the double-declining rate is 20 percent. Second, depreciation expense is computed by multiplying the rate by the book value of the asset at the beginning of each year. Since book value declines over time, the depreciation expense decreases each successive period.

This method *ignores* salvage value in the computation. However, the book value of the fixed asset at the end of its useful life cannot be less than its salvage value.

Example 4 Assume the same data as in Example 1. Since the straight-line rate is 12.5 percent (1/8), the double-declining-balance rate is (2 × 12.5 percent) = 25 percent. The depreciation expense is computed as follows:

Year	Book value at beginning of year ×	Rate (%) =	Depreciation expense	Year-end book value
1	$20,000	25%	$5,000	$15,000
2	15,000	25	3,750	11,250
3	11,250	25	2,813	8,437
4	8,437	25	2,109	6,328
5	6,328	25	1,582	4,746
6	4,746	25	1,187	3,559
7	3,559	25	890	2,669
8	2,669	25	667	2,002

Note: If the original estimated salvage value had been $2,100, the depreciation expense for the eighth year would have been $569 ($2,669−$2,100) = $569 rather than $667, since the asset cannot be depreciated below its salvage value.

Which Method Should Be Used? Of course, over the life of the fixed asset, the total depreciation charge will be the same no matter what depreciation method is used; only the timing of the tax savings will differ. The depreciation method used for financial reporting purposes should be realistic for that type of fixed assets. For example, depreciation on an automobile may be based on mileage.

The accelerated methods such as SYD and DDB are advantageous for tax purposes, since higher depreciation charges in the earlier years result in less income and thus less taxes in those years. The tax savings may then be invested for a return.

HOW IS IT USED AND APPLIED? Depreciation expense is reported on the income statement. Accumulated depreciation is a contra account to the fixed asset in order to determine its book value and is reported on the balance sheet. In this way, the profit of the reporting entity may reflect the physical deterioration and obsolescence of fixed assets. In addition, one can determine the worth of the fixed assets per the books.

WHO USES IT AND WHEN?

Accountants and Tax Preparers. Accountants and tax preparers must determine depreciation in preparing financial reports and tax returns.

Financial and Production Managers. Depreciation figures are used to evaluate the usefulness of a fixed asset and its expiration over time.

53 Direct Costs-to-Sales Ratios

DEFINITION. Direct costs include direct materials, direct labor, direct factory overhead, and other costs such as direct travel and computer usage. Direct costs relate *directly* to the product or service. Direct cost ratios are commonly employed in analyzing operational cost activity.

HOW IS IT COMPUTED?

1. Direct material to sales:

$$\frac{\text{Direct material}}{\text{sales}}$$

2. Direct labor to sales:

$$\frac{\text{Direct labor}}{\text{sales}}$$

3. Direct factory overhead to sales:

$$\frac{\text{Direct factory overhead}}{\text{sales}}$$

4. Other indirect costs to sales:

a. Direct travel to sales:

$$\frac{\text{Direct travel}}{\text{sales}}$$

b. Computer usage to sales:

$$\frac{\text{Computer usage}}{\text{sales}}$$

c. And so on.

Example The following information about a company is provided for analysis:

	19X1	19X2
Direct labor	$ 100,000	$ 200,000
Direct factory overhead	150,000	340,000
Sales	1,000,000	1,200,000

The relevant ratios are:

	19X1	19X2
Direct labor to sales	10%	16.7%
Factory overhead to sales	15	28.3

The increase in production costs relative to sales over the year indicates less efficiency and productivity in the production process than in the past. Cost excesses have occurred, which might indicate a lack of supervision and planning.

HOW IS IT USED AND BY WHOM?

Production Management. Production managers should analyze the ratios of production cost elements to sales. The reasons for changes in the ratios should be identified as a basis on which to estimate and plan production. If production costs increase significantly as a percentage of sales, it is a negative sign regarding the firm's manufacturing operations. In this case, managers should ask if cost control was lacking, and if it was, who was responsible. They must identify whether the problem is internal (e.g., poor supervision) or external (e.g., general economic problems) and take corrective action.

Transportation Management. If analysis shows that transportation costs have skyrocketed relative to sales, investigation should determine whether it is due to deficient traffic routing and planning or to increased fuel costs.

54 Discretionary-Cost Ratios

DEFINITION. Discretionary-cost ratios are used to analyze those costs that may easily be changed by management. Discretionary costs may be decreased when a company or department is having problems and desires a stable earnings trend. Discretionary costs include advertising, research and development, and repairs and maintenance.

HOW IS IT COMPUTED?

1. Discretionary costs/sales:

$$\frac{\text{Discretionary costs}}{\text{Sales}}$$

2. Discretionary costs/related asset:

$$\frac{\text{Discretionary costs}}{\text{Related asset}}$$

Example 1 A company's discretionary costs for two years are:

	19X1	19X2
Repairs and maintenance	$ 10,000	$ 6,000
Sales	100,000	110,000
Fixed assets	200,000	230,000

The ratios are:

	19X1	19X2
Repairs and maintenance/sales	10%	5.5%
Repairs and maintenance/fixed assets	5%	2.6%

The declining trend in the ratio of repairs and maintenance to both sales and fixed assets indicates that the net income of the company is overstated and there is inadequate maintenance of fixed assets, leading to possible future breakdowns. Although there are short-term benefits, the situation suggests that its continuance would have a detrimental effect in future years.

Analytical Example The following relationship exists between advertising and sales:

	19X1	19X2	19X3
Sales	$120,000	$150,000	$100,000
Advertising	11,000	16,000	8,000

19X1 is the most typical year. Increasing competition is expected in 19X4.

Advertising to sales is 9.2 percent in 19X1, 10.7 percent in 19X2, and 8.0 percent in 19X3. In terms of base dollars, 19X1 is assigned 100. In 19X2, the index number is $16,000/$11,000 = 145.5; and in 19X3 it is $8,000/$11,000 = 72.7. These are negative indicators regarding 19X3. Advertising is at a lower level than in previous years. In fact, advertising should have risen due to the expected increased competition.

HOW IS IT USED AND BY WHOM?

Financial Analysts, Business Managers, and Financial Managers. *Financial analysts* recognize that a pull-back in discretionary costs results in overstated earnings from an analytical point of view. This move may have a long-term negative effect because management is starving the company of needed expenditures. Thus, *business managers* should note that cost-reduction programs may sometimes eliminate those costs necessary to compete and prosper effectively.

The *financial manager*, however, cannot always conclude that any reduction in discretionary costs is improper. The reduction may be necessary when the prior corporate strategy is deficient or ill-conceived. Further, a reduction in discretionary costs (e.g., advertising) may be appropriate when a major competitor has gone out of business.

Credit and Loan Officers. Credit and loan officers should determine if the present level of discretionary costs conforms with the company's prior trends and with current and future requirements. Index numbers may be used in comparing current discretionary expenditures with base-year expenditures. A vacillating trend in discretionary costs to revenue may indicate that the company is smoothing earnings by altering its discretionary costs. A substantial increase in discretionary costs may have a positive impact on corporate earning power and future growth.

55 Dividend Ratios

DEFINITION. Dividend ratios compare dividends to the company's net income and market price of stock.

HOW IS IT COMPUTED?

$$\text{Dividend yield} = \frac{\text{Dividends per share}}{\text{Market price per share}}$$

$$\text{Dividend payout} = \frac{\text{Dividends per share}}{\text{Earnings per share}}$$

Example A company's common stock account for 19X3 and 19X2 showed $45,000 of common stock at $10 par value. Additional data are as follows:

	19X3	19X2
Dividends	$2,250.00	$3,600.00
Market price per share	20.00	22.00
Earnings per share	2.13	2.67

Computations of dividend ratios follow:

$$\text{Dividends per share} = \frac{\text{Dividends}}{\text{Outstanding shares}}$$

$$= \frac{\$2,250}{4,500 \text{ shares}} = \$0.50 \quad \text{for 19X3}$$

$$= \frac{\$3,600}{4,500 \text{ shares}} = \$0.80 \quad \text{for 19X2}$$

$$\text{Dividend yield} = \frac{\text{Dividends per share}}{\text{Market price per share}}$$

$$= \frac{\$0.50}{\$20.00} = 0.03 \quad \text{for 19X3}$$

$$= \frac{\$0.80}{\$22.00} = 0.04 \quad \text{for 19X2}$$

$$\text{Dividend payout} = \frac{\text{Dividends per share}}{\text{Earnings per share}}$$

$$= \frac{\$0.50}{\$2.13} = 0.23 \quad \text{for 19X3}$$

$$= \frac{\$0.80}{\$2.67} = 0.30 \quad \text{for 19X2}$$

The decline in dividends per share, dividend yield, and dividend payout from 19X2 to 19X3 will be viewed negatively by stockholders.

HOW IS IT USED AND BY WHOM?

Investors. Stockholders, who are interested in receiving dividends, typically prefer high dividend ratios. A reduction in the dividend ratios will cause stockholders to be concerned—particularly stockholders relying on a fixed income, such as an older couple. Stockholders may be tempted to sell their shares in a company that has cut its dividend.

Management. A growth company retains its earnings for future growth; hence, dividend payout is minimal or nonexistent. However, by reinvesting dividends in the company, appreciation in the market price of stock can be achieved.

56 Dollar-Cost Averaging

DEFINITION. Dollar-cost averaging is an investment method in which a constant dollar amount of stock is bought at regularly spaced intervals—a time diversification strategy. This method may be used for stock deemed to be a good long-term investment.

HOW IS IT COMPUTED?

$$\text{Average price} = \frac{\text{Total market price per share}}{\text{Total number of investments}}$$

By investing a fixed amount each time, more shares are purchased at a low price and fewer shares are purchased at a high price. This approach typically results in a lower average cost per share because the investor buys more shares of stock with the same dollars.

Example An investor invests $100,000 per month in ABC Company and engages in the following transactions:

Date	Investment	Market price per share	Shares purchased
6/1	$100,000	$40	2,500
7/1	100,000	35	2,857
8/1	100,000	34	2,941
9/1	100,000	38	2,632
10/1	100,000	50	2,000

The investor has purchased fewer shares at higher prices and more shares at lower prices. The average price per share is:

$$\frac{\$197}{5} = \$39.40$$

With the $500,000 investment, however, 12,930 shares have been bought, resulting in a cost per share of $38.67. On October 1, the market price of the stock ($50) exceeds the average cost of $38.67, reflecting an attractive gain.

HOW IS IT USED AND BY WHOM?

Individual, Corporate, and Institutional Investors. The dollar-cost averaging approach is advantageous when a stock price moves within a narrow range. If there is a decrease in stock price, the investor will incur less of a loss with this approach than otherwise. If there is an increase in stock price, the investor will gain, but less than with another stock-buying approach.

Drawbacks to dollar-cost averaging are (1) higher transaction costs and (2) its inability to work when stock prices are moving continuously either upward or downward.

Dollar-cost averaging is a conservative investment strategy, since it avoids the temptation to buy when the market is high or sell when the market is low. A conservative stock may be acquired with relatively little risk, benefiting from long-term price appreciation. Further, with dollar-cost averaging, the investor is not stuck with too many shares at high prices. In addition, in a bear market many shares may be purchased at very depressed prices.

57 Du Pont Formulas

DEFINITION. The Du Pont system combines the income statement and balance sheet into either of two summary measures of performance—return on investment (ROI) or return on equity (ROE). There are two versions of the Du Pont System.

THE ORIGINAL DU PONT FORMULA. The first version of the Du Pont formula breaks down return on investment (ROI) into net profit margin and total asset turnover.

How Is It Computed?

$$\text{ROI} = \frac{\text{Net profit after taxes}}{\text{Total assets}} = \frac{\text{Net profit after taxes}}{\text{Sales}} \times \frac{\text{Sales}}{\text{Total assets}}$$

$$= \text{Net profit margin} \times \text{Total asset turnover}$$

Example 1 Consider the following financial data:

Total assets	$100,000
Net profit after taxes	18,000

Then,

$$\text{ROI} = \frac{\text{Net profit after taxes}}{\text{Total assets}} = \frac{\$18,000}{\$100,000} = 18\%$$

Also assume sales of $200,000.
  Alternatively,

$$\text{Net profit margin} = \frac{\text{Net profit after taxes}}{\text{Sales}} = \frac{\$18,000}{\$200,000} = 9\%$$

$$\text{Total asset turnover} = \frac{\text{Sales}}{\text{Total assets}} = \frac{\$200,000}{\$100,000} = 2 \text{ times}$$

Therefore,

$$\text{ROI} = \text{net profit margin} \times \text{total asset turnover} = 9\% \times 2 \text{ times} = 18\%$$

Exhibit 57.1 shows the relationships of factors that influence ROI.

How Is It Used and Applied? The Du Pont formula provides a lot of insights to financial managers on how to improve company profitability and investment strategy. Specifically, it has several advantages over the orig-

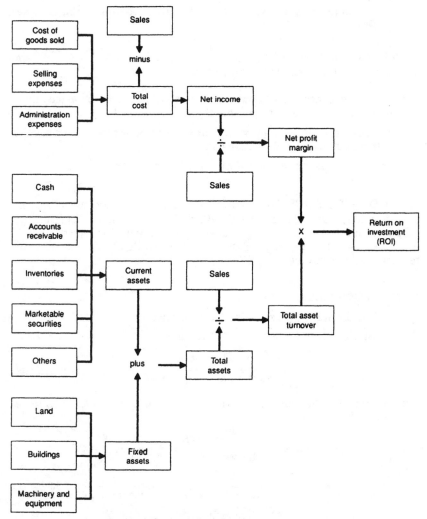

Exhibit 57.1 Relationships of factors influencing ROI.

inal formula (i.e., net profit after taxes/total assets) for profit planning. They are:

1. The importance of turnover as a key to overall return on investment is emphasized. In fact, turnover is just as important as profit margin in enhancing overall return.

2. The importance of sales, which is not in the original formula is explicitly recognized.

3. The breakdown stresses the possibility of trading margin and turnover, since they complement each other. Weak margin can be complemented by strong turnover, and vice versa.

4. It shows how important turnover is as a key to profit making. In effect, these two factors are equally important in overall profit performance.

5. The formula indicates where there are weaknesses—margin, turnover, or both.

Who Uses It and When? Financial managers can take various actions to improve ROI. For example, they could:

1. Reduce expenses (e.g., improve productivity, automate, or cut down on discretionary expenses), thereby increasing net profit
2. Reduce assets (e.g., improve inventory control or speed up receivable collections) without decreasing sales
3. Increase sales while maintaining profit margin

THE MODIFIED DU PONT FORMULA. The second version of the Du Pont formula, also called the modified Du Pont formula, ties together the ROI and the degree of financial leverage as measured using the equity multiplier, which is the ratio of total assets to stockholders' equity, to determine the return on equity (ROE).

How Is It Computed?

$$\text{ROE} = \frac{\text{Net profit after taxes}}{\text{Stockholders' equity}} = \frac{\text{Net profit after taxes}}{\text{Total assets}}$$

$$\times \frac{\text{Total assets}}{\text{Stockholders' equity}} = \text{ROI} \times \text{Equity multiplier}$$

Example 2 For the company in Example 1, assume stockholders' equity of $45,000. Then:

$$\text{Equity multiplier} = \frac{\text{Total assets}}{\text{Stockholders' equity}} = \frac{\$100,000}{\$45,000} = 2.22$$

$$= \frac{1}{(1 - \text{debt ratio})} = \frac{1}{(1 - 0.55)} = \frac{1}{0.45} = 2.22$$

$$\text{ROE} = \frac{\text{Net profit after taxes}}{\text{Stockholders' equity}} = \frac{\$18,000}{\$45,000} = 40\%$$

$$\text{ROE} = \text{ROI} \times \text{equity multiplier} = 18\% \times 2.22 = 40\%$$

If the company used only equity, the 18 percent ROI would equal ROE. However, 55 percent of the firm's capital is supplied by creditors ($45,000/$100,000 = 45% is the equity-to-asset ratio; $55,000/$100,000 = 55% is the debt ratio). Since the 18 percent ROI all goes to stockholders, who put up only 45 percent of the capital, the ROE is higher than 18 percent. This example indicates that the company was using leverage (debt) favorably.

How Is It Used and Applied? The use of the equity multiplier to convert the ROI to the ROE reflects the impact of the leverage (use of debt) on stockholders' return. It enables the company to break its ROE into a profit-margin portion (net profit margin), an efficiency-of-asset-utilization portion (total asset turnover), and a use-of-leverage portion (equity multiplier).

Who Uses It and When? *Financial managers* have the task of determining just what combination of asset return and leverage will work best in the company's competitive environment. Most companies try to keep at least a level equal to what is considered "normal" within the industry. *Division managers* have a responsibility of improving their performance by appropriately mixing margin and turnover. They need to know where their weaknesses are in an effort to improve their performance. They will be evaluated on the basis of their ROI.

Exhibit 57.2 shows the Du Pont and modified Du Pont formulas.

58 Earnings per Share

DEFINITION. Earnings per share (EPS) is the ratio of the company's earnings to each share held by the investing public.

HOW IS IT COMPUTED? Dual presentation of EPS is made as follows:

Primary EPS =

$$\frac{\text{Net income} - \text{preferred dividends}}{\text{Weighted-average common stock outstanding} + \text{common stock equivalents}}$$

$$\text{Fully diluted EPS} = \frac{\text{Net income} - \text{preferred dividends}}{\substack{\text{Weighted-average common stock outstanding} + \\ \text{common stock equivalents} + \text{other fully diluted securities}}}$$

Weighted-average common stock outstanding takes into account the number of months in which those shares were outstanding.

Common stock equivalents are securities that can become common stock at a later date, such as stock options, stock warrants, and convertible securities (i.e., when the yield is less than two-thirds of the average Aa corporate bond yield at the time of issuance).

Other fully diluted securities are convertible securities with a yield equal to or greater than two-thirds of the average Aa corporate bond yield at the time of issuance.

Example A company's net income for the year is $200,000, and preferred dividends are $20,000. On 1/1/19X1, 10,000 common shares were issued, and on 4/1/19X1, 2,000 additional shares were issued. A stock option exists for 3,000 common shares. A $10,000 convertible bond is not a common stock equivalent, but rather an "other fully diluted security." Each $1,000 bond is convertible into 500 common shares. The dual presentation of EPS follows:

Weighted-average common stock outstanding =

$$\left(10,000 \times \frac{3}{12}\right) + \left(12,000 \times \frac{9}{12}\right) = 11,500$$

$$\text{Primary EPS} = \frac{\$200,000 - \$20,000}{11,500 + 3,000} = \$12.41$$

The common shares exchangeable for the convertible bond is:

$$\frac{\$10,000}{\$1,000} = 10 \text{ bonds} \times 500 \text{ shares} = 5,000$$

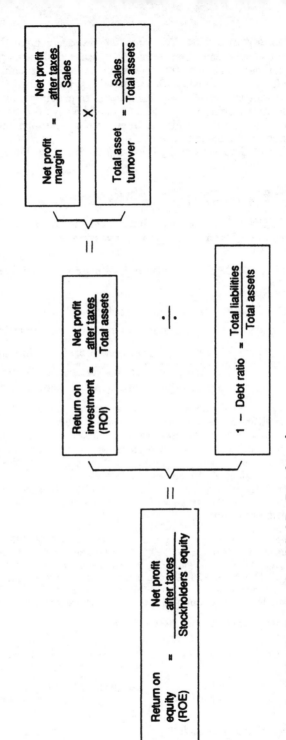

Exhibit 57.2 The Du Pont and modified Du Pont formulas.

$$\text{Net profit margin} = \frac{\text{Net profit after taxes}}{\text{Sales}}$$

$$\text{Total asset turnover} = \frac{\text{Sales}}{\text{Total assets}}$$

$$\text{Return on investment (ROI)} = \frac{\text{Net profit after taxes}}{\text{Total assets}}$$

$$1 - \text{Debt ratio} = \frac{\text{Total liabilities}}{\text{Total assets}}$$

$$\text{Return on equity (ROE)} = \frac{\text{Net profit after taxes}}{\text{Stockholders' equity}}$$

$$\text{Fully Diluted EPS} = \frac{\$200,000 - \$20,000}{11,500 + 3,000 + 5,000} = \frac{\$180,000}{19,500} = \$9.23$$

HOW IS IT USED AND BY WHOM?

Investors. Investors are interested in using EPS as a measure of the operating success of a company. A higher EPS will likely result in higher dividends per share and market price per share.

Management. Management wants a higher EPS because it reflects management's success in running the business.

Creditors. Creditors look negatively upon a company with declining profitability, since the decline may infer that the company has encountered financial difficulties, suggesting that there could be a greater risk of nonpayment of the amount owed.

Accountants. The independent certified public accountant auditing a client firm may view a sudden drop in EPS as a sign of potential business failure that could spur third-party lawsuits.

59 EBIT-EPS Approach to Capital Structure

DEFINITION. The EBIT-EPS approach to capital structure is a practical tool for use by financial managers to evaluate alternative financing plans by investigating these plans' effect on earnings per share (EPS) over a range of earnings before income taxes (EBIT). Use of this tool is a practical effort to move toward achieving an optimal capital structure that results in the lowest overall cost of capital.

HOW IS IT COMPUTED? The primary objective is to determine the EBIT breakeven, or indifference points between the various alternative financing plans being compared. The indifference point identifies the EBIT level at which the EPS will be the same regardless of the financing plan chosen by the financial manager. This indifference point has major implications for capital structure decisions. At EBIT amounts in excess of the EBIT indifference level, the more heavily levered financing plan will generate a higher EPS. At EBIT amounts below the EBIT indifference level, the financing plan involves less leverage and will generate a higher EPS. Therefore, it is of critical importance for the financial manager to know the EBIT indifference level. The indifference points between any two methods of financing can be determined by solving for EBIT in the following equality:

$$\frac{(\text{EBIT} - I)(1 - t) - \text{PD}}{S_1} = \frac{(\text{EBIT} - I)(1 - t) - \text{PD}}{S_2}$$

where I = interest rate
   t = tax rate

PD = preferred stock dividends

S_1 and S_2 = number of shares of common stock outstanding after financing for plan 1 and plan 2, respectively

Example ABC company, with long-term capitalization consisting entirely of $5 million in stock, wants to raise $2 million for the acquisition of special equipment by (1) selling 40,000 shares of common stock at $50 each, (2) selling bonds at 10 percent interest, or (3) issuing preferred stock with an 8 percent dividend. The present EBIT is $800,000, the income tax rate is 50 percent, and 100,000 shares of common stock are now outstanding. To compute the indifference points, we begin by calculating EPS at a projected EBIT level of $1 million.

	All common	All debt	All preferred
EBIT	$1,000,000	$1,000,000	$1,000,000
Interest		200,000	
Earnings before taxes (EBT)	$1,000,000	$ 800,000	$1,000,000
Taxes	500,000	400,000	500,000
Earnings after taxes (EAT)	$ 500,000	$ 400,000	$ 500,000
Preferred stock dividend			160,000
Earnings available to common stockholders	$ 500,000	$ 400,000	$ 340,000
Number of shares	140,000	100,000	100,000
EPS	$3.57	$4.00	$3.40

Now connect the EPSs at the EBIT level of $1 million with the EBITs for each financing alternative on a horizontal axis to obtain the EPS-EBIT graphs (see Exhibit 59.1). Next, plot the EBIT necessary to cover all fixed fi-

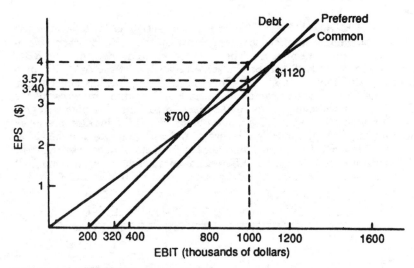

Exhibit 59.1 EBIT/EPS graph.

106

nancial costs for each financing alternative on the horizontal axis. For the common stock plan, there are no fixed costs, so the intercept on the horizontal axis is zero. For the debt plan, there must be an EBIT of $200,000 to cover interest charges. For the preferred stock plan, there must be an EBIT of $160,000/(1 − 0.5) = $320,000 to cover $160,000 in preferred stock dividends at a 50 percent income tax rate; so $320,000 becomes the horizontal axis intercept.

In this example, the indifference point between all common and all debt is:

$$\frac{(EBIT - I)(1 - t) - PD}{S_1} = \frac{(EBIT - I)(1 - t) - PD}{S_2}$$

$$\frac{(EBIT - 0)(1 - 0.5) - 0}{\$140,000} = \frac{(EBIT - \$200,000)(1 - 0.5) - 0}{\$100,000}$$

Rearranging yields:

$$0.5(EBIT)(\$100,000) = 0.5(EBIT)(\$140,000) - 0.5\ (\$200,000)(\$140,000)$$

$$\$20,000\ EBIT = \$14,000,000,000$$

$$EBIT = \$700,000$$

Similarly, the indifference point between all common and all preferred is:

$$\frac{(EBIT - I)(1 - t) - PD}{S_1} = \frac{(EBIT - I)(1 - t) - PD}{S_2}$$

$$\frac{(EBIT - 0)(1 - 0.5) - 0}{\$140,000} = \frac{(EBIT - 0)(1 - 0.5) - \$160,000}{\$100,000}$$

Rearranging yields:

$$0.5(EBIT)(\$100,000) = 0.5(EBIT)(\$140,000) - \$160,000(\$140,000)$$

$$\$20,000\ EBIT = \$22,400,000,000$$

$$EBIT = \$1,120,000$$

Based on the above computations and observing Exhibit 59.1, we can draw the following conclusions:

1. At any level of EBIT, debt is better than preferred stock, since it gives a higher EPS.
2. At a level of EBIT above $700,000, debt is better than common stock. If EBIT is below $700,000, the reverse is true.
3. At a level of EBIT above $1,120,000, preferred stock is better than common. At or below that point, the reverse is true.

It is important to realize that financial leverage is a double-edge sword. It can magnify profits, but it can also increase losses. The EBIT-EPS approach helps financial managers examine the impact of financial leverage as a financing method. Investment performance is crucial to the successful application of any leveraging strategy.

HOW IS IT USED AND APPLIED? The use of financial leverage has two effects on the earnings that flow to the firm's common stockholders: (1) an increased risk in earnings per share (EPS) due to the use of fixed financial obligations; and (2) a change in the level of EPS at a given EBIT associated with a specific capital structure. The first effect is measured by the degree of financial leverage. The second effect is analyzed by means of EBIT-EPS analysis. This analysis is a practical approach that enables the financial

manager to evaluate alternative financing plans by investigating their effect on EPS over a range of EBIT levels.

WHO USES IT AND WHEN?

Chief Financial Officers (CFOs). The EBIT-EPS approach to capital structure is a practical tool for use by the CFO in order to evaluate alternative financing plans by investigating the plans' effect on EPS over a range of EBIT levels. Using this tool, the CFO can find a desirable capital structure (or financing mix) that results in the lowest overall cost of capital and reduces financial risk.

60 Economic Order Quantity

DEFINITION. The economic order quantity (EOQ) is a calculation that shows a relationship among order size, order cost, and carrying cost of inventory—three aspects of inventory planning decisions that involve trade-offs. The higher the EOQ, the higher the carrying cost but the lower the ordering cost. At the EOQ amount, total ordering cost equals total carrying cost.

HOW IS IT COMPUTED?

1. Total number of orders $= \dfrac{S}{EOQ}$

   where S = total usage or demand
   EOQ = economic order quantity

2. Total order cost $= \dfrac{S}{EOQ} \times O$

   where O = cost per order

Ordering costs include the costs of placing the order and receiving goods. Examples are freight charges and clerical costs. *Note:* Cost of scheduling is included for produced items. Order cost is assumed to be constant for each order, regardless of the number of units in that order.

3. Total carrying cost $= \dfrac{EOQ}{2} \times C$

   where C = carrying cost per unit

   $\dfrac{EOQ}{2}$ = average inventory quantity for the period

Carrying costs include the storage, handling, property tax, and insurance costs, as well as the required return rate on the inventory investment. It is assumed constant per unit of inventory.

4. Total inventory cost $= \left(\dfrac{S}{\text{EOQ}} \times O\right) + \left(\dfrac{\text{EOQ}}{2} \times C\right)$

5. EOQ $= \sqrt{\dfrac{2SO}{C}}$

Example 1 Suppose that:

Usage = 500 units per month.
O = $20 per order.
C = $10 per unit.
Then:

$$\text{EOQ} = \sqrt{\dfrac{(2)(500)(20)}{10}} = \sqrt{2000} = 45 \text{ units} \qquad \text{(rounded)}$$

Number of times per month to place an order $= \dfrac{S}{\text{EOQ}} = \dfrac{500}{45} = 11 \qquad \text{(rounded)}$

An order should be placed about every 3 days (30/11).

Example 2 A company buys sets of steel at $40 per set from an outside vendor. The company will sell 6400 sets evenly throughout the year, and desires a 16 percent return on its inventory investment. In addition, rent, taxes, and so on, for each set in inventory is $1.60. The ordering cost is $100 per order.

Carrying cost per dozen = 0.16($40) + $1.60 = $8.00

$$\text{EOQ} = \sqrt{\dfrac{2(6400)(\$100)}{\$8}} = \sqrt{160{,}000} = 400 \text{ sets}$$

Total inventory costs = Carrying cost + Ordering cost

$$= C\left(\dfrac{\text{EOQ}}{2}\right) + O\left(\dfrac{S}{\text{EOQ}}\right)$$

$$= \$8\left(\dfrac{400}{2}\right) + \$100\left(\dfrac{6400}{400}\right)$$

$$= \$1600 + \$1600 = \$3200$$

Total number of orders per year $= \dfrac{S}{\text{EOQ}} = \dfrac{6400}{400} = 16 \text{ orders}$

HOW IS IT USED AND BY WHOM?

Purchasing Agents. EOQ aids in inventory planning. Management determines the EOQ amount to know how much is the optimum amount to order each time in order to minimize total inventory costs.

61 Economic Production Run Size

DEFINITION. Economic production run size is an optimum production run quantity that minimizes the sum of carrying and setup costs. Its computation is exactly the same as economic order quantity (see No. 60), except that the ordering cost in the EOQ formula is replaced by the setup cost. The setup cost is the cost incurred each time a batch is produced. It includes engineering cost of setting up the production runs or machines, paperwork cost of processing the work order, and ordering cost to provide raw materials for the batch.

HOW IS IT COMPUTED?

$$\text{Economic production run size} = \sqrt{\frac{2SD}{C}}$$

where C = carrying cost per unit
S = setup cost per order
D = annual demand (requirements) in units

Example Assume ABC Store sets up production of steel at $100 per set. ABC will sell 6400 sets evenly throughout the year. ABC desires a 16 percent return on investment (cost of borrowed money) on its inventory investment. In addition, rent, taxes, etc., for each set in inventory is $1.60. Then the carrying cost per dozen is 16% ($40) + $1.60 = $8.00.

$$\text{Economic production run size} = \sqrt{\frac{2(6400)(\$100)}{\$8.00}} = \sqrt{160,000} = 400 \text{ sets}$$

$$\text{Total production cost} = \text{Carrying cost} + \text{Setup cost}$$

$$= C\left(\frac{\text{run size}}{2}\right) + O\left(\frac{D}{\text{run size}}\right)$$

$$= \$8.00\left(\frac{400}{2}\right) + \$100\left(\frac{6400}{400}\right)$$

$$= \$1600 + 1600$$

$$= \$3200$$

$$\text{Total number of runs per year} = \frac{D}{\text{run size}} = \frac{6400}{400} = 16 \text{ runs}$$

HOW IS IT USED AND APPLIED?   Production managers need to know the run size that results in the lowest production costs in order to develop a budget for material purchases, labor hiring, and overhead spending.

WHO USES IT AND WHEN?

Production Managers.   To develop an appropriate production budget, production supervisors need to have a good understanding of economic production size and the optimum number of runs.

62 Effective Annual Yield

DEFINITION.   The effective annual yield is the real rate of interest on debt securities such as a bond, discount loan, or certificate of deposit (CD).

HOW IS IT COMPUTED? The effective annual yield means several things:

1. It is the *yield to maturity (YTM)* on a bond, which differs from the coupon (nominal) yield. (See also No. 22, Bond Yield.)

2. It is the real rate of interest on a discount loan, equal to the nominal interest rate divided by the actual proceeds.

Example 1 Eva took out a $10,000, 1-year, 10 percent discounted loan. The effective interest rate is:

$$\frac{\$1,000}{\$10,000 - \$1,000} = \frac{\$1,000}{\$9,000} = 11\%$$

In this discount loan, the actual proceeds are only $9000, which effectively raised the cost of the loan.

3. It is the effective interest rate, better known as the *annual percentage rate (APR)*. Different types of investments use different compounding periods. For example, most bonds pay interest semiannually. Some banks pay interest quarterly. If an investor wishes to compare investments with different compounding periods, he or she needs to put them on a common basis. APR is used for this purpose and is computed as follows:

$$APR = \left(1 + \frac{r}{m}\right)^m - 1.0$$

where r = stated, nominal, or quoted rate
$\quad\quad m$ = number of compounding periods per year

Example 2 A bank offers 6 percent interest, compounded quarterly. The APR is:

$$APR = (1 + \frac{0.06}{4})^4 - 1.0 = (1.015)^4 - 1.0 = 1.0614 - 1.0 = 0.0614 = 6.14\%$$

This means that one bank offering 6 percent with quarterly compounding, while another bank offering 6.14 percent with annual compounding, will both be paying the same effective rate of interest.

HOW IS IT USED AND APPLIED? Banks compete for deposits by offering attractive yields. To compare certificates of deposit (CDs), look at the effective annual yield, which takes into account the effects of compounding. The figures in Exhibit 62.1 indicate how much difference compounding can make on the rate of interest paid. For example, the annual return on a 6 percent CD with annual compounding is 6 percent, but the same CD with quarterly compounding could yield as much as 6.14 percent.

Banks calculate interest in various ways, so true yield varies widely on CDs with the same maturity and interest rate. Note that true yields are not always spelled out in bank advertising, but banks normally post the true yields inside bank offices, list them on window displays, or make them available over the phone.

Exhibit 62.1 Nominal and effective interest rates with different compounding periods

Nominal rate	Effective annualized yield				
	Annually	Semiannually	Quarterly	Monthly	Daily
6%	6%	6.09%	6.14%	6.17%	6.18%
7	7	7.12	7.19	7.23	7.25
8	8	8.16	8.24	8.30	8.33
9	9	9.20	9.31	9.38	9.42
10	10	10.25	10.38	10.47	10.52
11	11	11.30	11.46	11.57	11.62
12	12	12.36	12.55	12.68	12.74

WHO USES IT AND WHEN?

Investors, Depositors, and Financial Planners. Investors, depositors, and financial planners need to know the true return on their investments, rather than the nominal, coupon return. Financial calculators are widely available to calculate the effective annual yield so that real rates of return can be compared.

63 Effective Interest Rate

DEFINITION. The effective interest rate is the real rate of interest on a loan, expressed as an annual percentage applicable for the life of the loan.

HOW IS IT COMPUTED?

$$\text{Effective interest rate} = \frac{\text{Nominal interest on face of loan}}{\text{Net proceeds of loan}}$$

For a discounted loan, which is a common form, interest is deducted immediately in arriving at the net proceeds—which increases the effective interest rate. A bank may require a compensating balance, i.e., a deposit that offsets the unpaid loan. In this case, no interest is earned on the compensating balance, which is stated as a percentage of the loan. A compensating balance also increases the effective interest rate.

Example A company takes out a $10,000, 1-year, 10 percent discounted loan. The compensating balance is 5 percent. The effective interest rate is:

$$\frac{\$1,000}{\$10,000 - \$1,000 - \$500} = \frac{\$1,000}{\$8,500} = 11.8\%$$

HOW IS IT USED AND BY WHOM?

Corporate Borrowers. Company officers compute the effective interest rate to determine the true cost of borrowing.

64 Effective Tax Rate

DEFINITION. The effective tax rate is the average tax rate paid by an individual or corporate taxpayer.

HOW IS IT COMPUTED?

$$\text{Effective tax rate} = \frac{\text{Tax}}{\text{Taxable income}}$$

Example If the tax is $20,000 on taxable income of $80,000, the effective tax rate is:

$$\frac{\$20,000}{\$80,000} = 25\%$$

HOW IS IT USED AND BY WHOM?

Corporate Financial Managers and Individuals. The effective tax rate is used to determine the impact of tax on an entity's taxable income. Knowledge of the effective tax rate is also useful in tax planning.

65 Elasticity of Demand

DEFINITION. One of the most important concepts in gauging demand is the determination of elasticity, which tells how sensitive quantity demand is to a change in a factor in the demand function. The principal factors in demand elasticity are:

1. The price of the good (in the case of price elasticity)
2. Income (in case of income elasticity)
3. The price of a substitute product (in the case of cross-elasticity)
4. Advertising (in the case of promotional elasticity)

Only price elasticity is discussed explicitly here, since other elasticity concepts are similar with respect to their calculations and implications.

HOW IS IT COMPUTED? Price elasticity, denoted by e_p, is the ratio of a percentage change in quantity demanded (Q) to a percentage change in price (p):

$$e_p = \frac{dQ/Q}{dp/p} = \left(\frac{dQ}{dp}\right)\left(\frac{p}{Q}\right)$$

where dQ/dp is the slope of the demand function $Q = Q(p)$. The price elasticity of demand is classified into three categories:

If $e_p > 1$, demand is elastic.

If $e_p = 1$, demand is unitary.

If $e_p < 1$, demand is inelastic.

Example   The demand function is given as $Q = 200 - 6p$. The price elasticity at $p = 4$ is computed as follows. First,

$$Q = 200 - 6(4) = 176$$

Since $dQ/dp = -6$, the e_p at $p = 4$ is:

$$e_p = -6\left(\frac{4}{176}\right) = -0.136$$

which means that a 1 percent change in price will bring about a 0.14 percent change in demand. The product under study is considered to be price inelastic, since the e_p is less than 1 in absolute value.

HOW IS IT USED AND APPLIED?   Economists have established the following relationships between price elasticity (e_p) and total revenue (TR), which can aid a firm in setting its price:

Price	$e_p > 1$	$e_p = 1$	$e_p < 1$
Price rises	TR falls	No change	TR rises
Price falls	TR rises	No change	TR falls

Firms need to be aware of the elasticity of their own demand curves when they set product prices. For example, a profit-maximizing firm would never choose to lower its price in the inelastic range of its demand curve—such a price decrease would only decrease total revenue (see the above table) and at the same time increase costs, since output would rise. The result would be a drastic decrease in profits. In fact, when costs are rising and the demand is inelastic, the firm would have no difficulty passing on the increases by raising the price to the customer.

When there are many substitutes and demand is elastic, increasing prices may lead to a reduction in total revenue rather than an increase. The result may be lower profits rather than higher ones.

Similarly, managers are sometimes surprised by the lack of success of price reductions, though this merely reflects the fact that demand is relatively inelastic. In such a case, they may have to rely on other marketing efforts such as advertising and sales promotion in order to increase market share.

WHO USES IT AND WHEN?

Marketing Managers and Business Economists.   Marketing managers and business economists must ascertain how competitive their products are in the marketplace in order to determine the products' market share. The concept of elasticity aids managers in setting prices. Various elasticity measures allow marketing managers to see how effective each of the demand determinants (i.e., advertising, price change, and external factors) is going to be. In this way marketing resources may be utilized more profitably and efficiently.

66 Equity Ratios

DEFINITION. Equity ratios are used to evaluate a company's capital structure. The inherent financial stability of the entity and the risk of insolvency to which it is susceptible are traceable to its equity structure.

HOW IS IT COMPUTED? There are 11 commonly used equity ratios:

1. Investors' capital-to-sales ratio:

$$\frac{\text{Stockholders' equity}}{\text{Sales}}$$

2. Equity capital to noncurrent assets:

$$\frac{\text{Equity capital}}{\text{Noncurrent assets}}$$

3. Retained earnings to stockholders' equity:

$$\frac{\text{Retained earnings}}{\text{Stockholders' equity}}$$

4. Return on common equity:

$$\frac{\text{Net income} - \text{preferred dividends}}{\text{Average common stockholders' equity}}$$

5. Authorized shares to issued shares:

$$\frac{\text{Authorized shares}}{\text{Issued shares}}$$

6. Convertible securities (bonds and preferred stock) to common stock:

$$\frac{\text{Convertible securities}}{\text{Common stock}}$$

7. Stock options to total shares outstanding:

$$\frac{\text{Stock options}}{\text{Total shares outstanding}}$$

8. Trend in retained earnings:

$$\frac{\text{Change in retained earnings}}{\text{Beginning retained earnings}}$$

9. Net income to preferred dividends:

$$\frac{\text{Net income}}{\text{Preferred dividends}}$$

10. Preferred stock to total stockholders' equity:

$$\frac{\text{Preferred stock at stated value (or liquidation value)}}{\text{Total stockholders' equity}}$$

11. Equity growth rate:

$$\frac{\text{Net income} - \text{preferred dividends} - \text{common dividends}}{\text{Average common stockholders' equity}}$$

Example Several of these equity ratios are used in this example, which examines a company's performance for two years.

	19X1	19X2
Sales	$ 2,000,000	$ 2,900,000
Net income	1,000,000	1,400,000
Preferred dividends	100,000	120,000
Stockholders' equity	10,000,000	10,300,000

Relevant ratios are:

	19X1	19X2
Investors' capital to sales	5	3.6
Return on common equity	9%	12.4%
Net income to preferred dividends	10	11.6

Comparing ratios for these two years, the decline in the investors' capital ratio is favorable because it indicates greater revenue being earned from stockholders' equity investment. The analysis shows that the return on common stockholders' equity has improved substantially over the year, an increase of 37.7 percent. The increase in the ratio of net income to preferred dividends from 19X1 to 19X2 indicates that more earnings are available to common stockholders as possible dividends.

HOW IS IT USED AND BY WHOM?

Management. Managers use the investors' capital-to-sales ratio to indicate the proportion of sales financed by stockholders' equity. If management sees an increasing trend in retained earnings to capital, the condition is viewed as favorable because capital financing is being achieved from operational results (internally), thus reducing pressure on outside investor contributions.

When convertible bonds or convertible preferred stock are converted to common stock, bondholders or preferred stockholders are optimistic about the company; however, this conversion results in a drop in the market price of common stock as more shares are issued. The company has an advantage in this, however, since it will be able to omit the interest payment on bonds and the dividend payment on preferred stock.

The significance of the ratio of equity capital to noncurrent assets is that the stockholders' equity supports the noncurrent assets—that is, any surplus funds are available for current asset operating requirements. In general, the greater the ratio over 100 percent, the better is the firm's financial health with regard to satisfying creditor commitments and debts.

If analysis shows increasing retained earnings, this indicates that the company has been profitable.

Investors. If authorized shares significantly exceed issued shares, it is possible that a substantial additional issuance of securities may dilute stockholder interests. If new shares are issued, the market price of the stock will drop.

Investors should appraise whether stock options issued to executives are excessive and whether they are justified by managerial performance, since such issuance unfairly dilutes the stockholders' interests in the company. If the trend in the ratio of stock options to total shares outstanding has increased but profitability has decreased, a stock option issuance policy may not be consistent with company performance. Investors like to see a high return on common stockholders' equity ratio.

A high ratio of net income to preferred dividends is a positive signal, since it shows that more income will be left over for distribution to common stockholders.

The ratio of preferred stock to total stockholders' equity is important because preferred stock has a preference position with a claim on assets ahead of the common stock. Investors must understand the implications of this position.

The equity growth rate shows the percentage increase in common equity—that is, the growth rate arising from the retention of earnings, which assumes a constant dividend payout over time. This calculation reveals earnings growth without company dependence on external financing. These increased funds, in turn, will earn the rate of return that the company can obtain on its assets and thus contribute to earnings growth.

67 Equivalent Taxable Yield

DEFINITION. The equivalent taxable yield is the rate of return on a nontaxable investment as it would be on a taxable basis.

HOW IS IT COMPUTED?

$$\text{Equivalent taxable yield} = \frac{\text{Tax-free return}}{1 - \text{marginal tax rate}}$$

Example A municipal bond pays tax-free interest at 6 percent and the tax rate is 33 percent. The equivalent rate on a taxable instrument is:

$$\frac{0.06}{1 - 0.33} = \frac{0.06}{0.67} = 9.0\%$$

HOW IS IT USED AND BY WHOM?

Individuals in High Tax Brackets. Individuals use the equivalent taxable yield to determine what their tax-free rate of return would be on a taxable basis. This enables investors to compare alternative tax-free and taxable investments.

Managers of Governmental Institutions. Government managers can determine what tax-free interest rate to offer to attract investors to municipal bonds.

68 Estimated Expenses versus Cash Expenses

DEFINITION. The computation of estimated expenses versus cash expenses reveals the degree of uncertainty in company financial estimates, since estimated expenses are based on subjective interpretations that are uncertain, whereas cash expenses represent actual cash transactions.

HOW IS IT COMPUTED? Three computations are used:

1. Estimated expenses/total expenses
2. Estimated expenses/net sales
3. Estimated expenses/net income

Example A financial analyst assembles the following data for a company for 19X1 and 19X2:

	19X1	19X2
Cash and near-cash expenses (salaries, rent, telephone)	$ 40,000	$ 60,000
Noncash expenses (depreciation, amortization, bad debts)	70,000	120,000
Total expenses	$110,000	$180,000
Total revenue	$250,000	$310,000
Net income	$140,000	$130,000

Estimated expense items to total expenses is $70/$110 = 64 percent for 19X1 and $120/$180 = 67 percent for 19X2. Estimated expenses to total revenue is $70/$250 = 28 percent for 19X1 and $120/$310 = 39 percent for 19X2. Estimated expenses to net income is $70/$140 = 50 percent for 19X1 and $120/$130 = 92 percent for 19X2.

Uncertainty exists with regard to net income for 19X1 and 19X2 because of the high percentages of estimated income statement items. Further, a greater degree of estimation is associated with 19X2's income-measurement process.

HOW IS IT USED AND BY WHOM?

Financial Analysts. A financial analyst who is assessing the quality of a company's earnings is interested in appraising the degree of uncertainty of accounting estimates in the determination of net income. The more that subjective accounting estimates and judgments are used in arriving at earnings, the more uncertain is the net income figure.

The effects of quality of earnings can be identified by separating factual and interpretative information that enters into income determination. This involves isolating revenue and expense items representing cash and near-cash transactions versus revenue and expense items that involve subjective estimates and interpretations.

69 Expected Value and Standard Deviation

DEFINITION. Expected value is a weighted average using the probabilities as weights. For decisions involving uncertainty, the concept of expected value provides a rational means for selecting the best course of action. Whenever the expected value is discussed, standard deviation is the accompanying statistical datum.

Standard deviation is a statistic that measures the tendency of data to be spread out. Intuitively, it is a margin of error associated with a given expected value.

HOW IS EXPECTED VALUE COMPUTED? The expected value ($\bar{r}$) is found by multiplying the probability of each outcome by its payoff:

$$\bar{r} = \sum r_i p_i$$

where r_i is the outcome for the ith possible event and p_i is the probability of occurrence of that outcome.

Example 1 Consider the possible rates of return, depending on the states of the economy (i.e., recession, normal, and prosperity) that could be earned next year on a $50,000 investment in stock A or on a $50,000 investment in stock B.

State of economy	Return (r_i)	Probability (p_i)
	Stock A	
Recession	– 5%	.2
Normal	20%	.6
Prosperity	40%	.2
	Stock B	
Recession	10%	.2
Normal	15%	.6
Prosperity	20%	.2

The expected rates of returns are as follows.

For Stock A: $\bar{r} = (-5\%)(.2) + (20\%)(.6) + (40\%)(.2) = 19\%$

For Stock B: $\bar{r} = (10\%)(.2) + (15\%)(.6) + (20\%)(.2) = 15\%$

HOW IS STANDARD DEVIATION COMPUTED?

Standard Deviation as a Measure of Risk. As a measure of risk, the standard deviation, denoted by σ (read "sigma"), is defined and calculated as

$$\sigma = \sqrt{\frac{(r - \bar{r})^2}{n - 1}}$$

where $\bar{r}$ is the mean or expected value. In this case the r's are equally likely and therefore equally weighted. Note that we divide by $(n - 1)$.

Example 2 One and one-half years of quarterly returns are listed below for Amko Motors stock:

Time period	$r(\%)$	$(r - \bar{r})$	$(r - \bar{r})^2$
1	10	0	0
2	15	5	25
3	20	10	100
4	5	-5	25
5	-10	-20	400
6	20	10	100
	60		650

From this table, note that

$$\bar{r} = \frac{60}{6} = 10\%$$

$$\sigma = \sqrt{\frac{(r - \bar{r})^2}{n - 1}} = \sqrt{\frac{650}{6 - 1}} = \sqrt{130} = 11.40\%$$

The Amko Motors stock has returned on the average 10 percent over the last six quarters, and the variability about its average return is 11.40 percent. The high standard deviation (11.40 percent) relative to the average return of 10 percent indicates that the stock is very risky. Note that a spreadsheet program such as Lotus 1-2-3 has a built-in function key, @STD, for calculating standard deviation.

Standard Deviation as a Measure of Dispersion. Standard deviation is also a measure of the dispersion of a probability distribution. In this case, the smaller the deviation, the tighter is the distribution, and thus the lower is the riskiness of the investment. Standard deviation in this use is the square root of the mean of the squared deviations from the expected value ($\bar{r}$):

$$\sigma = \sqrt{\sum (r_i - \bar{r})^2 p_i}$$

where $\bar{r} = \Sigma r_i p_i$
To calculate σ, proceed as follows:

Step 1. Compute the expected rate of return ($\bar{r}$).

Step 2. Subtract each possible return from r to obtain a set of deviations $(r_i - \bar{r})$.

Step 3. Square each deviation, multiply the squared deviation by the probability of occurrence for its respective return, and sum these products to obtain the variance (σ^2): $\sigma^2 = \Sigma (r_i - \bar{r})^2 p_i$.

Step 4. Finally, take the square root of the variance to obtain the standard deviation (σ).

Example 3 In this example, standard deviations are computed for the data of Example 1. To complete the step-by-step procedure, it is convenient to set up a table, as follows:

Return (r_i)	Probability (p_i)	$r_i - p_i$ (step 1)	$(r_i - \bar{r})$ (step 2)	$(r_i - \bar{r})^2$ (step 3)	$(r_i - \bar{r})^2 p_i$
			Stock A		
– 5%	.2	– 1%	– 24%	576	115.2
20%	.6	12%	1%	1	0.6
40%	.2	8%	21%	441	88.2
		$\bar{r} = 19\%$			$\sigma^2 = 204$
					$\sigma = \sqrt{204}$ (step 4)
					$\sigma = 14.28\%$
			Stock B		
10%	.2	2%	– 5%	25	5
15%	.6	9%	0%	0	0
20%	.2	4%	5%	25	5
		$\bar{r} = 15\%$			$\sigma^2 = 10$
					$\sigma = \sqrt{10}$ (step 4)
					$\sigma = 3.16\%$

HOW IS IT USED AND APPLIED? In finance, standard deviation is used as an indicator of the risk involved in an investment, since it measures the variability of returns around the expected return from an investment. Financial managers can also use expected value and standard deviation to make important inferences from past data. Another application of standard deviation is in determining the variability in sales and earnings. Unstable or erratic sales and earnings mean uncertainty and therefore greater risk.

In using the standard deviation, it is important to compare risk, since it is only an absolute measure of dispersion (risk) and does not consider the dispersion of outcomes in relation to an expected return. In comparisons of securities with differing expected returns, for instance, the coefficient of variation (see No. 34) is often used.

WHO USES IT AND WHEN?

Investors and Financial Analysts. The expected return and its associated standard deviation are used as measures of risk in investment analysis. These measures aid in comparing investments such as stocks, bonds, and even mutual funds.

70 Exponential Smoothing

DEFINITION. Exponential smoothing is a popular technique for short-run forecasting by financial managers. It uses a weighted average of past data as the basis for a forecast. The procedure gives heaviest weight to more recent information and smaller weights to observations in the more distant past, since the future is more dependent on the recent past than on the distant past.

HOW IS IT COMPUTED? The formula for exponential smoothing is

$$\hat{y}_{t+1} = \alpha y_t + (1 - \alpha)\hat{y}_t$$

or, in words,

$$\hat{y}_{new} = \alpha y_{old} + (1 - \alpha)\hat{y}_{old}$$

where $\hat{y}_{new}$ = exponentially smoothed average to be used as the forecast
y_{old} = most recent actual data
$\hat{y}_{old}$ = most recent smoothed forecast
α = smoothing constant

The higher the α, the greater is the weight given to the more recent information.

Example The following data on sales are given:

Time period, t	Actual sales ($\times$ 1000), y_t
1	$60.0
2	64.0
3	58.0
4	66.0
5	70.0
6	60.0
7	70.0
8	74.0
9	62.0
10	74.0
11	68.0
12	66.0
13	60.0
14	66.0
15	62.0

To initialize the exponential smoothing process, it is necessary to have the initial forecast. The first smoothed forecast to be used can be

1. First actual observations.
2. An average of the actual data for a few periods

For illustrative purposes, let us use a six-period average as the initial forecast $\hat{y}_7$ with a smoothing constant of $\alpha = 0.40$. Then

$$\hat{y}_7 = \frac{y_1 + y_2 + y_3 + y_4 + y_5 + y_6}{6}$$

$$= \frac{60 + 64 + 58 + 66 + 70 + 60}{6} = 63$$

Note that $y_7 = 70$. Then $\hat{y}_8$ is computed as follows:

$$\hat{y}_8 = \alpha y_7 + (1 - \alpha)\hat{y}_7$$

$$= (0.40)(70) + (0.60)(63)$$

Similarly,

$$= 28.0 + 37.80 = 65.80$$

$$\hat{y}_9 = \alpha y_8 + (1 - \alpha)\hat{y}_8$$

$$= (0.40)(74) + (0.60)(65.80)$$

and

$$= 29.60 + 39.48 = 69.08$$

$$\hat{y}_{10} = \alpha y_9 + (1 - \alpha)\hat{y}_9$$

$$= (0.40)(62) + (0.60)(69.08)$$

$$= 24.80 + 41.45 = 66.25$$

By using the same procedure, the values of $\hat{y}_{11}$, $\hat{y}_{12}$, $\hat{y}_{13}$, $\hat{y}_{14}$, and $\hat{y}_{15}$ can be calculated. The following table compares actual sales and predicted sales using the exponential smoothing method.

Comparison of Actual Sales and Predicted Sales

Time period, t	Actual sales, y_t	Predicted sales, $\hat{y}_t$	Difference, $y_t - \hat{y}_t$	Difference², $(y_t - \hat{y}_t)^2$
1	$60.0			
2	64.0			
3	58.0			
4	66.0			
5	70.0			
6	60.0			
7	70.0	63.00	7.00	49.00
8	74.0	65.80	8.20	67.24
9	62.0	69.08	− 7.08	50.13
10	74.0	66.25	7.75	60.06
11	68.0	69.35	− 1.35	1.82
12	66.0	68.81	− 2.81	7.90
13	60.0	67.69	− 7.69	59.14
14	66.0	64.61	1.39	1.93
15	62.0	65.17	− 3.17	10.05
				307.27

Due to the negative and positive differences between actual sales and predicted sales, the forecaster can use a higher or lower smoothing constant, α, in order to adjust the prediction as quickly as possible to large fluctuations in the data series. For example, if the forecast is slow in reacting to increased sales (that is, if the difference is negative), the forecaster may want to try a higher value of α. For practical purposes, the optimal α may be picked by minimizing the *mean squared error* (MSE), defined as:

$$MSE = \frac{(y_t - \hat{y}_t)^2}{n - i}$$

where i = the number of observations used to determine the initial forecast

In our example, $i = 6$, so the mean squared error is

$$MSE = \frac{307.27}{15 - 6} = \frac{307.27}{9} = 34.14$$

The idea is to select the α that minimizes MSE, which is the average sum of the variations between the historical sales data and the forecast values for the corresponding periods.

Can a Computer Help?   A manager will sometimes be confronted with complex problems requiring large sample data, necessitating trial of many different values of α for exponential smoothing. A computer program is available to make this task easier. Exhibit 70.1 is a sample output from a computer program for exponential smoothing. Notice that the best α for this particular example is .9, because it gives the lowest MSE.

HOW IS IT USED AND APPLIED?   The exponential smoothing method is effective when there is randomness but no seasonal fluctuations in the data. The forecaster can use a higher or lower smoothing constant α in order to adjust the prediction as quickly as possible to large fluctuations in the data series. For example, if the forecast is slow in reacting to increased sales (that is, if the difference is negative), the forecaster may want to try a higher value. Finding the best α is the key to success in using this method.

WHO USES IT AND WHEN?

Sales Forecasters.   The method is effective when there is random demand and no seasonal fluctuation in the data. One disadvantage of the method, however, is that it does not include industrial or economic factors such as market conditions, prices, or the effects of competitors' actions.

Financial Forecasters.   Corporate financial planners may use this technique to project cash flows, earnings, and various balance sheet items. The exponential smoothing method is simple and effective, since it does not require a lot of data other than for the variable involved.

71 Fixed-Asset Ratios

DEFINITION.   Fixed-asset ratios reflect the productivity and efficiency of property, plant, and equipment in generating revenue and earnings. A high fixed-asset turnover reflects positively on the company's ability to utilize its fixed assets in business operations.

Exhibit 70.1 Printout of an exponential smoothing program.

```
      PLEASE ENTER THE NUMBER OF OBSERVATIONS.
?10
      ENTER YOUR DATA NOW.
      THE DATA SHOULD BE SEPARATED BY
      COMMAS.
?117,120,132,141,140,156,169,171,174,182
      ENTER THE NUMBER OF PERIODS OVER WHICH
YOU COMPUTE THE AVERAGE TO BE USED AS THE FIRST
FORECAST VALUE.
?1
      **********EXPONENTIAL SMOOTHING PROGRAM-SINGLE
SMOOTHING**********
                       JAE K. SHIM
```

PERIOD	ACUTAL VALUE	ESTIMATED VALUE	ERROR
1	117.00	.00	
2	120.00	117.00	

THE VALUE OF THE EXPONENTIAL SMOOTHER IS .1

3	132.00	117.30	14.70
4	141.00	118.77	22.23
5	140.00	120.99	19.01
6	156.00	122.89	33.11
7	169.00	126.20	42.80
8	171.00	130.48	40.52
9	174.00	134.54	39.46
10	182.00	138.48	43.52

THE TOTAL ABSOLUTE ERROR IN ESTIMATE IS 255.34
THE MEAN SQUARED ERROR IS 1136.48

THE VALUE OF THE EXPONENTIAL SMOOTHER IS .2

3	132.00	117.60	14.40
4	141.00	120.48	20.52
5	140.00	124.58	15.42
6	156.00	127.67	28.33
7	169.00	133.33	35.67
8	171.00	140.47	30.53
9	174.00	146.57	27.43
10	182.00	152.06	29.94

THE TOTAL ABSOLUTE ERROR IN ESTIMATE IS 202.24
THE MEAN SQUARED ERROR IS 690.23

THE VALUE OF THE EXPONENTIAL SMOOTHER IS .3

3	132.00	117.90	14.10
4	141.00	122.13	18.87
5	140.00	127.79	12.21
6	156.00	131.45	24.55
7	169.00	138.82	30.18
8	171.00	147.87	23.13
9	174.00	154.81	19.19
10	182.00	160.57	21.43

THE TOTAL ABSOLUTE ERROR IN ESTIMATE IS 163.66

(Continued)

PERIOD	ACTUAL VALUE	ESTIMATED VALUE	ERROR
THE VALUE OF THE EXPONENTIAL SMOOTHER IS .4			
3	132.00	118.20	13.80
4	141.00	123.72	17.28
5	140.00	130.63	9.37
6	156.00	134.38	21.62
7	169.00	143.03	25.97
8	171.00	153.42	17.58
9	174.00	160.45	13.55
10	182.00	165.87	16.13

THE TOTAL ABSOLUTE ERROR IN ESTIMATE IS 135.31
THE MEAN SQUARED ERROR IS 308.97

PERIOD	ACTUAL VALUE	ESTIMATED VALUE	ERROR
THE VALUE OF THE EXPONENTIAL SMOOTHER IS .5			
3	132.00	118.50	13.50
4	141.00	125.25	15.75
5	140.00	133.12	6.88
6	156.00	136.56	19.44
7	169.00	146.28	22.72
8	171.00	157.64	13.36
9	174.00	164.32	9.68
10	182.00	169.16	12.84

THE TOTAL ABSOLUTE ERROR IN ESTIMATE IS 114.16
THE MEAN SQUARED ERROR IS 226.07

PERIOD	ACTUAL VALUE	ESTIMATED VALUE	ERROR
THE VALUE OF THE EXPONENTIAL SMOOTHER IS .6			
3	132.00	118.80	13.20
4	141.00	126.72	14.28
5	140.00	135.29	4.71
6	156.00	138.12	17.88
7	169.00	148.85	20.15
8	171.00	160.94	10.06
9	174.00	166.98	7.02
10	182.00	171.19	10.81

THE TOTAL ABSOLUTE ERROR IN ESTIMATE IS 98.13
THE MEAN SQUARED ERROR IS 174.23

PERIOD	ACTUAL VALUE	ESTIMATED VALUE	ERROR
THE VALUE OF THE EXPONENTIAL SMOOTHER IS .7			
3	132.00	119.10	12.90
4	141.00	128.13	12.87
5	140.00	137.14	2.86
6	156.00	139.14	16.86
7	169.00	150.94	18.06
8	171.00	163.58	7.42
9	174.00	168.77	5.23
10	182.00	172.43	9.57

THE TOTAL ABSOLUTE ERROR IN ESTIMATE IS 85.76
THE MEAN SQUARED ERROR IS 140.55

(Continued)

```
              ACTUAL       ESTIMATED
PERIOD         VALUE         VALUE              ERROR
        THE VALUE OF THE EXPONENTIAL SMOOTHER IS .8
  3           132.00        119.40            12.60
  4           141.00        129.48            11.52
  5           140.00        138.70             1.30
  6           156.00        139.74            16.26
  7           169.00        152.75            16.25
  8           171.00        165.75             5.25
  9           174.00        169.95             4.05
 10           182.00        173.19             8.81
       THE TOTAL ABSOLUTE ERROR IN ESTIMATE IS 76.05
           THE MEAN SQUARED ERROR IS 117.91

        THE VALUE OF THE EXPONENTIAL SMOOTHER IS .9
  3           132.00        119.70            12.30
  4           141.00        130.77            10.23
  5           140.00        139.88              .02
  6           156.00        140.00            16.00
  7           169.00        154.40            14.60
  8           171.00        167.54             3.46
  9           174.00        170.65             3.35
 10           182.00        173.67             8.33
       THE TOTAL ABSOLUTE ERROR IN ESTIMATE IS 68.30
           THE MEAN SQUARED ERROR IS 102.23


                    SUMMARY RESULTS
    THE EXPONENTIAL SMOOTHER .1   WITH A MEAN SQUARED
                                    ERROR OF 1136.48
    THE EXPONENTIAL SMOOTHER .2   WITH A MEAN SQUARED
                                    ERROR OF 690.23
    THE EXPONENTIAL SMOOTHER .3   WITH A MEAN SQUARED
                                    ERROR OF 447.49
    THE EXPONENTIAL SMOOTHER .4   WITH A MEAN SQUARED
                                    ERROR OF 308.97
    THE EXPONENTIAL SMOOTHER .5   WITH A MEAN SQUARED
                                    ERROR OF 226.07
    THE EXPONENTIAL SMOOTHER .6   WITH A MEAN SQUARED
                                    ERROR OF 174.23
    THE EXPONENTIAL SMOOTHER .7   WITH A MEAN SQUARED
                                    ERROR OF 140.55
    THE EXPONENTIAL SMOOTHER .8   WITH A MEAN SQUARED
                                    ERROR OF 117.91
    THE EXPONENTIAL SMOOTHER .9   WITH A MEAN SQUARED
                                    ERROR OF 102.23
```

HOW IS IT COMPUTED?   Five types of fixed-asset ratios are commonly used:

1. Fixed-asset turnover:

$$\frac{\text{Sales}}{\text{Average fixed assets}}$$

2. Return on fixed assets:

$$\frac{\text{Net income}}{\text{Average fixed assets}}$$

3. Fixed assets to short-term debt:

$$\frac{\text{Fixed assets}}{\text{Short-term debt}}$$

4. Fixed assets to stockholders' equity:

$$\frac{\text{Fixed assets}}{\text{Stockholders' equity}}$$

5. Funded capital ratio:

$$\frac{\text{Long-term debt} + \text{owners' equity}}{\text{Fixed assets}}$$

Example The following data for a company is given:

	19X1	19X2
Sales	$500,000	$ 600,000
Net income	200,000	180,000
Fixed assets	700,000	1,000,000
Short-term debt	300,000	400,000

Relevant ratios are:

	19X1	19X2
Fixed-asset turnover	71.4%	60.0%
Return on fixed assets	28.6%	18.0%
Fixed assets to short-term debt	2.33	2.5

Fixed assets are less productive and less profitable in 19X2, as indicated by the lower turnover rate and rate of return. There is less short-term debt relative to fixed assets, however, which is a good sign for short-term creditors.

HOW IS IT USED AND BY WHOM?

Management. The turnover ratio is helpful in evaluating a company's ability to use its asset base effectively in order to generate revenue. A low ratio may be due to many factors, and it is important for management to identify the underlying reasons. Managers may ask, for example, whether investment in assets is excessive when compared to the value of output produced. If it is, the company might want to consolidate its present operation, perhaps by selling some of its assets and investing the proceeds for a higher return or using them to expand into a more profitable area.

If the return on fixed assets is acceptable to management, the proper investment decision is to maintain and improve production facilities. Similarly, if the return in the industry is high or if the industry is in the process of growth, management might consider investing in new equipment. On the other hand, if the return on fixed assets is unsatisfactory, the company would be justified in not maintaining capital. Similarly, if the industry is in a state of decline, management might restrict equipment replacement and repair.

A higher ratio of fixed assets to stockholders' equity may mean a buildup in inactive fixed assets, resulting in excessive costs—such as taxes, insurance, maintenance, and storage—which will raise the breakeven point.

The funded capital ratio reveals the extent to which fixed assets are financed by long-term commitments of both creditors and investors.

A high ratio of sales to floor space for machinery indicates the efficient utilization of space.

Creditors. A company with significant short-term debt may be unable to meet its current obligations if most of its money is tied up in long-term assets. Financing fixed assets with current debt is a precarious financing strategy; instead, assets should be financed with liabilities of similar maturity.

72 Fixed-Charge Coverage

DEFINITION. The fixed-charge coverage ratio indicates whether a company is able to meet its fixed commitments (e.g., interest, rent) from profits and cash earnings.

HOW IS IT COMPUTED. Fixed-charge coverage analysis utilizes two ratios:

1. Income before taxes and fixed charges/fixed charges
2. Cash flow provided from operations and fixed charges/fixed charges

Example The following information is given:

	19X1	19X2
Income before taxes	$3,600,000	$5,900,000
Cash flow provided from operations	3,000,000	5,000,000
Fixed charges	1,000,000	1,200,000

Relevant ratios are:

	19X1	19X2
Fixed-charge coverage based on income before tax	4.6	5.9
Fixed-charge coverage based on cash flow from operations	4.0	5.2

The analysis shows that the company is much better able to meet its fixed charges based on earnings and out of cash flow from operations in 19X2 than in 19X1. For example, in 19X2, for every $1 in fixed charges there was $5.90 of earnings and $5.20 in cash flow from operations. This indicates that creditors are better protected in terms of being paid interest, rent, and other fixed obligations.

HOW IS IT USED AND BY WHOM?

Management and Creditors. The fixed-charge coverage ratio is useful in gauging a company's ability to satisfy its fixed costs. A low ratio indicates increased risk, because when business activity falls, the firm may be unable to meet fixed charges. In analyzing fixed charges, it is better to consider cash flow from operations than from net income, since cash is used to meet fixed payments. A high fixed-charge ratio reflects favorably on the company's ability to refinance obligations as they mature.

In analyzing these ratios for a given company, it should be determined whether that entity has stability in both operations and funds flow. Such stability affords more confidence in the firm's ability to meet its fixed commitments.

The coverage ratios are influenced by the level of earnings and by the level of fixed charges, which depend significantly on the debt-to-equity relationship within the capitalization.

73 Flexible-Budget Variance

DEFINITION. A flexible budget shows budgeted cost figures at various capacity levels (e.g., expected, optimistic, and pessimistic), and requires the separation of fixed and variable costs. A flexible budget enables the comparison of actual and budgeted results at virtually any level of activity, and is useful for analyzing both manufacturing and nonmanufacturing activities.

HOW IS IT COMPUTED?

Variance = budget versus actual at a particular capacity level

If idle capacity exists, total variable costs will increase with increased production but total fixed costs will remain the same.

Example The following shows how a company would prepare a flexible budget to reflect a range of performance expectations

	Pessi-mistic	Ex-pected	Opti-mistic	Full capacity
Units	8,000	10,000	11,000	15,000
Capacity level relative to expected	80%	100%	110%	
Variable costs	$48,000	$60,000	$66,000	
Fixed costs	$90,000	$90,000	$90,000	

Assuming that 8000 units were actually produced, with actual costs of $50,000 in variable costs and $91,000 in fixed costs, the flexible budget variance would be:

	Actual	Budget	Variance	
Variable	$50,000	$48,000	$2,000	Unfavorable
Fixed	91,000	90,000	1,000	Unfavorable

HOW IS IT USED AND BY WHOM?

Cost Analysts and Budget Analysts. The flexible budget allows management to plan more effectively by assessing costs at different capacity levels. Production managers and sales managers, for example, can foresee which operating strategies may be most suitable and what costs may be expected.

74 Foreign-Exchange Gains and Losses

DEFINITION. Foreign-currency gains and losses represent unstable elements under economic conditions where the foreign-exchange rate is erratic. Ratios involving foreign-currency gains and losses provide insight into the impact that fluctuations may have on overall company financial health. The degree of vacillation in the foreign-exchange rate may be measured by its percentage change over time and/or its standard deviation.

HOW IS IT COMPUTED? A determination can be made whether foreign-currency gains and losses contribute to variability in the earnings stream by use of three ratios:

1. Foreign-currency gains and losses to net income

2. Foreign-currency gains and losses to total revenue

3. Foreign earnings to net income.

Example A company's comparative income statements for three years provide the basis for analysis:

	19X1	19X2	19X3
Foreign-currency gains and losses	$1,000,000	$2,000,000	$ 400,000
Net income	4,000,000	4,300,000	3,900,000
Revenue	7,000,000	7,200,000	6,800,000

Relevant ratios are:

	19X1	19X2	19X3
Foreign-currency gains and losses to net income	25.0%	46.5%	10.3%
Foreign-currency gains and losses to revenue	14.3	27.8	5.9

The trend in foreign-currency gains and losses in this case is erratic in terms of absolute dollars and as a ratio of net income and revenue. Further, earnings quality in 19X2 was poor because of the high percentage of foreign-currency gain to net income (46.5%). The figures show that such gain lack repeatability, as evidenced by the significantly lower percentage of foreign-currency gain to net income (10.3%) in 19X3.

HOW IS IT USED AND BY WHOM?

Financial Analysts and Financial Managers. Since the exchange rates of some countries are more unstable than those of others, analysts should know in which countries the company is operating. For those countries with erratic exchange rates, management should ask if such instability is long term or short term. Long-run instability would mean that there is a greater likelihood of continued vacillation in earnings arising from foreign currency transactions.

If foreign earnings are a high percentage of net income, a determination should be made whether those earnings are derived from politically and economically unstable foreign countries. If they are, a greater degree of risk exists with regard to these sources of earnings. Steps should be taken to minimize such risk exposure, particularly when a low rate of return is being earned.

75 Forward Premium (or Discount) on a Forward Exchange Contract

DEFINITION. The *forward* rate is the exchange rate for *later* delivery of currencies exchanged, whereas the *spot* rate is the exchange rate for *immediate* delivery of currencies exchanged. Forward rates may be greater than the current spot rate (premium) or less than the current spot rate (discount).

HOW IS IT COMPUTED?

Forward premium (or discount) =

$$\frac{\text{Forward rate} - \text{spot rate}}{\text{Spot rate}} \times \frac{12}{\text{Length of forward contract in months}} \times 100$$

Example The forward rate on a 90-day forward contract in British pounds was 1.6528, while the spot rate today was 1.6430. The percent premium is:

$$\frac{1.6528 - 1.6430}{1.6430} \times \frac{12}{3} \times 100 = 2.3859\%$$

Management. The forward premium (discount) computation aids managers in evaluating foreign-currency exposure and planning to minimize exchange risks.

76 Funded Debt (Long-Term Debt) to Operating Property

DEFINITION. For utilities, the funded debt-to-operating property ratio is a key financial tool used to compare long-term debt to operating property. Operating property consists of all the utility's property and plant less a depreciation allowance.

HOW IS IT COMPUTED?

$$\text{Funded debt to operating property} = \frac{\text{Funded debt}}{\text{Operating property}}$$

Example The following compares a utility's performance in two years.

	19X3	19X4
Funded debt	$1,882,247	$1,995,398
Operating property	$4,189,238	$4,235,786
Funded debt to operating property	44.93%	47.11%

The increased ratio over the course of the year indicates that the utility is at greater risk due to the higher degree of debt relative to operating property.

HOW IS IT USED AND APPLIED? The funded debt-to-operating ratio is a measure of debt coverage and an indicator of the sources of funding. Utilities normally have a very large amount of long-term debt with highly specialized assets. The larger the ratio, the more risk is implied as the investment return of operating property becomes overly stretched.

WHO USES IT AND WHEN?

Financial Analysts and Underwriters? The funded debt-to-operating property ratio measures investment risk for utilities and is used to assess the debt-financing ability of a particular utility.

77 Funds-Flow Adequacy Ratio

DEFINITION. The funds-flow adequacy ratio reveals the extent to which a company can generate sufficient funds from operations to meet budgeted capital expenditures, increase inventories, and pay cash dividends.

HOW IS IT COMPUTED?

$$\frac{\text{Five-year sum of sources of funds from operations}}{\text{Five-year sum of capital expenditures, inventory additions, and cash dividends}}$$

Typically, a 5-year total is used to eliminate cyclical and other distortions.

Example The following figures from a 5-year period are used to analyze funds-flow adequacy for a specific company:

Capital expenditures	$ 800,000
Additions to inventory	400,000
Cash dividends	100,000
Funds from operations	1,500,000

The funds-flow adequacy ratio is:

$$\frac{\$1,500,000}{\$1,300,000} = 1.15$$

A ratio of 1 shows that the business has covered its needs based on attained levels of growth without having to resort to external financing. A ratio of less than 1 indicates that there may be inadequate internally generated funds to maintain dividends and current operating growth levels.

HOW IS IT USED AND BY WHOM?

Financial Management. Management uses this ratio to indicate whether internally generated funds are sufficient to assure growth.

Creditors. Use of this ratio indicates to creditors a company's ability to obtain internal sources of funds.

78 Future (Compound) Value

DEFINITION. Future value (also called "compounding") is the value of an investment at a future date based on a rate of interest being paid at stated time intervals. Future value includes not only the earned rate of interest, but also the compounding effect of earning interest on the interest already accrued. Interest may be compounded at different intervals, such as daily. The more often the compounding, the higher is the future value.

HOW IS IT COMPUTED? Financial calculators marketed by several manufacturers, (e.g., Hewlett-Packard, Sharp, Texas Instruments) have a "future (compound) value" function. Future value is also incorporated as a built-in function in spreadsheet programs such as Lotus 1-2-3.

1. The formula for future value for 1 year is:

$$FV_1 = P(1 + i)$$

where i = interest rate per time period

P = principal amount at time 0 or the present time

FV_1 = future (compound) value at the end of year 1

2. The future value for at the end of year n for any sum compounded at interest rate i is:

$$FV_n = P(1 + i)^n$$

where n = the number of years

3. *Future-value interest factors* (FVIFs) simplify extended future-value calculations by providing a table with FVIFs for \$1 at interest rate i for n years. An example is given in Table 1 of the Appendix. The formula for this calculation is:

$$FV_n = P \times FVIF(i,n)$$

where CVIF = compound-value interest factor

Example Florence deposits \$1000 in a savings account earning 8 percent interest compounded annually. At the end of 1 year, Florence's \$1000 deposit will be worth the following:

$$FV_1 = P(1 + i)$$

$$= \$1000(1 + 0.08)$$

$$= \$1080$$

At the end of 5 years, Florence's initial \$1000 deposit in a savings account earning 8 percent interest compounded annually will be worth:

$$FV_n = P(1 + i)^n$$

$$= \$1000(1 + 0.08)^5$$

$$= \$1469.32$$

Alternatively, one can make the same calculation using compound-value interest factors. Using the FVIF at 8 percent for 5 years:

$$FV_n = P \times FVIF(i,n)$$

$$= \$1000(1.469)$$

$$= \$1469.00$$

HOW IS IT USED AND APPLIED? Future-value calculations are widely used to determine what a sum of money invested at interest rate i will be worth in n years. Future-value computation can also be used to determine a growth rate, how many years it will take to reach a financial goal, and what interest rate is being charged on a loan.

WHO USES IT AND WHEN?

Managers and Financial Analysts. Future-value computations are used to help decide where to invest a certain sum of money. This calculation is used every time a decision must be made about a long-term investment, whether the investment is in government bonds, a savings account, or any other interest-bearing financial instrument.

Individuals. Future-value computation is used when deciding on an optimum investment vehicle—for example, a bank versus a mutual fund versus buying a stock versus buying a bond. Future-value computations are also extremely important when determining how much will be accumulated in a pension fund within a certain period of time at a certain interest rate at specified compounding intervals.

79 Future Value of an Annuity

DEFINITION. Computation of the future value of an annuity (FVA) is based on the concept that an annual annuity payment is reinvested at a particular rate of interest. This mathematical technique tells how much an investment will be worth at the end of the annuity period.

Two types of annuities are discussed below: the ordinary annuity with the payment at the end of the year, and the annuity due when the payment is made at the beginning of the year. In addition, the discussion examines the future difference in value between these two annuities.

ORDINARY ANNUITY

How Is It Computed? Financial calculators from several manufacturers will calculate future (compound) value (see No. 78). In addition, the function is built into spreadsheet programs such as Lotus 1-2-3.

There are two formulas for the computation of the future value of an ordinary annuity, a long method and a short method.

1. Long method:

$$FVA = A(1 + i)^{n-1} + A(1 + i)^{n-2} + \cdots + A(1 + i)^1 + A(1 + i)^0$$

$$= A\left[\frac{(1 + i)^n - 1}{i}\right] = A \times FVIFA$$

where FVA = future value of the annuity for an interest rate and time period
i = interest rate
n = number of years of the annuity
A = amount of money received periodically
FVIFA = future-value interest factor for the annuity

2. Short method: This formula is a simplification of the long formula and relies on accessing a table that provides these factors for the sum of an annuity of $1 per period for n periods:

$$FVA = A \times FVIFA(i,n)$$

Future-value interest factors for an annuity are given in Table 2 of the Appendix.

Example 1 Michael receives an annual annuity of $2000 that is invested at 10 percent immediately upon receipt of the annual payment. At the end of the 5-year annuity, Michael will have accumulated the following sums.

1. Long method:

$$FVA = A(1 + i)^{n-1} + A(1 + i)^{n-2} + \cdots + A(1 + i)^1 + A(1 + i)^0$$

$$= \$2,000(1.10)^4 + \$2,000(1.10)^3 + \$2,000(1.10)^2 + \$2,000(1.10)^1 +$$

$$\$2,000(1.10)^0$$

$$= \$2,000(1.4641) + \$2,000(1.331) + \$2,000(1.21) + \$2,000(1.1) +$$

$$\$2,000(1)$$

$$= \$2,928.2 + \$2,662 + \$2,420 + \$2,200 + \$2,000$$

$$= \$12,210.2$$

2. Short method: Using the future-value interest factor for an annuity (FVIFA) of 5 years paying 10 percent interest considerably simplifies the problem and gives the same answer as the long method:

$$FVA = A \times FVIFA(i,n) = \$2,000 \times FVIFA(10\%, 5 \text{ years})$$

$$= \$2,000 \times 6.1051$$

$$= \$12,210.2$$

Using either method, Michael will have \$12,210.20 at the end of the annual annuity if it is invested at 10 percent.

ANNUITY DUE

How Is It Computed?   The formula for computing the future value of an annuity due must take into consideration one additional year of compounding, since the payment comes at the beginning of the year. Therefore, the future-value formula must be modified to take this into consideration by compounding it for one more year:

1. Long method:

$$FVA = [A(1 + i)^{n-1} + A(1 + i)^{n-2} + \ldots$$

$$+ A(1 + i)^1 + A(1 + i)^0](1 + i) = A\left[\frac{(1 + i)^n - 1}{i}\right] - 1 = A$$

$$\times FVIFA(i,n) - 1$$

2. Short method: Using the future-value interest factor for an annuity (FVIFA) of 5 years paying 10 percent interest modified for an annuity due, the formula is

$$FVA = A \times FVIFA(i,n)(1 + i)$$

Example 2   Using the same investment as Example 1, the future-value computations for the annuity due would be as follows:

1. Long method:

$$FVA = [\$2,000(1.10)^4 + \$2,000(1.10)^3 + \$2,000(1.10)^2 + \$2,000(1.10)^1 +$$

$$\$2,000(1.10)^0](1.10)$$

$$= [\$2,000(1.4641) + \$2,000(1.331) + \$2,000(1.21) + \$2,000(1.1) +$$

$$\$2,000(1)](1.10)$$

$$= (\$2,928.2 + \$2,662 + \$2,420 + \$2,200 + \$2,000)(1.10)$$

$$= \$12,210.2(1.10)$$

$$= \$13,431.22$$

2. Short method: Using the future-value interest factor for an annuity (FVIFA) of 5 years paying 10 percent interest modified for an annuity due:

$$\text{FVA} = A \times \text{FVIFA}(i,n)(1 + i) = \$2,000 \times \text{FVIFA}(10\%, 5 \text{ years}) + (1 + 0.1)$$

$$= \$2,000 \times 6.1051 \times 1.10$$

$$= \$13,431.22$$

FUTURE-VALUE DIFFERENCE BETWEEN ORDINARY ANNUITY AND ANNUITY DUE. The future-value difference between the ordinary annuity and an annuity due in our examples is $\$13,431.22 - \$12,210.20 = \$1,221.02$. Generally speaking, an annuity due is preferable over an ordinary annuity, since an amount equivalent to an additional year of compounding is received.

HOW IS IT USED AND APPLIED? Future-value determination based on periodic equal payments will give the accumulated amount in a fund such as a retirement account, sinking fund, or a bank account. The computation enables a distinction between the accumulated principal and interest, and a determination of the equal annual cash payment, interest rate, or number of periods.

WHO USES IT AND WHEN?

Individuals. The future annuity computation reveals what equal annual payments will be worth at a future date. For example, an individual might want to calculate how much income is generated after 30 years of depositing $2000 a year into an IRA account, or the annual deposit necessary to generate $1 million after 20 years.

Pension and Annuity Fund Managers. The formula is used to explain to fund members the worth of their annuities. It also shows the effect of different assumed interest rates on an accumulated balance.

Annuity Salespersons and Managers. This statistical methodology must be understood by annuity salespersons and managers in order to increase sales and to demonstrate the importance of the annuity concept for building wealth.

80 Geometric Average Return

DEFINITION. Geometric average return is a measure of return over a single holding period or over multiple periods. When an investor holds an investment for more than one period, it is important to understand how to compute the average of the successive rates of return. The other measure of multiperiod average (mean) returns is *arithmetic average return* (see No. 12). The arithmetic average return, however, can be quite misleading in multiperiod return calculations.

HOW IS IT COMPUTED?   A more accurate measure of the actual return generated by an investment over multiple periods is the **geometric average return**. The geometric return over n periods is computed as follows:

$$\text{Geometric return} = \sqrt[n]{(1 + r)(1 + r)\cdots(1 + r)} - 1$$

Since it is cumbersome to calculate the nth root (although there is a formula for approximating it), we will only illustrate the two-period return calculation $(n = 2)$.

Example   Consider the following data, where the price of a stock doubles in one period and depreciates back to the original price. Assume no dividends.

	Time period		
	$t = 0$	$t = 1$	$t = 2$
Price (end of period)	$50	$100	$50

The *holding period returns (HPR)* for periods 1 and 2 are computed as follows:

$$\text{Period 1 } (t = 1)\text{:}\qquad \text{HPR} = \frac{\$0 + (\$100 - \$50)}{\$50} = \frac{\$50}{\$50} = 100\%$$

$$\text{Period 2 } (t = 2)\text{:}\qquad \text{HPR} = \frac{\$0 + (\$50 - \$100)}{\$100} = \frac{-\$50}{\$100} = -50\%$$

Therefore, the arithmetic average return is the average of 100% and -50%, which is 25%, as shown below:

$$\frac{100\% + (-50\%)}{2} = 25\%$$

Obviously, the stock purchased for $50 and sold for the same price two periods later did not earn 25 percent; it clearly earned zero return. The geometric average return provides the correct return.

Note that $n = 2$, $r_1 = 100\% = 1$, and $r_2 = -50\% = -0.5$. Then,

$$\text{Geometric return} = \sqrt{(1 + 1)(1 - 0.5)} - 1$$

$$= \sqrt{(2)(0.5)} - 1$$

$$= \sqrt{1} - 1 = 1 - 1 = 0\%$$

WHO USES IT AND WHEN?

Investors.   When an investor holds an investment for more than one period, it is important to understand how to compute the average of the successive rates of return. The arithmetic average return, however, can be quite misleading in multiperiod return calculations. Investors must use the geometric mean return measure to be able to make correct decisions.

81 Gordon's Dividend Growth Model

DEFINITION. The value of a common stock is the present value of all future cash inflows expected to be received by the investor. The cash inflows expected to be received are dividends and the future price at the time of the sale of the stock.

Since common stock has no maturity date and is held for many years, a more general, multiperiod model is needed. The general common-stock valuation model (Gordon's dividend growth model) is defined as follows:

$$P_0 = \sum_{t=1}^{\infty} \frac{D_t}{(1+r)^t}$$

where D_t = dividend in period t
P_0 = current market price of stock
r = constant annual growth rate in dividends
t = number of periods

HOW IS IT COMPUTED?   In the case of constant growth, if dividends are assumed to grow at a constant rate of g every year [i.e., $D_t = D_0(1 + g)^t$], then the general model simplifies to:

$$P_0 = \frac{D_1}{r-g}$$

In words,

$$\text{Common stock value} = \frac{\text{Dividend in year 1}}{(\text{Required rate of return}) - (\text{growth rate})}$$

Example   Consider a common stock that paid a $3 dividend per share at the end of the last year and is expected to pay a cash dividend every year at a growth rate of 10 percent. Assume that the investor's required rate of return is 12 percent. The value of the stock is:

$$D_1 = D_0(1 + g) = \$3(1 + 0.10) = \$3.30$$

$$P_0 = \frac{D_1}{r-g} = \frac{\$3.30}{0.12 - 0.10} = \$165$$

HOW IS IT USED AND APPLIED?   This model is most applicable to the valuation of common stocks of very large or broadly diversified firms.

WHO USES IT AND WHEN?

Investors.   This model can be used to price a stock whose dividend records have been stable and are expected to grow at a stable rate.

82 Gross Income Multiplier

DEFINITION.   The gross income multiplier is one method of determining the price of income-producing property. Other methods are the *net income* multiplier (NIM) (see No. 127) and the *capitalization rate* (see No. 27). This rule-of-thumb valuation, or pricing formula, is also used for acquiring companies.

HOW IS IT COMPUTED? The gross income multiplier is obtained by dividing the asking price (or market value) of the property by the current gross rental income.

Example Assume that current gross rental income is $23,600 and the asking price is $219,000. Then the gross income multiplier is

$$\frac{\$219,000}{\$23,600} = 9.28$$

HOW IS IT USED AND APPLIED? A property in a similar neighborhood may be valued at "eight times annual gross." Thus, if its annual gross rental income amounts to $23,600, the value is taken as 8 × $23,600 = $188,800, which means that the property may be overvalued.

Applications of this approach in other industry sectors include the following:

1. In the publishing industry, new, fast-growing magazines are worth 5 to 10 times before-tax annual earnings.
2. Radio stations sell for 7.5 times earnings or cash flows.
3. Insurance agencies sell for 150 percent of annual commissions.
4. Automobile repair garages sell for three times average monthly receipts.

WHO USES IT AND WHEN?

Real Estate Investors, Appraisers, and Realtors. The real estate industry uses this approach to determine an approximate market value of a property. This approach should be used with caution, however, since different properties have different operating expenses that must be taken into account in determining value.

Corporate Strategists and Raiders. This rule-of-thumb pricing formula can be used for purchasing companies; however, reliance on this technique alone can result in gross oversimplification of the market value of a property.

83 Gross Profit Variance

DEFINITION. Gross profit analysis is used to determine the causes of a change in gross profit. Any variances that affect gross profit are reported to management so that corrective steps may be taken. The causes of a gross profit variance include (1) changes in unit sales price and cost; (2) changes in the volume of products sold; and (3) changes in the sales mix.

HOW IS IT COMPUTED? Computation methodology for gross profit variances for a *single product* follow:

Sales price variance = (actual price − budget price) × actual sales

Cost price variance = (actual cost − budget cost) × actual sales

Sales volume variance = (actual sales − budget sales) × budget price

Cost volume variance = (actual sales − budget sales)

$$× \text{ budget cost per unit}$$

Total volume variance = sales volume variance − cost volume variance

Computation of gross profit variances for *multiple products* varies from the above.

The total volume variance in a multiple-product situation is comprised of sales mix variance and sales quantity variance.

Sales mix variance = (actual sales at budgeted mix − budget sales at

budgeted mix × budget contribution margin (or gross margin) per unit

Sales quantity variance = (actual sales at budgeted mix − budget sales at

budgeted mix) × budgeted contribution margin (or gross margin) per unit

Total volume variance = sales mix variance + sales quantity variance

or

(actual sales at actual mix − budgeted sales at

budgeted mix) × budgeted contribution margin

(or gross marigin) per unit

In analyzing multiple products, the sales price variance and the cost price variance are calculated the same as for a single product.

Frequently, taking a contribution-margin approach for the analysis is superior to using the gross profit approach, since "gross profit" includes a deduction for fixed costs that may be beyond the control of a particular level of management.

Example A retail company sells two items—Model X and Model Y. For the years 19X1 and 19X2, the company realized gross profit of $246,640 and $211,650, respectively. Some executives were unsure why gross profit dropped in 19X2, despite the fact that total sales volume in dollars and in units was higher in 19X2 than in 19X1. The company's operating results for 19X1 and 19X2 are shown below. No fixed costs were included in the cost of goods sold per unit.

	Model X				Model Y			
Year	Selling price	Cost of goods sold per unit	Sales (in units)	Sales revenue	Selling price	Cost of goods sold per unit	Sales (in units)	Sales revenue
1	$150	$110	2,800	$420,000	$172	$121	2,640	$454,080
2	160	125	2,650	424,000	176	135	2,900	510,400

The analysis explains why gross profit declined by $34,990, and includes a detailed variance analysis of price changes and changes in volume for both sales and cost. The total volume variance is subdivided into changes in price and changes in quantity.

Sales price and sales volume variances measure the impact on the firm's contribution margin (or gross margin) of changes in the unit selling price and sales volume. In computing these variances, all costs are held constant in order to stress changes in price and volume. Cost price and cost volume variances are computed in the same manner, holding price and volume constant. All these variances for the company are computed below:

Sales Price Variance		
Actual sales for 19X2:		
Model X (2,650 × $160)	$424,000	
Model Y (2,900 × $176)	510,000	$934,400
Actual sales at 19X1 prices:		
Model X (2,650 × $150)	$397,500	
Model Y (2,900 × $172)	498,800	896,300
		$ 38,100 F

Sales Volume Variance		
Actual 19X2 sales at 19X1 prices		$896,300
Actual 19X1 sales (at 19X1 prices):		
Model X (2,800 × $150)	$420,000	
Model Y (2,640 × $172)	454,080	874,080
		$ 22,220 F

Cost Price Variance		
Actual cost of goods sold for 19X2:		
Model X (2,650 × $125)	$331,250	
Model Y (2,900 × $135)	391,500	$722,750
Actual 19X2 sales at 19X1 costs:		
Model X (2,650 × $110)	$291,500	
Model Y (2,900 × $121)	350,900	642,400
		$ 80,350 U

Cost Volume Variance		
Actual 19X2 sales at 19X1 costs		$642,400
Actual 19X1 sales (at 19X1 costs):		
Model X (2,800 × $110)	$308,000	
Model Y (2,640 × $121)	319,440	627,440
		$ 14,960 U

Total volume variance = Sales volume variance − cost volume variance

$7,260 F = $22,220 F − $14,960 U

The total volume variance is computed as the sum of a sales mix variance and a sales quantity variance as follows:

Sales Mix Variance

	19X2 actual sales at 19X1 mix[a]	19X2 actual sales at 19X2 mix	Difference	19X1 gross profit per unit	Variance ($)
Model X	$2,857	$2,650	207 U	$40	$ 8,280 U
Model Y	2,693	2,900	207 F	51	10,557 F
	$5,550	$5,550			$ 2,277 F

[a]This is the 19X1 mix (used as standard or budget) proportions of 51.47% (or 2800/5440 = 51.47%) and 48.53% (or 2640/5440 = 48.53%) applied to the actual 19X2 sales figure of 5550 units.

Sales Quantity Variance

	19X2 actual sales at 19X1 mix[a]	19X1 actual sales at 19X1 mix	Difference	19X1 gross profit per unit	Variance ($)
Model X	$2,857	$2,800	57 F	$40	$2,280 F
Model Y	2,693	2,640	53 F	51	2,703 F
	$5,550	$5,440			$4,983 F

[a]This is the 19X1 mix (used as standard or budget) proportions of 51.47% (or 2800/5440 = 51.47%) and 48.53% (or 2640/5440 = 48.53%) applied to the actual 19X2 sales figure of 5550 units.

A favorable total volume variance is due to a favorable shift in the sales mix (that is, from Model X to Model Y) and also to a favorable increase in sales volume (by 110 units), which is shown as follows:

Sales mix variance	$2,277	F
Sales quantity variance	4,983	F
	$7,260	F

There remains, however, the decrease in gross profit of $34,990, which can be explained as follows:

	Gains		Losses	
Gain due to increased sales price	$38,100	F		
Loss due to increased cost			$80,350	U
Gain due to increase in units sold	4,983	F		
Gain due to shift in sales mix	2,277	F		
	$45,360	F	$80,350	U

Hence, the net decrease in gross profit is $80,350 - $45,360 = $34,900 U.

Despite the increase in sales price and volume and the favorable shift in sales mix, the company ended up losing $34,990 in 19X2, compared to 19X1. The major reason for this comparative loss was the tremendous increase in cost of goods sold, as indicated by an unfavorable cost price variance of $80,350. The costs for both Model X and Model Y went up quite significantly over 19X1, suggesting that the company has to take a close look at its cost picture. Even though only variable costs were included in cost of goods sold per unit, both variable and fixed costs should be analyzed in an effort to cut down on controllable costs. In doing that, it is essential that responsibility be clearly fixed to given individuals. In a retail business, operating expenses such as advertising and employee payroll must also be closely scrutinized.

HOW IS IT USED AND BY WHOM?

Marketing Managers and Cost Analysts. Changes in gross profit may be examined by marketing managers and cost analysts, either in terms of the entire company or by product line. In an effort to improve profitability, analyzing the change in the character of sales or the mix of sales is just as important as the increase in total volume. For example, if the total volume in the budget is constant, but a larger proportion of high-margin products are sold than were budgeted, then higher profits will result.

Gross profit (or contribution margin) is usually the joint responsibility of the managers of the sales department and the production department, with the sales department manager responsible for the sales revenue component and the production department manager accountable for the cost-of-goods-sold component. The sales department manager must hold fast to prices, volume, and mix; the production department supervisor must control the costs of materials, labor, and factory overhead and quantities; the purchasing manager must purchase materials at budgeted prices; and the personnel manager must employ the right people at the right wage rates.

It is the task of top management, however, to ensure that the target profit is met. The internal audit department must ensure that budgetary figures for sales and costs are being adhered to by all the departments which are, directly or indirectly, involved in contributing to making profit.

Although the sales mix variance is part of profit analysis, the production mix variance for materials and labor is an important part of cost variance analysis. The analysis of standard cost variances, however, should be understood as part of what is broadly known as *profit analysis*. In industries where each cost element can be substituted for one another and where production is at or near full capacity, how different types of materials and classes of labor are combined will affect the extent to which costs are controlled and gross profit maximized.

Taken as a whole, the analysis of profit involves careful evaluation of all facets of variance analysis—that is, sales variances and cost variances. The effect of changes in mix, volume, and yield on profits must especially be separated and analyzed. The analysis of these variances provide management with added dimensions to responsibility accounting, since it provides additional insight into what caused the increase or decrease in profits or why the actual profit deviated from the target profit. Analyzing the change in gross profit via an effective responsibility accounting system based on the control of costs and sales variances is a step toward maximization of profits.

84 Growth Rate

DEFINITION. Growth rate is the percentage change in earnings per share, dividends per share, sales, market price of stock, or total assets, compared to a base-year amount. It is also the compounded annual rate at which the value of a security increases. In economics, it is the annual growth rate in gross national product (GNP) of the economy, expressed as a percentage over the previous year. The growth rate generally indicates whether the economy is in a period of prosperity, recession, or stability.

HOW IS IT COMPUTED? The compound annual rate of growth can be computed as

$$F_n = P \cdot \text{FVIF}\ (i,n)$$

where F_n = future value in period n
P = a present sum of money or base-period value
$\text{FVIF}(i,n)$ = future value factor at a specified interest rate for a stated number of periods.

$$\text{FVIF}(i,n) = \frac{F_n}{P}$$

Example Assume that a company has earnings per share of \$2.50 in 19X1, and 10 years later the earnings per share have increased to \$3.70. The compound annual rate of growth in earnings per share is computed as follows:

$$F_{10} = \$3.70 \quad \text{and} \quad P = \$2.50$$

Therefore,

$$\text{FVIF}(i,10) = \frac{\$3.70}{\$2.50} = 1.48$$

From Table 1 in the Appendix, a FVIF of 1.48 at 10 years is at $i = 4\%$. The compound annual rate of growth is therefore 4 percent.

HOW IS IT USED AND APPLIED? The growth rate is used in many ways. Applications include:

- Growth rate in earnings or dividends (g) required for Gordon's dividend growth model (see No. 81):

$$P_0 = \frac{D_1}{r - g}$$

where P_0 = current price of a security
D_1 = expected dividend at the end of the first year
r = investor's required rate of return

- Mutual funds, which are frequently ranked on the basis of 5- or 10-year compound annual returns
- Growth rates in GNP, used to indicate whether the economy is in a recession or achieving prosperity

CAN A COMPUTER HELP?   Spreadsheet programs such as Lotus 1-2-3 have a routine for this growth calculation. Furthermore, many financial calculators have preprogrammed formulas and perform many present-value and future-value applications (e.g., Radio Shack EC5500, Hewlett-Packard 10B, Sharp EL733, and Texas Instruments BA35).

WHO USES IT AND WHEN?

Investors and Security Analysts.   Investors and analysts need to know the rate of growth in earnings and dividends in order to determine the theoretical value of a stock.

Fund Managers.   Fund managers often use the growth rate, because their performance is frequently rated on 5- or 10-year growth rates.

Business Economists and Forecasters.   It is vital for sales forecasters to be up to date on the state of the nation's economy; thus economists and forecasters utilize the growth-rate calculation for much of their analysis.

85 High–Low Method

DEFINITION.   The high–low method is an algebraic method that attempts to estimate the constant and slope of the equation using only the highest and lowest pairs of the sample data. For example, for planning, control, and decision-making purposes, mixed (or semivariable) costs need to be separated into their variable and fixed components.

Since the mixed costs include both fixed and variable elements, the analysis takes the following mathematical form, which is called a cost–volume formula (flexible budget formula or cost function):

$$Y = a + bX$$

where Y = the mixed cost to be broken up
$\quad X$ = any given measure of activity, such as direct labor hours, machine hours, or production volume
$\quad a$ = the fixed-cost component
$\quad b$ = the variable rate per unit of X

The separation of the mixed cost into its fixed and variable components is the same as estimating the parameter values a and b in the cost–volume formula. Another method available for this purpose is the least-squares method (regression analysis). (See No. 105, Least-Squares Regression.)

HOW IS IT COMPUTED?   The high–low method, as the name indicates, uses two extreme data points to determine the values of a (the fixed-cost portion) and b (the variable rate) in the equation $Y = a + bX$. The extreme data points are the highest representative X–Y pair and the lowest representative X–Y pair. The activity level X, rather than the mixed-cost item Y, governs their selection.

The high–low method is explained, step by step, as follows:

Step 1: Select the highest pair and the lowest pair.

Step 2: Compute the variable rate, b, using the formula:

$$\text{Variable rate} = \frac{\text{Difference in cost } Y}{\text{Difference in activity } X}$$

Step 3: Compute the fixed-cost portion as:

$$\text{Fixed-cost portion} = \text{total mixed cost} - \text{variable cost}$$

Example NB Publishing Company decides to relate total factory overhead costs to direct labor hours (DLH) to develop a cost–volume formula in the form $Y = a + bX$. Twelve monthly observations are collected. They are given in Exhibit 85.1 and plotted in Exhibit 85.2.

The high–low points selected from the monthly observations are

	X		Y	
High	23 hours	$25	(May pair)
Low	7	14	(September pair)
Difference	16 hours	$11	

Thus

$$\text{Variable rate } b = \frac{\text{Difference in } Y}{\text{Difference in } X} = \frac{\$11}{16 \text{ hours}} = \$0.6875 \text{ per DLH}$$

Exhibit 85.1 Monthly observations.

Month	Direct labor hours, X (000 omitted)	Factory overhead, Y (000 omitted)
January	9 hours	$ 15
February	19	20
March	11	14
April	14	16
May	23	25
June	12	20
July	12	20
August	22	23
September	7	14
October	13	22
November	15	18
December	17	18
Total	174 hours	$225

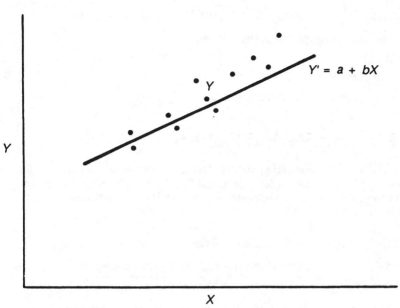

Exhibit 85.2 Actual (Y) versus estimated (Y').

The fixed-cost portion is computed as

	High	Low
Factory overhead (Y)	$25	$14
Variable expense ($0.6875/DLH)	(15.8125)	(4.8125)
	$9.1875	$9.1875

Therefore, the cost–volume formula for factory overhead is 9.19 fixed plus $0.69 per DLH.

HOW IS IT USED AND APPLIED? The high–low method is simple and easy to use. It has the disadvantage, however, of using two extreme data points, which may not be representative of normal conditions. The method may yield unreliable estimates of a and b in the formula. In such a case, it is best to drop them and to choose two other points that are more representative of normal situations. Use of this method is also potentially dangerous for a seasonal business, where the seasonality drives the high and low points.

The scatter diagram plotted should be checked for this possibility. It is important to make sure that there is a linear relationship between Y and X.

WHO USES IT AND WHEN?

Cost and Managerial Accountants. The breakdown of mixed costs into their fixed and variable portions is essential for the development of contribution-margin data. Contribution margin, which is sales minus variable costs (see No. 36), has various applications:

1. Breakeven, cost–volume–profit (CVP), and sales mix analyses
2. Appraisal of divisional performance
3. Flexible budgeting
4. Short-term choice decisions
5. Transfer pricing decisions

86 Holding-Period Return

DEFINITION. Holding-period return (HPR) is the total return earned from holding an investment for a period of time. It is determined from current income (dividend income, rental income, or interest income) and capital gain or loss.

HOW IS IT COMPUTED? Holding-period return is computed as:

$$HPR = \frac{\text{Current income} + \text{capital gain (or loss)}}{\text{Purchase price}}$$

Example 1 Consider the following investment in stock A and B over a 1-year period of ownership:

	Stock A	Stock B
Purchase price (beginning of year)	$100	$100
Cash dividend received (during the year)	$10	$15
Sales price (end of year)	$108	$98

Combining the capital gain (or loss) with the current income, the total return on each investment is summarized below:

Return	Stock A	Stock B
Cash dividend	$10	$15
Capital gain (loss)	8	(2)
Total return	$18	$13

Then the HPR is:

$$HPR \text{ (stock A)} = \frac{\$10 + (\$108 - \$100)}{\$100} = \frac{\$10 + \$8}{\$100}$$

$$= \frac{\$18}{\$100} = 18\%$$

$$HPR \text{ (stock B)} = \frac{\$15 + (\$98 - \$100)}{\$100} = \frac{\$15 - \$2}{\$100}$$

$$= \frac{\$13}{\$100} = 13\%$$

How Is It Computed for a Mutual Fund? In the case of a mutual fund, the return is distributed in three ways: dividends, capital gain distribution, and appreciation in net asset value (NAV). The holding-period return incorporates all factors:

$$HPR = \frac{\text{Dividends} + \text{capital gain distributors} + (\text{ending NAV} - \text{beginning NAV})}{\text{Beginning NAV}}$$

where NAV = net asset value and (ending NAV - beginning NAV) represents price appreciation.

Example 2 Assume that a mutual fund paid dividends of $0.50 and capital gain distributions of $0.35 per share over the course of the year, and had a price (NAV) at the beginning of the year of $6.50 that rose to $7.50 per share by the end of the year. The holding period return (HPR) is:

$$HPR = \frac{\$0.50 + \$0.35 + (\$7.50 - \$6.50)}{\$6.50} = \frac{\$1.85}{\$6.50} = 28.46\%$$

HOW IS IT USED AND APPLIED? The holding-period return is a measure of the annual rate of return on an investment. In the case of a mutual fund, the return is distributed in three ways: dividends, capital gain distribution, and appreciation in net asset value (NAV). NAV indicates only the current market value of the underlying portfolio. An investor also receives capital gains and dividends. Therefore, the performance of a mutual fund must be judged on the basis of these three.

WHO USES IT AND WHEN?

Investors and Fund Managers. Investors and fund managers look at 5 or 10 years of HPRs in selecting their investment. In addition to a stable return record, a risk factor, measured by beta or other factors, must be weighed against the return.

87 Horizontal Analysis

DEFINITION. Horizontal analysis is a time series analysis of financial statements covering more than one accounting period. Horizontal analysis looks at the percentage change in an account over time.

HOW IS IT COMPUTED?

$$\text{Percentage change} = \frac{\text{dollar change}}{\text{base-year amount}} = \frac{(\text{year 2} - \text{year 1})}{\text{year 1}}$$

Example Horizontal analysis across two years yields the following outcome: If sales in 19X8 and 19X9 were $100,000 and $300,000, respectively, the increase is $200,000/$100,000 = 200 percent.

Financial Analysts, Investors, and Management. By examining the magnitude and direction of a financial statement item, the analyst or manager is able to evaluate the reasonableness of the trend. Trend analysis identifies areas of wide divergence, and alerts analysts to the need for further evaluation. For example, a large increase in sales returns and allowances coupled with a decrease in sales would be a cause of concern. An analyst might compare these results with those of competitors to investigate whether the problem is industrywide, or particular to the company.

88 Housing-Affordability Measures

DEFINITION. Housing-affordability measures are used to determine how much one can afford to spend for a home. The basic calculations involve how much one can pay each month for the long-term expenses of owning a home (e.g., mortgage payments, maintenance and operating expenses, insurance, and property taxes), and how much cash is available for the initial costs of the purchase (e.g., the down payment, points, and closing costs).

HOW IS IT COMPUTED?

1. *Thirty-five percent rule:* A borrower can afford no more than 35 percent of his or her monthly take-home pay.

2. *Multiple-of-gross-income rule:* The price should not exceed two and a half times the family's gross annual income.

3. *Percent-of-monthly-gross-income rule:* The monthly mortgage payment, property taxes, and insurance should not exceed 25 percent of the family's monthly gross income.

Example 1 Your gross annual income is $33,000 per year, and your take-home pay is $2095 per month. Under the 35 percent rule, you can afford a monthly payment of $733.

Example 2 Your annual gross income is $80,000. The maximum price you can afford to pay for a house is:

$$2\frac{1}{2} \times \$80,000 = \$200,000$$

Example 3 You and your spouse have annual gross income of $60,000. Your monthly payment for mortgage, property taxes, and insurance should not exceed:

$$25\% \times \$5000 = \$1250$$

HOW IS IT USED AND BY WHOM?

Individuals. In personal financial planning, housing-affordability measures are used to determine how much one can pay for a home and how much one can meet in monthly payments.

Lenders. The rules of thumb are used by lenders to determine a borrower's ability to afford a house.

89 Index-Number Trend Series

DEFINITION. In an index-number trend series, an index is assigned to a base year and values for other years are computed by reference to the base year.

HOW IS IT COMPUTED? A base year that is most *representative* (typical, normal) of the entity's operations is selected and assigned an index of 100. All index numbers are computed with reference to the base year.

$$\text{Index} = \frac{\text{Current-year amount}}{\text{Base-year amount}}$$

Warning: As with the computation of year-to-year percentage changes, certain fluctuations in a series, such as changes from negative to positive amounts, *cannot* be expressed by means of index numbers.

Example The base year is 19X1 and sales for that year are $600,000. An index number of 100 is assigned to 19X1. Sales for 19X2 and 19X3 are $660,000 and $500,000, respectively. The appropriate index numbers are:

$$19\text{X}2: \quad \frac{\$660,000}{\$600,000} = 110$$

$$19\text{X}3: \quad \frac{\$500,000}{\$600,000} = 83$$

A manager who sees this type of sharp drop in sales in 19X3 should research the reasons and find the responsible parties.

HOW IS IT USED AND BY WHOM?

Financial Analysts and Financial Management. When comparing accounts covering more than 3 years, the year-to-year method of comparison may become too cumbersome. Often the best way to look at a long-term trend is through the use of index numbers. Financial analysts and management can identify any financial statement accounts or items that appear to be out of line. If the trend is illogical or signals a problem, the item should be investigated. Where possible, managers should take corrective action.

90 Index of Bearish Sentiment

DEFINITION. The Index of Bearish Sentiment is a technical investment analysis tool published by Investors Intelligence. It is based on a reversal of the recommendations of investment advisory services—i.e., whatever the investment advisory service recommends, the opposite should be done.

HOW IS IT COMPUTED?

$$\text{Index} = \frac{\text{Bearish investment advisory services}}{\text{Total number of investment advisory services}}$$

Example Of 250 investment advisory services, 110 are bearish on the stock market. The Index of Bearish Sentiment is:

$$\frac{110}{250} = 44\%$$

Investors Intelligence believes that when 42 percent or more of the advisory services are bearish, as in this example, the market will go up. On the other hand, when 17 percent or fewer of the services are bearish, Investors Intelligence believes that the market will go down.

HOW IS IT USED AND BY WHOM?

Investors. The index is used by investors to predict the future direction of the securities market using the contrary-opinion approach. If bearish sentiment exists, the market is expected to go up.

Investors Intelligence believes that advisory services are trend followers rather than anticipators.

A movement toward 10 percent means that the Dow Jones Industrial Average is about to go from bullish to bearish. When the index approaches 60 percent, the Dow Jones Industrial Average is about to go from bearish to bullish.

91 Indirect Labor to Direct Labor

DEFINITION. The ratio of indirect labor to direct labor monitors indirect labor planning and control.

HOW IS IT COMPUTED?

$$\frac{\text{Indirect labor}}{\text{Direct labor}}$$

Example The following quarterly information is available for a company.

	Quarter				
	1	2	3	4	Annual
Indirect labor	$ 50,000	$ 52,000	$ 56,000	$ 62,000	$220,000
Direct labor	125,000	130,000	135,000	140,000	530,000
Ratio of indirect labor to direct labor	40.0%	40.0%	41.5%	44.3%	41.5%

The ratios for the first two quarters in this example are constant. In the last two quarters there was an increase in the percentage of indirect labor incurred relative to direct labor. This trend is favorable because it indicates that management has maintained a desirable relationship between indirect and direct personnel.

Management's preliminary operating plan can *project* indirect labor by multiplying direct labor requirements by the average ratio, which is 41.5% in this example.

HOW IS IT USED AND BY WHOM?

Management. A pool of qualified personnel, both direct and indirect, are needed in any organization to conduct the tasks and services required to accomplish the organization's goals. Labor planning and control are crucial at all supervisory levels to produce competitive products and/or to perform profitable services. Management can use this ratio to evaluate and monitor indirect personnel requirements through the impact of these requirements on operations, earnings, and overhead costs.

92 Inflation Adjustments

DEFINITION. Inflation adjustments are those adjustments of accounts or items that reflect the impact of inflation-driven changes in the purchasing power of the dollar over time—for example, adjustments to the historical cost figures for net income, nonmonetary assets, and nonmonetary liabilities.

INFLATION-ADJUSTED EARNINGS. To the degree that net income includes inflationary profits, reported earnings are overstated in an economic sense, because such profits result from changes in the price level and/or replacement cost rather than from operational performance. Use of inflation-adjusted earnings state income more accurately.

How Is It Computed?

1. Consumer Price Index (CPI)-adjusted net income to report net income

2. Replacement-cost (current-cost) net income to reported net income

These ratios reveal the impact of inflation on reported results. If the amount reported in the income statement is materially higher than the inflation-adjusted net income measure(s), the quality of earnings is poor. The wider the difference, the lower is the quality of net income.

Example 1 Company K's income statement for 19X1 shows a net income of $4,000,000. A footnote titled "Inflation" reveals that constant-dollar net income is $3,500,000 and current-cost net income is $3,200,000. Company L, a competitor, reports net income for 19X1 of $2,000,000. A related footnote discloses that constant-dollar net income is $1,900,000 and current-cost net income is $1,800,000.

Ratios showing inflationary effects for the companies follow:

	Company K	Company L
Constant-dollar net income to net income	87.5%	95.0%
Current-cost net income to net income	80.0%	90.0%

Company K's quality of earnings is lower than that of Company L, as evidenced by its lower ratios of (1) constant-dollar net income to net income and (2) current-cost net income to net income. In effect, Company K's historically determined net income relative to inflation-adjusted profits is proportionately overstated compared to that of Company L. The more a company's net income exceeds the inflationary adjusted net income, the lower is its quality of earnings. The absolute dollar amount of reported net income is irrelevant.

INFLATION-ADJUSTED ASSETS

How Is It Computed?

1. Historical cost × (average CPI for current year/CPI at acquisition date). The CPI takes into account general inflation, because it considers the change in prices of goods and services.

2. Replacement cost of assets. Replacement cost takes into account the current value of a specific item.

Example 2 On 1/1/19X1, a company bought land at a price of $200,000. The CPI on that date was 140. The average CPI index for 19X9 was 200. The replacement cost was $260,000. On 12/31/19X9, the inflation-adjusted value of the land was as follows:

1. Based on CPI:

$$\$200,000 \times \frac{200}{140} = \$285,714$$

2. Based on replacement cost:

$$\$260,000$$

Although the land is on the books at $200,000 using historical cost, it is worth $285,714 in today's CPI dollars or $260,000 based on its specific current value.

HOW IS IT USED AND BY WHOM?

Financial Management. Financial management is able to determine actual company earnings and net assets by taking changes in the purchasing power of the dollar into account. By taking inflation into account, more informed decisions are made.

Investors and Creditors. Investors and creditors are in a better position to appraise the financial health and operating performance of a company when they consider current prices and current values.

Individual. When informed of the degree to which inflation has financially affected a private individual, that person can assess their real purchasing power today relative to that of prior years.

93 Instability Index in Earnings

DEFINITION. The instability index in earnings reveals the variability in a company's earnings stream. The index reflects the deviation of actual income from trend income.

HOW IS IT COMPUTED?

$$I = \sqrt{\frac{\sum (y - y^T)^2}{n}}$$

where y^T = trend earnings for period t, and is calculated from

$$y^T = a + bt$$

where a = dollar intercept
b = slope of trend line
t = time period

A simple trend equation solved by computer is used to determine trend income.

HOW IS IT USED AND BY WHOM?

Financial Analysts. The financial analyst computes the instability index in earnings as a basis on which to evaluate a company's quality of earnings. A wide fluctuation in earnings is disadvantageous, since it implies corporate instability.

94 Insurance Reimbursement

DEFINITION. Casualty insurance reimburses the holder for the fair market value of property lost subject to a formula. Typically, there is a coinsurance clause so that the insured bears part of the loss.

HOW IS IT COMPUTED?

$$\frac{\text{Face of policy}}{\text{Coinsurance rate} \times \text{fair market value of property}}$$

$$\times \text{ fair market value of loss} = \text{possible reimbursement}$$

Insurance reimbursement is based on the lowest amount of either the face of the policy, the fair market value of the loss, or possible reimbursement.

Example The following demonstrates this calculation based on three different cases:

Case	Face of policy	Fair market value of property	Fair market value of loss
A	$ 4,000	$10,000	$ 6,000
B	6,000	10,000	10,000
C	10,000	10,000	4,000

The insurance reimbursement calculation (assuming 80 percent coinsurance) follows:

Case A: $\dfrac{\$4,000}{0.8 \times \$10,000} \times \$6,000 = \$3,000$ insurance reimbursement

Case B: $\dfrac{\$6,000}{0.8 \times \$10,000} \times \$10,000 = \$7,500$ insurance reimbursement

Case C: $\dfrac{\$10,000}{0.8 \times \$10,000} \times \$4,000 = \$5,000$ insurance reinbursement

HOW IS IT USED AND BY WHOM?

Insurers and Property Owners. Insurers and owners of destroyed property use the formula to compute the amount of insurance reimbursement due because of a casualty loss.

95 Interest Computation

DEFINITION. Interest is the amount charged by a lender to a borrower for the use of funds. The interest rate is typically expressed on an annual basis.

HOW IS IT COMPUTED?

Interest = principal × interest rate × period of time

Example The interest on a $10,000, 8 percent loan for 9 months is calculated as follows:

$$\$10,000 \times 8\% \times \frac{9}{12} = \$600$$

HOW IS IT USED AND BY WHOM?

Individuals, Corporate Borrowers, Loan Officers, and Financial Managers. Individual and corporate borrowers as well as loan officers need to determine the cost of money in a debt agreement. By knowing the cost of borrowing, a corporate financial manager can better plan a corporate strategy to obtain an adequate return on the company's money and to provide sufficient funds to meet all principal and interest payments.

96 Interest Coverage (Times Interest Earned) Ratio

DEFINITION. The interest coverage ratio reflects the number of times interest expense is covered by earnings or cash flow. The ratio reveals the magnitude of the decline in income that a firm can tolerate and still be able to meet its interest payments.

HOW IS IT COMPUTED?

$$1. \frac{\text{Income before taxes and interest}}{\text{Interest}}$$

$$2. \frac{\text{Cash flow from operations and interest}}{\text{Interest}}$$

Example Interest coverage is analyzed for a company based on the following information from two years of operation:

	19X1	19X2
Income before taxes	$100,000	$105,000
Cash flow from operations	80,000	82,000
Interest expense	20,000	28,000

Relevant ratios are:

	19X1	19X2
Interest coverage based on earnings	6	4.8
Interest coverage based on cash flow from operations	5	3.9

The decline in interest coverage from 19X1 to 19X2 is a negative indicator for the company, since less earnings and cash flow from operations are available to meet interest charges. This drop in the ratio in the second year would be of concern to creditors.

In 19X2, there was $4.80 in income before taxes and interest for every $1.00 spent on interest. Further, $3.90 in cash earnings was the amount available to cover each $1.00 in interest expenses.

HOW IS IT USED AND BY WHOM?

Management and Creditors. A company that is unable to meet its interest charges is in a precarious financial situation. The trend in the coverage ratios indicates how much interest-bearing debt burden the company can handle.

It is better to use cash flow from operations than income before taxes as a basis on which to compare interest expense, since cash flow indicates the amount of actual cash that can be used to meet interest charges.

A potential creditor would like to see high ratios for a company, because high ratios indicate that the company is able to meet its interest obligations with room to spare.

97 Interest-Rate Swaps

DEFINITION. An interest-rate swap is an agreement between two parties either to pay each other's debt payments or to receive payments from each other's securities over time. The parties in an interest-rate swap agree to exchange cash for a specified period of time at designated intervals.

Interest-rate swaps are a method of taking advantage of possible global market inefficiencies.

The *notional amount* is the basic amount on which all interest payments are computed.

The *payment exchange* is the date on which interest and principal payments occur.

HOW IS IT COMPUTED? The interest rate on the money borrowed by Firm A is exchanged with international Firm B in order to receive a mutually advantageous interest rate. The net annual interest benefit is computed by multiplying the loan principal times the difference between the avoided interest cost and the swap interest cost:

Net annual benefit = loan × avoided interest cost − swap interest cost

Example A large American corporation with an excellent credit rating, AAA, is seeking a $75 million variable-rate loan. It can either sell fixed-rate bonds at a rate of 8.5 percent or obtain a variable-rate loan in the Euromarket at the London Interbank Offered Rate (LIBOR), the market rate for Eurodollar deposits, plus 0.5 percent. In France, a large plastics company also needs the equivalent of $75 million for recapitalization. It could sell bonds, but at the rate of 10.5 percent. It could also borrow money in the variable-rate LIBOR market plus 0.5 percent, but it desires fixed-rate financing.

A financial intermediary arranges for an interest-rate swap between the two companies. The U.S. firm sells $75 million in bonds at 8.5 percent, and the French firm agrees to borrow $75 million at LIBOR plus 0.5 percent. The firms then swap interest-rate payments for the next 15 years by paying the 0.5 percent LIBOR premium plus the 8.5 percent rate the American firm pays to its bondholders, for a total of 9 percent. The U.S. firm agrees to pay the French firm a net variable rate of LIBOR. The interest-payment exchange occurs every 6 months in order to make the financing charges in a timely manner. How does this benefit both firms?

Consider the difference for the American firm with and without the interest-rate swap:

Without the swap agreement:
| Pays Euro banks | $75 million × (LIBOR + 0.005) |

With the swap agreement:
Pays French firm	$75 million × (LIBOR)
Receives from French firm	$50 million × 0.09
Pays bondholders	$50 million × 0.085

Net annual benefit = loan × avoided interest cost − swap interest cost

$$= \$75,000,000 \times (0.095 - 0.085)$$

$$= \$75,000,000 \times 0.010 = \$750,000$$

In this case, the American firm makes 0.5 percent from the difference between the bond rate paid and the rate received from the French firm plus the 0.5 percent LIBOR premium charge.

Now consider the difference for the French firm:

Without the swap agreement:
| Pays Euro banks | $75 million × 0.105 |

With the swap agreement:
Pays U.S. firm	$75 million × 0.09
Receives from U.S. firm	$75 million × LIBOR
Pays variable-rate bondholders	$75 million × (LIBOR + 0.005)

Net annual benefit = loan × avoided interest cost − swap interest cost

$$= \$75,000,000 \times [0.105 - (0.090 + 0.005)]$$

$$= \$75,000,000 \times (0.105 - 0.095)$$

$$= \$750,000$$

The French firm receives fixed-rate financing at an effective cost of 9.5 percent compared with the original 10.5 percent. The interest-rate swap provides both the American and French firms an annual interest-cost benefit of $750,000.

HOW IS IT USED AND APPLIED?   The international form of interest-rate swaps takes advantage of international interest-rate differences, normally using the Eurodollar London Interbank Offered Rate and the Eurodollar market. Swaps are a method of permitting a company facing high domestic loan-interest rates to take advantage of another country's lower interest rates while providing tangible benefits to the other company.

There are other forms of the interest-rate swap. Interest-rate swaps may be used on new or existing debt (or other securities). Sometimes firms will swap out an older, fixed-rate portfolio for a newer, variable-rate portfolio using the same notional amount. The underlying assets or liabilities of the company remain unchanged, but the swap replaces unwanted assets at one interest rate with assets at a different interest rate. The basic type of interest rate a firm desires, including long-term unchanging rates, can be structured with an interest-rate swap.

Another use of swaps is when a bank wants to swap the interest return on a portfolio of fixed-rate mortgages for a fixed-rate mortgage return with another bank. This allows the bank to hedge against fluctuations in the interest rates on the variable-rate mortgage portfolio. The two banks agree on a notional amount and the specific interest rates each pays the other on the payment-exchange date.

WHO USES IT AND WHEN?

Banks, Underwriters, and Treasurers/Controllers. Interest-rate swaps assist large firms in restructuring their debt as well as achieving favorable financing for new capital needs.

The risk in an interest-rate swap is that one of the parties could default on the payments. Firms that engage in interest-rate swaps therefore must make certain that the other party is creditworthy and able to fulfill the terms of the contract.

98 Internal Rate of Return (Time-Adjusted Rate of Return)

DEFINITION. The internal rate of return is the return earned on a business proposal—that is, the discount rate equating the present value of cash inflows to the initial investment. The internal rate of return (IRR) assumes that cash inflows are reinvested at the internal rate.

INTERNAL RATE OF RETURN WHERE UNEQUAL CASH INFLOWS EXIST

How Is It Computed? This computation uses the trial-and-error method while working through the present-value tables (see the Appendix). Step-by-step, the IRR is computed as follows:

1. Compute net present value at the cost of capital, denoted as r_1.
2. See if net present value is positive or negative.
3a. If net present value is positive, use a higher rate (r_2) than r_1.
3b. If net present value is negative, use a lower rate (r_2) than r_1.
3c. The exact internal rate of return at which net present value equals zero is sometimes between the two rates.
4. Compute net present value using r_2.
5. Perform interpolation for the exact rate.

Example 1 A project costing $100,000 is expected to generate the following cash inflows:

Year	Cash inflow
1	$50,000
2	30,000
3	20,000
4	40,000

Using trial and error, the interest rate is calculated as follows:

Year	At 16%	Present value	At 18%	Present value
1	0.862	$ 43,100	0.847	$ 42,350
2	0.743	22,290	0.718	21,540
3	0.641	12,820	0.609	12,180
4	0.552	22,080	0.516	20,640
		$ 100,290		$ 96,710
Investment		− 100,000		− 100,000
Net present value		$ 290		− $ 3,290

The internal rate of return on this project is a little more than 16 percent, because at that rate the net present value of the investment is approximately zero.

INTERNAL RATE OF RETURN WHERE EQUAL CASH INFLOWS EXIST

How Is It Computed? The internal rate of return is computed first by determining a factor (which happens to be the same as the *payback period*) and then looking up the rate of return in a table of the present value of an annuity of $1 (see Table 4 in the Appendix).

Example 2 Assume that $100,000 is invested in a proposal that will produce annual cash inflows of $15,000 for the next 20 years. Then

$$\frac{\$100,000}{\$15,000} = 6.6667$$

Consult the present value of an annuity of $1 table (see Table 4 in the Appendix). Looking across 20 years, find the factor closest to 6.6667—i.e., 6.6231, in the 14 percent column.

Example 3 Assume the following investment:

Initial investment	$12,950
Estimated life	10 years
Annual cash inflows	$ 3,000
Cost of capital	12%

The calculation of internal rate of return (IRR), including the interpolation to achieve the exact rate, is:

$$\text{Present value of annuity factor} = \frac{\$12,950}{\$3,000} = 4.317$$

The value 4.317 is somewhere between 18 and 20 percent in the 10-year line of the present value of an annuity of $1 table. Using interpolation,

	Present value of annuity factor	
18%	4.494	4.494
IRR		4.317
20%	4.192	
	0.302	0.177

Therefore,

$$\text{IRR} = 18\% + \frac{0.177}{0.302}(20\% - 18\%)$$

$$= 18\% + 0.586(2\%) = 18\% + 1.17\% = 19.17\%$$

Because the internal rate of return (19.17%) exceeds the cost of capital (12%), this analysis concludes that the project should be accepted.

HOW IS IT USED AND BY WHOM?

Financial Management and Project Analysts. If the IRR is greater than the cost of capital, the project should be accepted.

The advantages of using the IRR method are that it does not consider the time value of money and, therefore, is more exact and realistic than the accounting rate of return method.

The shortcomings of this method are that (1) it is time-consuming to compute, especially when cash inflows are not even (although most business calculators have a program for calculating IRR), and (2) it fails to recognize the varying sizes of investment in competing projects and their respective dollar profitabilities.

99 Intrayear Compounding

DEFINITION. Intrayear compounding refers to interest that is compounded more frequently than once a year—for example, interest compounded quarterly, daily, or even continuously.

HOW IS IT COMPUTED? If interest is compounded m times a year, the general formula for solving the future value is:

$$F_n = P\left(1 + \frac{i}{m}\right)^{n \cdot m} = P \cdot \text{FVIF}(i/m, n \cdot m)$$

where FVIF = the future value interest factor, found in Table 1 in the Appendix
P = principal
i = interest rate
n = number of years
m = number of compounding periods within a year

The formula reflects more frequent compounding $(n \cdot m)$ at a lower interest rate per period (i/m). For example, for semiannual compounding $(m = 2)$, the above formula becomes

$$F_n = P\left(1 + \frac{i}{2}\right)^{n \cdot 2} = P \cdot \text{FVIF}(i/2, n \cdot 2)$$

As m approaches infinity, the term $(1 + i/m)^{n \cdot m}$ approaches $e^{i \cdot n}$ where e is approximately 2.71828. F_n then becomes

$$F_n = P \cdot e^{i \cdot n}$$

The future value increases as m increases. Thus, continuous compounding results in the maximum possible future value at the end of n periods for a given rate of interest.

Example 1 Assume that a deposit of $10,000 is made into an account offering an annual interest rate of 20 percent. Assume that the money is kept on deposit for 5 years, with the interest compounded quarterly. The accumulated amount at the end of the fifth year is calculated as follows:

$$F_n = P\left(1 + \frac{i}{m}\right)^{n \cdot m} = P \cdot \text{FVIF}(i/m, n \cdot m)$$

where P = $10,000
$\quad i/m$ = 20%/4 = 5%
$\quad n \cdot m$ = 5 × 4 = 20

Therefore,

$$F_5 = \$10,000(1 + 0.05)^{20} = \$10,000 \cdot \text{FVIF}(5\%, 20)$$

$$= \$10,000(2.653) = \$26,530$$

Example 2 Assume that P = $1000, i = 8 percent, and n = 2 years. Then, with annual compounding $(m = 1)$:

$$F_2 = \$1000(1 + 0.08)^2 = \$1000 \cdot \text{FVIF}(8\%, 2)$$

$$= \$1000(1.166)$$

$$= \$1166.00$$

With semiannual compounding $(m = 2)$,

$$F_2 = \$1000\left(1 + \frac{0.08}{2}\right)^{2.2}$$

$$= \$1000(1 + 0.04)^4 = \$1000 \cdot \text{FVIF}(4\%, 4)$$

$$= \$1000(1.170)$$

$$= \$1170.00$$

With quarterly compounding $(m = 4)$,

$$F_2 = \$1000\left(1 + \frac{0.08}{4}\right)^{2.4}$$

$$= \$1000(1 + 0.02)^8 = \$1000 \cdot \text{FVIF}(2\%, 8)$$

$$= \$1000(1.172)$$

$$= \$1172.00$$

And with continuous compounding,

$$F_2 = \$1000(2.71828)^{.25} = \$1175.00$$

As this example shows, the more frequently interest is compounded, the greater is the amount accumulated. This is true for any interest rate for any period of time.

HOW IS IT USED AND BY WHOM?

Depositors and Investors. Interest based on intrayear compounding reveals to depositors and investors the amount of the real rate of return on the funds invested.

100 Inventory Ratios

DEFINITION. Inventory ratios reveal the turnover and age of inventory. Types of inventory include raw materials, work-in-process (partially completed goods), and finished goods (completed goods). Knowing whether excess inventory exists is critical, since corporate funds that are being tied up in inventory could be invested elsewhere. Excess inventory is also associated with a high carrying cost for storing goods as well as risk of obsolescence.

HOW IS IT COMPUTED?

1. Inventory turnover $= \dfrac{\text{Cost of goods sold}}{\text{Average inventory}}$

   where

   Average inventory $= \dfrac{\text{Beginning inventory} + \text{ending inventory}}{2}$

   If the year-end inventory figures are not representative because of cyclical effects, a quarterly or monthly average should be used.

2. Number of days inventory held (age of inventory) $= \dfrac{365}{\text{Inventory turnover}}$

3. Sales to inventory:

   $$\dfrac{\text{Sales}}{\text{Inventory}}$$

Example 1 A company reports the following data on its finished goods inventory for a two-year period:

	12/31/19X1	12/31/19X2
Finished goods	$10,000	$15,000
Cost of sales	70,000	80,000

Assume that as of January 1, 19X1, finished goods inventory is $9,000.

The inventory turnover and the number of days inventory is held are calculated below:

	19X1	19X2
Inventory turnover	($70,000/$9,500) = 7.4	($80,000/$12,500) = 6.4
Age of inventory	(365/7.4) = 49 days	(365/6.4) = 57 days

Example 2 A company provides the following data on two years performance:

	19X1	19X2
Sales	$200,000	$290,000
Total inventories	40,000	43,000

The percentage increase in sales is 45%, while the advance in total inventories is only 7.5%. This analysis indicates that the company has good inventory control.

HOW IS IT USED AND BY WHOM?

Management. Good inventory management leads to maximum return at minimum risk. A buildup of inventory may indicate to management an uncertainty regarding future sales. Inventory buildup, which may occur at the plant, at the wholesaler site, or at the retailer site, is indicated when inventory increases at a rate much greater than the rate of increase in sales. A high ratio of sales to inventory means more efficient utilization of inventory in generating revenue.

The turnover rate for each major inventory category and for each department should be ascertained by management. A low turnover rate may point to either (1) overstocking, (2) obsolescence, or (3) deficiencies in the product line or marketing effort. In some instances, however, a low rate of turnover is appropriate, such as cases where higher inventory levels occur in anticipation of rapidly rising prices (i.e., oil). A high turnover rate may indicate that the company does not maintain adequate inventory levels—a situation that could lead to a loss in business if inventory is unavailable. Also, the turnover rate may be unrepresentatively high if a company uses its "natural year-end" to calculate turnover, since the inventory balance at that time of year would be exceptionally low.

A decline in raw materials coupled with an increase in work-in-process and finished goods indicate a future production slowdown.

Creditors. A company with a poor inventory turnover is viewed by creditors as having greater liquidity risk.

101 Investment Income to Investments

DEFINITION. The ratio of investment income to investments reveals the rate of return earned on the investment portfolio.

HOW IS IT COMPUTED?

$$\frac{\text{Investment income (dividend income and/or interest income)}}{\text{Investments at carrying value}}$$

Example A company reports the following data for the calendar years 19X1 and 19X2:

	19X1	19X2
Investments	$30,000	$33,000
Income from investments (dividend and interest income)	4,000	3,200

The ratio of investment income to total investments declined from 13.3% ($4,000/$30,000) in 19X1 to 9.7% ($3,200/$33,000) in 19X2.

HOW IS IT USED AND BY WHOM?

Financial Analysts, Financial Managers, and Stockholders. If the ratio declines, there is greater realization risk in the portfolio. Thus, the financial analyst would view the company being analyzed as having a lower-quality asset. The corporate financial manager would be concerned with a drop in investment income because less of a return would be earned and the value of the quality of the investment portfolio might have deteriorated. For example, if a company cuts back on paying out dividends to its stockholders, the implication is that this might have been precipitated by financial difficulties.

102 Investment Turnover

DEFINITION. Investment turnover is the return earned on capital invested in a business.

HOW IS IT COMPUTED?

$$\text{Investment turnover} = \frac{\text{Sales}}{\text{Stockholders' equity} + \text{long-term liabilities}}$$

Example The following information is provided for a company:

Sales	$3,000,000
Stockholders' equity (net worth)	2,000,000
Long-term liabilities	500,000
Short-term liabilities	400,000

The investment turnover is calculated as:

$$\frac{\$3,000,000}{\$2,500,000} = 1.2$$

The analysis shows that for every $1.00 of capital invested, $1.20 in sales are generated.

HOW IS IT USED AND BY WHOM?

Investors, Long-Term Creditors, and Management. The ratio indicates the revenue generated on the amount invested. A high ratio indicates good use of the funds placed in the business. A low ratio indicates that the company is not putting the funds to good use.

103 Lawsuit Damages to Sales

DEFINITION. The ratio of lawsuit damages to sales examines litigation losses suffered by a business.

HOW IS IT COMPUTED? The ratio is:

$$\frac{\text{Lawsuit losses}}{\text{Total sales}}$$

Example A company reports the following information for two consecutive years:

	19X1	19X2
Lawsuit losses	$ 100,000	$ 400,000
Sales	2,000,000	2,200,000

The relevant ratios are:

	19X1	19X2
Lawsuit losses to sales	0.05	0.18

The significant increase in lawsuit damages relative to sales indicates possible product liability problems, which might put a serious drain on cash flow and profitability. Excessive legal exposure indicates high risk.

Management, Creditors, and Investors. A company that has legal problems may fail or be seriously impaired. The assessment of damages and legal costs may have a devastating effect. In addition, criminal penalties may be involved in addition to civil penalties.

104 Learning Curve

DEFINITION. The learning curve is based on the proposition that labor hours decrease in a definite pattern as labor operations are repeated. More specifically, it is based on the statistical finding that as cumulative production doubles, cumulative average time required per unit will be reduced by some constant percentage, ranging typically from 10 percent to 20 percent.

By convention, learning curves are referred to in terms of the complements of their improvement rates. For example, an 80 percent learning curve denotes a 20 percent decrease in unit time with each doubling of repetitions.

As an illustration, a project is known to have an 80 percent learning curve. It has just taken a laborer 10 hours to produce the first unit. Then each time the cumulative output doubles, the time per unit for that amount should be equal to the previous time multiplied by the learning percentage.

Unit	Unit time (hours)
1	10
2	0.8(10) = 8
4	0.8(8) = 6.4
8	0.8(6.4) = 5.12
16	0.8(5.12) = 4.096

An 80 percent learning curve is shown in Exhibit 104.1.

HOW IS IT COMPUTED? The learning-curve model is:

$$y_n = an^{-b}$$

where y_n = time for the nth unit

a = time for the first unit (in the illustration above, 10 hours)

b = index of the rate of increase in productivity during learning (log learning rate/log 2)

To be able to utilize linear regression, we need to convert this power (or exponential) function form into a linear form by taking a log of both sides, which yields:

$$\log y_n = \log a - b \log n$$

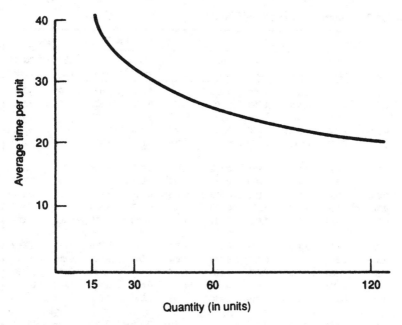

Exhibit 104.1 Learning curve.

The learning rate, which is indicated by b, is estimated using least-squares regression (see No. 105) with the sample data on y and n. Note that

$$b = \frac{\log \text{(learning rate)}}{\log 2}$$

which means that

$$\log \text{(learning rate)} = b \times \log 2$$

The unit time (i.e., the number of labor hours required) for the nth unit can be computed using the estimated model:

$$y_n = an^{-b}$$

Example 1 For an 80 percent curve with $a = 10$ hours, the time for the third unit is:

$$y_3 = 10(3^{-\log 0.8/\log 2}) = 10(3^{(0.3219)}) = 7.02$$

Fortunately, it is not necessary to grind through this model each time a learning calculation is to be made; values (n^b) can be found using Exhibit 104.2. The time for the nth unit can be quickly determined by multiplying the table value by the time required for the first unit.

Example 2 NB Contractors, Inc., is negotiating a contract involving production of 20 jets. The initial jet required 200 labor-days of direct labor. Assuming an 80 percent learning curve, we will determine the expected number of labor-days for (1) the twentieth jet, and (2) all 20 jets, as follows:

Exhibit 104.2 Learning-curve coefficients.

Unit number	70% Unit time	70% Total time	75% Unit time	75% Total time	80% Unit time	80% Total time	85% Unit time	85% Total time	90% Unit time	90% Total time
1	1.000	1.000	1.000	1.000	1.000	1.000	1.000	1.000	1.000	1.000
2	0.700	1.700	0.750	1.750	0.800	1.800	0.850	1.850	0.900	1.900
3	0.568	2.268	0.634	2.384	0.702	2.502	0.773	2.623	0.846	2.746
4	0.490	2.758	0.562	2.946	0.640	3.142	0.723	3.345	0.810	3.556
5	0.437	3.195	0.513	3.459	0.596	3.738	0.686	4.031	0.783	4.339
6	0.398	3.593	0.475	3.934	0.562	4.299	0.657	4.688	0.762	5.101
7	0.367	3.960	0.446	4.380	0.534	4.834	0.634	5.322	0.744	5.845
8	0.343	4.303	0.422	4.802	0.512	5.346	0.614	5.936	0.729	6.574
9	0.323	4.626	0.402	5.204	0.493	5.839	0.597	6.533	0.716	7.290
10	0.306	4.932	0.385	5.589	0.477	6.315	0.583	7.116	0.705	7.994
11	0.291	5.223	0.370	5.958	0.462	6.777	0.570	7.686	0.695	8.689
12	0.278	5.501	0.357	6.315	0.449	7.227	0.558	8.244	0.685	9.374
13	0.267	5.769	0.345	6.660	0.438	7.665	0.548	8.792	0.677	10.052
14	0.257	6.026	0.334	6.994	0.428	8.092	0.539	9.331	0.670	10.721
15	0.248	6.274	0.325	7.319	0.418	8.511	0.530	9.861	0.663	11.384
16	0.240	6.514	0.316	7.635	0.410	8.920	0.522	10.383	0.656	12.040
17	0.233	6.747	0.309	7.944	0.402	9.322	0.515	10.898	0.650	12.690
18	0.226	6.973	0.301	8.245	0.394	9.716	0.508	11.405	0.644	13.334
19	0.220	7.192	0.295	8.540	0.388	10.104	0.501	11.907	0.639	13.974
20	0.214	7.407	0.288	8.828	0.381	10.485	0.495	12.402	0.634	14.608
21	0.209	7.615	0.283	9.111	0.375	10.860	0.490	12.892	0.630	15.237
22	0.204	7.819	0.277	9.388	0.370	11.230	0.484	13.376	0.625	15.862
23	0.199	8.018	0.272	9.660	0.364	11.594	0.479	13.856	0.621	16.483
24	0.195	8.213	0.267	9.928	0.359	11.954	0.475	14.331	0.617	17.100
25	0.191	8.404	0.263	10.191	0.355	12.309	0.470	14.801	0.613	17.713
26	0.187	8.591	0.259	10.449	0.350	12.659	0.466	15.267	0.609	18.323
27	0.183	8.774	0.255	10.704	0.346	13.005	0.462	15.728	0.606	18.929
28	0.180	8.954	0.251	10.955	0.342	13.347	0.458	16.186	0.603	19.531
29	0.177	9.131	0.247	11.202	0.338	13.685	0.454	16.640	0.599	20.131
30	0.174	9.305	0.244	11.446	0.335	14.020	0.450	17.091	0.596	20.727
31	0.171	9.476	0.240	11.686	0.331	14.351	0.447	17.538	0.593	21.320
32	0.168	9.644	0.237	11.924	0.328	14.679	0.444	17.981	0.590	21.911
33	0.165	9.809	0.234	12.158	0.324	15.003	0.441	18.422	0.588	22.498
34	0.163	9.972	0.231	12.389	0.321	15.324	0.437	18.859	0.585	23.084
35	0.160	10.133	0.229	12.618	0.318	15.643	0.434	19.294	0.583	23.666
36	0.158	10.291	0.226	12.844	0.315	15.958	0.432	19.725	0.580	24.246
37	0.156	10.447	0.223	13.067	0.313	16.271	0.429	20.154	0.578	24.824
38	0.154	10.601	0.221	13.288	0.310	16.581	0.426	20.580	0.575	25.399
39	0.152	10.753	0.219	13.507	0.307	16.888	0.424	21.004	0.573	25.972
40	0.150	10.902	0.216	13.723	0.305	17.193	0.421	21.425	0.571	26.543

Using Exhibit 104.2 with $n = 20$ and an 80 percent learning rate, we find:

$$\text{Unit} = 0.381 \qquad \text{Total} = 10,485$$

Therefore,

1. Expected time for the twentieth jet = 200(0.381) = 76.2 labor-days.
2. Expected total time for all 20 jets = 200(10.485) = 2097 labor-days.

HOW IS IT USED AND APPLIED? Learning-curve theory has found useful applications in many areas, including:

1. Budgeting, purchasing, and inventory planning
2. Scheduling labor requirements
3. Setting incentive wage rates
4. Pricing new products
5. Negotiated purchasing

Example 3 illustrates the use of the learning-curve theory for the pricing of a contract.

Example 3 Big Mac Electronics Products, Inc., finds that new product production is affected by an 80 percent learning effect. The company has just produced 50 units of output at 100 hours per unit. Costs were as follows:

Materials: 50 units @ $20	$1000
Labor and labor-related costs:	
Direct labor: 100 hours @ $8	800
Variable overhead: 100 hours @ $2	200
	$2000

The company has just received a contract calling for another 50 units of production. It wants to add a 50 percent markup to the cost of materials and labor and labor-related costs. To determine the price for this job, the first step is to build the learning-curve table.

Quantity	Total time (hours)	Average time (per unit)
50	100	2 hours
100	160	1.6 (0.8 × 2 hours)

Thus, the new 50-unit job will require 60 hours. The contract price is:

Materials: 50 units @ $20	$1000
Labor and labor-related costs:	
Direct labor: 60 hours @ $8	480
Variable overhead: 60 hours @ $2	120
	$1600
50 percent markup	800
Contract price	$2400

WHO USES IT AND WHEN?

Cost Analysts, Production Managers, and Contract Directors. Businesspeople use learning-curve theory in setting wage rates and contract prices, and also in determining labor requirements for a job or project.

Budget Director. Budget directors must take into account the learning rate in budgeting direct and indirect labor costs.

105 Least-Squares Regression

DEFINITION. The least-squares method is widely used in regression analysis to estimate the parameter values in a regression equation. Regression analysis is a statistical procedure for estimating mathematically the average relationship between the dependent variable and the independent variable(s). *Simple regression* involves only one independent variable, such as price *or* advertising in a demand function. *Multiple regression* involves two or more variables, such as *both* price and advertising in the prediction of sales.

A simple linear regression will be assumed to illustrate the least-squares method, which means that the relationship $Y = a + bX$ is assumed.

HOW IS IT COMPUTED? The regression method includes all the observed data and attempts to find a line of best fit. To find this line, a technique called the least-squares method is used.

To explain the least-squares method, we define the error as the difference between the observed value and the estimated one and denote it by u (see Exhibit 105.1). In equation form,

$$u = Y - Y'$$

where Y = observed value of the dependent variable
    Y' = estimated value based on $Y' = a + bX$

The least-squares criterion requires that the line of best fit be such that the sum of the squares of the errors (or the vertical distance in Exhibit 105.1 from the observed data points to the line) is a minimum, i.e.,

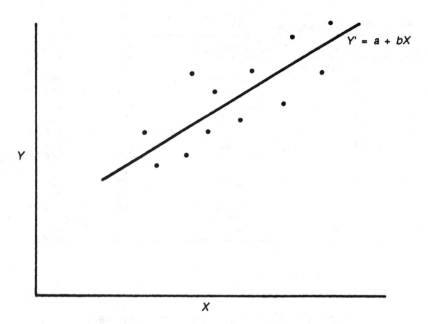

Exhibit 105.1 Y and Y'.

$$\text{minimum:} \quad \sum u^2 = \sum (Y - Y')^2$$

Using differential calculus, the following equations, called *normal equations*, are obtained:

$$\sum Y = na + b\sum X$$

$$\sum XY = a\sum X + b\sum X^2$$

Solving the equations for b and a yields

$$b = \frac{n\sum XY - (\sum X)(\sum Y)}{n\sum X^2 - (\sum X)^2}$$

$$a = \overline{Y} - b\overline{X}$$

where $\overline{Y} = \Sigma Y/n$ and $\overline{X} = \Sigma X/n$.

Example To illustrate the computations of b and a, refer to the data in Exhibit 105.2. All the sums required are computed and shown below.
From Exhibit 105.2:

$$\sum X = 174 \quad \sum Y = 225 \quad \sum XY = 3414 \quad \sum X^2 = 2792$$

$$\overline{X} = \frac{\sum X}{n} = \frac{174}{12} = 14.5 \quad \overline{Y} = \frac{\sum Y}{n} = \frac{225}{12} = 18.75$$

Substituting these values into the equation for b:

Exhibit 105.2 Least-squares calculations.

Direct labor hours, X	Factory overhead, Y	XY	X^2
9 hours	$ 15	135	81
19	20	380	361
11	14	154	121
14	16	224	196
23	25	575	529
12	20	240	144
12	20	240	144
22	23	506	484
7	14	98	49
13	22	286	169
15	18	270	225
17	18	306	289
174 hours	$225	3414	2792

$$b = \frac{n\sum XY - (\sum X)(\sum Y)}{n\sum X^2 - (\sum X)^2} = \frac{(12)(3414) - (174)(225)}{(12)(2792) - (174)^2} = \frac{1818}{3228} = 0.5632$$

Then

$$a = \overline{Y} - b\overline{X} = 18.75 - (0.5632)(14.5) = 18.75 - 8.1664 = 10.5836$$

Thus,

$$Y' = 10.5836 + 0.5632X$$

CAN A COMPUTER HELP? Spreadsheet programs such as Lotus 1-2-3 include regression routines that can be used without difficulty. As a matter of fact, the parameter values a and b are not computed manually. Exhibit 105.3 shows, step by step, how to use the Lotus regression command. Other statistics that appear are discussed under No. 160, Regression Statistics.

HOW IS IT USED AND APPLIED? Before attempting a least-squares regression approach, it is extremely important to plot the observed data on a diagram called a scattergraph (see Exhibit 105.4), to make sure that a linear (straight-line) relationship exists between Y and X in the past sample. If for any reason a nonlinear relationship is detected in the sample, the assumed linear relationship—$Y = a + bX$—will not give a good fit.

WHO USES IT AND WHEN?

Forecasters and Policymakers. Simple regression and multiple regression are powerful statistical techniques that are most widely used by businesspeople and economists. In order to obtain a good fit and to achieve

Exhibit 105.3 Spreadsheet regression calculation.

```
Step 1 Enter the data on Y and X as shown below

                    (Y) Factory        (X) Direct Labor
                    Overhead (00)          Hr. (00)
                          9                  15
                         19                  20
                         11                  14
                         14                  16
                         23                  25
                         12                  20
                         12                  20
                         22                  23
                          7                  14
                         13                  22
                         15                  18
                         17                  18

Step 2 Press "/Data Regression"
Step 3 Define Y and X range
Step 4 Define output range
Step 5 Hit Go

This will produce the following regression output:

                     Regression Output
        Constant                 10.58364  ←  a = 10.58364
        Std Err of Y Est          2.343622
        R Squared                 0.608373
        No. of Observations           12
        Degrees of Freedom            10
        X Coefficient(s) 0.563197           ←  b = 0.563197
        Std Err of Coef. 0.142893

The result shows:
        Y' = 10.58364 + 0.563197 X
```

a high degree of accuracy, businesspeople should be familiar with statistics relating to regression, such as r squared (r^2) and t value.

See also No. 122, Multiple Regression; No. 123, Multiple-Regression Tests; No. 160, Regression Statistics; and No. 182, Simple Regression.

106 Leverage Ratios and Financial Leverage

DEFINITION. Leverage ratios reveal the extent of debt within a company's capital structure and the company's ability to pay the debt. Financial leverage results from the company's use of debt financing, financial leases, and preferred stock.

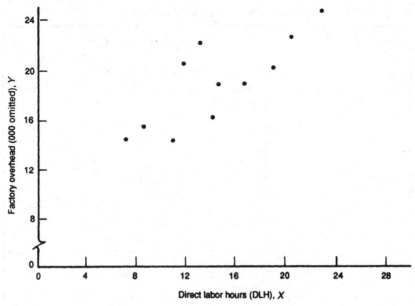

Exhibit 105.4 Scattergraph.

HOW IS IT COMPUTED? Ten leverage ratios are commonly used in analyzing a company's financial position:

1. Debt/equity ratio $= \dfrac{\text{Total liabilities}}{\text{Total stockholders' equity}}$

   The usefulness of the debt/equity ratio is enhanced if securities are valued at their year-end market value rather than book value. If year-end values are not representative, average market prices can be used.

2. $\dfrac{\text{Long-term debt}}{\text{Stockholders' equity}}$

3. Debt ratio $= \dfrac{\text{Total liabilities}}{\text{Total assets}}$

4. Capital structure ratio $= \dfrac{\text{Average long-term debt}}{\text{Long-term debt plus owners' equity}}$

5. $\dfrac{\text{Owners' equity}}{\text{Borrowed capital}}$

   Owners' equity includes the owners' investment (primarily capital stock) plus retained earnings.

6. $\dfrac{\text{Interest}}{\text{Borrowed capital}}$

$$7. \quad \frac{\text{Average working capital}}{\text{Average funded debt}}$$

$$8. \quad \frac{\text{Average current liabilities}}{\text{Owners' equity}}$$

$$9. \quad \text{Financial leverage index} = \frac{\text{Return on common equity}}{\text{Return on total assets}}$$

$$10. \quad \text{Financial leverage ratio} = \frac{\text{Total assets}}{\text{Common stockholders' equity}}$$

Example Leverage-ratio information is derived from a company's balance sheet. A partial balance sheet for a company follows:

Long-term liabilities	$500,000
Total liabilities	700,000
Stockholders' equity	300,000
Cash flow provided from operations	100,000

The company's ratios are:

Long-term debt to stockholders' equity	1.67
Cash flow to long-term liabilities	0.2
Total liabilities to stockholders' equity	2.33

These are compared to average norms taken from competitors:

Long-term debt to stockholders' equity	0.8
Cash flow to long-term liabilities	0.3
Total liabilities to stockholders' equity	1.5

After comparing the company's ratios with the industry norms, it is clear that the firm's solvency is worse than its competitors. The company has a much greater extent of total debt and long-term liabilities in its capital structure and has lower cash flow to cover its debt.

HOW IS IT USED AND BY WHOM?

Creditors and Management. In analyzing company performance, a high ratio of total liabilities to total stockholders' equity (financial leverage) implies a great deal of risk because it may be difficult for the company to satisfy its interest and principal payments and also obtain reasonable levels of further financing. A high debt/equity ratio is an especially acute problem for companies with cash problems, particularly during times when adverse business conditions exist. Carrying excessive amounts of debt will result in less financial flexibility for the company since it is more difficult to obtain funds in a tight money market. Also, having to pay high fixed interest charges can also cause earnings instability.

A favorable leverage situation occurs when the return on borrowed funds exceeds the interest cost, provided that the firm is not in debt over its head. A desirable debt/equity ratio depends on many variables, including the rates of other companies in the industry, the access to further debt financing, and the stability of earnings.

A ratio in excess of 1 for long-term debt to stockholders' equity indicates a higher long-term debt participation as compared to equity capital.

The debt ratio (total liabilities to total assets) shows the percentage of total funds obtained from creditors. The ratio is an indicator of how much debt may be comfortably taken on, given the company's situation. Creditors would rather see a low debt ratio because there is then a greater cushion for creditor losses if the firm goes bankrupt.

Potential creditors are reluctant to give financing to a company with a high debt position; however, the size of debt taken on may be satisfactory, depending on the nature of a particular business. For example, a utility can afford a higher debt ratio than a manufacturer because its earnings can be controlled by rate adjustments.

If analysis shows that interest on borrowed capital has increased, it is important to search out the reason. Is it due to lenders demanding a higher interest rate because of increased corporate risk? Is it because market interest rates have risen sharply?

The ratio of current liabilities to owners' equity is used to measure whether short-term creditors are furnishing excessive capital resources to support operations relative to materials, supplies, and services. The reasonableness of the ratio depends on such factors as the turnover rate of inventory and receivables, liquidity status, and so forth.

Where a lot of debt exists, a sharp drop in sales or in receivables turnover may mean that the business will be unable to meet its debt obligations. Substantial interest on borrowed funds may even exceed earnings, resulting in a loss; however, even though debt might be high, the company may still safely meet its obligations—for example, there may be a quick turnover in current assets to make timely debt payments, some current liabilities may be stretched or due dates extended, long-term debt may be restructured for later payment, or a substantial boost in cash earnings may occur.

If borrowed capital exceeds invested capital, proprietary risk is shared with the creditors, and the creditors have risk regarding their payment. In general, invested capital should exceed borrowed capital. Analyzing the trend in the ratio of owners' capital to borrowed capital reveals a company's financial policy and objectives. This provides insight into management's financing preferences, such as whether management is inclined toward taking excess risk.

The effect of leverage on operating results is positive when the return on equity capital exceeds the return on total assets. Leverage is positive when the return on assets is higher than the cost of debt.

The financial leverage ratio measures the relationship between total assets and the common equity capital that finances them. In a company that uses leverage profitably, a higher financial leverage ratio will enhance the return on equity; at the same time, the risk inherent in a change in profitability is also greater.

If analysis of a company shows a recurring trend of equity at book value that exceeds equity at market value, this may signal financial weakness in the company and restricted financial capability. This adversely affects the ability to sell equity capital or to raise new debt capital. An excess of market value of equity securities over book value, on the other hand, is a strong protecting factor for bondholders and other creditors. It points to an ability to raise equity capital, reflecting financial strength.

The ratio of working capital to funded debt is used to determine whether a company could liquidate its long-term debt obligations from working capital. Even if a company shows sufficient profitability, it may not have adequate liquid funds to pay long-term debt obligations.

107 Life Insurance Adequacy

DEFINITION. The multiple-of-income approach helps one to determine the amount of life insurance needed.

HOW IS IT COMPUTED?

Multiplier × gross annual income

The multiplier depends on personal desires and family conditions. For example, if there are children and a nonworking spouse, the multiplier should be higher. The multiplier usually ranges from 5 to 10 times one's annual gross income.

Example Your annual gross income is $65,000 and you want to take out the most life insurance within the recommended range. The policy should be for $650,000.

HOW IS IT USED AND BY WHOM?

Individuals. A person may use the multiple-of-income method to select the amount of life insurance to carry.

Life Insurance Agents. The insurance broker may use this method to recommend a suitable amount of insurance for a client.

108 Linear Programming

DEFINITION. Linear programming (LP) is a mathematical technique designed to determine an optimal decision (or an optimal plan) from among a large number of possibilities. The optimal decision is the one that meets the specified objective of the company, subject to various restrictions or constraints. It concerns itself with the problem of allocating scarce resources among competing activities in an optimal manner. The optimal decision yields the highest return, contribution margin, or revenue, or the lowest cost or risk. A linear programming model consists of two important ingredients:

1. *Objective function:* The company must define the specific objective to be achieved.
2. *Constraints:* Constraints are in the form of restrictions on availabil-

ity of resources or meeting minimum requirements.

As the name linear programming indicates, both the objective function and constraints must be in linear form.

HOW IS IT FORMULATED AND COMPUTED?

To formulate an LP problem, certain steps are followed:

1. Define the decision variables for which the computation will solve.

2. Express the objective function and constraints in terms of these decision variables. All the expressions must be in linear form.

There are basically two ways to solve an LP problem:

1. *The graphical method:* This method is limited to two (or three in a few cases) decision variables.

2. *The simplex method:* Most computer software utilizes this method.

Example This technique will be used first in this example to find the optimal investment mix.

The JKS Growth and Income Fund (JKS) is an open-end mutual fund with an objective of maximum total return from capital growth accompanied by a relatively high and stable level of investment income. The fund has a policy of remaining invested largely in a diversified portfolio of corporate stocks and bonds. The fund's investment policy states that stock investments are to be emphasized, representing at least three times the amount of bond holdings. To reduce downside risk, at least 20 percent of the fund's total portfolio must be invested in bonds. Like many funds, JKS cannot use leverage (or borrowing) to enhance investor return. As a result, stock plus bond investments cannot total more than 100 percent of the portfolio. Finally, the current expected return on investment is 12 percent for stocks (S) and 9 percent for bonds (B). JKS wants to determine the optimal portfolio percentage holdings of stocks (S) and bonds (B).

In this example, the goal is to maximize the mutual fund investors' expected return, R, subject to the various constraints on the fund's investment policies. The relevant LP problem is:

$$\text{Maximize:} \quad R = 0.12S + 0.09B$$
$$\text{Subject to:} \quad S - 3B \geq 0 \quad \text{or} \quad S \geq 3B$$
$$B \geq 0.2$$
$$S + B \leq 1$$
$$S, B \geq 0$$

where R = the investor's expected return
S = the portfolio share in company stocks
B = the portfolio share in bonds

Using a popular LP software called LINDO (Linear Discrete Optimization), as shown in Exhibit 108.1, the following solution is obtained: $S = 0.8 = 80$ percent, $B = 0.2 = 20$ percent, and $R = 0.114 = 11.4$ percent.

HOW IS IT USED AND APPLIED?

LP is used when a firm wishes to find an optimal product mix, which is the combination that maximizes its total contribution margin within the allowed budget and production capacity.

Exhibit 108.1 LINDO output.

```
MAX .12 S + .09 B
SUBJECT TO
        2)  S - 3 B > = 0
        3)  B > = .2
        4)  S + B < = 1
END

:g0
LP OPTIMUM FOUND AT STEP 4

OBJECTIVE FUNCTION VALUE

1)    .114000000  ←  R = 11.4%
```

VARIABLE	VALUE	REDUCED COST	
S	.800000	.000000 ⎫	$S = 0.8 = 80\%$
B	.200000	.000000 ⎭	$B = 0.2 = 20\%$

ROW	SLACK OR SURPLUS	DUAL PRICES
2)	.200000	.000000
3)	.000000	-.030000
4)	.000000	.120000

```
NO. ITERATIONS =  4

DO RANGE (SENSITIVITY) ANALYSIS?
? yes

RANGES IN WHICH THE BASIS IS UNCHANGED:
```

OBJ COEFFICIENT RANGES

VARIABLE	CURRENT COEF	ALLOWABLE INCREASE	ALLOWABLE DECREASE
S	.120000	INFINITY	.030000
B	.090000	.030000	INFINITY

RIGHTHAND SIDE RANGES

ROW	CURRENT RHS	ALLOWABLE INCREASE	ALLOWABLE DECREASE
2	.000000	.200000	INFINITY
3	.200000	.050000	.200000
4	1.000000	INFINITY	.200000

The firm may also use LP to determine a least-cost combination of input materials while meeting production requirements, employing production capacities, and using available employees.

Other applications of LP include:

1. Developing an optimal budget

2. Determining an optimal investment portfolio

3. Scheduling jobs to machines

4. Determining a least-cost shipping pattern

5. Scheduling flights

6. Gasoline blending

WHO USES IT AND WHEN?

Managers. Whenever managers want to find the optimal solution to a resource-constrained problem, the LP formulation fits right in. Although LP is a complex computation, the computation problem no longer exists, since many reasonably priced, user-friendly LP software packages are available.

109 Liquid Assets to Take-Home Pay

DEFINITION. The ratio of liquid assets to take-home pay tells an individual whether your current earnings are sufficient to pay current bills. The rule of thumb is that liquid assets should be equal to 6 months of take-home pay.

HOW IS IT COMPUTED?

$$\frac{\text{Liquid assets}}{\text{Take-home pay}}$$

Example Your liquid assets are $50,000 and your monthly take-home pay is $20,000. Therefore, you can cover the loss of monthly take-home pay for 2.5 months. You need a larger liquid balance in assets.

HOW IS IT USED AND BY WHOM?

Individuals. The ratio is used in personal financial planning. A higher ratio enables a person to better protect himself so that he is able to pay his bills even if for some reason monthly take-home pay stops. For example, in a recessionary period such as in the early 1990s, many individuals were laid off from their jobs. A lower multiple is justified if the individual has good loss-of-income protection (for example, insurance policy, union contract).

Lenders. The ratio gives a lender a basis on which to decide whether to extend credit to a loan applicant.

110 Liquidity Index

DEFINITION. The liquidity index is the number of days that current assets are removed from cash.

HOW IS IT COMPUTED?

Current asset amount × days removed from cash = total

$$\text{Index} = \frac{\text{total}}{\text{amount}} = \text{number of days}$$

Example Following is a calculation of a liquidity index from information provided by a company:

Current asset	Amount	×	Days removed from cash	=	Total
Cash	$ 20,000	×	0	=	0
Accounts receivable	50,000	×	30	=	$1,500,000
Inventory	80,000	×	50	=	4,000,000
Total	$150,000				$5,500,000

$$\text{Index} = \frac{\$5,500,000}{\$150,000} = 36.7 \text{ days}$$

HOW IS IT USED AND BY WHOM?

Financial Analysts, Creditors, Financial Managers, and Lenders. The liquidity index is used by financial analysts, creditors, and financial management to determine a company's liquidity. The index reveals how many days it would take to convert the current assets to cash. A company with poor liquidity is viewed negatively by lenders, since it may not be able to meet its debt payments when due. Financial managers would be concerned with deficient liquidity, since the company may fail to operate because of inadequate funds. When liquidity problems exist, management must take corrective steps.

111 Loan-Loss Coverage Ratio

DEFINITION. The loan-loss coverage ratio helps to determine the quality of assets and a bank's provision for nonperforming loans. It is computed by dividing pretax income (before security transactions) plus the bank's provision for loan losses by net charge-offs. Lower bank earnings and higher charge-offs during the late 1980s and early 1990s caused substantial ratio declines, resulting in many bank failures and huge losses due to problem loans.

HOW IS IT COMPUTED?

$$\text{Loan-loss coverage ratio} = \frac{[\text{pretax income (before security transactions)} + \text{provision for loan losses}]}{\text{net charge-offs}}$$

Example The calculation of the loan-loss coverage ratio for the XYZ Bank & Trust follows:

	19X3	19X4
Pretax income (before security transactions) (A)	$1,289,453	$ 898,647
Provision for loan losses (B)	742,947	1,347,970
Net charge-offs (C)	764,348	1,457,876
Loan-Loss coverage ratio [(A + B)/C]	2.66	1.54

XYZ Bank & Trust experienced a fall in the loan-loss coverage ratio from 2.66 in 19X3 to 1.54 in 19X4 because of falling pretax income and an increase in the provision for loan losses and net charge-offs. The bank's performance deteriorated during this period.

HOW IT IT USED AND BY WHOM?

Bank Regulators, Bank Management, and Financial Analysts. The loan-loss coverage ratio helps to determine the quality of a bank's assets and the degree of its protection from losses due to problem loans.

Any increase in charge-offs is particularly important, as an increase indicates the total amount of nonperforming loans, forcing a bank to make a greater provision for loan losses.

112 Loans to Deposits

DEFINITION. The loans-to-deposits ratio provides a basic measure of the loan coverage that banks have in terms of the loan deposit base. The greater the ratio of loans to deposits, the greater is the liquidity risk of the bank.

HOW IS IT COMPUTED? The formula for the loans-to-deposits ratio is:

$$\text{Loans-to-deposits ratio} = \frac{\text{average net loans}}{\text{average deposits}}$$

Example The ratio is calculated based on two years of a bank's activity:

	19X4	19X5
Average net loans	$ 8,792	$ 7,229
Average deposits	$14,238	$13,228
Loans to deposits	61.75%	54.65%

The trend reveals that the loan portfolio of this bank declined more sharply than its average deposit base.

HOW IS IT USED AND APPLIED?

Bank Regulators, Bank Analysts, Depositors, and Stockholders. Loans to deposits is a type of asset-to-liability ratio. This debt-coverage ratio is used as an indicator of a bank's liquidity. Stockholders and depositors are interested in the ratio of loans to deposits as an indication of a bank's financial stability.

Bank loans are made from deposits. Although loans typically have fixed periods, deposits are volatile and easily withdrawn; thus, it is important to know the percentage to which loans comprise deposits in order to understand the implications of their coverage.

113 Maintenance and Repair Index

DEFINITION. The maintenance and repair index shows how much maintenance and repair time was required for each direct hour of labor. The ratio is best applied to compare departments or to compare groups of similar machinery.

HOW IS IT COMPUTED? The maintenance and repair index is found as:

$$\frac{\text{Maintenance and repair hours}}{\text{Total direct labor hours}}$$

Example The following company information provides a basis for computing this index:

	19X1	19X2
Maintenance and repair hours	200	600
Total direct labor hours	10,000	9,400
Maintenance and repair hours to total direct labor	2%	6%

The analysis shows that the increase in the ratio from 19X1 to 19X2 is unfavorable. It indicates that more maintenance and repairs are being required, which suggests that the company is sustaining more problems with its machinery.

HOW IS IT USED AND BY WHOM?

Production Managers. The extent of repairs necessary relative to direct labor input may reflect the quality of manufacturing equipment. An increasing trend in the percentage may indicate that the company has had to cope with an increasing number of machinery breakdowns.

114 Margin Requirement

DEFINITION. The purchase of securities on credit for which a minimum down payment must be made is called a margin requirement. Interest is charged by the broker on the unpaid balance.

HOW IS IT COMPUTED?

1. Amount paid for stock = 50 percent of purchase price

2. Amount paid for corporate bonds = 70 percent of purchase price

3. Amount paid for U.S. government securities = 90 percent of purchase price

An investor must put up more cash for equity securities than for bonds because of the greater risk in equity investments. Securities bought on margin will be held by the broker in "street name"—that is, in the name of the brokerage firm.

Example You buy on margin 100 shares of ABC Company at a market price of $60 per share. The brokerage commission is $150. Your minimum down payment is:

$$50\% \times \$6150 = \$3075$$

If the interest rate is 12 percent, the annual interest charge will be:

$$\$3075 \times 12\% = \$369$$

HOW IS IT USED AND BY WHOM?

Investors and Bankers. A brokerage firm typically charges a borrowing investor 2 percent more than is charged by the bank. If the value of the portfolio declines enough to jeopardize the brokerage loan, a "margin call" will be made to put up additional money on securities, or sell some stock. A margin account requires a minimum of $2000 in cash (or equity in securities) on deposit.

Buying on margin gives the investor the opportunity to improve his or her return through leverage (buying on credit). The investor makes only partial payment for a stock that has appreciated in value. However, the investor's loss can also be magnified if the value of the security portfolio declines.

There is also a *maintenance margin requirement,* representing the minimum percentage equity that an investor must maintain in a stock or bond purchased using borrowed funds. The New York Stock Exchange and the National Association of Securities Dealers both require a maintenance margin of 25 percent of the market value of securities. Many brokerage firms require more, typically 30 percent.

115 Marginal Cost and Marginal Revenue

DEFINITION. Marginal cost (MC) is the change in total cost associated with a unit change in quantity. Marginal revenue (MR) is the rate of change in total revenue with respect to quantity sold. The calculation of MR indicates to a firm how total sales will change if there is a change in the quantity sold of a firm's product. In economics, marginal revenue must equal marginal cost in order for profit to be maximized, or MR = MC.

In a discrete range of activity—the activity in which firms operate in actual business—MR is equivalent to incremental (or differential) revenue

(IR). MC is also viewed as being equivalent to incremental (or differential) cost (IC), which is the increment in cost between the two alternatives or two discrete volumes of output. Therefore, in reality, decisions affecting this type of activity should be made only when IR > IC.

HOW IS IT COMPUTED?   The marginal cost of the five-hundredth unit of output can be calculated by finding the difference between total cost at 499 units of output and total cost at 500 units of output. Thus, MC is the additional cost of one more unit of output, calculated as:

$$MC = \frac{\text{change in total cost}}{\text{change in quantity}}$$

MC is also the change in total variable cost associated with a unit change in output, because total cost changes even though total fixed cost remains unchanged. MC may also be considered the rate of change in total cost as the quantity (Q) of output changes; it is simply the first derivative of the total cost (TC) function. Thus,

$$MC = \frac{d\text{TC}}{dQ}$$

Similarly, the marginal revenue of the five-hundredth unit of output can be calculated by finding the difference between total revenue at 499 units of output and total revenue at 500 units of output. MR is thus the additional revenue derived from one more unit of output. It is calculated as:

$$MR = \frac{\text{change in total revenue}}{\text{change in quantity}}$$

MR may also be thought of as the rate of change in total revenue as the quantity (Q) of output changes and is simply the first derivative of the total revenue (TR) function. Thus,

$$MR = \frac{d\text{TR}}{dQ}$$

For profit to be maximized, MR must equal MC.

Example   Consider the following TR and TC functions:

$$TR = \$1,000Q - \$5Q^2 \quad \text{and} \quad TC = \$20,000 + \$200Q$$

MR and MC are:

$$MR = \frac{d\text{TR}}{dQ} = \$1,000 - \$10Q \quad \text{and} \quad MC = \frac{d\text{TC}}{dQ} = \$200$$

At the profit-maximizing output level, MR = MC; thus

$$MR = \$1,000 - \$10Q = \$200 = MC$$

Solving for Q gives

$$Q = 980 \text{ units}$$

which is the profit-maximizing quantity of output.

HOW IS IT USED AND APPLIED? Marginal analysis utilizing the concepts of marginal revenue and marginal cost is a key principle in decision making that can be applied to financial and investment decisions. The analysis suggests that financial and investment decisions should be made and actions taken only when marginal revenues equals marginal costs. If this condition exists, a given decision should maximize the firm's profits.

WHO USES IT AND WHEN?

Managers. Managers at any level who have to make functional decisions—such as marketing, operational, production, purchasing, financing, investment, and personnel decisions—must always weigh the marginal cost to be incurred against the marginal revenue to be derived from that decision. In practice, since decision makers typically work with incremental data (rather than marginal data), they have to weigh the incremental cost associated with the decision against the incremental revenue to be gained.

116 Market-Index Model

DEFINITION. The number of data inputs for even a moderate-size portfolio using an investment portfolio selection model can be quite staggering. William Sharpe developed a model that drastically reduced the data requirements necessary to perform portfolio analysis. Sharpe's model is called the *market-index* (or *single-index*) *model.*

HOW IS IT COMPUTED? Sharpe suggests that all securities are linearly related to a market index. This relationship can be expressed through the following equation:

$$r_j = a + b\, r_m + u_j$$

where r_j = return on security j
$\quad r_m$ = return on the market portfolio (such as Standard & Poors 500)
$\quad a$ = alpha
$\quad b$ = beta

Beta is the index of systematic risk that represents the individual security's relationship with the market, the random error u_j represents the unsystematic or non-market-related return of an individual asset.

Rather than computing the covariances of all combinations of securities in a portfolio, the Sharpe model assumes that all securities are related to one another through their relationship with a market index such as the Standard & Poor's 500.

Example Spreadsheet programs such as Lotus 1-2-3 can help in computing beta, since the program contains the regression analysis routine. Exhibit 116.1 is a sample output of such a program.

HOW IS IT USED AND APPLIED? Beta measures a security's volatility relative to an average security. Stated another way, it is a measure of a

Exhibit 116.1 Beta output: Spreadsheet result for the model $r_j = a + br_m$.

Year	rj (%)	rm (%)
19x1	-5	10
19x2	4	8
19x3	7	12
19x4	10	20
19x5	12	15

Regression Output:

Constant	$-6.51363 \leftarrow a = -6.51363$
Std Err of Y Est	5.796289
R Squared	0.431202
No. of Observations	5
Degrees of Freedom	3
X Coefficient(s)	$0.931818 \leftarrow b = 0.931818$
Std Err of Coef.	0.617886

The equation is: $r_j = -6.51 + .93\ r_m$
Therefore, the beta is 0.93

security's return over time to that of the overall market. (See also No. 19, Beta.)

WHO USES IT AND WHEN?

Financial Managers. Financial managers use beta to determine the approximate cost of equity capital. (See also No. 41, Cost of Capital.)

Investors and Securities Analysts. Beta for a particular stock is useful in predicting how much the security will go up or down, provided that securities analysts and investors feel that they know which way the market will go. Beta helps to figure out the risk and the expected return. Note that beta values are easily available through periodicals or publications such as *Value Line Investment Survey*.

117 Materiality of Options

DEFINITION. Corporations often provide stock option plans by which employees and management can purchase corporate stock at substantially below the market price at some future time. Stock options are issued by corporations as a motivational incentive to encourage productivity, profits, and loyalty.

Although stock options do not require the corporation to make a cash outlay, their extensive use does represent a possible dilution of value for present stockholders. The materiality of options represents the extent to which stock options dilute the equity value of the shares of common stock already issued and outstanding. Generally speaking, if the percentage of stock options outstanding exceeds 5 percent of the common stock outstanding, the stock options outstanding are considered to be material and important to current stockholders.

In a noncompensatory plan, there is an effort to raise capital and to increase ownership of the stock by employees and management by selling the stock at a reasonable but not excessive discount.

A compensatory stock option plan is characterized as offering an opportunity to buy the corporation's stock at a substantial discount—a practice considered by many to be a form of direct compensation.

HOW IS IT COMPUTED?

$$\text{Materiality of options} = \frac{\text{stock options outstanding}}{\text{shares of common stock outstanding}}$$

Example The materiality of options for a specific company is calculated below based on two years of information:

	19X2	19X3
Options outstanding, December 31	249,342	352,512
Number of common shares outstanding, December 31	12,245,789	14,345,642
Materiality of options	2.04%	2.45%

Since the materiality of options is shown to be less than 5 percent in both years, the options are not considered to be material to the profit-per-share analysis of the company.

HOW IS IT USED AND APPLIED? The objective of a stock option plan for the management and employees of a company is to provide a motivational incentive. Note that the additional cash flow from stock options exercised does provide small improvements in liquidity and reduction in debt.

WHO USES IT AND WHEN?

Management and Financial Analysts. The materiality of options determines the effect of options on the stock outstanding. For example, management would use materiality of options when considering whether or not to offer new or additional stock options to corporate officers and employees.

Stockholders. If analysis shows the materiality of options to be excessive, stockholders would recognize that the issuance of materially more shares at a low price would significantly dilute the interest of existing stockholders in the company.

118 Median

DEFINITION. The median is the middle value of a list of numbers when the numbers in the data set are arranged by order of importance—that is, it is the midpoint in a range of values.

HOW IS IT COMPUTED? The formula for the position occupied by the median item is:

$$\frac{n + 1}{2}$$

where n is the number of items.

Example An employer has nine employees, all of whom earn different hourly wages. The employer wants to determine the median wage of his employees, whose wages are listed below:

Unsorted Hourly Wages of Employees

Employee	Hourly wage rate
1	$3.75
2	5.25
3	4.25
4	6.25
5	6.50
6	4.00
7	4.50
8	5.75
9	8.00

The procedural steps to calculate the median follow:

1. Sort the data:

Sorted Hourly Wage for Employees

Employee	Hourly wage rate
1	3.75
6	4.00
3	4.25
7	4.50
2	5.25
8	5.75
4	6.25
5	6.50
9	8.00

2. Locate the median item position:

$$\text{Median item position} = \frac{n + 1}{2}$$

$$\frac{n + 1}{2} = \frac{9 + 1}{2} = \frac{10}{2} = \text{fifth position}$$

3. Ascertain the value of the component occupying the median position. By a simple process of observation, we determine that employee 2 is in the median position, receiving $5.25 per hour.

HOW IS IT USED AND APPLIED? The median is an essential measure of central tendency used in financial analysis when it is necessary to eliminate large deviations. For example, in a seasonal industry such as the manufacturer and sale of snow skis, it may be essential to identify the midpoint sales month.

WHO USES IT AND WHEN?

Managers and Financial Analysts. Median analysis is used to obtain a representative of the data set without a distortion due to large deviations. Since median analysis of a data set permits the analyst to focus on the midpoint, median analysis is perfectly suitable when seeking the midpoint in sales figures or income data that has only a few extremely small or large observations. Use of the median may be misrepresentative, however, if the values of the observed items do not cluster at the center of the data set. In this case, modal analysis may be more appropriate (see No. 120, Mode).

119 Mix and Yield Variances

DEFINITION. Mix and yield variances are computed to gain insight into the utilization of material and productivity of labor. *Mix* refers to the relative proportion of various ingredients of input factors such as materials and labor. *Yield* is a measure of productivity. The material mix variance indicates the impact on material costs of the deviation from the standard mix. The labor mix variance measures the impact on labor costs of changes in the labor mix.

HOW IS IT COMPUTED? The material quantity variance is comprised of a material mix variance and a material yield variance. The material mix variance measures the impact on material costs of the deviation from the standard mix; the material yield variance reflects the impact on material costs of the deviation from the standard input material allowed for actual production.

The material mix variance is computed by holding the total input units constant at their actual amount.

Material mix variance = (actual units used at standard mix

– actual units used at actual mix) × standard unit price

The material yield variance is computed by holding the mix constant at the standard amount.

Material yield variance = (actual units used at standard mix

– actual output at standard mix) × standard unit price

The computations for labor mix and yield variances are the same as those for materials. If there is no mix, the yield variance is the same as the quantity (or usage) variance.

Labor mix variance = (actual hours used at standard mix

– actual hours used at actual mix) × standard hourly rate

Labor yield variance = (actual hours used at standard mix

— actual output hours at standard mix) × standard hourly rate

Example Assume that a company produces a compound, composed of materials alpha and beta, which is marketed in 20-pound bags. Material alpha can be substituted for material beta. Standard cost and mix data are determined as follows:

	Unit price	Standard unit	Standard mix proportions
Material alpha	$3	5 pounds	25%
Material beta	4	15	75
		20 pounds	100%

Processing each 20 pounds of material requires 10 hours of labor. The company employs two types of labor—"skilled" and "unskilled"—working on two processes, assembly and finishing. The following standard labor cost is calculated to produce a 20-pound bag:

	Standard hours	Standard wage rate	Total	Standard mix proportions
Unskilled	4	$2.00	$ 8	40%
Skilled	6	3.00	18	60
Total	10	$2.60	$26	100%

At standard cost, labor averages $2.60 per unit. During the month of December, 100 20-pound bags were produced with the following labor costs:

	Actual hours	Actual rate	Actual wages
Unskilled	380	$2.50	$ 950
Skilled	600	3.25	1950
Total	980		$2900

Material records show

	Beginning inventory	Purchases	Ending inventory
Material alpha	100 pounds	800 @ $3.10	200 pounds
Material beta	225	1350 @ $3.90	175

The following variances can now be determined from standard costs:

1. Material purchase price
2. Material mix
3. Material quantity
4. Labor rate

5. Labor mix

6. Labor efficiency

Computation of these variances follows:

1. Material purchase price variance

	Material price per unit			Actual quantity purchased	Variance ($)
	Standard	Actual	Difference		
Material alpha	$3	$3.10	$.10 U	800 pounds	$ 80 U
Material beta	4	3.90	.10 F	1350	135 F
					$ 55 F

2. Material mix variance

	Units that should have been used at standard mix[a]	Actual units at actual mix[b]	Differ-ence	Standard unit price	Variance ($)
Material alpha	525 pounds	700 pounds	175 U	$3	$525 U
Material beta	1575	1400	175 F	4	700 F
	2100 pounds	2100 pounds			$175 F

[a]This is the standard mix proportions of 25 percent and 75 percent applied to the actual material units used of 2100 pounds.

[b]Actual units used = beginning inventory + purchase − ending inventory. Therefore,

Material alpha: 700 pounds = 100 + 800 − 200
Material beta: 1400 pounds = 225 + 1350 − 175

The material mix variance measures the impact on material costs of the deviation from the standard mix. Therefore, this variance is computed by holding the total quantity used constant at its actual amount and allowing the material mix quantity to vary between the actual mix and standard mix. As shown, due to a favorable change in mix, a favorable material mix variance of $175 results:

3. Material quantity variance

	Units that should have been used at standard mix	Standard units at standard mix	Differ-ence	Standard unit price	Variance ($)
Material alpha	525 pounds	500 pounds	25 U	$3	$ 75 U
Material beta	1575	1500	75 U	4	300 U
	2100 pounds	2000 pounds			$375 U

The total material variance is the sum of the three variances:

Purchase price variance	$ 55	F
Mix variance	175	F
Quantity variance	375	U
	$145	U

The increase of $145 in material costs in this example is due solely to an unfavorable quantity variance of 100 pounds of materials alpha and beta. The unfavorable quantity variance, however, is largely compensated for by favorable mix and price variances. The analysis shows that the company should look for ways to cut down on its waste and spoilage.

The labor cost increase of $2900 − $2600 = $300 is attributable to these causes:

- An increase of $0.50 per hour in the rate paid to skilled labor and $0.25 per hour in the rate paid to unskilled labor
- An unfavorable mix of skilled and unskilled labor
- A favorable labor efficiency variance of 20 hours

Three labor variances are computed as follows:

4. Labor rate variance

	Labor rate per hour			Actual hours used	Variance ($)
	Standard	Actual	Difference		
Unskilled	$2	$2.50	$0.50 U	380	$190 U
Skilled	3	3.25	$0.25 U	600	150 U
					$340 U

5. Labor mix variance

	Actual hours at standard mix[a]	Actual hours at actual mix	Difference	Standard rate	Variance ($)
Unskilled	392	380	12 F	$2	$24 F
Skilled	588	600	12 U	3	36 U
	980	980			$12 U

[a]This assumes the standard proportions of 40 percent and 60 percent applied to the 980 actual total labor hours used.

6. Labor efficiency variance

	Actual hours at standard mix	Standard hours at standard mix	Difference		Standard rate	Variance ($)	
Unskilled	392	400	8	F	$2	$16	F
Skilled	588	600	12	F	3	36	F
	980	1000				$52	F

The total labor variance is the sum of these three variances:

Rate variance	$340	U
Mix variance	12	U
Efficiency variance	52	F
Total	$300	U

which is proved to be:

7. Total labor variance

	Actual hours used	Actual rate	Total actual cost	Standard hours allowed	Standard rate	Total standard cost	Variance ($)	
Unskilled	380	$2.50	$ 950	400	$2	$ 800	$150	U
Skilled	600	3.25	1950	600	3	1800	150	U
			$2900			$2600	$300	U

The unfavorable labor variance, as evidenced by the cost increase of $300, may be due to: overtime necessary because of poor production scheduling, which results in a higher average labor cost per hour; and/or unnecessary use of more expensive skilled labor. If this is the case, the company should put more effort into better production scheduling.

HOW IS IT USED AND BY WHOM?

Management and Production Managers. Mix and yield variances are used by management in evaluating material and labor. The probable causes of unfavorable mix variances that should be investigated by management include capacity restraints, force substitution, poor production scheduling, lack of certain types of labor, and certain materials in short supply.

The probable causes of unfavorable yield variances are the use of low-quality materials and/or labor, the existence of faulty equipment, the use of improper production methods, and an improper or costly mix of materials and/or labor.

120 Mode

DEFINITION. The mode is the most commonly occurring value in a data set. It is a meaningful statistic only when a particular value clearly occurs more frequently than any of the others.

HOW IS IT COMPUTED? The mode is determined by observation, usually in the form of a graphic. On such a graph, the modal value is the value at the point of highest density of activity.

Example The *simple mode* is shown in Exhibit 120.1.
   Bimodal distribution occurs in certain cases. For example, if a stock exchange wishes to find the modal values of the distribution of weekly sales volume, the graph may be drawn as shown in Exhibit 120.2.

HOW IS IT USED AND APPLIED? There are a wide variety of financial applications for modal analysis; including the evaluation of a product's peak selling periods when there are two clear distinctions. Modal analysis can be very useful with any financial or other data graph to display the most commonly occurring value. Modal analysis is useful with sales, income, utilization rates, population, and other data where there is a clearly occurring value. Use of a mode graph can be extremely effective in making presentations.

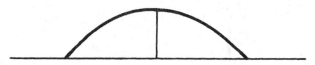

Exhibit 120.1   Simple mode.

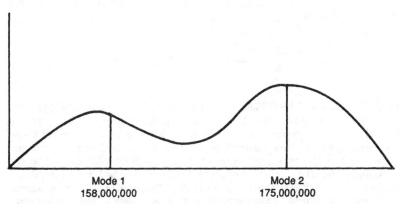

Mode 1
158,000,000

Mode 2
175,000,000

Exhibit 120.2   Bimodal distribution of average weekly stock sale volume.

Managers and Financial Analysts. Modal analysis is used to demonstrate the most commonly occurring value in a data set, but it is useful only when the value of a given variable occurs more frequently than others in the same data set. Examples are peak selling periods, utilization rates, or activity rates.

121 Moving Average

DEFINITION. A moving average is an average that is updated as new information is received. For example, a financial manager employs the most recent observations to calculate an average, which is used as the forecast for the next period.

HOW IS IT COMPUTED? For a moving average, simply take the most recent observations to calculate an average, and update these observations continually as new data becomes available.

Example Assume that a financial manager has the following cash inflow data:

Month	Cash collections (000)
April	20
May	21
June	24
July	22
August	26
September	25

Using a five-month moving average, predicted cash collection for October is computed as follows:

$$\frac{21 + 24 + 22 + 26 + 25}{5} = \frac{118}{5} = 23.60 \quad \text{or} \quad \$23,600$$

HOW IS IT USED AND APPLIED? The moving average is used as a prediction model. Forecasters can choose the number of periods to use on the basis of the relative importance attached to old data versus current data. For example, compare two possibilities—a five-month and three-month period. In terms of the relative importance of new-versus-old data, the old data receives a weight of 4/5 and current data a weight of 1/5. In the second possibility, the old data receives a weight of 2/3, while current observations receive 1/3 weight. This example is a special case of the exponential smoothing method, in which a smoothing constant represents the weight given to the most recent data (see No. 70, Exponential Smoothing).

Business Economists and Forecasters. Business forecasters can be very effective using this analysis once the right number of observations to be averaged has been selected. In order to pick the right number of observations, analysts may have to experiment with different moving-average periods.

122 Multiple Regression

DEFINITION. Multiple regression attempts to estimate statistically the average relationship between the dependent variable (e.g., sales) and two or more independent variables (e.g., price, advertising, income).

HOW IS IT FORMULATED? Multiple regression analysis takes the following form:

$$Y = b_0 + b_1X_1 + b_2X_2 \cdots + b_kX_k + u$$

where Y = dependent variable
X = independent (explanatory) variable
b = regression coefficient
u = error term

When a simple regression is not good enough to provide a satisfactory fit (as indicated typically by a low r^2), a manager should use multiple regression for the analysis. Presented below are examples of both simple and multiple regressions and their spreadsheet printouts.

Example 1 In this case, a manager is trying to develop an estimated regression equation for factory overhead costs.
Assume the following data:

Factory overhead costs, Y	Direct labor hours, X_1	Machine hours, X_2
$3200	26	50
2001	15	35
2700	18	40
3135	21	45
2964	20	40

First, two simple regression results are presented (one variable at a time):

Simple regression 1: $Y' = a + bX_1$

Simple regression 2: $Y' = a + bX_2$

Then, a multiple regression result is presented:

$$Y' = b_0 + b_1X_1 + b_2X_2$$

A Lotus 1-2-3 regression printout is shown as Exhibit 122.1. As can be seen, there was only a slight increase in r^2, from 76.8% in simple regression 1 and 75.91% in simple regression 2 to 77.50%. Apparently, the extra indepen-

Exhibit 122.1 Simple and multiple regression results for cost–volume formula.

Factory Overhead Cost (Y)	Direct Labor Hours (X1)	Machine Hours (X2)
3200	26	50
2001	15	35
2700	18	40
3135	21	45
2964	20	40

Simple regression 1: Y' = a + b X1

Regression Output:

Constant	700	$\leftarrow a$
Std Err of Y Est	270.7224	
R Squared	0.767950	$\leftarrow r^2$
No. of Observations	5	
Degrees of Freedom	3	

X Coefficient(s)	105	$\leftarrow b$
Std Err of Coef.	33.32363	
T-value	3.150916 (calculated independently)	

Y' = 700 + 105 X1 with r2 = 0.767950 = 76.80%

Simple regression 2: Y' = a + b X2

Regression Output:

Constant	−324.153	$\leftarrow a$
Std Err of Y Est	275.8156	
R Squared	0.759137	$\leftarrow r^2$
No. of Observations	5	
Degrees of Freedom	3	

X Coefficient(s)	74.38461	
Std Err of Coef.	24.19063	
T-value	3.074935 (calculated independently)	

Y' = − 324.15 + 74.38 X2 with r2 = 0.759137 = 75.91%

Multiple regression: Y' = a + b X1 + c X2

Regression Output

Constant	254.5	$\leftarrow b_0$
Std Err of Y Est	326.5095	
R Squared	0.774974	$\leftarrow r^2$
No. of Observations	5	
Degrees of Freedom	2	

X Coefficient(s)	63.75	30.25	$\leftarrow b_1, b_2$
Std Err of Coef.	169.9209	121.0729	
T-value	0.375174	0.249849 (calculated independently)	

Y' = 254.5 + 63.75 X1 + 30.25 X2 with r2 = 0.774974 = 77.50%

dent variable added little new explanatory power. Furthermore, t-values for both independent variables came out to be much less than 2 (approximately 0.38 and 0.25, respectively), which means that both variables together in the same regression equation were not statistically significant. All this indicates that either simple regression was good enough for the purpose of developing the cost–volume formula.

Example 2 The LA Company wants to identify trends in demand so that funds available for investment, and related expenditures, can be allocated efficiently. The company tries three different models: (1) a constant-change model, which is a linear trend equation; (2) a constant-growth model; and (3) a simple econometric model that incorporates explanatory factors besides trend.

Exhibit 122.2 shows all three results as they appear on a Lotus 1-2-3 regression output.

For a more detailed discussion on statistics, see No. 160, Regression Statistics, and No. 123, Multiple-Regression Tests.

HOW IS IT USED AND APPLIED?   Multiple-regression analysis is used to do the following:

1. To find the overall association between the dependent variable and a host of explanatory variables. For example, overhead costs are explained by volume, productivity, and technology.

2. To attempt to identify the factors that influence the dependent variable. For example, factors critically affecting sales include price, advertising, taste, and competition.

3. To use it as a basis for providing sound forecasts of the dependent variable. For example, sometimes cash collections from customers are forecasted from credit sales of prior months, since cash collections lag behind sales.

WHO USES IT AND WHEN?

Forecasters and Policymakers.   Multiple regression is a powerful statistical technique that is perhaps most widely used by businesses and economists. In order to obtain a good fit and achieve a high degree of accuracy, users should be familiar with the ways to handle many econometric problems surrounding the multiple regression. The problems include multicollinearity, homoscedasticity, and autocorrelation. Users need to know how to interpret and analyze regression statistics such as $\bar{r}^2$, t-values, F-tests, and the Durbin-Watson statistic. (See also No. 160, Regression Statistics, and No. 123, Multiple-Regression Tests.)

123 Multiple-Regression Tests

DEFINITION.   In using multiple regression, managers must look for the following statistics and perform various statistical tests, each of which is discussed below:

- t-statistic
- $\bar{r}^2$, and F statistics

Exhibit 122.2 Multiple regression analysis.

Sales (Y)	GNP (X1)	Tractor Sales T-Bill (X2)	Time (X3)	Log Sales (Log Y)
1102.16	1688.9	7.10	43	3.042244
1092.53	1671.3	7.01	42	3.038433
1064.92	1663.5	7.56	41	3.027316
1052.74	1662.4	8.16	40	3.022321
1044.31	1645.2	10.40	39	3.018829
1015.75	1638.8	9.94	38	3.006786
993.66	1610.9	9.44	37	2.997237
1017.20	1572.5	8.80	36	3.007406
998.89	1553.3	9.13	35	2.999517
986.72	1525.2	8.40	34	2.994193
967.50	1490.1	8.11	33	2.985650
961.12	1480.7	7.91	32	2.982777
951.24	1485.7	9.32	31	2.978290
921.58	1489.3	12.42	30	2.964533
913.01	1485.8	12.81	29	2.960475
934.99	1506.9	11.75	28	2.970806
913.17	1525.8	15.05	27	2.960551
903.33	1512.5	14.90	26	2.955846
906.66	1510.1	14.39	25	2.957444
891.65	1477.9	13.61	24	2.950194
922.27	1464.2	9.15	23	2.964858
915.71	1461.4	9.62	22	2.961757
897.52	1496.2	13.35	21	2.953044
904.71	1489.3	11.84	20	2.956509
922.57	1486.6	9.67	19	2.964999
912.60	1469.2	9.38	18	2.960280
913.99	1472.6	9.38	17	2.960941
916.93	1468.4	8.57	16	2.962336
916.26	1448.8	7.31	15	2.962018
918.31	1437.0	6.48	14	2.962989
809.61	1400.0	6.39	13	2.908275
977.15	1388.4	6.11	12	2.989961
892.60	1385.8	5.50	11	2.950656
886.17	1363.3	4.84	10	2.947517
875.18	1341.3	4.63	9	2.942097
858.59	1315.4	4.67	8	2.933785
847.57	1303.3	5.15	7	2.928175
840.74	1295.8	5.16	6	2.924661
837.22	1287.2	4.92	5	2.922839
814.76	1259.7	5.63	4	2.911029
799.99	1248.4	6.33	3	2.903084
791.62	1221.0	5.39	2	2.898516
777.73	1206.3	5.75	1	2.890828

(Continued)

```
                Simple Regression Result 1
─────────────────────────────────────────────────────────
                  Constant Change Model
                    Regression Output:
Constant                        820.5275  ← a
Std Err of Y Est                32.18917
R Squared                       0.601492  ← r²
No. of Observations                   32
Degrees of Freedom                    30
X Coefficient(s)   4.147102  b
Std Err of Coef.   0.616293
t-value            6.729101 (calculated independently)

     Thus, Y' = 820.53 + 4.15 X3 with R Squared = 60.15%


                Simple Regression Result 2
─────────────────────────────────────────────────────────
                  Constant Growth Model
                    Regression Output:
Constant                        2.913950  ← a
Std Err of Y Est                0.016022
R Squared                       0.604007  ← r²
No. of Observations                   32
Degrees of Freedom                    30
X Coefficient(s)   0.002075  ← b
Std Err of Coef.   0.000306
t-value            6.764546 (calculated independently)

    Thus, Log Y = 2.91 + 4.15 X3 with R Squared = 60.40%


                Multiple Regression Result
─────────────────────────────────────────────────────────
                 Simple Econometric Model
                    Regression Output:
Constant                        224.5181  ← b₀
Std Err of Y Est                23.14612
R Squared                       0.807686  ← r²
No. of Observations                   32
Degrees of Freedom                    28
X Coefficient(s) 0.501877   -8.97865   2.036930   ← b₁,b₂,b₃
Std Err of Coef. 0.110761    2.139940  1.153795
t-values         4.531160   -4.19574   1.765416
      Thus Y' = 224.52 +  0.50 X1  -8.98 X2 + 2.04 X3
         t-values:       (4.53)    (-4.20)    (1.77)
                       R2 = 80.76%
```

- Multicollinearity
- Autocorrelation (serial correlation) detected by the Durbin-Watson statistic
- Homoscedasticity

t Statistic.   The *t* statistic is discussed in No. 160, Regression Statistics, but is taken up here because it is more valid in multiple regressions than in simple regressions. The t statistic shows the significance of each explanatory variable in predicting the dependent variable. It is desirable to have as large (either positive or negative) a t statistic as possible for each independent variable. Generally, a t statistic greater than $+2.0$ or less than -2.0 is acceptable. Explanatory variables with low t values can usually be eliminated from the regression without substantially decreasing r^2 or increasing the standard error of the regression. In a multiple-regression situation, the t statistic is defined as

$$t \text{ statistic} = \frac{b_i}{s_{b_i}}$$

where b = regression coefficient
  i = ith independent variable
  s_b = standard error of the regression coefficient

$\bar{r}^2$ and F Statistics.

A more appropriate test for goodness of fit for multiple regressions is $\bar{r}^2$,

$$\bar{r}^2 = 1 - (1 - r^2)\left(\frac{n - 1}{n - k}\right)$$

where n = number of observations
  k = number of coefficients to be estimated

An alternative test of the overall significance of a regression equation is the F test. Virtually all computer programs for regression analysis show an F statistic. Note that the Lotus 1-2-3 regression command does *not* calculate this statistic.

The F statistic is defined as

$$F = \frac{(y' - \bar{y})^2/k}{(y - y')^2/(k - k - 1)} = \frac{\text{explained variation}/k}{\text{unexplained variation}/(n - k - 1)}$$

If the F statistic is greater than the table value, it is concluded that the regression equation is statistically significant in overall terms.

Multicollinearity.

When using more than one independent variable in a regression equation, there is sometimes a high correlation between the independent variables themselves. Multicollinearity occurs when these variables interfere with each other. Multicollinearity is the condition that exists when the independent variables are highly correlated with each other. In the presence of multicollinearity, the estimated regression coefficients may be unreliable. The presence of multicollinearity can be tested by investigating the correlation between the independent variables.

Multicollinearity can be recognized when:

- The t statistics of two seemingly important independent variables are low.

- The estimated coefficients on explanatory variables have the opposite sign from that which would logically be expected.

There are two ways to get around the problem of multicollinearity:

- One of the highly correlated variables may be dropped from the regression.
- The structure of the equation may be changed using one of the following methods:

1. Divide both the left- and right-hand-side variables by some series that will leave the basic economic logic but remove multicollinearity.
2. Estimate the equation on a first-difference basis.
3. Combine the collinear variables into a new variable that is their weighted sum.
4. Keep one variable and drop the rest of the variables that are highly correlated.

Autocorrelation and the Durbin-Watson Statistic. Autocorrelation is another major pitfall that is often encountered in regression analysis. It occurs where there is a correlation between successive errors. When autocorrelation exists (i.e., the error terms are not independent), the standard errors of the regression coefficients are seriously underestimated. The problem of autocorrelation is usually detected by the Durbin-Watson statistic. Roughly speaking,

Durbin-Watson statistic	Autocorrelation
Between 1.5 and 2.5	No autocorrelation
Below 1.5	Positive autocorrelation
Above 2.5	Negative autocorrelation

Autocorrelation usually indicates that an important part of the variation of the dependent variable has not been explained. *Recommendation:* The best solution to this problem is to search for other explanatory variables to include in the regression equation.

Homoscedasticity. Homoscedasticity (or constant variance) is one of the assumptions required in a regression in order to make valid statistical inferences about population relationships. Homoscedasticity requires that the standard deviation and variance of the error terms be constant for all x's, and that the error terms are drawn from the same population. This indicates that there is a uniform scatter or dispersion of data points about the regression line. If the assumption does not hold, the accuracy of the regression coefficient (s) is open to question.

HOW IS IT COMPUTED? CAN A COMPUTER HELP? It is important to note that Lotus 1-2-3 does not calculate many statistics such as $\bar{r}^2$, the F statistic, or the Durbin-Watson statistic. Regression packages must be used, such as Statistical Analysis System (SAS), STATPACK, or Statistical Packages for Social Scientists (SPSS), all of which offer PC versions.

Example Cypress Consumer Products Corporation wishes to develop a forecasting model for its dryer sales by using multiple-regression analysis. The marketing department has prepared the following sample data:

Month	Sales of washers (x_1)	Disposable income (x_2)	Savings (x_3)	Sales of dryers (y)
January	$45,000	$16,000	$71,000	$29,000
February	42,000	14,000	70,000	24,000
March	44,000	15,000	72,000	27,000
April	45,000	13,000	71,000	25,000
May	43,000	13,000	75,000	26,000
June	46,000	14,000	74,000	28,000
July	44,000	16,000	76,000	30,000
August	45,000	16,000	69,000	28,000
September	44,000	15,000	74,000	28,000
October	43,000	15,000	73,000	27,000

The computer statistical package called STATPACK, which is one of the easiest programs to use, is employed to develop the regression model.

Exhibit 123.1 contains the input data and output that results using three explanatory variables. To help in understanding the listing, illustrative comments are added whenever applicable.

1. *The forecasting equation.* From the STATPACK output it is seen that

$$y' = -45.796 + 0.597x_1 + 1.177x_2 + 0.405x_3$$

Suppose that in November the company expects

$$x_1 = \text{sales of washers} = \$43.00$$

$$x_2 = \text{disposable income} = \$15,000$$

$$x_3 = \text{savings} = \$75,000$$

Then the forecast sales for the month of November would be

$$y' = -45.796 + 0.597(43) + 1.177(15) + 0.405(75)$$

$$= -45.796 + 25.671 + 17.655 + 30.375 - 27.905 \text{ or } \$27,905$$

2. *The coefficient of determination.* Note that the STATPACK output gives the value of r, not r^2 (and not $\bar{r}^2$, for that matter). In this example, $r = 0.99167$, so

$$r^2 = (0.99167)^2 = 0.983$$

In the case of multiple regression, $\bar{r}^2$ is more appropriate, as was discussed previously.

$$\bar{r}^2 = 1 - (1 - r^2)\left(\frac{(n-1)}{(n-k)}\right)$$

$$= 1 - (1 - 0.983)\left(\frac{10-1}{10-3}\right) = 1 - 0.017\left(\frac{9}{7}\right)$$

$$= 1 - 0.0219 = 0.978$$

This reveals that 97.8 percent of total variation in sales of dryers is ex-

Exhibit 123.1 STATPACK input and output.

```
RUN***STATPACK

STATPACK

ARE YOU A STATPACK EXPERT

?* NO

THE RESPONSE 'SOS' MAY BE ENTERED IN ORDER TO GAIN
ADDITIONAL INFORMATION ABOUT THE RESPONSE NEEDED BY
STATPACK. SOS MAY BE ENTERED ONLY IF THE QUESTION IS
FOLLOWED BY THE CHARACTERS ?*

SPECIFY THE NAMES OF THE INPUT AND OUTPUT FILES(FORM:IN,OUT)
?**,* ← Indicates that all input and output will be on the screen
or printer.

WHAT ANALYSIS DO YOU WISH TO PERFORM
?* MULTIPLE REGRESSION

HOW MANY ROWS IN YOUR DATA MATRIX   ← How many observations?
?* 10

HOW MANY COLUMNS   ← How many variables?
?* 4

NOW, ENTER EACH ROW
?45,16,71,29
?42,14,70,24
?44,15,72,27
?45,13,71,25
?43,13,75,26
?46,14,74,28
?44,16,76 (28)  ← Entered incorrectly
?45,16,69,28
?44,15,74,28
?43,15,73,27

DO YOU WISH TO PRINT THE DATA JUST READ IN
?* NO

DO YOU WISH TO CHANGE SOME VALUES
?* YES

TYPE EDIT CODE
?* SOS

THE FOLLOWING CODES SIGNIFY TYPES OF EDIT FEATURES..
0-NO MORE EDIT
1-REPLACE AN INDIVIDUAL VALUE
2-REPLACE AN ENTIRE ROW
3-ADD A ROW
4-DELETE A ROW
5-SORT DATA (DESCENDING)
6-SORT DATA (ASCENDING)
?* 1
```

(Continued)

```
TYPE ROW NUMBER, COLUMN NUMBER, AND NEW VALUE
?7,4,30  ← Corrected input value for July

TYPE EDIT CODE
?* 0

DO YOU WISH TO PRINT THE DATA MATRIX
?* YES
        45.000          16.000          71.000          29.000
        42.000          14.000          70.000          24.000
        44.000          15.000          72.000          27.000
        45.000          13.000          71.000          25.000
        43.000          13.000          75.000          26.000
        46.000          14.000          74.000          28.000
        44.000          16.000          76.000          30.000
        45.000          16.000          69.000          28.000
        44.000          15.000          74.000          28.000
        43.000          15.000          73.000          27.000

SPECIFY THE DEPENDENT VARIABLE
?* 4

HOW MANY INDEPENDENT VARIABLES
?* 3

SPECIFY THESE VARIABLES
? 1,2,3
```

| | | STD.ERROR | |
VARIABLE	REG.COEF.	COEF. $\leftarrow s_b$	COMPUTED T
1	0.59697	0.08113	7.35866
2	1.17684	0.08 07	13.99748
3	0.40511	0.04223	9.59200

INTERCEPT -45.79634
MULTIPLE CORRELATION $0.99167 \leftarrow r$
STD.ERROR OF ESTIMATE $0.28613 \leftarrow s_e$

ANALYSIS OF VARIANCE FOR THE REGRESSION

SOURCE OF VARIATION	D.F	SUM OF SQ.	MEAN SQ.	F
ATTRIBUTABLE TO REGRESSION	3	29.109	9.703	118.515
DEVIATION FROM REGRESSION	6	0.491	0.082	
TOTAL	9	29.600		

plained by the three explanatory variables. The remaining 2.2 percent was unexplained by the estimated equation.

3. *The standard error of the estimate* (s_e). This is a measure of dispersion of actual sales around the estimated equation. The output shows $s_e = 0.28613$.

4. *Computed* t. From the output is read:

	t Statistic
x_1	7.35866
x_2	13.99748
x_3	9.59200

All t values are greater than a rule-of-thumb table t value of 2.0. (Strictly speaking, with $n - k - 1 = 10 - 3 - 1 = 6$ degrees of freedom and a level of significance of, say, 0.01, Table 7 in the Appendix shows that the table t value is 3.707.) For a two-sided test, 0.005 was the level of significance looked up in this table. In any case, the conclusion is that all three explanatory variables selected were statistically significant.

5. F *test*. From the output, it is seen that

$$F = \frac{\text{explained variance}/k}{\text{unexplained variance}/(n - k - 1)} = \frac{29.109/3}{0.491/6}$$

$$= \frac{9.703}{0.082} = 118.515 \quad \text{which is given in the printout.}$$

At a significance level of 0.01, the F value is far above the value of 9.78 (from Table 9 in the Appendix), so it can be concluded that the regression as a whole is highly significant.

6. *Conclusion*. Based on statistical considerations, it is shown that:

- The estimated equation had a good fit.
- All three variables are significant explanatory variables.
- The regression as a whole is highly significant.
- The model developed can be used as a forecasting equation with a great degree of confidence.

HOW IS IT USED AND APPLIED? The following is a checklist of how to choose the best forecasting equation. Choosing among alternative forecasting equations involves two basic steps: (1) eliminate the obvious losers; (2) select the winner from among the remaining contenders.

1. *How to eliminate losers*. Losers are eliminated by asking a series of questions:

- Does the equation make sense? Equations that do not make sense intuitively or from a theoretical standpoint must be eliminated.
- Does the equation have explanatory variables with low t statistics? These equations should be reestimated or dropped in favor of equations in which all independent variables are significant. This test will eliminate equations in which multicollinearity is a problem.
- How about a low $\bar{r}^2$? The $\bar{r}^2$ can be used to rank the remaining equations in order to select the best candidates. A low $\bar{r}^2$ could mean that (*a*) a wrong functional form was fitted; (*b*) an important explanatory vari-

able is missing; or (c) other combinations of explanatory variables might be more desirable.

2. *How to choose the best equation.* To choose the best equation, look for the

- Best Durbin-Watson statistic. Given equations that survive all previous tests, the equation with the Durbin-Watson statistic closest to 2.0 can be a basis for selection.
- Best forecasting accuracy. Examining the forecasting performance of the equations is essential for selecting one equation from among those that have not been eliminated. The equation whose prediction accuracy is best in terms of MAD (mean absolute deviation) or MSE (mean squared error) generally provides the best basis for forecasting.

WHO USES IT AND WHEN?

Forecasters and Policy Makers. Multiple regression is a powerful statistical technique that is perhaps most widely used by businesspeople and economists. In order to obtain a good fit and achieve a high degree of accuracy, users should be familiar with the ways to handle many problems surrounding the multiple regression, including multicollinearity, homoscedasticity, and autocorrelation. Users need to know how to interpret and analyze regression statistics such as $\bar{r}^2$, t values, F tests, and the Durbin-Watson statistic.

See also No. 160, Regression Statistics.

124 Naive Forecasting Models

DEFINITION. Naive forecasting models are based exclusively on historical observation of sales or other variables such as earnings and cash flows being forecast. These models do *not* attempt to explain the underlying causal relationships that produce the variables being forecast.

Naive models may be classified into two groups. One group consists of simple projection models. These models require inputs of data from recent observations, but no statistical analysis is performed. The second group is comprised of models that, while naive, are complex enough to require a computer. Traditional methods such as classical decomposition, moving average, and exponential smoothing models are some examples. (See No. 121, Moving Average, and No. 70, Exponential Smoothing.)

The advantages of naive forecasting models are that they are inexpensive to develop, store data, and operate. The disadvantages are that they do not consider possible causal relationships that underlie the forecasted variable.

HOW IS IT COMPUTED? A simple example of a naive model type is to use the actual sales of the current period as the forecast for the next period. Assume that y_{t+1} is the forecast value and y_t is the actual value. Then:

$$y_{t+1} = y_t$$

If trends are considered, then:

$$y_{t+1} = y_t + (y_t - y_{t-1})$$

This model adds the latest observed absolute period-to-period change to the most recent observed level of the variable.

If it is desirable to incorporate the rate of change rather than the absolute amount, then:

$$y_{t+1} = y_t \left(\frac{y_t}{y_{t-1}} \right)$$

Example Consider the following sales data for 19X1:

Month	Monthly sales of product
1	$3050
2	2980
3	3670
4	2910
5	3340
6	4060
7	4750
8	5510
9	5280
10	5504
11	5810
12	6100

Forecasts will be developed for January 19X2 based on the three models:

$$y_{t+1} = y_t = \$6100$$

$$y_{t+1} = y_t + (y_t - y_{t-1}) = \$6100 + (\$5810 - \$5504) = \$6100 + \$306 = \$6406$$

$$y_{t+1} = y_t \left(\frac{y_t}{y_{t-1}} \right) = \$6100 \left(\frac{\$6100}{\$5810} \right) = \$6100(1.05) = \$6405$$

HOW IS IT USED AND APPLIED? Naive models can be applied, with very little need of a computer, to develop forecasts for sales, earnings, and cash flows.

WHO USES IT AND WHEN?

Business Economists and Forecasters. Forecasters use various prediction methods. The naive models described above must be used in conjunction with more complex naive models such as classical decomposition and exponential smoothing and more sophisticated models such as regression analysis and the Box-Jenkin model. The object is to pick the model (or models) that will best forecast performance.

125 Net Asset Value

DEFINITION. The value of a mutual fund share is measured by net asset value (NAV):

$$\text{NAV} = \frac{\text{fund's total assets} - \text{liabilities}}{\text{number of shares outstanding in the fund}}$$

HOW IS IT COMPUTED?   For simplicity, assume that a fund owns 100 shares each of General Motors (GM), Xerox, and International Business Machines (IBM). Assume also that on a particular day, the market values below existed. The NAV of the fund (assuming the fund has no liabilities) is calculated as follows.

GM:—$90 per share × 100 shares	$ 9,000
Xerox:—$100 per share × 100 shares	10,000
IBM:—$160 per share × 100 shares	16,000
Value of the fund's portfolio	$35,000
Number of shares outstanding in the fund	1,000
Net asset value (NAV) per share ($35,000/1,000)	$ 35

If an investor owns 5 percent of the fund's outstanding shares, or 50 shares (5% × 1000 shares), then the value of the investment is $35 × 50 = $1750.

HOW IS IT USED AND APPLIED?   The performance of a mutual fund must be judged on the basis of three types of returns. NAV represents one component of the return on mutual fund investments. However, NAV indicates only the current market value of the underlying portfolio. An investor also receives capital gains and dividends, and this must be taken into account.

WHO USES IT AND WHEN?

Fund Managers and Investors.   Investors monitor the closing daily change of a fund as reported in the financial pages of a newspaper, which provides an indicator of the return earned by investors on their money. Fund managers make every effort to increase the NAV, since their performance is evaluated partly on its change. It is also important for managers to remember that there are additional measures of a fund's quality, such as beta (see No. 19) and risk-adjusted return.

126 Net-Cost Method

DEFINITION.   The net-cost method is a method publicized by insurance agents for cash-value life insurance. The net cost of a life insurance policy considers premiums, accumulated cash value, and dividends. The net cost is computed for a specified point in time during the life of the policy.

HOW IS IT COMPUTED?

Net cost = total premiums to be paid − accumulated cash value

− accrued dividends

Example You are considering the purchase of a $100,000 cash-value life insurance policy. Your annual premiums will be $1664, and the policy will have a cash value at the end of 20 years of $25,008. Total dividends accumulated for 20 years will be $9300. The net cost of the policy after 20 years will be:

$$(\$1664 \times 20) - \$25,008 - \$9300 = -\$1028$$

Since the net cost is negative, the policy will pay for itself and is therefore beneficial to carry.

HOW IS IT USED AND BY WHOM?

Individuals. In personal financial planning, individuals can determine how much a life insurance policy will cost them.

Insurance Agents. Insurance brokers can compute the net cost and explain its benefit to potential policyholders.

127 Net Income Multiplier

DEFINITION. The net income multiplier (NIM) is another method of determining the price of income-producing property. The other methods are the *gross income multiplier* (GIM, see No. 82) and the *capitalization rate* (see No. 27).

HOW IS IT COMPUTED?

$$\text{NIM} = \frac{\text{purchase price}}{\text{net operating income (NOI)}}$$

Where NOI is the gross income less allowances for vacancies and operating expenses, except depreciation and debt payments.

Example Assume that NOI = $18,618 and the asking price = $219,000. The net income multiplier is calculated as follows:

$$\frac{\$219,000}{\$18,618} = 11.76$$

HOW IS IT USED AND APPLIED? A property in a similar neighborhood may be valued at "10 times annual net." Thus, if its annual gross rental income amounts to $18,618, the value is taken as 10 × $18,618 = $186,180, which means that the property may be overvalued.

WHO USES IT AND WHEN?

Real Estate Investors, Appraisers, and Realtors. Professionals involved in real estate can use this approach to determine an approximate market value for a property. This approach is better than the GIM approach since it takes into account vacancies and operating expenses.

128 Net Savings

DEFINITION. Net savings is total income less expenses. It reveals financial health and indicates if there is excess discretionary income to save.

HOW IS IT COMPUTED?

Net savings = total income − total expenses

In general, families save about 4 percent of disposable income.

Example Your total income is $12,000 and your expenses are $7000. Your net savings is $5000.

HOW IS IT USED AND BY WHOM?

Individuals. Savings are important in personal financial planning. Are your savings enough? Are your spending habits excessive, and in what areas? Are living expenses unusually high, and why? The relationship between your income and your expenses may give you ideas on ways to readjust your expenses.

The amount you save depends on the importance of savings in your financial plan and your income level. As your income increases, the percentage of income saved also typically increases. This is because, at higher incomes, many expenses (for example, food) do not increase at the same pace as income. Hence, it becomes easier to save.

129 Net Worth

DEFINITION. Net worth (or equity) refers to either an individual's net assets or the total stockholders' equity interest in a business.

HOW IS IT COMPUTED?

Individual net worth: Net worth = assets − liabilities − tax provision

Assets and liabilities are reported at their current values.

Corporation net worth: Net worth = assets − liabilities

Example This example calculates net worth for both an individual and a corporation:

For an *individual,* assume that the current value of a person's assets and liabilities are $700,000 and $200,000, respectively. The tax provision is $60,000. Net worth is then:

Net worth = $700,000 − $200,000 − $60,000 = $440,000

For a *corporation,* if corporate assets and liabilities are $20,000,000 and $6,000,000, then net worth is:

$20,000,000 − $6,000,000 = $14,000,000

HOW IS IT USED AND APPLIED?

Individuals. Net worth represents a person's financial worth. Net worth may be used as the basis to determine if an individual is able to obtain a bank loan, buy a house, and so forth. Individual net worth is also the basis for estate planning and taxes.

Corporations. Net worth reveals the equity interest of the stockholders in the business. A company with a high net worth is more financially secure and thus favorably looked upon by investors and creditors.

130 Noncurrent Assets to Noncurrent Liabilities

DEFINITION. The ratio of noncurrent assets to noncurrent liabilities represents primarily the relationship between property, plant, and equipment and long-term debt.

HOW IS IT COMPUTED?

$$\frac{\text{Noncurrent assets}}{\text{Noncurrent liabilities}}$$

Example The following balance sheet information is available for 19X1 and 19X2.

	19X1	19X2
Property, plant, and equipment	$800,000	$700,000
Long-term liabilities	400,000	500,000

The ratio of noncurrent assets to noncurrent liabilities is 2 for 19X1 and 1.4 for 19X2. The trend in the ratio has declined from 19X1 to 19X2, indicating a possible solvency problem.

HOW IS IT USED AND BY WHOM?

Long-Term Creditors. A decline in the coverage of long-term debt by noncurrent assets may trigger an alarm for long-term creditors, such as bondholders, bankers, and long-term suppliers, since fewer long-term assets are available to cover debt when it is due.

Long-term debt will ultimately be paid out of long-term assets; hence, a high ratio indicates protection for long-term creditors.

Financial Management. A lower ratio of noncurrent assets to noncurrent liabilities means that it may be more difficult for the company to borrow over the long term. Also, managers might anticipate that company could be charged a higher interest rate to obtain necessary financing.

131 Normal Distribution

DEFINITION. The normal distribution is the most popular probability distribution used for statistical decision making in business. A normal distribution, shown in Exhibit 131.1, has the following important characteristics:

1. The curve has a single peak.
2. The curve is bell-shaped.
3. The mean (average) lies at the center of the distribution, and the distribution is symmetrical around the mean.
4. The two tails of the distribution extend indefinitely and never touch the horizontal axis.
5. The shape of the distribution is determined by its mean (μ) and standard deviation (σ).

Since the normal distribution is symmetric, it has the valuable advantage that a known percentage of all possible values of x lie within a certain number of standard deviations of the mean, as illustrated in Exhibit 131.2. For example, 68.27 percent of the values of any normally distributed variable lie within the interval (μ, σ).

HOW IS IT COMPUTED? The probability of the normal distribution as given above is difficult to work with in determining areas under the curve; each set of x values generates another curve (as long as the means and standard deviations are different). To facilitate computations, every set of x values

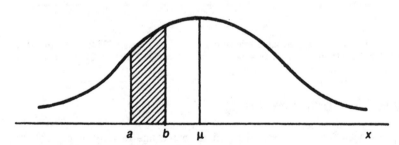

Exhibit 131.1 Normal distribution.

Percent (%):	99.73%	99%	95.45%	95%	90%	68.27%
Number of $\pm\sigma$'s:	3.00	2.58	2.00	1.96	1.645	1.00

Exhibit 131.2 Area under the curve.

is translated to a new axis—a z axis—with the translation defined as

$$z = \frac{x - \mu}{\sigma}$$

The resulting values, called z values, are the values of a new variable called the *standard normal variate, z*. The translation process is shown in Exhibit 131.3.

The new variable z is normally distributed with a mean of zero and a standard deviation of 1. Tables of areas (see Table 6 in the Appendix) under this standard normal distribution have been compiled and widely published, so that areas under any normal distribution can be found by translating the x values to z values and then using the tables for the standardized normal.

Example Assume that the total book value of an inventory is normally distributed with μ = $5000 and σ = $1000. Management may want to know the percentage of the population that lies between $3000 and $7000. To answer, two x values must be translated to z values using the z formula:

$$z_1 = \frac{\$3000 - \$5000}{\$1000} = -2$$

$$z_2 = \frac{\$7000 - \$5000}{\$1000} = +2$$

Exhibit 131.2 shows that 95.45 percent of the population lies between these two values. This means that total book value will lie between $3000 and $7000 with 95.45 percent confidence.

HOW IS IT USED AND APPLIED? Applications of the normal distribution in business and finance are numerous, including:

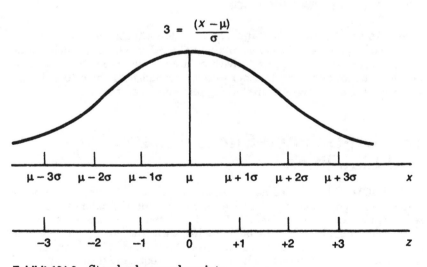

Exhibit 131.3 Standard normal variate.

1. Capital budgeting under risk
2. Probability of meeting a delivery date. [See also No. 155, **Program Evaluation and Review Technique (PERT)**.]
3. Determination of safety stock
4. Cost–Volume–Profit (CVP) analysis under uncertainty

WHO USES IT AND WHEN?

Financial Analysts and Project Analysts.   Whenever the probability distribution underlying a variable under consideration is normal, managers will be able to make probabilistic statements about the characteristics of the variable. Examples of some of the questions that can be answered in business are: (1) What is the chance of the company at least breaking even? (2) What is the chance that the firm will make at least a certain amount of money? (3) What is the probability that a project will meet its deadline?

132 Odd-Lot Index

DEFINITION.   The odd-lot index is an index of the ratio of odd-lot purchases to odd-lot sales. Odd-lot trading reflects popular opinion. Volume is usually expressed in number of shares rather than dollars.

HOW IS IT COMPUTED?

$$\frac{\text{Odd-lot purchases}}{\text{Odd-lot sales}}$$

Example   On the New York Stock Exchange, 18 million odd-lot shares are purchased and 20 million odd-lot shares are sold. The ratio is 0.90.

HOW IS IT USED AND BY WHOM?

Investors and Portfolio Managers.   The odd-lot theory rests on the rule of contrary opinions. You determine what *small investors* are doing and you do the *opposite,* since small investors are usually wrong because they lack investment expertise. In other words, knowledgeable investors should sell when the small traders are buying and buy when they are selling.

133 Off-Balance-Sheet Assets and Liabilities

DEFINITION.   Unrecorded assets either represent resources of the business or are expected to have future economic benefit. Off-balance-sheet assets include tax-loss carryforward benefits, anticipated rebates, and purchase commitments where the business has a contract to buy an item at a price significantly less than the going rate. Unrecorded liabilities are those not reported on the balance sheet but possibly requiring future payments or services. Examples are lawsuits, rental commitments, and cosigned loans.

HOW IS IT COMPUTED?

1. Off-balance-sheet assets/total assets
2. Off-balance-sheet liabilities/total liabilities

Example A company reports the following information:

	19X1	19X2
Off-balance-sheet liabilities	$ 200,000	$ 500,000
Total liabilities	1,000,000	1,300,000

The relevant ratios are:

	19X1	19X2
Off-balance-sheet liabilities to total liabilities	0.20	0.38

The increase in unrecorded liabilities may cause concern because of possible future payment. For example, there may have been renegotiation of claims under government contracts.

HOW IS IT USED AND BY WHOM?

Management, Creditors, and Investors. Off-balance-sheet assets are positive attributes of financial position even though they are not presented on the balance sheet. Of course, a going concern is assumed, since in a distress situation unrecorded assets could generally not be realized. Off-balance-sheet liabilities are negative attributes of financial position, because they may require the use of corporate resources.

134 Operating Assets Ratio

DEFINITION. The operating assets ratio analyzes the percentage of a company's assets used to generate revenue.

HOW IS IT COMPUTED?

$$\text{Operating assets ratio} = \frac{\text{operating assets}}{\text{total assets}}$$

Example A company reports the following information for 19X1 and 19X2:

	19X1	19X2
Operating assets	$100,000	$200,000
Total assets	500,000	600,000

The relevant ratios are:

	19X1	19X2
Operating assets to total assets	20%	33.3%

Analysis shows that there has been an increase in the productive assets over the year, which should result in improved operations, and greater productive capacity, and therefore greater revenue.

HOW IS IT USED AND BY WHOM?

Management. The operating assets ratio isolates those assets that are actively employed in *current* operations. Such assets exclude both past-oriented and future-oriented assets. Past-oriented assets arise from prior errors, inefficiencies, or losses because of competitive factors or changes in business plans. Past-oriented assets, such as obsolete goods, idle plants, receivables under litigation, delinquent receivables, and nonperforming loans (no interest being recognized), have not yet been formerly recognized in the accounts. Future-oriented assets, such as land held for speculation and factories under construction, are acquired for corporate growth or for generating future sales. Nonoperating assets reduce profits and return on investment, because there is no benefit to current operations—that is, they neither generate sales nor reduce costs. Nonoperating assets are a "drain" on the company and may require financing.

135 Operating Cycle

DEFINITION. The operating cycle is the number of days taken to translate cash to inventory to accounts receivable and back to cash.

HOW IS IT COMPUTED?

Operating cycle = age of inventory

+ collection period on accounts receivable

Example Assume that for a particular company, inventory is held for 85 days, while it takes 45 days to collect from accounts receivable. The operating cycle is:

HOW IS IT USED AND BY WHOM?

Financial Managers. The operating cycle is of interest to financial management because it reveals how long cash is tied up in inventory and receivables. A shorter operating cycle is desired because the freed cash can be invested to add to the returns.

Creditors, Suppliers, and Loan Officers. Short-term creditors are interested in knowing the operating cycle of a company since a shorter period indicates that cash will be more readily available to meet short-term obligations. Suppliers and loan officers are more assured of repayment with a shorter operating cycle.

136 Operating Leverage

DEFINITION. Operating leverage refers to the existence of fixed costs in a company's cost structure, and is used as a measure of operating risk.

HOW IS IT CALCULATED? The following ratios may be used to measure operating leverage:

1. Fixed cost/total cost
2. Percentage change in operating income/percentage change in sales volume, or

$$\frac{\text{Change in profit/profit}}{\text{Change in quantity/quantity}}$$

3. Net income/fixed charges

ANALYTICAL IMPLICATIONS. An increase in (1) and (2) or a decrease in (3) indicates higher fixed charges for a company. This situation indicates greater operating risk for the company, because it will have to meet its fixed cost commitments, which cannot be cut to meet declining sales volume in the short term.

Higher fixed charges also result in greater earnings instability, because high leverage magnifies changes in earnings that result from small changes in sales.

Example 1 Operating leverage is calculated based on data from the following comparative income statements:

	19X0	19X1
Net income	$100,000	$102,000
Fixed cost	40,000	55,000
Variable cost	25,000	27,000
Total cost	65,000	82,000

The company's operating leverage in 19X1 relative to 19X0 was higher, as evidenced by the increase in the ratio of fixed costs to total cost and the decrease in the ratio of the net income to fixed costs.

	19X0	19X1
Fixed cost to total cost	61.5%	67.1 %
Net income to fixed cost	2.5	1.86

Example 2 Financial management wants to evaluate its operating leverage, based on the following data:

Selling price per unit	= $2.00
Fixed cost	= $50,000
Variable cost per unit	= $1.10

Profit is determined as follows:

Sales volume	Dollar sales	−	Fixed costs	−	Variable costs	= Profit
$100,000	$200,000	−	$50,000	−	$110,000	= $40,000
130,000	260,000	−	50,000	−	143,000	= 67,000

The ratio of the percentage change in operating income to the percentage change in sales volume is:

$$\frac{(\$67,000 - \$40,000)/\$40,000}{(130,000 - 100,000)/100,000} = \frac{\$27,000/\$40,000}{30,000/100,000} = \frac{67.5\%}{30.0\%} = 2.25$$

HOW IS IT USED AND BY WHOM?

Financial Management and Financial Analysts. Managers and analysts are interested in knowing the degree of operating leverage of a company. A high operating leverage means greater fixed cost commitments that have to be met even when sales volume declines. Managers and analysts must be aware that high degrees of operating leverage in combination with highly elastic product demand will result in high levels of variability in earnings, although such a condition may be inherent in the industry (e.g., the airline and auto industries).

Financial managers should note that the effects of operating leverage diminish as revenue increases above the breakeven point, since the bases to which increases in earnings are compared become progressively larger. Hence, financial managers should examine the relationship between sales and the breakeven point.

Financial analysts should note that a company with a high breakeven point is quite vulnerable to economic declines. A high ratio of variable cost to total cost indicates greater earnings stability, because variable cost can be adjusted more easily than fixed cost to meet a decline in product demand.

137 Operating Revenue-to-Operating Property Ratio

DEFINITION. The operating revenue-to-operating property ratio is a form of asset turnover, showing the role of fixed assets in generating operating revenues.

HOW IS IT COMPUTED?

$$\text{Operating revenue to operating property} = \frac{\text{total operating revenues}}{\text{operating property}}$$

Example This ratio is computed based on two years of information about a company:

	19X8	19X9
Total operating revenues	$2,543,298	$2,622,402
Operating property	4,189,238	4,235,786

The relevant ratios are:

	19X8	19X9
Operating revenue to operating property	60.71%	61.91%

The increase in the ratio over the year indicates more efficient utilization of operating property in generating revenue—that is, the company has been more productive.

HOW IS IT USED AND APPLIED?
The operating revenue-to-operating property ratio is an important measure for capital-intensive companies such as utilities, as it gives an indication of the ability of investment to generate income. The higher the percentage return, the more productive is the company's operating property.

WHO USES IT AND WHEN?

Financial Analysts, Financial Managers, and Securities Analysts. The ratio is used when trying to measure an entity's operating revenue performance as it relates to its fixed plant. It is also used to assess the debt-financing ability of the business.

138 Opportunity Cost

DEFINITION. Opportunity cost is the revenue forfeited by rejecting an alternative use of time or facilities.

HOW IS IT COMPUTED?

Opportunity cost = annual return rate foregone × fraction of year

× capital invested

Example A company has money tied up in accounts receivable because of a collection problem. The funds tied up for a 3-month period were $400,000. The company earns 10 percent per annum. The opportunity cost is:

$$\$400,000 \times 10\% \times \frac{3}{12} = \$10,000$$

HOW IS IT USED AND BY WHOM?

Management. Management uses opportunity-cost analysis when choosing among alternatives in making decisions. The opportunity cost is a consideration in whether to, for example, increase production, liberalize credit policy, or manufacture a different product. Its significance in decision making is that the best outcome can be sought, since this analysis considers what it would cost if the best available alternative is *not* taken. The opportunity-cost approach is used to solve short-term, nonroutine decision problems.

139 Opportunity Cost of Not Taking a Discount

DEFINITION. The opportunity cost of not taking a discount is the return foregone from an alternative use of funds or time.

HOW IS IT COMPUTED?

$$\text{Opportunity cost of not taking a discount} = \frac{\text{discount foregone}}{\text{use of proceeds}}$$

$$\times \frac{360}{\text{days use of money}}$$

Example A company buys $500,000 of merchandise on credit terms of 2/10, net/30. The company does not pay within 10 days and thus loses the discount. The opportunity cost is:

$$\frac{0.02 \times \$500,000}{0.98 \times \$500,000} \times \frac{360}{20} = \frac{\$10,000}{\$490,000} \times \frac{360}{20} = 36.7\%$$

The analysis of this computation is that financial management would surely have been better off taking advantage of the discount by borrowing $490,000 at the prime interest rate.

HOW IS IT USED AND BY WHOM?

Financial Managers. Financial management can use the formula to determine the opportunity cost of not paying for a purchase within the prescribed discount period. Management can then compare this opportunity cost to the going interest rate for financing.

Creditors. Management that does not take the discount typically shows a lack of financial astuteness, because the cost of paying in full is usually higher than the cost of borrowing money.

140 Payback Period

DEFINITION. The payback period is the number of years it takes to recover an initial investment. Analyzing the payback period of an investment assists in evaluating a project's risk and liquidity.

HOW IS IT COMPUTED?

1. *Payback period.*

$$\text{Payback period} = \frac{\text{initial investment}}{\text{annual cash inflow}}$$

2. *Discounted payback period.* This computation takes into account the time value of money. It is calculated by adding the present value of each year's cash inflows until they equal the initial investment. The payback period will be longer using the discounted method, because money is worth less over time.

3. *Payback reciprocal.* This is the reciprocal of the payback time.

$$\text{Payback reciprocal} = \frac{1}{\text{payback period}}$$

The payback reciprocal gives a quick but accurate estimate of the *internal rate of return* (*IRR*) on an investment when the project life is more than twice the payback period and the cash inflows are uniform during every period.

Example 1 A company is considering offering a new product, which will initially cost the company $250,000. Expected cash inflows are $80,000 for the next 5 years. The company wants its money back in 4 years. The payback analysis is as follows:

$$\text{Payback period} = \frac{\text{initial investment}}{\text{annual cash inflow}} = \frac{\$250,000}{\$80,000} = 3.125$$

Because the payback period (3.125) is less than the cutoff payback period (4), the company should offer the new product.

Example 2 A company invests $40,000 and receives the following cash inflows:

Year 1	$15,000
Year 2	$20,000
Year 3	$28,000

$$\$35,000 + \frac{\$5,000}{\$28,000}$$

$$2 \text{ years} + 0.18 = 2.18 \text{ years}$$

$$\text{Payback period} = 2.18 \text{ years}$$

If there are unequal cash inflows each year, to determine the payback period, add up the annual cash inflows to determine the amount of the cash outlay. The answer is the length it takes to recover the initial investment.

Example 3 Assume the same facts as in Example 2 and a cost of capital of 10 percent. Then

$$\text{Discounted payback} = \frac{\text{initial cash outlay}}{\text{discounted annual cash inflows}}$$

Year 1		Year 2		Year 3
$15,000	+	$20,000	+	$28,000
× 0.9091		× 0.8264		× 0.7513
$13,637	+	$16,528	+	$21,036

$$\$30,165 + \frac{\$9835}{\$21,036}$$

$$2 \text{ years} + 0.47 = 2.47 \text{ years}$$

HOW IS IT USED AND BY WHOM?

Management. The payback period is one of the methods management uses to select among alternative proposals. A shorter payback period is desirable because it indicates less risk, improved liquidity, and faster rate of return. A benefit of payback is that it permits companies that have a cash problem to evaluate the turnover of scarce resources in order to recover those funds invested more quickly.

Some believe that payback should not be used in unstable, uncertain industries subject to rapid technological change because the future is so unpredictable that there is no point in guessing what cash flows will be more than 2 years from the present.

Advantages of payback are that it is easy to use and understand, handles investment risk effectively, and can be used as a supplement to other, more sophisticated techniques since it does indicate risk.

Deficiencies of payback analysis are that it ignores the time value of money, does not consider cash flows received after the payback period, and does not measure profitability.

141 Pension Formulas

DEFINITION. A pension plan is a contractual agreement in which the employer provides benefits to employees upon retirement. Pension plan formulas assist in determining the employer's cost and the funding of pension benefits.

HOW IS IT COMPUTED?

1. Pension expense equals:
   + Service cost (pension expense assigned for services rendered in the current year)
   + Amortization of prior service cost (pension expense assigned for services rendered before the adoption of the plan)
   − Return on pension plan assets (return rate multiplied by the fair value of plan assets at the beginning of the year.)
   + Interest on projected benefit obligation (interest rate multiplied by the projected benefit obligation at the beginning of the year. The projected benefit obligation is the present value of future pension benefits based on expected future salary levels.)
   − or + Actuarial gains or losses (difference between estimates and actual experience)

2. Deferred pension liability = pension expense exceeds cash funded
   Deferred pension asset = pension expense is less than cash funded

3. Accumulated benefit obligation—12/31
   Less: fair value of pension plan assets—12/31
   Minimum pension liability
   Less: deferred pension liability
   Additional pension liability

   Note: Accumulated benefit obligation is the present value of future pension benefits based on current salary levels.

Example The following company information is used to analyze the company's pension plan for 19X5:

Service cost	$ 800,000
Prior service cost—1/1/19X5	2,000,000
Amortization period for prior service cost is 10 years	
Fair market value of pension plan assets—1/1/19X5	4,000,000
Fair market value of pension plan assets—12/31/19X5	4,300,000
Projected benefit obligation—1/1/19X5	6,000,000
Accumulated benefit obligation—12/31/19X5	5,000,000
Actuarial gain	50,000
Funding for the period	1,000,000
Return rate	10%
Interest rate	12%

Pension expense to the company is calculated as follows:

Service cost		$ 800,000
Amortization expense on prior service cost ($2,000,000/10)		200,000
Return on plan assets ($4,000,000 × 10%)		(400,000)
Interest on projected benefit obligation ($6,000,000 × 12%)		720,000
Actuarial gain		50,000
Pension expense		$1,370,000
Deferred pension liability = pension expense – cash funded ($1,370,000 – $1,000,000)	$370,000	
Accumulated benefit obligation—12/31/19X5		$5,000,000
Less: Fair market value of pension plan assets—12/31/19X5		4,300,000
Minimum pension liability		$ 700,000
Less: Deferred pension liability		370,000
Additional pension liability		$ 330,000

HOW IS IT USED AND BY WHOM?

Management and Pension Officers. Management wants to know its pension cost, since this represents a major expense to the company, and pension expense is tax deductible. Management needs to ask if there are adequate corporate funds to satisfy pension requirements. Depending on the pension cost, the company may want to alter its pension policy and requirements, and move toward larger employee contributions. It is critical to understand if there is inadequate pension funding, since this would show the liability exposure of the company.

142 Percent Earned on Operating Property

DEFINITION. The percent earned on operating property relates net earnings to a company's assets (for example, net property and plant).

HOW IS IT COMPUTED?

$$\text{Percent earned on operating property} = \frac{\text{net income}}{\text{operating property}}$$

Example The ratio is computed based on the following information:

	19X2	19X3
Net income	$ 543,298	$ 622,402
Operating property	$4,189,238	$4,235,786

The percent earned on operating property is 12.96% for 19X2 and 14.69% for 19X3. The increase in the ratio between 19X2 and 19X3 is favorable because it indicates a greater return being earned on operating property, demonstrating improved productivity.

HOW IS IT USED AND BY WHOM?

Financial Analysts and Financial Management. The ratio measures a company's profit performance as it relates to operating assets. It is also used to assess debt-financing capability.

143 Percent-of-Sales Method for Financial Forecasting

DEFINITION. Percentage of sales is the most widely used method for projecting a company's financing needs. This method involves estimating the various expenses, assets, and liabilities for a future period as a percent of the sales forecast and then using these percentages, together with the projected sales, to construct pro-forma balance sheets.

Forecasts of future sales and their related expenses provide the firm with the information needed to project its future needs for financing.

HOW IS IT COMPUTED? The basic steps involved in projecting financing needs are as follows:

1. Project the firm's sales. The sales forecast is the most important initial step. Most other forecasts (budgets) follow the sales forecast.

2. Project additional variables such as expenses.

3. Estimate the level of investment in current and fixed assets required to support the projected sales.

4. Calculate the firm's financing needs.

The following example illustrates how to develop a pro-forma balance sheet and determine the amount of external financing needed.

Example 1 Assume that sales for 19X1 = $20, projected sales for 19X2 = $24, net income = 5 percent of sales, and the dividend payout ratio = 40 percent. The steps for the computations are outlined as follows, with the results shown in Exhibit 143.1:

Step 1: Express those balance sheet items that vary directly with sales as a percentage of sales. Any item such as long-term debt that does not vary directly with sales is designated "n.a.," or "not applicable."

Step 2: Multiply these percentages by the 19X2 projected sales, $24, to obtain the projected amounts as shown in the last column.

Step 3: Insert figures for long-term debt, common stock, and paid-in-capital from the 19X1 balance sheet.

Step 4: Compute 19X2 retained earnings as shown in Note *b.*

Step 5: Sum the asset accounts, obtaining total projected assets of $7.2, and also add projected liabilities and equity to obtain $7.12, the total fi-

Exhibit 143.1 Pro-forma balance sheet (in millions of dollars).

	Present (19X1)	Percent of Sales (19X1 Sales = $20)	Projected (19X2 Sales = $24)	
Assets				
Current assets	$2.0	10	$24 × 10% = $2.4	
Fixed assets	4.0	20	4.8	
Total assets	$6.0		$7.2	
Liabilities and stockholders' equity				
Current liabilities	$2.0	10	$2.4	
Long-term debt	2.5	n.a.[a]	2.5	
Total liabilities	$4.5		$4.9	
Common stock	$0.1	n.a.[a]	$0.1	
Paid-in-capital	0.2	n.a.[a]	0.2	
Retained earnings	1.2		1.92[b]	
Total equity	$1.5		$2.22	
Total liabilities and stockholders' equity	$6.0		$7.12	Total financing provided
			0.08[c]	External financing needed
			$7.2	Total

Notes:
[a]Not applicable. These figures are assumed not to vary with sales.
[b]19X2 retained earnings   = 19X1 retained earnings + projected net income − cash dividends paid
     = $1.2 + 5%($24) − 40%[5%($24)]
     = $1.2 + $1.2 − $0.48 = $2.4 − $0.48 = $1.92
[c]External financing needed = (projected total liabilities + projected equity)
     = $7.2 − ($4.9 + $2.22) = $7.2 − $7.12 = $0.08.

nancing provided. Since liabilities and equity must total $7.2, but only $7.12 is projected, there is a shortfall of $0.08 "external financing needed."

Short-Cut Formula. Although the forecast of additional funds required can be made by setting up a pro-forma balance sheet as described above, it is often easier to use the following formula:

External funds needed (EFN) = Required increase in assets

     − Spontaneous increase in liabilities − Increase in retained earnings

$$\text{EFN} = \left(\frac{A}{S}\right)\Delta S - \left(\frac{L}{S}\right)\Delta S - (\text{PM})(\text{PS})(1 - d)$$

where A/S = assets that increase spontaneously with sales as a percentage of sales

L/S = liabilities that increase spontaneously with sales as a percentage of sales

ΔS = change in sales

PM = profit margin on sales

PS = projected sales

d = dividend payout ratio

Example 2 For the data in Example 1,

$$\frac{A}{S} = \frac{\$6}{\$20} = 30\%$$

$$\frac{L}{S} = \frac{\$2}{\$20} = 10\%$$

$$\Delta S = \$24 - \$20 = \$4$$

$$PM = 5\% \text{ on sales}$$

$$PS = \$24$$

$$d = 40\%$$

Plugging these figures into the formula yields:

$$EFN = 0.3(\$4) - 0.1(\$4) - (0.05)(\$24)(1 - 0.4)$$

$$= \$1.2 - \$0.4 - \$0.72 = \$0.08$$

Thus, the amount of external financing needed is $800,000, which can be raised by issuing notes payable, bonds, stocks, or any combination of these financing sources.

HOW IS IT USED AND APPLIED?   The major advantage of the percent-of-sales method of financial forecasting is that it is simple and inexpensive to use. To obtain a more precise projection of the firm's future financing needs, however, the preparation of a cash budget is required. One important assumption behind the use of the method is that the firm is operating at full capacity. This means that the company has not sufficient productive capacity to absorb a projected increase in sales, requiring an additional investment in assets.

WHO USES IT AND WHEN?

Financial Officers.   Financial officers need to determine the next year's funding requirements in particular, the portion that must be raised externally. This way management can have a head start in arranging a least-cost financing plan.

144 Personal Debt to Personal Assets

DEFINITION.   The ratio of total debt to total assets is used to determine how much of an individual's assets is financed.

HOW IS IT COMPUTED?

$$\frac{\text{Personal debt}}{\text{Personal assets}}$$

Example An individual's total liabilities are $30,000, and his total assets are $50,000. The debt/asset ratio is 0.60. This means that for every $0.60 in total debt, the person has total assets of $1. A lower ratio is preferred, since it is better not to owe too much money. A lower ratio would also be preferable if the market value of the person's assets fluctuates greatly.

HOW IS IT USED AND BY WHOM?

Individuals. The ratio is used in personal financial planning. If debt exceeds assets, a person may have difficulty paying bills. This may ultimately lead to personal bankruptcy and result in a devastating effect on the individual's credit rating.

Lenders. If an individual is already "over his head" in debt, a lender may be reluctant to extend additional credit.

145 Portfolio Theory

DEFINITION. Most financial assets are not held in isolation but are held as part of a portfolio. Therefore, risk-return analysis should not be confined to single assets only. It is important to know the expected return on the portfolio (not just the return on one asset) and the level of the portfolio's risk.

HOW IS IT COMPUTED? The expected return on a portfolio (r_p) is the weighted-average return of the individual securities in the portfolio, the weights being the fraction of the total funds invested in each asset. The formula is:

$$r_p = w_1 r_1 + w_2 r_2 + \cdots + w_n r_n$$

$$= \sum w_j r_j$$

where the r_j's are the expected returns in individual securities, the w's are the fractions, n is the number of assets in the portfolio, and $\Sigma w_j = 1.0$.

Example 1 A portfolio consists of assets A and B. Asset A makes up one-third of the portfolio and has an expected return of 18 percent. Asset B makes up the other two-thirds of the portfolio and is expected to earn 9 percent. What is the expected return on the portfolio?

Asset	Return (r_j)	Fraction (w_j)	$w_j r_j$
A	18%	$\frac{1}{3}$	$\frac{1}{3} \times 18\% = 6\%$
B	9%	$\frac{2}{3}$	$\frac{2}{3} \times 9\% = 6\%$
			$r_p = 12\%$

Unlike returns, the riskiness of a portfolio (σ_p) is not simply a weighted average of the standard deviations of the individual securities in the portfolio. In a two-asset portfolio, the portfolio risk is defined as:

$$\sigma_p = \sqrt{W_A^2\sigma_A^2 + W_B^2\sigma_B^2 + 2W_A \cdot W_B \cdot \rho_{AB} \cdot \sigma_A \cdot \sigma_B}$$

where σ_A and σ_B are the standard deviations of the possible returns from security A and security B, respectively; W_A and W_B are the weights of fractions of total funds invested in security A and security B; and ρ_{AB} is the correlation coefficient between security A and security B. By the way, the correlation coefficient is the measurement of joint movement between two securities.

Example 2 Assume the following:

Asset	σ	w
A	20%	⅓
B	10%	⅔

The portfolio risk is then:

$$\sigma_p = \sqrt{W_A^2\sigma_A^2 + W_B^2\sigma_B^2 + 2W_A \cdot W_B \cdot \rho_{AB} \cdot \sigma_A \cdot \sigma_B}$$

$$= \sqrt{(⅓)^2(0.2)^2 + (⅔)^2(0.1)^2 + 2\rho_{AB}(⅓)(⅔)(0.2)(0.1)}$$

$$= \sqrt{0.0089 + 0.0089\rho_{AB}}$$

(a) Now assume that the correlation coefficient between A and B is $+1$ (a perfectly positive correlation)—that is, when the value of asset A increases in response to market conditions, the value of asset B follows at exactly the same rate as asset A. The portfolio risk when $\rho = +1$ then becomes:

$$\sigma_p = \sqrt{0.0089 + 0.0089\rho_{AB}} = \sqrt{0.0089 + 0.0089(1)} = \sqrt{0178} = 0.1334 = 13.34\%$$

(b) If $\rho = 0$, the assets lack correlation and the portfolio risk is simply the risk of the expected returns on the assets, i.e., the weighted average of the standard deviations of the individual assets in the portfolio. Therefore, when $\rho_{AB} = 0$, the portfolio risk for this example is:

$$\sigma_p = \sqrt{0.0089 + 0.0089\rho_{AB}} = \sqrt{0.0089 + 0.0089(0)} = \sqrt{0.0089} = 0.0943$$

$$= 9.43\%$$

(c) If $\rho = -1$ (a perfectly negative correlation coefficient), then as the price of A rises, the price of B declines at the very same rate. In such a case, risk is completely eliminated. Therefore, when $\rho_{AB} = -1$, the portfolio risk is

$$\sigma_p = \sqrt{0.0089 + 0.0089\rho_{AB}} = \sqrt{0.0089 + 0.0089(-1)} = \sqrt{0.0089 - 0.0089}$$

$$= 0 = 0$$

When we compare the results of (a), (b), and (c), a positive correlation between assets is seen to increase a portfolio's risk above the level found at zero correlation, while a perfectly negative correlation eliminates that risk.

As can be seen in the formula, the portfolio risk—measured in terms of σ_p— is not the weighted average of the individual asset risks in the portfolio.

The third term in the formula (ρ_{AB}) makes a significant contribution to the overall portfolio risk.

The formula basically shows that the portfolio risk can be minimized or completely eliminated by diversification. The degree of reduction in portfolio risk depends on the correlation between the assets being combined. Generally speaking, by combining two perfectly negatively correlated assets ($\rho = -1.0$), risk can be eliminated completely. In the real world, however, most securities are negatively, but not perfectly, correlated.

In fact, in the real world, most assets are positively correlated. The portfolio risk can still be reduced by combining even positively correlated assets.

Example 3 To illustrate the point of diversification, assume that data on the following three securities are as follows:

Year	Security X (%)	Security Y (%)	Security Z (%)
19X1	10	50	10
19X2	20	40	20
19X3	30	30	30
19X4	40	20	40
19X5	50	10	50
r_j	30	30	30
σ	14.14	14.14	14.14

Note here that securities X and Y have a perfectly negative correlation, and securities X and Z have a perfectly positive correlation. Notice what happens to the portfolio risk when X and Y and X and Z are combined. Assume that funds are split equally between the two securities in each portfolio.

Year	Portfolio XY (50%–50%)	Portfolio XZ (50%–50%)
19X1	30	10
19X2	30	20
19X3	30	30
19X4	30	40
19X5	30	50
r_p	30	30
σ_p	0	14.14

Again, the two perfectly negative correlated securities (XY) result in a zero overall risk.

The central theme of portfolio theory is that rational investors behave in a way reflecting their aversion to taking increased risk without being compensated by an adequate increase in expected return. Also, for any given expected return, most investors will prefer a lower risk and, for any given level of risk, a higher return to a lower return.

Markowitz showed how to calculate a set of "efficient" portfolios. Investors try to find the optimum portfolio by using the indifference curve, which shows the investor's trade-off between risk and return. By matching the indifference curve showing the risk-return trade-off with the best investments available in the market as represented by points on the efficient frontier, investors are able to find an optimum portfolio.

HOW IS IT USED AND APPLIED?   For even a moderate-sized portfolio, the formulas for portfolio return and risk require estimation of a large number of input data. Concern with the computational burden in deriving these estimates led to the development of the following *Sharpe's market index model:*

$$r_j = a + br_m$$

where r_j = return on security j
  r_m = return on the market portfolio
  b = beta or systematic risk of a security

Beta is a measure of systematic (or uncontrollable) risk. It is widely used to measure the volatility of a stock or mutual fund. (See also No. 19, Beta, and No. 116, Market-Index Model.)

WHO USES IT AND WHEN?

Investors and Financial Analysts.   Investors use beta to measure the risk of a security or mutual fund. Generally speaking, the higher the beta, the higher is the uncontrollable risk.

146 Preferred Stock to Total Stockholders' Equity

DEFINITION.   Preferred stock to total stockholders' equity shows the percentage of stockholder equity that is comprised of preferred stock.

HOW IS IT COMPUTED?

$$\frac{\text{Preferred stock}}{\text{Total stockholders' equity}}$$

Example   A company reports the following information pertaining to stockholders' equity:

	19X1	19X2
Preferred stock	$ 300,000	$1,000,000
Total stockholders' equity	3,000,000	4,000,000

The ratio of preferred stock to total stockholders' equity is therefore 10 percent for 19X1 and 25 percent for 19X2.

This analysis shows that the company had a substantial increase in preferred stock relative to total stockholders' equity in 19X2, which could imply that the company is having difficulty floating its common stock in the marketplace. Perhaps stockholders want more security because they know preferred stock has preference over common stock in liquidation and in the distribution of earnings.

HOW IS IT USED AND BY WHOM?

Investment Analysts. If a company issues preferred stock for the first time or if it issues substantial preferred stock in the current year, this action may indicate that the company has problems when issuing its common stock. This is a negative sign, since the investing public may be viewing the company's common stock as too risky.

Financial Management. If a company's convertible preferred stock is converted into common stock, this action means that preferred stockholders are optimistic about the company. This will result, however, in a drop in market price of common stock as more shares are issued. On the plus side, the company will be able to omit the dividend payment on preferred stock.

147 Present Value

DEFINITION. Present value is a method for determining the current value of money based on a future yield; it is also called discounting. The concept of present value assumes that money received or paid out in the future is not worth as much as money today. Investing a discrete value of money necessarily implies an opportunity cost. Thus, given some future value, FV_n, what is the equivalent value of money today or its present value, PV?

HOW IS IT COMPUTED? Financial calculators offered by several manufacturers calculate present value. In addition, it is incorporated as a built-in function in spreadsheet programs such as Lotus 1-2-3.

1   Universal Formula. The formula for computing present value is:

$$PV = FV_n \frac{1}{(1 + i)^n}$$
$$= FV_n \cdot \text{PVIF}(i,n)$$

where i = interest rate per time period
$\quad n$ = number of years
$\quad PV$ = principal amount at the present time
$\quad FV_n$ = future (compound) value at the end of year n
$\quad \text{PVIF}$ = present-value interest factor (see below)

2   Present-Value Interest Factors (PVIFs). Using PVIFs, available in tables, simplifies the computation of present value by eliminating the necessity of determining the reciprocals of the future (compound)-value interest factors, $1/(1 + i)^n$. Table PVIFs will be used in this discussion (see Table 3 in the Appendix). The formula for using PVIFs is:

$$PV = FV_n \times \text{PVIF}(i,n)$$

where PVIF = present-value interest factor for $1 at interest rate i for n years

Example 1 An individual has an opportunity to receive $30,000 four years from now. The interest rate is 12 percent. The most that should be paid for this investment is:

$$PV = FV_n \times \text{PVIF}(i,n)$$
$$= \$30,000 \times 0.6355$$
$$= \$19,065$$

Example 2 An individual borrows $10,000 today and will repay $15,387 in 5 years. The individual wants to know the interest rate being charged before the decision is made to accept the money:

$$PV = FV_n \times \text{PVIF}(i,n)$$
$$\$10,000 = \$15,387 \times \text{PVIF}(i,5)$$
$$\frac{\$10,000}{\$15,387} = \text{PVIF}(i,5)$$
$$0.6499 = \text{PVIF}(i,5)$$

Reading across the 5-year row in the present-value interest factor of $1 table, 0.6499 is found in the 9 percent column. Thus, the effective interest rate on the loan is 9 percent per year, compounded annually.

HOW IS IT USED AND APPLIED? The determination of the present value of money is crucial in evaluating the choice of a future investment. It is also used in the discounting process to determine the rate of interest actually being charged on a loan or other financing arrangement. The number of periods involved in a financing situation may also be computed.

WHO USES IT AND WHEN?

Managers and Financial Analysts. Present-value analysis is used to assess the financial attractiveness of investments. This important technique is used in making capital budgeting decisions to select the optimum alternative long-term investment opportunity. It helps to identify where money should be placed, whether leasing or buying is the best option, whether a business should be kept or sold, a new product introduced, or equipment replaced with new equipment. Time-value-of-money analysis compares proposals on the same basis, converting everything into present value (year 0) dollars, so that the proposal with the highest present value is identified.

Individuals. Present-value tables are used to make financial decisions when there are competing choices such as which job to take or whether to seek graduate education.

148 Present Value of an Annuity

DEFINITION. The present value of an annuity is a method of discounting an annuity to determine its worth in present-day dollars. It shows the amount of the lump-sum payment that would have to be received today to equal the annuity.

This analysis accommodates two types of annuities—ordinary annuities in which the equal payment comes at the end of the year, and annuities due in which the equal payment is made at the beginning of the year.

ORDINARY ANNUITY

How Is It Computed?   Financial calculators offered by several manufacturers calculate present value. In addition, it is incorporated as a built-in function in spreadsheet programs such as Lotus 1-2-3.

The formulas for the computation of the present value of an ordinary annuity are as follows:

1. Long method:

$$PVA = A\left(\frac{1}{1+i}\right) + A\left(\frac{1}{1+i}\right)^2 + \cdots + A\left(\frac{1}{1+i}\right)^n$$

where PVA = present value of an annuity for an interest rate and time period (PVIFA)
A = amount of periodic payment
i = interest rate

2. Short method:

$$PVA = A \times PVIFA(i,n)$$

The present-value interest factor for an annuity (PVIFA) is a simplification of the long formula and relies on accessing a table (see Table 4 in the Appendix) that provides these factors for the present value of an annuity of $1 per period for n periods. Use of this formula eliminates the need to determine the reciprocals of the compound value interest factors, $1/(1 + i)^n$; it will be used in this discussion.

Example 1   Judy has been offered a 5-year annuity of $2000 a year or a lump-sum payment today. Since Judy wants to invest the money in a security paying 10 percent interest, she decides to take the lump-sum payment today. How large should the lump-sum payment be to equal the 5-year, $2000 annual annuity at 10 percent interest?

Using the present-value interest factor for an ordinary annuity (PVIFA) of 5 years paying 10 percent interest provides an easy solution:

$$PVA = A \times PVIFA(i,n) = \$2000 \times PVIFA(10\%, 5 \text{ years})$$
$$= \$2000 \times 3.79908$$
$$= \$7598.16$$

The lump-sum payment today for Judy should be $7598.16 to equal the 5-year, $2000 annual annuity at 10 percent interest.

ANNUITY DUE

How Is It Computed?   The formula for the computation of the present value of an annuity due must take into consideration one additional year of compounding since the payment occurs at the beginning of the year. Therefore, the future value formula must be modified as follows:

1. Long method:

$$PVA = [A\left(\frac{1}{1+i}\right) + A\left(\frac{1}{1+i}\right)^2 + \cdots + A\left(\frac{1}{1+i}\right)^n](1 + i)$$

2. Short method:

$$PVA = A \times PVIFA(i,n)(1 + i)$$

using the present-value interest factor for an annuity (PVIFA).

Example 2 Using the same information as in the previous example and the present-value interest factor for an annuity (PVIFA) of 5 years paying 10 percent interest modified for an annuity due:

$PVA = A \times PVIFA(i,n)(1 + i) = \$2000 \times PVIFA(10\%, 5 \text{ years}) (1 + 0.1)$

$\quad = \$2000 \times 3.79908 \times 1.10$

$\quad = \$8357.97$

PRESENT-VALUE DIFFERENCE BETWEEN ORDINARY ANNUITY AND ANNUITY DUE. The present-value difference between an ordinary annuity and an annuity due is substantial. In the above examples, the difference is $8357.97 - $7598.16 = $759.81. Generally, an annuity due is preferable over an ordinary annuity, since an additional year of compounding is essentially received.

HOW IS IT USED AND APPLIED? Present value of an annuity is used to compute what an annuity is worth in today's money at a particular rate of interest for a designated time period. Present value of an annuity is also used to determine the equal annual payment, interest rate, and the length of time.

WHO USES IT AND WHEN?

Managers. Present-value-of-annuity computations enable selection of the best mutually exclusive proposal or project, revealing which alternative is most financially advantageous. It can be applied to situations involving loans, leases, equity or debt investments, capital expansion, product-line selection, and so forth.

Consumers. Annuities and their current worth are important to look at when analyzing pension plans, insurance policies, and investments. Present value enables determination of the price to pay for an investment, such as a bond that pays semiannual interest. Discounting applications also reveal the interest rate that is being charged on a loan, and the number of years necessary to pay off that loan.

149 "Pressing" Current Liabilities to "Patient" Current Liabilities

DEFINITION. "Pressing" current to "patient" current liabilities is a ratio that describes the degree of flexibility that a company has in regard to meeting it debt payment. "Pressing" liabilities are those that must be paid without excuse, such as taxes and loans payable. "Patient" liabilities are those that offer some flexibility when corporate financial difficulties exist (e.g., accounts payable). For example, in times of corporate financial difficulty, the supplier may postpone or even modify the amount of the debt.

HOW IS IT COMPUTED?

$$\frac{\text{Pressing current liabilities}}{\text{Patient current liabilities}}$$

Example Assume that a company's current liabilities are comprised of the following:

	19X1	19X2
Accounts payable	$400,000	$350,000
Taxes payable	50,000	60,000
Bank loans payable	200,000	220,000
Commercial paper	50,000	60,000

The ratios of pressing debt to patient debt are:

	19X1	19X2
"Pressing" debt to "patient" debt	$\dfrac{\$300,000}{\$400,000} = 0.75$	$\dfrac{\$340,000}{\$350,000} = 0.97$

The higher ratio of pressing to patient short-term debt indicates that the company has greater liquidity risk in the second year than in the first.

HOW IS IT USED AND BY WHOM?

Financial Managers. If more "pressing" current liabilities exist, a potential problem could occur during times of financial adversity, because short-term creditors would demand to be paid. Loan agreements, for example, may stipulate that the principal of the loan will be paid even if an interest payment is not. On the other hand, having more "patient" current liabilities will work to the company's advantage, as it irons out renegotiated payment arrangements.

Short-Term Creditors. If the company has many "pressing" current liabilities, there is less chance of a short-term creditor being paid on time; thus, creditors must monitor the trend in this ratio.

150 Price-to-Book Value Ratio

DEFINITION. The ratio of price to book value compares the market price of a stock to its book value.

HOW IS IT COMPUTED?

$$\frac{\text{Market price per share}}{\text{Book value per share}}$$

Market price is based on current prices, whereas book value is based on historical prices. Market price per share should generally be higher than book value per share, as a result of inflation and good corporate performance over the years.

Example A company's market price per share is $20 and its book value per share is $25. The price-to-book value ratio is:

$$\frac{\$20}{\$25} = 0.8$$

The analytical implication of this low ratio may be that the company has not been performing well. If analysts see that a company's market price is below its book value, the situation could suggest that the company is having financial and operating problems. Some analysts, however, feel a buying opportunity may exist when book value is above market price, because the company stock may be undervalued.

HOW IS IT USED AND BY WHOM?

Financial Management. A higher ratio is more desirable, since it shows that the stock market places a high value on the company. In some businesses, the book value per share may typically be higher than the market price per share, such as the case for many banks.

Investors. If investors believe that the market price of a company is too high relative to its book value, they may sell the stock; alternatively, if they feel that the stock is undervalued in the market, investors will be encouraged to buy stock.

151 Price–Earnings Ratio (Multiple)

DEFINITION. The price–earnings (P/E) ratio (also called the P/E multiple, or the earnings multiplier) is a company's market price per share divided by its earnings per share. It reflects the company's relationship to its stockholders.

HOW IS IT COMPUTED?

$$\text{Price-earnings ratio} = \frac{\text{market price per share}}{\text{earnings per share}}$$

A high P/E multiple for a company is good because it indicates that the investing public considers the company in a favorable light. A steady decrease in the P/E ratio reflects decreasing investor confidence in the growth potential of the company.

The P/E ratio varies among companies in an industry as well as among companies in different industries; thus, a company's price-earnings ratios should be compared to the P/E ratios of competing companies in the same industry to obtain a relative measure of comparison. Some companies have P/E multiples, reflecting high earnings growth expectations. Young, fast-growing companies often have high-P/E stocks, with multiples over 20.

The P/E ratio of a company is listed in financial advisory reports and in the financial pages of daily newspapers, notably *The Wall Street Journal*. In April 1990, some P/E ratios of Fortune 500 companies were:

American Telephone and Telegraph	16
General Electric	14
General Motors	7

Industry P/E ratios may also be found in financial advisory services such as Standard and Poors, Moody's, and Robert Morris Associates.

Example Assume that the market price per share of stock is $20 and $24, respectively, for the years 19X8 and 19X9. The earnings per share for those years are $2 and $3, respectively. The price-earnings ratios are computed as follows:

		19X8	19X9
P/E ratio =	$\dfrac{\text{market price per share}}{\text{earnings per share}}$	$\dfrac{\$20}{\$2} = 10$	$\dfrac{\$24}{\$3} = 8$

The decline in the price-earnings ratio in this case from 10 to 8 may have one or more of the following implications:

- Investors have less confidence in the company. Possible reasons are the company's deteriorating financial health (e.g., declining growth rate, negative cash flow), increased risk and instability, industry-wide problems, management problems, negative economic situation, and adverse political environment.
- The company's earnings may have been overstated (poor quality of earnings) and thus are discounted by investors.

WHO USES IT AND WHEN?

Investors. The P/E ratio is useful in appraising the investment potential of a company—for example, investors may use it in deciding whether or not to invest in the company. Investors also use the P/E ratio as an indicator of how the company's stock price is performing.

Some investors believe that if a company's P/E ratio is too low relative to its industry, the stock may be undervalued and represent an acquisition opportunity. A high P/E ratio is desirable because it indicates that investors highly value a company's earnings. On the other hand, some investors believe that if the P/E ratio is too high relative to industry averages, the stock may be overvalued and should be sold. Of course, many other financial and economic factors have to be taken into account in making this decision.

Financial Analysts. Financial analysts who believe that the company will generate future profit at higher levels than at present may value the stock higher than its current earnings may justify.

Management. Management is interested in the P/E ratio to determine how the company is perceived by the investing public.

152 Price (Rate, Spending) Variance

DEFINITION. The price (rate, spending) variance compares the difference between the standard price and actual price for materials issued to production or labor hours incurred.

HOW IS IT COMPUTED?

Price variance = (actual price versus standard price) × actual quantity

The price variance may be computed for materials and labor.

Example Assume the following company standards:

Direct material: 5 pounds @ $4 per pound	$20 per unit
Direct labor: 3 hours @ $12 per hour	$36 per unit

Company volumes are:

Production	9,800 units
Purchases: 50,000 pounds @ $3	$150,000
Direct labor: 22,000 hours @ $10	$220,000

The material price variance is:

$$(\$3 \text{ versus } \$4) \times 50{,}000 = \$50{,}000 \quad \text{Favorable}$$

The labor price variance is:

$$(\$10 \text{ versus } \$12) \times 22{,}000 = \$44{,}000 \quad \text{Favorable}$$

HOW IS IT USED AND BY WHOM?

Management, Purchasing Managers, and Personnel Directors. Management uses the material price variance to evaluate the activity of its purchasing department and to understand the impact of raw material cost changes on company profitability. To correct for an unfavorable material price variance, management can increase selling price, substitute cheaper materials, change a production method or specification, or engage in a cost-reduction program. Management cannot control material price variances when higher prices are the result of inflation or market shortages.

Where salary rates are set by union contract, the labor price variance will usually be minimal, since the standard labor rate is based on the contracted hourly wage rate. Possible reasons for a labor price variance include the following:

Reason	Party responsible
Use of overpaid or excessive number of workers	Production manager or union contract
Poor job descriptions	Personnel
Overtime	Production planning

If there is a shortage of skilled workers, it may be impossible to avoid an unfavorable labor price variance.

153 Profit Margin

DEFINITION. The profit margin reveals the profitability generated from sales. Profit is typically expressed in terms of net income and gross profit. Profit may be improved by generating additional revenue or by cutting costs.

HOW IS IT COMPUTED?

1. $\text{Net profit margin} = \dfrac{\text{net income}}{\text{net sales}}$

2. $\text{Gross profit margin} = \dfrac{\text{gross profit}}{\text{net sales}}$

$$\text{Gross profit} = \text{sales} - \text{cost of sales}$$

Profit margin may vary greatly within an industry, because it is subject to sales, cost controls, and pricing.

Example Analysis of a company's profit margin is based on the following information:

	19X2	19X3
Gross profit	$15,000	$20,000
Net income	8,000	9,600
Sales	65,000	80,000

Relevant ratios are:

	19X2	19X3
Net profit margin	0.12	0.12
Gross profit margin	0.23	0.25

The net profit margin is shown to be constant, indicating that the earning power of the business has remained static. The improvement in gross profit is probably due to increased sales and/or better control of cost of sales. A lack of control in operating expenses is most likely the reason that gross profit margin is up but net profit margin is constant, even though sales have increased.

HOW IS IT USED AND BY WHOM?

Financial Management. The profit margin indicates the success of management in generating earnings from its operations. The higher the profit margin on each sales dollar generated, the better the company is doing financially. Profit may also be increased by controlling expenses. A high profit margin is desirable because it indicates that the company is earning a good return on its cost of merchandise sold and operating expenses.

Investors and Creditors. By examining a company's profit margin relative to previous years and to industry norms, one can evaluate the company's operating efficiency and pricing strategy as well as its competitive status within the industry. The ratio of income to sales is important to investors and creditors because it indicates the financial success of the business. The "bottom line" is what counts. Profit margin reveals the entity's ability to generate earnings at a particular sales level.

Investors will be reluctant to invest in an entity with poor earning potential, since the market price of stock and future dividends will be adversely affected. Creditors will also shy away from companies with deficient profitability, since the amounts owed to them may not be paid.

154 Profitability Index

DEFINITION. The profitability index is used to differentiate the net present values of competing proposals. It compares the initial cash investment to the discounted value of future net cash inflows. The index is used to rank projects in order of their attractiveness.

HOW IS IT COMPUTED?

$$\text{Profitability index} = \frac{\text{present value of cash inflows}}{\text{present value of cash outflows}}$$

Rule of thumb: Accept a proposal with a profitability index equal to or greater than 1. If the index is less than 1, the company is losing money on the proposal.

Warning: A higher profitability index does not always coincide with the project with the higher net present value. Thus, it eliminates the distortive effect of size.

Example 1 Assume that the following information is provided about two proposals:

	Proposal A	Proposal B
Initial investment	$100,000	$10,000
Present value of cash inflows	500,000	90,000

The net present value of Proposal A is $400,000 and that of Proposal B is $80,000. Based on net present value, Proposal A appears better than Proposal B; however, this would be an incorrect conclusion, because a budget constraint exists. The profitability index should be used in evaluating proposals when budget constraints exist. In this case, Proposal B's profitability index of 9 far surpasses Proposal A's index of 5. The net result is that Proposal B should be selected over Proposal A.

Example 2 A *contingent proposal* is one that requires acceptance of another, related proposal. Hence, the proposals must be looked at together, and a profitability index should be computed for the group, as indicated below:

Project	Investment	Present value	Profitability	Index ranking
A	$ 70,000	$112,000	1.6	1
B	100,000	145,000	1.45	2
C	110,000	126,500	1.15	5
D	60,000	79,000	1.32	3
E	40,000	38,000	0.95	6
F	80,000	95,000	1.19	4

The budget constraint is $250,000. Projects A, B, and D should be selected, as indicated by the following calculations.

Project	Investment	Present value
A	$ 70,000	$112,000
B	100,000	145,000
D	60,000	79,000
	$230,000	$336,000

where net present value = $336,000 − $230,000 = $106,000

Example 3 Consider the following proposals:

Proposal	Present value of cash outflow	Present value of cash inflow
A	$160,000	$210,000
B	60,000	40,000
Total	$220,000	$250,000

The combined profitability index is:

$$\text{Profitability index} = \frac{\$250,000}{\$220,000} = 1.14$$

HOW IS IT USED AND BY WHOM?

Financial Management and Project Analysts. In capital budgeting, the profitability index is used to rank competing proposals to determine a priority order given a budget constraint. Proposals of different dollar magnitude are ranked on a comparative basis.

Capital rationing takes place when a business is not able to invest in projects that have a net present value greater than or equal to zero. Typically, the firm establishes an upper limit to its capital budget based on budgetary constraints. *Special note:* With capital rationing, the project with the highest ranking index rather than the highest net present value should be selected for investment.

155 Program Evaluation and Review Technique (PERT)

DEFINITION. Program Evaluation and Review Technique (PERT) is a useful management tool for planning, scheduling, costing, coordinating, and controlling complex projects such as:

- Formulation of a master budget
- Development of PERT-derived sales forecasts
- Scheduling the closing of accounting books
- Construction of buildings
- Installation of computers
- Assembly of a machine
- Research and development activities

HOW IS IT COMPUTED? The PERT technique involves the diagrammatic representation of the sequence of activities comprising a project by means of a network. The network (1) visualizes all of the individual tasks (activities) to complete a given job or program; (2) points out interrelationships; and (3) consists of activities (represented by arrows) and events (represented by circles), as shown in Exhibit 155.1.

1. *Arrows* represent "tasks" or "activities," which are distinct segments of the project that require time and resources.

2. *Nodes (circles)* symbolize "events," or milestone points in the project, and represent the completion of one or more activities and/or the initiation of one or more subsequent activities. An event is a point in time and does not consume any time in itself.

In a real-world situation, the estimates of completion times of activities will seldom be certain. To cope with the uncertainty in activity time estimates, PERT proceeds by estimating three possible duration times for each activity. As shown in Exhibit 155.1, the numbers on the arrows represent these three time estimates for activities needed to complete the various events. These time estimates are:

- The most optimistic time, which we shall call a
- The most likely time, which we shall call m
- The most pessimistic time, which we shall call b

Example The most optimistic time for completing activity B is 1 day, the most likely time is 2 days, and the most pessimistic time is 3 days. The next step is to calculate an expected time, which is determined as follows:

$$t_e \text{ (expected time)} = \frac{a + 4m + b}{6}$$

For example, for activity B, the expected time is

$$t_e = \frac{1 + 4(2) + 3}{6} = \frac{12}{6} = 2 \text{ days}$$

As a measure of variation (uncertainty) about the expected time, the standard deviation is calculated as follows:

$$\sigma = \frac{b - a}{6}$$

For example, the standard deviation of completion time for activity B is:

$$\sigma = \frac{3 - 1}{6} = \frac{2}{6} = 0.33 \text{ day}$$

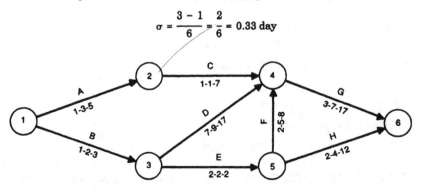

Exhibit 155.1 PERT network diagram.

Expected activity times and their standard deviations are computed in this manner for all the activities of the network and arranged in tabular form as shown below.

Activity	Predecessors	a	m	b	t_e	σ
A	None	1	3	5	3.0	0.67
B	None	1	2	3	2.0	0.33
C	A	1	1	7	2.0	1.00
D	B	7	9	17	10.0	1.67
E	B	2	2	2	2.0	0.00
F	E	2	5	8	5.0	0.67
G	C, D, F	3	7	17	8.0	2.33
H	E	2	4	12	5.0	1.67

A *path* is a sequence of connected activities, such as path 1–2–4–6 in Exhibit 155.1. It is important to determine the *critical path* for a project—that is, the path that takes the longest amount of time. The sum of the estimated times for all activities on this critical path represents the total time required to complete the project. These activities are "critical" because any delay in their completion will cause a delay in the project. Activities that are not on the critical path are not critical, since they will be worked on simultaneously with critical-path activities and their completion could be delayed up to a point without delaying the project as a whole.

It is important to determine the minimum amount of time needed for the completion of the project. Thus, the activities along the critical path must be shortened to speed up the project. An easy way to find the critical path involves the following two steps:

1. Identify all possible paths of a project and calculate their completion times.
2. Pick the one with the longest amount of completion time, which is the critical path.

(When the network is large and complex, a more systematic and efficient approach is required—an approach whose description is best reserved for an advanced management science text.) In the following example, the critical path is B–D–G, which means that it will take 20 days to complete the project.

Path	Completion time
A–C–G	3 + 2 + 8 = 13 days
B–D–G	2 + 10 + 8 = 20 days
B–E–F–G	2 + 2 + 5 + 8 = 17 days
B–E–H	2 + 2 + 5 = 9 days

The next important step is to determine the chances that the project will be completed within the contract time (e.g., 21 days). To solve this issue, the standard deviation of total project time around the expected time is determined as follows:

Standard deviation (project)

= $\sqrt{\text{sum of the squares of the standard deviations of all critical-path activities}}$

Using the standard deviation and table of areas under the normal distribution curve (Table 6 in the Appendix), the probability of completing the project within any given time period can be determined.

Using the formula above, the standard deviation of completion time (the path B–D–G) for the project is:

$$\sqrt{(0.33)^2 + (1.67)^2 + (2.33)^2} = \sqrt{0.1089 + 2.7889 + 5.4289} = \sqrt{8.3267}$$

$$= 2.885 \text{ days}$$

Assume that the expected delivery time is 21 days. The first step is to compute z, which is the number of standard deviations from the mean represented by our given time of 21 days. The formula for z is:

$$z = \frac{\text{delivery time} - \text{expected time}}{\text{standard deviation}}$$

Therefore,

$$z = \frac{21 \text{ days} - 20 \text{ days}}{2.885 \text{ days}} = 0.35$$

The next step is to find the probability associated with the calculated value of z by referring to a table of areas under a normal curve. From Table 6 in the Appendix, we see that the probability is .63683, which means that there is close to a 64 percent chance that the project will be completed in less than 21 days.

To summarize what has been obtained:

1. The expected completion time of the project is 20 days.
2. There is a better than 60 percent chance of finishing before 21 days.

The chances of meeting any other deadline can also be obtained, if desired:

1. Activities B–D–G are on the critical path; they must be watched more closely than the others, for if they fall behind, the whole project will fall behind.

2. If extra effort is needed to finish the project on time or before the deadline, resources (such as money and labor) must be borrowed from activities that are not on the critical path.

3. It is possible to reduce the completion time of one or more activities, but this will require extra cost expenditures. The benefit of reducing the total completion time of a project by accelerating efforts on certain activities must be balanced against the extra cost of doing so. A related problem is to determine which activities must be accelerated to reduce the total project completion time. The critical-path method (CPM), also known as PERT/COST, is widely used to deal with this subject.

It should be noted that PERT is a technique for project management and control. It is not an optimizing decision model, since the decision to undertake a project is initially assumed. It will not help in evaluating an investment project according to its attractiveness or time specifications.

HOW IS IT USED AND APPLIED? Questions that can be answered us-

ing PERT include:

* When will the project be finished?
* What is the probability that the project will be completed by a given time?

This technique is also useful in producing estimates based on subjective opinions, such as executive opinions or salesforce polling. Of course, the PERT methodology for forecasting requires that the expert provide three estimates: most pessimistic, most likely, and most optimistic.

WHO USES IT AND WHEN?

Project Managers. It is essential for a project manager to determine when a project will be finished and the likelihood that the project will be completed by a given time. Thus, a project manager will be able to ascertain ways (such as adding more money and labor) to achieve the deadline in case the deadline is not likely to be met.

Sales Forecasters. Sales forecasters often depend on expert opinions to develop forecasts—a case in which the PERT-derived method can be very effective in smoothing out a wide range of expert forecasts. For example, suppose that the company's economist believes that if the economy is prosperous, then next year's sales will be $330,000 and if the economy is in recession, sales will be $300,000. The most likely projection is $310,000. The PERT method generates an expected sales as follows:

$$\frac{\$300,000 + 4(\$310,000) + \$330,000}{6} = \$311,667$$

with a standard deviation of

$$\sigma = \frac{\$330,000 - \$300,000}{6} = \$5,000$$

If the forecaster is 95 percent confident that the true value of the forecasted sales lies between ±2 standard deviations from the expected sales of $311,667, then the true value can be expected to fall between $301,667 and $321,667 [$311,667 ± 2($5,000)].

156 Quality of Earnings

DEFINITION. Quality of earnings is the *realistic* earnings of a company that conform to economic reality. Quality of earnings is a multifaceted concept that embraces many accounting and financial considerations and involves both quantitative and qualitative elements. Quantitative elements, such as cash flow, are subject to measurement; qualitative elements, such as the quality of management, cannot be measured objectively. This discussion considers only the quantitative aspects that are subject to computation.

HOW IS IT COMPUTED?

Reported net income
Add: Items unrealistically deducted from earnings
Less: Items unrealistically added to earnings
Equals: Quality of earnings

There is no absolute "true" (real) earnings figure; however, the "quality of earnings" figure (adjusted earnings) should be more representative of a company's operational activity than reported net income.

Example A company reports sales of $1,000,000 and net income of $400,000. Included in the net income figure is $50,000 in research and development costs, or 5 percent of sales. In past years, however, the company's research and development cost relative to sales was 8 percent. Competing companies are showing 8 percent this year as well. Thus, an analyst can conclude that research and development should be realistically 8% × $1,000,000 = $80,000. Hence, R&D is understated by $80,000 − $50,000 = $30,000.

The adjusted earnings follows:

Reported net income	$400,000
Less: Understatement of R&D	30,000
Equals: Quality of earnings	$370,000

In this example, there is only one adjustment. Of course, many adjustments would typically be required.

HOW IS IT USED AND BY WHOM?

Financial Analysts and Investors. Earnings quality is relative rather than absolute; it refers to comparing the attributes of reported earnings among companies in an industry. Analytical points to consider are:

1. The "quality of earnings" encompasses much more than the mere understatement or overstatement of net income; it refers also to such factors as the stability of income statement components, the realization risk of assets, and the maintenance of capital.

2. Quality of earnings affects the P/E ratio, the bond rating, the cost of financing, and the availability of financing.

3. Identical earnings of competing companies may possess different degrees of quality. The key to evaluating a company's earnings quality is to compare its earnings profile (that is, the mixture and the degree of favorable and unfavorable characteristics associated with reported results) with the earnings profile of other companies in the same industry. Investment and credit analysts attempt to assess earnings

quality in order to render the earnings comparable, and to determine the level of valuation that should be placed on those earnings.

157 Quantity Discount Model (EOQ with Quantity Discounts)

DEFINITION. The economic order quantity (EOQ) model does not take into account quantity discounts, which is not realistic in many real-world applications. Usually, the more ordered, the lower is the unit price paid. Quantity discounts are price reductions for large orders offered to buyers to induce them to buy in large quantities. If quantity discounts are offered, the buyer must weigh the potential benefits of reduced purchase price and fewer orders that will result from buying in large quantities against the increase in carrying costs caused by higher average inventories. The quantity discount model assists in making this decision.

HOW IS IT COMPUTED? The buyer's goal is to select the order quantity that will minimize total costs, where total cost is the sum of carrying cost, ordering cost, and product cost:

Total cost = carrying cost + ordering cost + product cost

$$= C\left(\frac{Q}{2}\right) + O\left(\frac{D}{Q}\right) + PD$$

where C = carrying cost per unit
O = ordering cost per order
D = annual demand (requirements) in units
P = unit price
Q = order quantity

A step-by-step approach in computing EOQ with quantity discounts is summarized below.

1. Compute the economic order quantity (EOQ) when price discounts are ignored and the corresponding costs using the new cost formula given above. Note that

$$\text{EOQ} = \sqrt{\frac{2OD}{C}}$$

2. Compute the costs for those quantities greater than the EOQ at which price reductions occur.

3. Select the value of Q that will result in the lowest total cost.

Example Assume that ABC Store buys sets of steel at $40 per set from an outside vendor. ABC will sell 6400 sets evenly throughout the year. ABC desires a 16 percent return on investment (cost of borrowed money) on its inventory investment. In addition, rent, taxes, and other costs for each set in inventory is $1.60. The ordering cost is $100 per order. Then the carrying cost per dozen is 16%($40) + $1.60 = $8.00.

Assume further that ABC store has been offered the following price discount schedule:

Order quantity (Q)	Unit price (P)
1–499 sets	$40.00
500–999 sets	39.90
1000 or more sets	39.80

First, the EOQ with no discounts is computed as:

$$EOQ = \sqrt{\frac{2(6,400)(\$100)}{\$8.00}} = \sqrt{160,000} = 400 \text{ sets}$$

$$\text{Total cost} = \$8.00\left(\frac{400}{2}\right) + \$100\left(\frac{6,400}{400}\right) + \$40.00(6,400)$$

$$= \$1,600 + 1,600 + 256,000 = \$259,200$$

Exhibit 157.1 provides cost information for different order quantities.

The value that minimizes the sum of the carrying cost and the ordering cost but not the purchase cost is EOQ = 400 sets. As can be seen in Exhibit 157.2, the further the figures move away from the 400 point, the greater will be the sum of the carrying and ordering costs. Thus, 400 is the only candidate for minimum total cost value within the first price range, $Q = 500$ is the only candidate within the $39.90 price range, and $Q = 1000$ is the only candidate within the $39.80 price bracket. These three quantities are evaluated in Exhibit 157.1 and illustrated in Exhibit 157.2. The EOQ with price discounts is 500 sets. Hence, ABC store is justified in going to the first price break, but the extra carrying cost of going to the second price break more than outweighs the savings in ordering and in the cost of the product itself.

HOW IS IT USED AND APPLIED? There are both favorable and unfavorable features of buying in large quantities. The advantages are lower unit costs, lower ordering costs, fewer stockouts, and lower transportation costs. The disadvantages are higher inventory carrying costs, greater capital requirements, and a higher probability of obsolescence and/or deterioration.

WHO USES IT AND WHEN?

Purchasing Managers. Whenever quantity (or price) discounts are offered, the purchasing manager must weigh the potential benefits of re-

Exhibit 157.1 Annual costs with varying order quantities.

Order quantity	400	500	1,000
Ordering cost: $100 × (6,400/order quantity)	$ 1,600	$ 1,280	$ 640
Carrying cost:$8 × (order quantity/2)	1,600	2,000	4,000
Product cost: unit price × 6,400	256,000	255,360	254,720
Total cost	$259,200	$258,640	$259,360

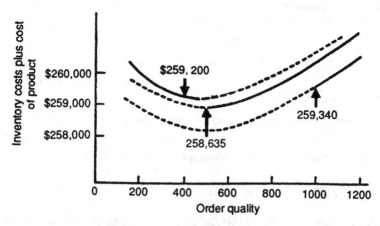

Exhibit 157.2 Inventory costs and quantities.

duced purchase price and fewer orders that will result from buying in large quantities against the increase in carrying costs caused by higher average inventories. The purchasing manager should receive credit for achieving the overall savings resulting from quantity buying.

158 Quantity (Usage, Efficiency) Variance

DEFINITION. The quantity (usage, efficiency) variance reveals the excess or deficient usage of material or labor in production, and links this usage to cost consequence.

HOW IS IT COMPUTED?

Quantity variance = (actual quantity versus standard quantity)

× standard price

The quantity variance is computed for both material and labor.

If the actual cost or quantity exceeds the standard cost or quantity, the variance is unfavorable.

Example Assume the following standards from a particular company:

Direct material: 5 pounds @ $4 per pound	$20 per unit
Direct labor: 3 hours @ $12 per hour	$36 per unit

Company volumes are:

Production: 9800 units

Direct material used: 44,000 pounds
Direct labor: 22,000 hours @ $10 = $220,000

Then the material quantity variance is:

(Actual quantity versus standard quantity) × standard price

$$= (44{,}000 \text{ versus } 49{,}000) \times \$4 = \$20{,}000$$

The labor quantity variance is:

(Actual quantity versus standard quantity) × standard price

$$= (22{,}000 \text{ versus } 29{,}400) \times \$12 = \$88{,}800$$

In both cases in this analysis, the quantity variances are favorable.

HOW IS IT USED AND BY WHOM?

Production Management.   Material and labor efficiency standards are typically estimated by engineers based on an analysis of the production process. The material quantity variance is typically the responsibility of the production department, but the purchasing department is responsible for acquiring inferior goods to economize on cost.

The reasons and responsible parties for unfavorable material quantity variances are:

Reason	Party responsible
Improper specifications, insufficient quantities, failure to buy regularly	Purchasing
Poor mix of materials, poorly trained workers, improperly adjusted machines, poor production scheduling or design, lack of proper tools or machines, unexpected volume changes	Production manager
Failure to detect defective goods	Receiving
Inefficient labor, poor supervision, waste on the production line	Foreman

To control against an unfavorable labor efficiency variance due to inadequate materials or sales orders, a daily direct labor report should be prepared. The causes and responsible parties for unfavorable labor efficiency variances are:

Cause	Party responsible
Poor-quality workers, poor training	Personnel or training
Inefficient flow of materials, wrong mixture of labor for a given job, inferior tools, idle time from production delays	Foreman
Employee unrest	Personnel or foreman
Improper functioning of equipment	Maintenance
Insufficient material supply or poor quality	Purchasing

An unfavorable labor efficiency variance may indicate that better machinery is needed, plant layout should be revised, improved operating methods are needed, and/or better employee training and development are required.

159 Realization Risk in Assets

DEFINITION. Realization risk is the risk associated with receiving cash from assets. The quality of a company's assets is related to the degree of certainty associated with the amount and timing of the realization of assets. A change in asset quality—that is, a change in realization—will signal a change in a company's profits and cash flow.

HOW IS IT COMPUTED? High-risk assets generally include intangible assets and deferred charges. Two computations are utilized to assess realization risk:

1. High-risk assets to total assets:

$$\frac{\text{High-risk assets}}{\text{Total assets}}$$

2. High-risk assets to sales:

$$\frac{\text{High-risk assets}}{\text{Sales}}$$

Example 1 A company reports total assets of $9,000,000 and sales of $10,000,000. Included in the former are the following assets that the analyst deems to be of high risk:

Deferred moving costs	$400,000
Deferred plant rearrangement costs	200,000
Receivables for claims under a government contract	100,000
Goodwill	300,000

The analysis follows:

$$\text{High-risk assets to total assets} = \frac{\$1,000,000}{\$9,000,000} = 11.1\%$$

$$\text{High-risk assets to sales} = \frac{\$1,000,000}{\$10,000,000} = 10\%$$

The realization risk of each major asset category should also be evaluated by the company.

Example 2 A company reports receivables of $4,000,000. Included therein are the following high-risk receivables:

Notes receivable arising from extensions of unpaid balances from delinquent customers	$100,000
Advances to politically and economically unstable foreign governments	200,000

Analysis shows that $300,000 or 7.5% of the receivables reported in the balance sheet are of dubious quality.

HOW IS IT USED AND BY WHOM?

Financial Analysts and Investors. Analysts can evaluate and measure the quality of earnings by analyzing assets according to risk category. The greater the dollar frequency of a company's assets in the high-risk category, the lower is its quality of earnings. High asset-realization risk indicates poorer earnings quality for a company because of possible future charge-offs. For example, the future realization of accounts receivable has a higher degree of probability than the future realization of goodwill.

160 Regression Statistics

DEFINITION. Regression analysis is a statistical method that uses a variety of statistics to convey the accuracy and reliability of regression-analysis results. These statistics include:

1. Correlation coefficient (r) and coefficient of determination (r^2)

2. Standard error of the estimate (S_e)

3. Standard error of the regression coefficient (S_b) and t statistic

HOW IS IT COMPUTED?

Correlation Coefficient (r) and Coefficient of Determination (r^2). The correlation coefficient r measures the degree of correlation between Y and X. The range of values it takes on is between -1 and $+1$. More widely used, however, is the coefficient of determination, designated r^2 (read as r-squared). Simply put, r^2 tells the level of quality of the estimated regression equation—a measure of "goodness of fit" in the regression. Therefore, the higher the r^2, the more confidence can be placed in the estimated equation.

More specifically, the coefficient of determination represents the proportion of the total variation in Y that is explained by the regression equation. It has the range of values between 0 and 1.

Example 1 The statement "Factory overhead is a function of machine hours with $r^2 = 70$ percent," can be interpreted as "70 percent of the total variation of factory overhead is explained by the regression equation or the change in machine hours, and the remaining 30 percent is accounted for by something other than machine hours."

The coefficient of determination is computed as

$$r^2 = 1 - \frac{\sum(Y - Y')^2}{\sum(Y - \overline{Y})^2}$$

where Y = actual values
Y' = estimated values
$\overline{Y}$ = average (mean) value of y

In a simple regression situation, however, there is a shortcut method available:

$$r^2 = \frac{[n\sum XY - (\sum x)(\sum Y)]^2}{[n\sum X^2 - (\sum X)^2 \sqrt{n} \sum Y^2 - (\sum Y)^2]}$$

where n = number of observations
X = value of independent variable

Comparing this formula with the one for b (slope), the only additional information that needs to be computed for r^2 is $\sum Y^2$.

Example 2 To illustrate the computations of various regression statistics, use the same data used in No. 105, Least-Squares Regression. All the sums required are computed and shown below. Note that the Y^2 column is added to be used for r^2.

Direct labor hours, X	Factory overhead, Y	XY	X^2	Y^2
9 hours	$ 15	135	81	225
19	20	380	361	400
11	14	154	121	196
14	16	224	196	256
23	25	575	529	625
12	20	240	144	400
12	20	240	144	400
22	23	506	484	529
7	14	98	49	196
13	22	286	169	484
15	18	270	225	324
17	18	306	289	324
174 hours	$225	3414	2792	4359

From this table,

$$\sum X = 174 \quad \sum Y = 225 \quad \sum XY = 3414 \quad \sum X^2 = 2792$$

$$\bar{X} = \frac{\Sigma X}{n} = \frac{174}{12} = 14.5 \qquad \bar{Y} = \frac{\Sigma Y}{n} = \frac{225}{12} = 18.75$$

Using the shortcut method for r^2,

$$r^2 = \frac{(1,818)^2}{(3,228)[(12)(4,359) - (225)^2]} = \frac{3,305,124}{(3,228)(52,308 - 50,625)} = \frac{3,305,124}{(3,228)(1,683)}$$

$$= \frac{3,305,124}{5,432,724} = 0.6084 = 60.84\%$$

This means that about 60.84 percent of the total variation in total factory overhead is explained by direct labor hours (DLH) and the remaining 39.16 percent is still unexplained. A relatively low r^2 indicates that there is a lot of room for improvement in the estimated cost–volume formula ($Y' = \$10.5836 + \$0.5632X$). Machine hours or a combination of direct labor hours and machine hours might improve r^2.

Standard Error of the Estimate (S_e). The standard error of the estimate, designated S_e, is defined as the standard deviation of the regression. It is computed as

$$S_e = \sqrt{\frac{\Sigma(Y - Y')^2}{n - 2}} = \sqrt{\frac{\Sigma Y^2 - a\Sigma Y - b\Sigma XY}{n - 2}}$$

Statistics can be used to gain some idea of the accuracy of these predictions.

Example 3 Returning to our example data, S_e is calculated as

$$S_e = \sqrt{\frac{4359 - (10.5836)(225) - (0.5632)(3414)}{12 - 2}} = \sqrt{\frac{54.9252}{10}} = 2.3436$$

If 95 percent confidence in the prediction is desired, the confidence interval would be the estimated cost $\pm 2(2.3436)$.

Standard Error of the Regression Coefficient (S_b) and the t Statistic. The standard error of the regression coefficient, designated S_b, and the t statistic are closely related. S_b is calculated as:

$$S_b = \frac{S_e}{\sqrt{\Sigma(X - \bar{X})^2}}$$

or, in short-cut form,

$$S_b = \frac{S_e}{\sqrt{\Sigma X^2 - \bar{X}\Sigma X}}$$

S_b gives an estimate of the range where the true coefficient will "actually" fall.

The t statistics (or t value) is a measure of the statistical significance of an independent variable X in explaining the dependent variable Y. It is determined by dividing the estimated regression coefficient b by its standard error S_b. It is then compared with the table t value (see Table 7 in the Appendix). Thus, the t statistic measures how many standard errors the

262

coefficient is away from zero. Generally, any t value greater than $+2$ or less than -2 is acceptable. The higher the t value, the greater is the confidence that can be placed in the coefficient as a predictor. Low t values are indicators of low reliability of the predictive power of that coefficient.

Example 4 The S_b for our example is:

$$S_b = \frac{2.3436}{\sqrt{2792 - (14.5)(174)}}$$

$$= \frac{2.3436}{\sqrt{2792 - 2523}} = \frac{2.3436}{\sqrt{269}} = 0.143$$

Thus,

$$t \text{ statistic} = \frac{b}{S_b} = \frac{0.5632}{0.143} = 3.94$$

Since $t = 3.94 > 2$, the conclusion is that the b coefficient is statistically significant.

HOW IS IT USED AND APPLIED? The least-squares method is used to estimate both simple and multiple regressions, although in reality managers will confront multiple regression more often than simple regression. Computer software is used to estimate b's. A spreadsheet program such as Lotus 1-2-3 can be used to develop a model and estimate most of the regression statistics discussed thus far. Exhibit 160.1 shows the relevant statistics.

WHO USES IT AND WHEN?

Forecasters and Policymakers. Regression analysis is a powerful statistical technique that is widely used by businesspersons and economists. In order to obtain a good fit and to achieve a high degree of accuracy, analysts must be familiar with statistics relating to regression, such as r^2 and the t value, and be able to make further tests that are unique to multiple regression. (See also No. 105, Least-Squares Regression; No. 122, Multiple Regression; No. 123, Multiple-Regression Tests; and No. 182, Simple Regression.)

161 Reorder Point

DEFINITION. The reorder point is the inventory level at which it is appropriate to replenish stock. Determination of the reorder point considers the necessary lead time—the period between placing an order and receiving delivery.

HOW IS IT COMPUTED?

Reorder point = average usage per unit of lead time

$\times$ lead time + safety stock

First, multiply average daily (or weekly) usage by the lead time in days (or weeks), yielding the lead time demand. Then add the factor of safety stock

Exhibit 160.1 Spreadsheet regression calculation.

Step 1 Enter the data on Y and X as shown below

Y Factory Overhead (00)	X Direct Labor Hour (00)
15	9
20	19
14	11
16	14
25	23
20	12
20	12
23	22
14	7
22	13
18	15
18	17

Step 2 Press ''/Data Regression''
Step 3 Define Y and X ranges
Step 4 Define output range
Step 5 Hit ''Go''

This will produce the following regression output:

Regression Output

Constant	10.58364	$\leftarrow a$
Std Err of Y Est	2.343622	$\leftarrow S_e$
R Squared	0.608373	$\leftarrow r^2$
No. of Observations	12	
Degrees of Freedom	10	

X Coefficient(s)	0.563197	$\leftarrow b$
Std Err of Coef.	0.142893	$\leftarrow S_b$

$t = 3.94$ (calculated independently)

The result shows:

$Y' = 10.58364 + 0.563197X$
$r^2 = 0.608373 = 60.84\%$
$S_e = 2.343622$
$S_b = 0.142893$
t statistic $= 3.94$

All of the above are the same as these values as obtained manually.

to this calculation to provide for the variation in lead time demand to determine the point at which stock must be reordered. If average usage and lead time are both certain, it is not necessary to add safety stock, which then should be dropped from the formula.

Example A company has a yearly usage of 6400 units over a 50-week work period. The lead time is 2 weeks. A safety stock of 50 units is desired.

$$\text{Reorder points} = \left(\frac{6400}{50} \times 2\right) + 50 = 306 \text{ units}$$

This calculation shows that when the inventory level drops to 306 units, an order should be placed.

HOW IS IT USED AND BY WHOM?

Production/Operations Managers and Inventory Planners. The reorder point aids in inventory planning, since it reveals the inventory level at which a reorder is necessary at the economic order quantity (EOQ) amount.

162 Repairs and Maintenance Ratios

DEFINITION. Repairs and maintenance need to be conducted to ensure that fixed assets are in proper working condition. Repair and maintenance ratios demonstrate the level of investment that a company makes in these types of activities.

HOW IS IT COMPUTED? There are two common repair and maintenance ratios by which a company's commitment can be measured:

1. Repairs and maintenance to fixed assets:

$$\frac{\text{Repairs and maintenance}}{\text{Fixed assets}}$$

2. Repairs and maintenance to sales:

$$\frac{\text{Repairs and maintenance}}{\text{Sales}}$$

Example A company provides two years of data relative to its fixed assets:

	19X1	19X2
Fixed assets	$100,000	$ 90,000
Repairs and maintenance	4,000	2,000
Replacement cost	180,000	210,000

Improper maintenance of capital is indicated by an analysis—(1) the decline in the ratio of repairs and maintenance to fixed assets from 4 percent in 19X1 to 2.2 percent in 19X2; (2) the significant difference between replacement cost and historical cost; and (3) the decline in fixed assets over the year.

If the financial analyst concludes that a normal ratio of repairs and maintenance to fixed asset is 4 percent, the analyst would adjust the reported earnings downward by the incremental 1.8 percent of fixed assets (4.0% − 2.2%). This amounts to 1.8% × $90,000 = $1,620.

HOW IS IT USED AND BY WHOM?

Financial Management, Financial Analysts, and Operations Managers. The failure to perform adequate maintenance for productive assets and the failure to replace obsolete fixed assets with new and more efficient equipment will result in manufacturing and operating problems. By understanding the implications of these repair and maintenance ratios, users will be able to investigate possible problems, thus minimizing a risk that these failures would have a long-term negative effect on the company.

163 Residual Income

DEFINITION. Residual income is the operating income that an investment center is able to earn above some minimum return on its assets.

HOW IS IT COMPUTED?

Residual income = net operating income
      − (minimum rate of return on investment × total operating assets)

The minimum rate of return is often based on the company's weighted-average cost of capital.

Example Assume that a company's operating assets are $100,000,000, net operating income is $18,000,000, and the minimum return on assets is 13 percent. Residual income is

Net operating income	$18,000,000
Less: Minimum return × total operating assets:	
13% × $100,000,000	13,000,000
Residual income	$ 5,000,000

HOW IS IT USED AND BY WHOM?

Financial Managers. Residual income is an absolute amount of income rather than a rate of return, and it is used to evaluate divisional performance. An evaluation based on residual income encourages managers to accept investment opportunities that have rates of return greater than the charge for invested capital. Managers being evaluated using return on investment (ROI) may be reluctant to accept new investments that lower their current ROI even though the investments would be desirable for the entire company.

The advantages of using residual income in evaluating divisional performance include the following: (1) It is an economic income that takes into account the minimum return that must be earned on assets; (2) the minimum rate of return can vary depending on the riskiness of the division; (3) different assets can be required to earn different returns depending on their risk; (4) the same asset may be required to earn the same return regardless of the division it is in; and (5) the effect of maximizing dollars rather than a percentage leads to goal congruence.

A major disadvantage of residual income is that it cannot be used to compare divisions of different sizes; residual income tends to favor larger divisions due to the larger amount of dollars involved.

Financial Analysts.   Investment and credit analysts look favorably upon a higher residual income since it means that the company is not only earning a net income but that it is also covering the opportunity cost of tying up assets in the business.

The higher the ratio of residual income to net income, the better is the earnings quality. Residual income is viewed by many analysts as a better measure of true earnings than net income.

164 Return on Total Assets

DEFINITION.   Return on total assets (ROA) equals net income divided by total assets and measures the effectiveness of a firm's assets to create profits.

HOW IS IT COMPUTED?

$$\text{Return on total assets} = \frac{\text{net income}}{\text{average total assets}}$$

where

$$\text{Average total assets} = \frac{\text{beginning total assets} + \text{ending total assets}}{2}$$

Example   The following data shows a company's performance in two different years:

	19X5	19X6
Net income	$ 259,358	$ 384,346
Average total assets		
Beginning of year	1,548,234	1,575,982
End of year	1,575,982	1,614,932
Average total assets	$1,562,108	$1,595,457
Return on total assets	16.60%	24.09%

The analysis shows that there has been growth in the return on assets during the year, indicating greater productivity of assets in generating earnings.

HOW IS IT USED AND APPLIED? Return on total assets is probably the single most widely used measure of an entity's success. Along with return on stockholders' equity (ROE), it has been used to rank companies in the same industry. For managerial use, ROA should be viewed as the product of two important factors, net profit margin and total asset turnover:

$$ROA = \frac{\text{net income}}{\text{average total assets}} = \frac{\text{net income}}{\text{sales}} \times \frac{\text{sales}}{\text{average total assets}}$$

$$= \text{net profit margin} \times \text{total asset turnover}$$

WHO USES IT AND WHEN?

Managers and Investors. The return on assets indicates the productive utilization of business resources. (See also No. 57, Du Pont Formulas.)

165 Risk-Adjusted Discount Rate

DEFINITION. The risk-adjusted discount rate is a method for incorporating the project's level of risk into the capital budgeting process. The discount rate is adjusted upward to compensate for higher-than-normal risk *or* downward to compensate for lower-than-normal risk.

HOW IS IT COMPUTED?

1. An investment's value is determined by discounting the expected cash flows at a rate allowing for the risk associated with those cash flows.

2. The cost of capital (discount rate) is adjusted for a project's risk. A profitable investment is indicated by a positive net present value.

Example Assume the task of evaluating whether to accept Proposal A or Proposal B. Each proposal mandates an initial cash outlay of $12,000 and has a 3-year life. Annual net cash flows along with expected probabilities are as follows:

Expected annual cash inflow	Probability
Proposal A	
$ 5,800	.4
6,400	.5
7,000	.1
Proposal B	
$ 3,400	.3
8,000	.5
11,000	.2

The inflation rate and interest rate are estimated at 10 percent.

The analysis is shown in Exhibit 165.1. Proposal A has a lower risk since its cash flows show greater stability than those of Proposal B. Since Proposal A has less risk, it is assigned a discount rate of 8 percent, while Proposal B is assigned a 10 percent discount rate because of the greater risk. Proposal B should be selected, despite the fact that it carries more risk, because it has a higher risk-adjusted net present value.

HOW IS IT USED AND BY WHOM?

Project Management. If the results of the net present value calculated using the risk-adjusted discount rate are positive, the project should be accepted.

166 Risk Measures

DEFINITION. Risk measures are quantitative measures of risk that attempt to assess the degree of variation or uncertainty about earnings or return. There are several risk measures, including the standard deviation, the coefficient of variation, and beta. The standard deviation is a statistical measure of the dispersion of the probability distribution of possible returns. The smaller the deviation, the tighter the distribution, and thus, the lower is the riskiness of the investment.

Exhibit 165.1   Two proposals analyzed for risk-adjusted discount rate.

Cash flow	Probability	Probable cash flow
Proposal A		
$ 5,800	.4	$2,320
6,400	.5	3,200
7,000	.1	700
Expected annual cash inflow		$6,220
Proposal B		
$ 3,400	.3	$1,020
8,000	.5	4,000
11,000	.2	2,200
Expected annual cash inflow		$7,220

Year	Explanation	Amount	× Factor	=	Present value
	Proposal A				
0	Initial investment	− $12,000 × 1		=	− $12,000
1–3	Annual cash flow	+ 6,220 × 2.5771[a]		=	+ 16,030
	Net present value				+ $ 4,030
	Proposal B				
0	Initial investment	− $12,000 × 1		=	− $12,000
1–3	Annual cash flow	+ 7,220 × 2.4869[b]		=	+ 17,955
	Net present value				+ $ 5,955

[a] Using an 8% discount rate.
[b] Using a 10% discount rate.

One must be careful in using the standard deviation to compare risk because it is only an absolute measure of dispersion (risk) and does not consider the dispersion of outcomes in relationship to an expected return. In comparisons of securities with differing expected returns, the coefficient of variation is commonly used. The coefficient of variation (CV) is computed simply by dividing the standard deviation for a security by its expected value. The higher the coefficient, the more risky is the security. Beta measures a stock's or mutual fund's volatility relative to the general market. (See also No. 19, Beta; No. 34, Coefficient of Variation; and No. 69, Expected Value and Standard Deviation.)

HOW IS IT COMPUTED? To calculate the standard deviation and the coefficient of variation, the expected value, A, must first be computed. It is

$$\overline{A} = \sum_{i=1}^{n} A_i P_i$$

where A_i = value of the ith possible outcome
P_i = probability that the ith outcome will occur
n = number of possible outcomes

Then the absolute risk is measured by the standard deviation:

$$\sigma = \sum_{i=1}^{n} (A_i - \overline{A})^2 P_i$$

The relative risk is measured by the coefficient of variation, which is $\sigma/\overline{A}$.

Example The ABC Corporation is considering investing in one of two mutually exclusive projects. Depending on the state of the economy, the projects would provide the following cash inflows in each of the next 5 years:

State	Probability	Proposal A	Proposal B
Recession	.3	$1000	$ 500
Normal	.4	2000	2000
Boom	.3	3000	5000

To compute the expected value ($\overline{A}$), the standard deviation (σ), and the coefficient of variation, it is convenient to set up the following tables:

For Proposal A:

A_i ($)	P_i	$A_i P_i$ ($)	$(A_i - \overline{A})$ ($)	$(A_i - \overline{A})^2$ ($)
1,000	.3	300	− 1,000	1,000,000
2,000	.4	800	0	0
3,000	.3	900	1,000	1,000,000
		$\overline{A} = 2,000$		$\sigma^2 = 2,000,000$

Since $\sigma^2 = 2,000,000$, $\sigma = 1,414$. Thus,

$$\frac{\sigma}{\bar{A}} = \frac{\$1,414}{\$2,000} = 0.71$$

For Proposal B:

A_i (\$)	P_i	A_iP_i (\$)	$(A_i - \bar{A})$ (\$)	$(A_i - \bar{A})^2$ (\$)
500	.3	150	− 1,950	3,802,500
2,000	.4	800	− 450	202,500
5,000	.3	1,500	2,550	6,502,500
		2,450		$\sigma^2 = 10,507,500$

Since $\sigma^2 = 10,507,500$, $\sigma = \$3,242$. Thus,

$$\frac{\sigma}{\bar{A}} = \frac{\$3,242}{\$2,450} = 1.32$$

Therefore, Proposal A is relatively less risky than Proposal B, as indicated by the lower coefficient of variation.

HOW IS IT USED AND APPLIED? The following different sources of risk are involved in investment and financial decisions. Investors and decision makers must take into account the type of risk underlying an asset.

1. *Business risk:* Business risk is caused by fluctuations in earnings before interest and taxes (operating income). Business risk depends on variability in demand, sales price, input prices, and amount of operating leverage.

2. *Liquidity risk:* Liquidity risk represents the possibility that an asset may not be sold on short notice for its market value. If an investment must be sold at a high discount, then it is said to have a substantial amount of liquidity risk.

3. *Default risk:* Default risk is the risk that a borrower will be unable to make interest payments or principal repayments on debt. For example, there is a great amount of default risk inherent in the bonds of a company experiencing financial difficulty.

4. *Market risk:* Prices of all stocks are correlated to some degree with broad swings in the stock market. Market risk refers to changes in a stock's price that result from changes in the stock market as a whole, regardless of any fundamental change in a firm's earning power.

5. *Interest-rate risk:* Interest-rate risk refers to fluctuations in the value of an asset as the interest rates and conditions of the money and capital markets change. Interest-rate risk relates to fixed-income securities such as bonds. For example, if interest rates rise (fall), bond prices fall (rise).

6. *Purchasing-power risk:* Purchasing-power risk relates to the possibility that an investor will receive a lesser amount of purchasing power than was originally invested. Bonds are most affected by this

risk, since the issuer will be paying back in cheaper dollars during an inflationary period.

7. *Systematic and unsystematic risk:* Many investors hold more than one financial asset. The portion of a security's risk, called unsystematic risk, can be controlled through diversification. This type of risk is unique to a given security. Business, liquidity, and default risks fall in this category. Nondiversifiable risk, more commonly referred to as systematic risk, results from forces outside of the firm's control and are therefore not unique to the given security. Purchasing power, interest rate, and market risks fall into this category. This type of risk is measured by the beta coefficient.

WHO USES IT AND WHEN?

Investors and Financial Analysts.   Investors must weigh return (yield) against the potential risk associated with an investment vehicle. Risks of many investment instruments are rated by major investment advisories such as *Moody's* and *Standard and Poor's*. Beta measures a stock's or mutual fund's volatility relative to the general market, and is available in such publications as *Value Line Investment Survey*.

167 Rule of 72 and Rule of 69

DEFINITION.   The *rule of 72* is a rule-of-thumb method used to determine how many years it takes to double investment money. The *rule of 69*, which is very similar to the rule of 72, also states how long it takes an amount of money invested at r percent per period to double.

HOW IS IT COMPUTED?   Using the rule of 72, dividing the number 72 by the fixed rate of return gives the number of years it takes for annual earnings from the investment to double. That is,

$$\frac{72}{r} \quad \text{(in percent)}$$

Using the rule of 69,

$$\frac{69}{r} \text{ (in percent)} + 0.35 \text{ period}$$

Example   Richard bought a piece of property yielding an annual return of 25 percent. This investment will double in less than three years, because

$$\frac{72}{25} = 2.88 \text{ years}$$

Alternatively, using the rule of 69,

$$\frac{69}{25} + 0.35 = 2.76 + 0.35 = 3.11 \text{ years}$$

HOW IS IT USED AND APPLIED?   These are simply handy rules of thumb to determine how long it takes to double money in an investment.

WHO USES IT AND WHEN?

Investors.   Without looking up the present value and future value in tables or using a financial calculator, it is easy to see the number of years it will take for an investment to double.

168 Rule of 78

DEFINITION.   The rule of 78 was originally called the *rule of the sum of the digits*. It is a method that banks use to develop a loan amortization schedule. It results in a borrower paying more interest at the beginning of a loan when the borrower has the use of more of the money, and paying less and less interest as the debt is reduced. Therefore, it is important to know how much interest can be saved by prepaying a loan after a certain month and how much of the loan is still owed.

HOW IS IT COMPUTED?

Example   Allison borrows $3180 ($3000 principal and $180 interest) for 12 months, so her equal monthly payment is $3180/12 = $265. She wants to know how much interest she saves by prepaying the loan after 6 payments. Allison might guess $90 ($180 × 6/12), reasoning that interest is charged uniformly each month. Good guess, but wrong. Here is how the rule of 78 works:

1. First, add up all the digits for the number of payments scheduled to be made, in this case the sum of the digits 1 through 12:

$$1 + 2 + 3 + \cdots + 12 = 78$$

Generally, the sum of the digits (SD) can be found using the formula:

$$SD = \frac{n(n + 1)}{2} = \frac{12(12 + 1)}{2} = \frac{(12)(13)}{2} = \frac{156}{2} = 78$$

where n is the number of months. For example, the sum of the digits for a 4-year (48-month) loan is

$$\frac{(48)(48 + 1)}{2} = \frac{48(49)}{2} = 1176$$

(See the loan amortization schedule in Exhibit 168.1.)

2. In the first month, before making any payments, Allison has the use of the entire amount borrowed. She thus pays 12/78ths (or 15.39 percent) of the total interest in the first payment. In the second month, she pays 11/78ths (14.10 percent); in the third, 10/78ths (12.82 percent); and so on down to the last payment, 1/78th (1.28 percent). Thus, the first month's total payment of $265 includes $27.69 (15.39% × $180) in interest and $237.31 ($265 − $27.69) in principal. The twelfth and last payment of $265 contains $2.30 (1.28% × $180) in interest and $262.70 in principal.

3. In order to find out how much interest is saved by prepaying after the sixth payment, Allison merely adds up the digits for the remaining six pay-

Exhibit 168.1 Loan amortization schedule based on a loan of $3180 ($3000 principal and $180 interest).

Payment number	Fraction (percent) earned by lender	Monthly payment	Interest	Principal
1	12/78 (15.39%)	$ 265	27.69^a	$ 237.31^b
2	11/78 (14.10%)	265	25.39	239.61
3	10/78 (12.82%)	265	23.08	241.92
4	9/78 (11.54%)	265	20.77	244.23
5	8/78 (10.26%)	265	18.46	246.54
6	7/78 (8.97%)	265	16.15	248.85
7	6/78 (7.69%)	265	13.85	251.15
8	5/78 (6.41%)	265	11.54	253.46
9	4/78 (5.13%)	265	9.23	255.77
10	3/78 (3.85%)	265	6.92	258.05
11	2/78 (2.56%)	265	4.62	260.38
12	1/78 (1.28%)	265	2.30	262.70
78	78/78 (100%)	$3180	$180.00	$3000.00

^{a}$27.69 = $180.00 × 12/79(15.39%).
^{b}$237.31 = $265 − $27.69.

ments. Thus, using the above formula, 6(6 + 1)/2 = 21. This means that 21/78ths of the interest, or $48.46 (21/78 × $180), will be saved.

4. To calculate the amount of principal still owed, subtract the total amount of interest already paid ($180 − $48.46 = $131.54) from the total amount of payments made (6 × $265 = $1590), giving $1458.46. Then subtract this from the original $3000 principal, giving $1541.54 still owed.

5. Does it pay to pay off after the sixth payment? It depends on how much return Allison can get from investing elsewhere. In this example, she needs $1541.54 to pay off the loan to save $48.46 in interest. For loans of longer maturities, the same rules apply, though the actual sum of the digits will be different. Thus, for a 48-month loan, 48/1176ths of the total interest would be paid in the first month, 47/1176ths in the second month, and so on.

HOW IS IT USED AND APPLIED?   If there is no prepayment clause in a loan, a borrower might want to know how much interest can be saved by prepaying the loan after a certain month and how much of the loan is still owed.

WHO USES IT AND WHEN?

Borrowers and Lenders.   Without resorting to present-value tables or a financial calculator, a borrower is able to calculate the breakdown of a monthly payment into its principal and interest portions.

169 Safety Stock

DEFINITION.   When lead time and demand (or usage) are not certain (or variable), the firm must carry extra units of inventory, called *safety stock*, as protection against possible stock-outs. To determine the appropriate level of safety stock size, the service level or stock-out costs must be considered. Safety stock must be added to the *reorder point* (ROP), which tells when to place an order.

Service level can be defined as the probability that demand will not exceed supply during the lead time. Thus, a service level of 90 percent implies a probability of 90 percent that usage will not exceed supply during lead time. Exhibit 169.1 shows a service level of 90 percent.

To determine the optimal level of safety stock size, it is desirable to measure the costs of not having enough inventory, or stock-out costs.

We will discuss three cases for computing the safety stock. The first two do not recognize stock-out costs; the third case does.

HOW IS IT COMPUTED? In the case of uncertain usage and/or lead time, the reorder point (ROP) is computed as:

ROP = expected usage during lead time + safety stock

   = lead time × average usage per unit of time + safety stock

Case 1: Variable Usage Rate, Constant Lead Time

ROP = expected usage during lead time + safety stock

$$= \bar{u}\, LT + z\, \sqrt{LT}(\sigma_u)$$

where u = average usage rate
   LT = lead time
   σ_u = standard deviation of usage rate
   z = standard normal variate (See No. 131, Normal Distribution.)

Example 1 Norman's Pizza uses large cases of tomatoes at an average rate of 50 cans per day. Usage can be approximated by a normal distribution with a standard deviation of 5 cans per day. Lead time is 4 days. Thus,

$$\bar{u} = 50 \text{ cans per day}$$

$$LT = 4 \text{ days}$$

$$\sigma_u = 5 \text{ cans}$$

How much safety stock is necessary for a service level of 99 percent? What is the ROP?

For a service level of 99 percent, $z = 2.33$ (determined from normal distribution table, Table 6 in the Appendix). Thus,

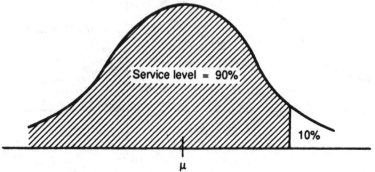

Exhibit 169.1 Service level of 90 percent.

$$\text{Safety stock} = 2.33\sqrt{4(5)} = 23.3 \text{ cans}$$
$$\text{ROP} = 50(4) + 23.3 = 223.3 \text{ cans}$$

Exhibit 169.2 shows a service level of 99 percent.

Case 2: Constant Usage Rate, Variable Lead Time

$$\text{ROP} = \text{expected usage during lead time} + \text{safety stock} = u\overline{LT} + zu(\sigma_{LT})$$

where u = constant usage rate
   LT = average lead time
   σ_{LT} = standard deviation of lead time

Example 2 SVL's hamburger shop uses 10 gallons of cola per day. Lead time is normally distributed, with a mean of 6 days and a standard deviation of 2 days. Thus,

$$u = 10 \text{ gallons per day.}$$
$$\overline{LT} = 6 \text{ days}$$
$$\sigma_{LT} = 2 \text{ days}$$

How much safety stock is necessary for a service level of 99 percent? What is the ROP?

For a service level of 99 percent, $z = 2.33$ (from the normal distribution table). Thus,

$$\text{Safety stock} = 2.33(10)(2) = 46.6 \text{ gallons}$$
$$\text{ROP} = 10(6) + 46.6 = 106.6 \text{ gallons}$$

Case 3: Incorporation of Stock-Out Costs.

This case specifically recognizes the cost of stock-outs or shortages, which can be quite expensive. Lost sales and disgruntled customers are examples of external costs. Idle machines and disrupted production scheduling are examples of internal costs.

The probability approach is illustrated to show how the optimal safety stock can be determined in the presence of stock-out costs.

Example 3 Assume that ABC Store buys sets of steel at $40 per set from an outside vendor. ABC will sell 6400 sets evenly throughout the year. The car-

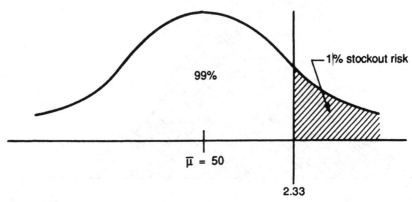

Exhibit 169.2 Service level of 99 percent.

rying cost per set is $8.00. If the lead time and demand are certain, the reorder point is:

$$\text{Reorder point} = 1 \text{ week} \times \frac{6400}{50 \text{ weeks}} = 1 \times 128 = 128 \text{ sets}$$

Assume that the total usage over a 1-week period is uncertain and expected to be:

Total usage	Probability
78	.2
128	.4
178	.2
228	.1
278	.1
	1.00

The stock-out cost is estimated at $12.00 per set. Exhibit 169.3 shows the computation of safety stock. The computation shows that the total costs are minimized at $1200 when a safety stock of 150 sets is maintained. Therefore, the reorder point is:

$$128 \text{ sets} + 150 \text{ sets} = 278 \text{ sets}$$

HOW IS IT USED AND APPLIED?   In reality, managers face either uncertain lead time or uncertain demand, or both. If they have knowledge about the probability distribution and the stock-out costs, however, they will be able to determine the optimal safety stock and the resulting reorder point.

Exhibit 169.3   Computation of safety stock.

Safety stock levels in units	Stock-out and probability	Average stock-out in units	Average stock-out costs	No. of orders	Total annual stock-out costs	Carrying costs	Total
0	50 with .2 100 with .1 150 with .1	35[a]	$420[b]	16	$6720[c]	0	$7140
50	50 with .1 100 with .1	15	180	16	2880	400[d]	3280
100	50 with .1	5	60	16	960	800	1760
150	0	0	0	16	0	1200	1200

[a]$50(.2) + 100(.1) + 150(.1) = 10 + 10 + 15 = 35$ units.
[b]35 units $\times$ $12.00 = $420.
[c]420×16 times = $6720.
[d]50 units $\times$ $8.00 = $400.

WHO USES IT AND WHEN?

Purchasing Managers.   Purchasing managers need to know two things:
(1) how much to order and (2) when to order. In the face of uncertain reality, managers must determine the safety stock to determine the reorder
point; otherwise, they will have to deal with the serious consequences of
shortages and lost customers.

170 Sales-Mix Analysis

DEFINITION. Breakeven and cost–volume–profit (CVP) analysis requires additional computations and assumptions when a company produces and sells more than one product. In multiproduct firms, sales mix is
an important factor in calculating the overall company breakeven point.
   Different selling prices and different variable costs result in different
unit contribution margin (CM) and CM ratios. As a result, the breakeven
points and CVP relationships vary with the relative proportions of the
products sold, called the *sales mix*. In breakeven and CVP analysis, it is
necessary to predetermine the sales mix and then compute a weighted-
average unit CM. It is also necessary to assume that the sale mix does not
change for a specified time period.

HOW IS IT COMPUTED?   There are two steps to finding a breakeven
point for each individual product or service.

Step 1: Compute the breakeven point for the company as a whole (or for
all products or services combined). The formula is:

Breakeven sales in units (or in dollars)

$$= \frac{\text{fixed costs}}{\text{weighted-average unit CM (or CM ratio)}}$$

Step 2: Divide the company's breakeven sales according to the present
sales mix.

Example 1 Assume that Company X has two products with the following
unit CM data:

	A	B
Selling price	$15	$10
Variable cost per unit	12	5
Unit CM	$ 3	$ 5
Sales mix	60%	40%
Fixed costs	$76,000	

   The weighted-average unit CM = ($3)(0.6) + ($5)(0.4) = $3.80. Therefore
the company's breakeven point in units is

$$\frac{\$76,000}{\$3.80} = 20,000 \text{ units}$$

which is divided as follows:

A:	20,000 units × 60% =	12,000 units
B:	20,000 units × 40% =	8,000
		20,000 units

Example 2 Assume that Company Y produces and sells three products with the following data:

	A	B	C	Total
Sales	$30,000	$60,000	$10,000	$100,000
Sales mix	30%	60%	10%	100%
Less: Variable costs	24,000	40,000	5,000	69,000
CM	$ 6,000	$20,000	$ 5,000	$ 31,000
CM ratio	20%	33 1/3%	50%	31%
Fixed costs				$ 18,600
Net income				$ 12,400

The CM ratio for Company Y is $31,000/$100,000 = 31 percent. Therefore the breakeven point in dollars is

$$\frac{\$18,600}{0.31} = \$60,000$$

which will be split in the mix ratio of 3:6:1 to give the following breakeven points for the individual products A, B, and C:

A:	$60,000 × 30% =	$18,000
B:	$60,000 × 60% =	36,000
C:	$60,000 × 10% =	6,000
		$60,000

One of the most important assumptions underlying CVP analysis in a multiproduct firm is that the sales mix will not change during the planning period. But if the sales mix changes, the breakeven point will also change.

HOW IS IT USED AND APPLIED? Contribution margin is a key to sales-mix decisions, especially in the short term. What matters in the short term is which product or service contributes most toward the company's overall fixed costs. Other things being equal, a shift of emphasis from a low-margin product or service to a high-margin product will enhance the company's overall profitability. The following example illustrates this point.

Example 3 Assume that total sales from Example 2 remain unchanged at $100,000 but that a shift is expected in mix from product B to product C, as follows:

	A	B	C	Total
Sales	$30,000	$30,000	$40,000	$100,000
Sales mix	30%	30%	40%	100%
Less: Variable costs	24,000	20,000[a]	20,000	64,000
CM	$ 6,000	$10,000	$20,000	$ 36,000
CM ratio	20%	33 1/3%	50%	36%
Fixed costs				$ 18,600
Net income				$ 17,400

[a] $20,000 = $30,000 × 66⅔%.

Note that the shift in sales mix toward the more profitable line C has caused the CM ratio for the company as a whole to go up from 31 percent to 36 percent. The new breakeven point will be $18,600/0.36 = $51,667. The breakeven dollar volume has decreased from $60,000 to $51,667. The improvement in the mix caused net income to go up, and vice versa. Again, the shift of emphasis from low-margin products to high-margin ones will increase the overall profits of the company.

Other applications of sales mix analysis include:

1. Keeping, adding, or dropping a certain business segment (e.g., product line, service, division, sales territory, department, salesperson, etc.)
2. Merging, acquiring, or divesting

WHO USES IT AND WHEN?

Managers. Sales-mix analysis is vital to the overall success of a company, and is needed at all levels of management. Top managers have to make an important strategic decision involving mergers, buyouts, acquisitions, and divestiture as part of diversification. Middle managers may have to decide on which segments to keep, drop, or add.

Store Branch Managers. Managers of retail store branches must constantly check their product mix. For example, they may have to decide which products to replace with high-margin beach products before beach season arrives.

Banks and Insurance Management. Banks would be concerned with which loan products to offer, drop, and add. Insurance companies have a keen interest in knowing what insurance (such as auto insurance) to drop in a certain metropolitan region.

171 Sales Returns and Allowances to Sales

DEFINITION. The ratio of sales returns and allowances to sales indicates how much of sales were returned or discounted because of customer dissatisfaction.

HOW IS IT COMPUTED?

$$\frac{\text{Sales returns and allowances}}{\text{Sales}}$$

Example A company reports the following information:

	19X1	19X2
Sales returns and allowances	$ 50,000	$ 80,000
Sales	1,000,000	1,100,000

The relevant ratios are:

	19X1	19X2
Sales returns and allowances to sales	0.05	0.07

The increased sales returns and allowances indicates possible problems with the company's merchandise. The reasons for the returns must be identified and corrective action taken.

HOW IS IT USED AND BY WHOM?

Management. The amount of sales returns and allowances is a good indicator of the quality of merchandise sold to customers. If returns and allowances are high relative to sales, it means that buyers are not satisfied. This has a negative effect on the reputation of the company's product line. Further, the company may have to pay the freight for returning the goods.

172 Sales to Current Assets

DEFINITION. The ratio of sales to current assets examines the extent to which revenue is generated from current assets.

HOW IS IT COMPUTED?

$$\frac{\text{Sales}}{\text{Current assets}}$$

Example A company reports the following information:

	19X1	19X2
Sales	$250,000	$400,000
Current assets	100,000	120,000

The relevant ratios are:

	19X1	19X2
Sales to current assets	2.5	3.33

The higher turnover rate may indicate deficient working capital. Perhaps current liabilities will become due before inventory and receivables turn to cash.

HOW IS IT USED AND BY WHOM?

Management, Credit Analysts, and Lenders. The amount of sales relative to current assets indicates the adequacy of current assets. A low turnover implies excessive current assets.

173 Sales to Current Debt

DEFINITION. The ratio of sales to current debt examines the degree to which short-term debt finances sales growth.

HOW IS IT COMPUTED?

$$\frac{\text{Sales}}{\text{Short-term debt}}$$

Example Assume that a company reports the following information:

	19X1	19X2
Sales	$100,000	$130,000
Short-term debt	40,000	40,000

The results of the computation are:

	19X1	19X2
Sales to short-term debt	2.5	3.25

The analysis shows that the company is making greater use of current debt in supporting its sales base.

Management, Credit Analysts, and Lenders. The amount of short-term credit a company is able to obtain from suppliers depends on its needs for goods and services—that is, on the level of sales. This ratio enables users to analyze the relationship between these factors. The advantage of having a larger amount of short-term credit is that it is relatively low cost and, in turn, reduces the investment in working capital.

174 Sales to Personnel

DEFINITION. The ratio of sales to personnel represents a comparison of sales dollars and/or sales volume generated relative to the number of employees. It provides insight into levels of employee productivity.

HOW IS IT COMPUTED?

1. $$\frac{\text{Sales}}{\text{Number of employees}}$$

2. $$\frac{\text{Sales volume}}{\text{Manpower}}$$

3. $$\frac{\text{Sales}}{\text{Salaries expense}}$$

Example Assume that a company's performance for year 1 is:

Unit sales	100,000
Dollar sales	$2,000,000
Number of employees	500
Salaries expense	$ 800,000

Calculation of this year's ratios are:

1. $$\frac{\text{Sales}}{\text{Number of employees}} = \frac{\$2,000,000}{500} = \$4,000$$

2. $$\frac{\text{Sales volume}}{\text{Manpower}} = \frac{100,000}{500} = 200$$

3. $$\frac{\text{Sales}}{\text{Salaries expense}} = \frac{\$2,000,000}{\$800,000} = \$1,600$$

Last year's figures were:

1. $$\frac{\text{Sales}}{\text{Number of employees}} = \$3,600$$

2. $$\frac{\text{Sales volume}}{\text{Manpower}} = 180$$

$$3. \ \frac{\text{Sales}}{\text{Salaries expense}} = \$1,500$$

All the productivity ratios of employee staff have improved this year relative to last year—a favorable sign since greater revenue is being derived from employee efforts.

HOW IS IT USED AND BY WHOM?

Management. The greater the revenue derived from employee time spent and payroll incurred, the more successful the business will be. Management wants to make maximum use of manpower in accomplishing corporate objectives. High ratios indicate good employee morale, training, and on-the-job performance.

175 Sales Variances

DEFINITION. Sales variances analyze the deviation between expected and actual selling price and volume. Reasons for deviation are examined to improve the marketing of the company's products and services.

HOW IS IT COMPUTED?

1. Sales price variance = (actual selling price versus budgeted selling price) × actual units sold
2. Sales volume variance = (actual quantity versus budgeted quantity) × budgeted selling price

Example Western Corporation's budgeted sales for 19X1 were:

Product A: 10,000 units at $6 per unit	$ 60,000
Product B: 30,000 units at $8 per unit	240,000
Expected sales revenue	$300,000

Actual sales for the year were:

Product A: 8,000 units at $6.20 per unit	$ 49,600
Product B: 33,000 units at $7.70 per unit	254,100
Actual sales revenue	$303,700

There is a favorable sales variance of $3,700, consisting of the sales price variance and the sales volume variance.
The sales price variances are:

Product A: ($6.20 versus $6.00) × 8,000	$1,600	Favorable
Product B: ($7.70 versus $8.00) × 33,000	9,900	Unfavorable
Sales price variance	$8,300	Unfavorable

The sales volume variances are:

Product A: (8,000 versus 10,000) × $6.00	$12,000	Unfavorable
Product B: (33,000 versus 30,000) × $8.00	24,000	Favorable
Sales volume variance	$12,000	Favorable

HOW IS IT USED AND BY WHOM?

Marketing Management and Business Planners. The sales variances (price and volume) are prepared for product sales reports and sales district reports to gauge the performance of the marketing function. The sales vice president is responsible for sales variances and must explain deviations to the president. The sales price variance indicates whether the product is being sold at a discount or a premium. Sales price variances may be due to uncontrollable market conditions or to managerial decisions.

The analysis of sales volume includes consideration of budgets, standards, sales plans, industry comparisons, and manufacturing costs. Note that high sales volume does not automatically mean high profits, since there may be high costs associated with the products.

An unfavorable sales volume variance may arise from poor marketing or price cuts by competing companies. If the unfavorable volume variance is coupled with a favorable price variance, the company may have lost sales by raising its prices.

The sales volume variance reflects the effect on the total budgeted contributed margin that is caused by changes in the total number of units sold. The variance may be caused by unpredictable product demand, lack of product demand, or poor sales forecasting.

An unfavorable total sales variance may signal a problem with the marketing manager, who controls sales, advertising, and often pricing. Another possible cause of the unfavorable sales situation may be a lack in quality control, substitution of poorer-quality components due to deficient purchasing, or deficient product design emanating from poor engineering.

176 Salesperson Variances

DEFINITION. Salesperson variances are used to determine the effectiveness of the sales force by looking at cost and time spent by these employees.

HOW IS IT COMPUTED? Several computations are utilized to gain insight into salesperson variances:

1. Total cost variance = actual cost versus standard cost
2. Variance in salesperson days = (actual days versus standard days) × standard rate per day

3. Variance in salesperson costs = (actual rate versus standard rate) × actual days

4. Total variance in calls = actual calls versus actual sales
   Total variance in calls = standard calls versus standard sale

5. Variance in calls = (actual calls versus standard calls) × standard sale

6. Variance in sales = (actual sales versus standard sale) × standard calls

7. Joint variance = (actual calls versus standard calls) × (actual sale versus standard sales)

Example 1 Assume the following sales data for a company:

Standard cost	$240,000
Standard salesperson days	2,000
Standard rate per salesperson day	$ 120
Actual cost	$238,000
Actual salesperson days	1,700
Actual rate per salesperson day	$ 140
Total cost variance:	
Actual cost	$238,000
Standard cost	240,000
Variance	$ 2,000 F

This analysis demonstrates a favorable variance.

The control variance is broken down into salesperson days and salesperson costs.

Variance in salesperson days = (actual days versus standard days)

$$× \text{ standard rate per day} = (1,700 \text{ versus } 2,000) × \$120 = \$36,000 \quad F$$

The variance is favorable because the territory was handled in fewer days than expected.

Variance in salesperson costs = (actual rate versus standard rate) × actual days

$$= (\$140 \text{ versus } \$120) × 1,700 = \$34,000 \quad U$$

An unfavorable variance results because the actual rate per day is greater than the expected rate per day.

Example 2 Assume that a salesperson called on 55 customers and sold each an average of $2800 worth of merchandise. The standard number of calls is 50, and the standard sale is $2400. Variance analysis of calls and sales follows:

Total variance:	
Actual calls × actual sale: 55 × $2,800	$154,000
Standard calls × standard sale: 50 × $2,400	120,000
Variance	$ 34,000
Variance in calls:	
(actual calls versus standard calls) × standard sale:	
(55 versus 50) × $2,400	$ 12,000 F

Variance in sales:
(actual sale versus standard sale) × standard
calls: ($2,800 versus $2,400) × 50 $20,000   F

Joint variance:
(actual calls versus standard calls) × (actual
sale versus standard sale): (55 versus
50) × ($2,800 versus $2,400) $ 2,000   F

HOW IS IT USED AND BY WHOM?

Sales Managers. Sales managers use salesperson variances to appraise the sales force within a territory, including time spent and expenses incurred. Sales managers can keep track of salesperson costs and compare them to budget figures to determine whether salespersons are using their time and calls effectively in generating profitable sales.

Cost variances for the selling function may be analyzed by geographic region, product, or type of personnel.

177 Savings to Income

DEFINITION. The amount held in demand savings accounts relative to take-home pay is a useful measure for personal financial planning.

HOW IS IT COMPUTED?

1. Conservative demand deposits = 6 months' income

2. Regular demand deposits = 3–5 months' income

3. Recommended demand deposits each pay period = 10 percent × take-home pay

Demand deposits are funds that are available immediately, such as in savings accounts, money market accounts, and checking accounts.

Example Your monthly take-home pay is $2200 and you want to save 15 percent of it. The desired amount of demand deposits is:

$$\$2200 \times 15\% = \$330$$

If you want to have in savings a conservative amount of money, your savings in the bank should be:

$$6 \times \$2200 = \$13,200$$

HOW IS IT USED AND BY WHOM?

Individuals. Individuals need to have a basic amount of money saved for ordinary living expenses and emergencies. If you put your last cent in stocks and bonds, you may have to sell them when they are down in price.

If your income fluctuates sharply, you should have more money in a savings account. You should also have a backup fund that can be tapped if needed. The backup fund should be about the same amount as your demand deposits. A backup fund may be in the form of a time deposit such as a certificate of deposit.

178 Selling Price Computation

DEFINITION. Computation of the selling price for a product or service depends on its cost and the desired profit markup. If idle capacity exists, a lower selling price may be warranted.

HOW IS IT COMPUTED? For a regular sale situation:

Selling price = actual cost (variable cost + fixed cost) + profit markup

For a special sale situation:

Selling price = variable cost + profit markup

A company should accept an order at below-normal selling price when idle capacity exists (since fixed cost remains constant), as long as there is a contribution margin on the order.

Example 1   Assume that a company's actual cost to produce a product is $20. The company desires a profit markup of 50 percent on cost. The selling price is calculated as follows:

Actual cost	$20
Profit markup (50% × $20)	10
Selling price	$30

Example 2   A company is operating at idle capacity. Therefore, its fixed costs are constant even with the new order. Variable cost per unit is $12, and the desired profit markup on variable cost is 30 percent. Total fixed cost is $100,000 and, since 10,000 units are currently being sold, the fixed cost per unit is $10. The selling price is calculated as:

Variable cost	$12.00
Plus: Profit markup (30% × $12)	3.60
Selling price	$15.60

The contribution margin and net income on an incremental order of 100 units priced at $15.60 each is:

Sales (100 × $15.60)	$1560
Less: Variable costs (100 × $12)	1200
Contribution margin (100 × $3.60)	$ 360
Less: Fixed cost	0
Net income	$ 360

Marketing Managers and Product Managers. The marketing manager must establish an appropriate selling price for a product or service—a price that considers the costs involved, desired profit markup, capacity utilization, supply/demand, and competitive factors. These financial considerations are imperative, since this pricing bears directly on the bottom line.

179 Shadow Price

DEFINITION. Shadow price in linear programming (LP) is an imputed value, not an actual value—that is, the maximum price that management is willing to pay for an extra unit of a given scarce resource. For example, a financial manager who has solved an LP problem might wish to know whether it pays to add capacity in hours in a particular department. The manager would be interested in the monetary value to the firm of adding, say, an hour per week of assembly time. This monetary value is usually the additional profit that could be earned. This amount is the shadow price. A shadow price is in a way an *opportunity cost*—the profit that would be lost by not adding an additional hour of capacity. To justify a decision in favor of a short-term capacity decision, the manager must be sure that the shadow price exceeds the actual price of that expansion.

HOW IS IT COMPUTED? Shadow prices are computed, step by step, as follows:

1. Add 1 hour (preferably, more than 1 hour to make it easier to show graphically) to the constraint of a given LP problem under consideration.

2. Resolve the problem and find the maximum objective function value.

3. Compute the difference between the objective function value of the original LP problem and the objective function value determined in step 2, which is the shadow price.

Example Shadow price is shown automatically on any LP software printout. See Exhibit 179.1 for a LINDO (Linear Discrete Optimization) output. (See also No. 108, Linear Programming.)

HOW IS IT USED AND APPLIED? Suppose that the shadow price of an hour of assembly capacity is $6.50, while the actual market price is $8.00. The analysis shows that it does not pay to add an additional hour of assembly capacity.

WHO USES IT AND WHEN?

Production Managers and Financial Managers. Managers may wish to know if an additional hour of capacity or dollar of working capital is justified. Proper justification exists when the shadow price exceeds the cost of acquiring an extra unit.

Exhibit 179.1 LINDO output of shadow-price computation.

```
:MAX 600A + 200B
>ST
>A<6
>B<10
>10A+20B<160
>300A+200B<2400
>END
:LOOK ALL

MAX   600A + 200B
SUBJECT TO
  2)   A<=6
  3)   B<=10
  4)   10A + 20B<= 160
  5)   300A + 200B< = 2400
:GO
 LP OPTIMUM FOUND   AT STEP    2


OBJECTIVE FUNCTION VALUE


1)    4200.00000
VARIABLE     VALUE           REDUCED COST
       A     6.000000            .000000
       B     3.000000            .000000

ROW       SLACK OR SURPLUS      DUAL PRICES    ←Shadow
 2)               .000000       300.000000      prices
 3)              7.000000           .000000
 4)             40.000000           .000000
 5)               .000000         1.000000

NO.ITERATIONS =   2

DO RANGE    (SENSITIVITY) ANALYSIS?  >
 4)             40.000000                 .000000
 5)               .000000              1.000000

NO.ITERATIONS =   2

  DO RANGE (SENSITIVITY) ANALYSIS? > YES
   RANGES IN WHICH THE BASIS IS UNCHANGED

                  OBJ COEFFICIENT RANGES
VARIABLE    CURRENT      ALLOWABLE      ALLOWABLE
            COEF         INCREASE       DECREASE
       A    600.000000   INFINITY       300.000000
       B    200.000000   200.000000     200.000000
```

180 Simple Interest

DEFINITION. Simple interest is interest paid only on the principal of a loan, with no compounding effect.

HOW IS IT COMPUTED? Simple interest is computed by multiplying the principal times the rate of interest per time period times the number of time periods. That is,

$$I = P \times i \times n$$

where I = simple interest in dollars
P = principal amount at the current time
i = interest rate per time period
n = number of time periods

Example 1 The simple interest on $1000 at 9 percent borrowed for 9 months is:

$$I = P \times i \times n$$

$$= \$1000 \times 9\% \times \frac{9}{12}$$

$$= \$67.50$$

Example 2 Sharron Cotter receives $50 every month from a bond fund paying 9 percent annual interest. How much is invested in the bond fund? Since P is the unknown, the formula must be rearranged to solve for P:

$$P = \frac{I}{i \times n}$$

$$= \frac{50}{0.09} \times \frac{1}{12}$$

$$= \frac{50}{0.0075}$$

$$= \$6666.67$$

Example 3 A 1-month interest payment on a $60,000 mortgage borrowed at 9.5 percent is:

$$I = P \times i \times n$$

$$= \$60,000 \times 9.5\% \times \frac{1}{12}$$

$$= \$475.00$$

HOW IS IT USED AND APPLIED? Simple interest is the basis for interest calculations such as in borrowing and leasing arrangements. Money has time value, and simple-interest calculations are a method of computing this value.

WHO USES IT AND WHEN?

Borrowers. Borrowers are concerned about simple interest because the payments reduce cash flow and profitability. Simple interest is a vitally important part of any business or personal financial decision, because it represents the cost of financing.

Creditors. To creditors, lending money results in interest revenue, which improves cash flow and net income. The interest rate charged depends on the risk of the loan, which in turn depends on the borrower's financial condition.

181 Simple (Accounting) Rate of Return

DEFINITION. Simple rate of return is a capital budgeting criterion that relates the returns generated by a project, as measured by average accounting income after taxes, to the average dollar size of the investment.

HOW IS IT COMPUTED?

$$\text{Simple rate of return} = \frac{\text{expected future annual net income}}{\text{average investment}}$$

Example A proposal requires an initial investment of $6500, has an estimated life of 20 years, and will generate expected annual net income of $675. The calculation of the simple rate of return is:

$$\frac{\$675}{\$6500/2} = \frac{\$675}{\$3250} = 20.8\%$$

HOW IS IT USED AND BY WHOM?

Financial Managers and Project Analysts. The simple rate of return is one method used to compare the profitability among alternative investment opportunities and proposals; however, drawbacks of the method include its failure to (1) consider cash flows, (2) take into account the time value of money, and (3) consider the payback period.

182 Simple Regression

DEFINITION. Simple regression is a type of regression analysis that involves one independent (explanatory) variable.

HOW IS IT FORMULATED AND COMPUTED? Simple regression takes the form:

$$Y = a + bX$$

where Y = dependent variable
X = independent variable

a = constant
b = slope

The least-squares estimation method is typically used to estimate the parameter values a and b.

Example Assume that data on VCR sales and advertising expenditures have been collected over the past seven periods. The linear regression equation can be estimated using the least-squares method. A Lotus 1-2-3 regression printout is shown in Exhibit 182.1. As shown in the exhibit, the sales/advertising regression for VCRs is estimated to be:

$$\text{VCR sales} = Y = 19.88 + 4.72X$$

$$r^2 = 0.7630 = 76.30\%$$

HOW IS IT USED AND APPLIED?

1. Total factory overhead is explained by only one activity variable (such as either direct labor hours or machine hours).

2. An asset's return is a function of the return on a market portfolio (such as Standard & Poor's 500); i.e., $r_j = a + br_m$, where b = beta.

3. Consumption is a function of disposable income; i.e., $C = a + bY_d$, where b = marginal propensity to consume.

Exhibit 182.1   Simple regression output.

```
VCR Sales


  Sales(Y) Advertising(X)
    (both in millions)
    37            4.5
    48            6.5
    45            3.5
    36            3
    25            2.5
    55            8.5
    63            7.5


              Regression Output:


    Constant              19.88222  ← a = 19.88222
    Std Err of Y Est      6.790423
    R Squared             0.763018
    No. of Observations      7
    Degrees of Freedom       5

    X Coefficient(s) 4.717344  ← b = 4.717344
    Std Err of Coef. 1.175716

The estimated sales forecasting equation is:
    Y' = 19.88 + 4.72 X with R Squared = 76.30%
```

4. Demand is a function of price; i.e., $Q_d = a - bP$.

WHO USES IT AND WHEN?

Forecasters and Policymakers. Simple regression and multiple regression are powerful statistical techniques that are perhaps most widely used by businesses and economists. In order to obtain a good fit and achieve a high degree of accuracy, users should be familiar with statistics relating to regression, such as r^2 and the t value. (See also No. 105, Least-Squares Regression; and No. 160, Regression Statistics.)

183 Simulation Model

DEFINITION. A simulation model is a system of mathematical equations, logic, and data that describes the relationships among financial and operating variables. A primary example of a simulation model is a financial model. A simulation model is one in which:

1. One or more financial variables appear (expenses, revenues, investment, cash flow, taxes, earnings, etc.).

2. The model user can manipulate (set and alter) the value of one or more financial variables.

3. The purpose of the model is to influence strategic decisions by revealing to the decision maker the implications of alternative values of these financial variables.

Financial models are basically "what-if" models. (The other type is an optimization model.) What-if models attempt to simulate the effects of alternative management policies and assumptions about the firm's external environment. They are basically a tool for management's laboratory.

Models can be deterministic or probabilistic. *Deterministic models* do not include any random or probabilistic variables, whereas *probabilistic models* incorporate random numbers and/or one or more probability distributions for variables such as sales and costs. Financial models can be solved and manipulated computationally to derive current and projected future implications and consequences. As a result of technological advances in computers (such as spreadsheets, financial modeling languages, graphics, database management systems, and networking), more and more companies are using modeling.

HOW IS IT DEVELOPED? Generally speaking, the model consists of three important ingredients:

* Variables
* Input parameter values
* Definitional and/or functional relationships

The development of financial models essentially involves two steps:

1. Definition of variables and input parameters

2. Model specification

Definition of Variables and Input Parameters. Fundamental to the specification of a financial model is the definition of the variables to be included in the model. There are basically three types of variables: policy variables (Z), external variables (X), and performance variables (Y).

Policy variables are the variables over which management can exert some degree of control. Policy variables are often called *control variables*. In finance, for example, such variables are cash-management policy, working-capital policy, debt-management policy, depreciation policy, tax policy, merger-acquisition decisions, the rate and direction of the firm's capital investment programs, the extent of its equity and external debt financing and the financial leverage represented thereby, and the size of its cash balances and liquid assets position. Policy variables are denoted by the symbol Z in Exhibit 183.1.

External variables are environmental variables that are external to the company but that influence the firm's decisions. For example, the firm is embedded in an industry environment, which is influenced by overall general business conditions. General business conditions exert influences on particular industries in several ways, such as having an impact on such variables as total volume of demand, product prices, labor costs, material costs, money rates, and general expectations. The symbol X represents the external variables in the Exhibit 183.1.

Performance variables measure the firm's economic and financial performance, which are usually endogenous. The symbol Y is used in Exhibit 183.1. The Ys are often called *output variables*. The output variables of a financial model would be the line items of the balance sheet, cash budget, income statement, or statement of cash flows. The manner in which the

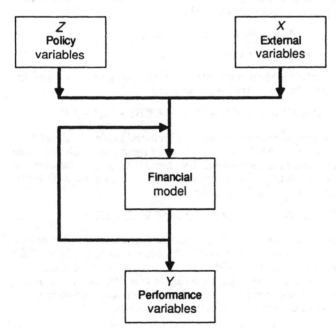

Exhibit 183.1 Financial model variables.

output variables of the firm is defined will depend on the goals and objectives of management. The variables basically indicate how management measures the performance of the organization or some segments of it. Management is likely to be concerned with (1) the firm's level of earnings, (2) growth in earnings, (3) projected earnings, (4) growth in sales, and (5) cash flow.

When a financial model is set up, it is common to face risk or uncertainty associated with particular projections. In that case some of the variables, such as sales, are treated as random variables with given probability distributions. The inclusion of random variables in the model transforms it from a deterministic model to a risk-analysis model. Note that the use of the risk-analysis model is rare in practice because of the difficulty involved in modeling and computation.

Input parameter values form a major part of the model. For example, in order to generate the balance sheet, the model needs to input beginning balances of various asset, liability, and stockholders' equity accounts. These input and parameter values are supplied by management. The ratio between accounts receivable and sales and financial decision variables, such as the maximum desired debt–equity ratio, are good examples of input parameters.

Once various variables and input parameters for the financial model have been defined, a set of mathematical and logical relationships linking the input variables to the performance variables must be specified. The relationships usually fall into two categories: definition equations and behavioral equations. *Definitional equations* take the form of accounting identities. *Behavioral equations* involve theories or hypotheses about the behavior of certain economic and financial events. They must be empirically tested and validated before they are incorporated into the financial model.

Definitional equations are exactly what their name implies—mathematical or accounting definitions. For example,

$$\text{Assets} = \text{liabilities} + \text{equity}$$

$$\text{Net income} = \text{revenues} - \text{expenses}$$

are fundamental definitions in accounting for the balance sheet and income statement, respectively. Another example is:

$$\text{CASH} = \text{CASH}(- 1) + \text{CC} + \text{OCR} + \text{DEBT} - \text{CD} - \text{LP}$$

This equation is a typical cash equation in a financial model. It states that ending cash balance (CASH) is equal to beginning cash balance [CASH(- 1)] plus cash collections from customers (CC) plus other cash receipts (OCR) plus borrowings (DEBT) minus cash disbursements (CD) minus loan payments (LP). As a final example,

$$\text{INV} = \text{INV}(- 1) + \text{MAT} + \text{DL} + \text{OVER} - \text{CGS}$$

states that ending inventory (INV) is equal to the beginning inventory [INV(- 1)] plus cost of materials used (MAT) plus cost of direct labor (DL) plus manufacturing overhead (OVER) minus cost of goods sold (CGS).

Behavioral equations describe the behavior of the firm in terms of the specific activities that are subject to empirical testing and validation. For example, the classical demand function in economics is:

$$Q = f(P)$$

or, more specifically,

$$Q = a - bP$$

which says simply that the quantity demanded is negatively related to the price. That is, the higher the price, the lower is the demand.

The firm's sales, however, are more realistically described as

$$SALES = f(P, ADV, I, GNP, Pc, etc.)$$

or, assuming a linear relationship among these variables,

$$SALES = a + bP + cADV + dI + eGNP + fPc + u$$

which says that sales are affected by such factors as price (P), advertising expenditures (ADV), consumer income (I), gross national product (GNP), prices of competitive goods (Pc), etc. (u is the error term). Given the data on SALES, P, ADV, I, GNP, and Pc, the parameter values a, b, c, d, e, and f can be estimated using linear regression. The statistical significance of each of the parameter estimates can be tested and the overall explanatory power of the model evaluated, measured by the t statistic and r^2, respectively.

In this way, the most influential factors that affect the sales of a particular product will be identified. With the best model chosen, financial management can simulate the effects on sales of alternative pricing and advertising strategies. It is also possible to experiment with alternative assumptions regarding external economic factors such as GNP, consumer income, and prices of competitive goods.

Model Specification. See Exhibit 183.2 for the basic structure of the model. (See also No. 39, Corporate Planning Models.)

In addition to the factors discussed previously (that is, definitional equations and behavioral equations), the financial model may include basic decision rules specified in a very general form. The decision rules are not written in the form of conventional equations. Rather, they are described algebraically using conditional operators, consisting of statements of the type: "IF...THEN...ELSE." For example, suppose that the following decision rule is desired: "If X is greater than 0, then Y is set equal to X multiplied by 5. Otherwise, Y is set equal to 0." The rule is expressed as:

$$Y = IF\ X\ GT\ 0\ THEN\ X*5\ ELSE\ 0$$

Example Suppose that a company wishes to develop a financing decision model, based on alternative sales scenarios. To attempt to determine an optimal financing alternative, financial managers might want to incorporate some decision rules into the model for a "what-if" or sensitivity analysis. Some examples of such decision rules are:

- The amount of dividends paid are determined on the basis of targeted earnings available to common stockholders and a maximum dividend payout ratio as specified by management.
- After calculating the amount of external funds needed to meet changes in assets as a result of increased sales, dividends, and maturing debt, the amount of long-term debt to be floated is selected on the basis of a prespecified leverage ratio.
- The amount of equity financing to be raised is chosen on the basis of funds

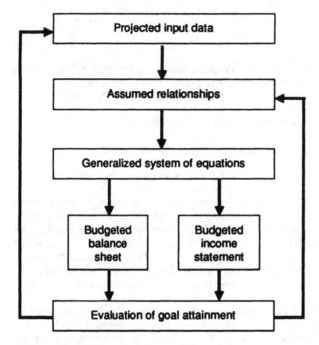

Exhibit 183.2 Corporate financial model.

needed that are not financed by new long-term debt, but that is constrained by the responsibility to meet minimum dividend payments.

In the model just described, simultaneity is quite evident. A sales figure is used to generate earnings, and this in turn leads to, among other items, the level of long-term debt required. The level of debt affects the interest expense incurred within the current period and therefore earnings. Furthermore, as earnings are affected, so are the prices at which new shares are issued, the number of shares to be sold, and thus earnings per share. Earnings per share then "feeds back" into the stock price calculation.

A *lagged model structure* is common in financial modeling. Balance sheet equations or identities are virtually all of this type; for example,

Capital = capital(− 1) + net income + contributions − cash dividends

More interestingly,

$$CC = a*SALES + b*SALES(-1) + c*SALES(-2)$$

where CC = cash collections from customers
a = percentage received within the current period
b = percentage received with one-period lag
c = percentage received with two-period lag

HOW IS IT USED AND APPLIED?   Basically, a financial model is used to generate projected financial statements such as the income statement, balance sheet, and statement of cash flow. Such a model can be called a budgeting model, since essentially a master budget is developed with such a model. Applications and uses of the model are numerous, including:

- Projection of financial statements or development of budgets
- Financial forecasting and analysis
- Cash budgeting
- Capital expenditure analysis
- Tax planning
- Exchange-rate analysis
- Analysis for mergers and acquisitions
- Labor contract negotiations
- Capacity planning
- Cost–volume–profit analysis
- New-venture analysis
- Lease/purchase analysis
- Evaluation of performance by segments
- Market analysis
- New-product analysis
- Development of long-term strategy
- Planning for financial requirements
- Risk analysis
- Cash-flow analysis
- Cost and price projections

WHO USES IT AND WHEN?

Financial Analysts, Budget Analysts, and Corporate Strategists. Financial analysts and budgeting personnel use a simulation model in order to generate pro-forma financial statements (budgets); corporate strategists use it to see the impact of changes in policy variables on the future profitability of the firm (such as the impact of a change in foreign-exchange rate or a leverage buyout).

184 Sinking Fund Computation

DEFINITION. Sinking fund computation is a calculation that can be used to find the annual deposit (or payment) necessary to accumulate a future sum. A sinking fund is a sum of money dedicated to fund a particular purpose, such as retiring a portion of a bond issue at the time it is due, or having sufficient funds for capital expansion.

HOW IS IT COMPUTED? The formula for computing a sinking fund problem is:

$$S = A\left[\frac{(1 + i)^n - 1}{i}\right] = R \times \text{CVIFA}_{(i,n)}$$

where S_n = compound sum of an n-period ordinary annuity
A = annual amount of money to be deposited to create sinking fund in n years
i = interest rate the sinking-fund account earns
n = number of years the sinking fund will exist
CVIFA = compound sum of annuity interest factor

Solving for A, we obtain:

$$\text{Sinking fund amount} = A = \frac{S_n}{\text{CVIFA}_{(i,n)}}$$

Example A company needs to create a $15 million sinking fund at the end of 8 years at 10 percent interest to retire $15 million in outstanding bonds. The amount that should be deposited in the account at the end of each year is:

$$S_n = A\left[\frac{(1+i)^n - 1}{i}\right] = A \times \text{CVIFA}_{(10\%,\,8)}$$

$$A = \frac{\$15,000,000}{\text{CVIFA}_{(10\%,\,8)}}$$

$$= \frac{\$15,000,000}{11.436}$$

$$= \$1,311,647.42$$

Thus, if the company deposits $1,311,647.42 at the end of each year for the next 8 years in an account earning 10 percent interest, it will accumulate the $15 million needed to retire the bonds.

HOW IS IT USED AND APPLIED? The compound sum of annuity interest factor methodology is used for creating a sinking fund at the end of each year for a certain number of years by compounding funds at a given rate of interest.

WHO USES IT AND WHEN?

Business Managers, Comptrollers, Treasurers, and Financial Analysts. Businesspeople may need to make sinking fund computations in order to accumulate a desired sum at a future date so as to pay off debt or buy capital assets. A sinking fund provision may also be incorporated into a loan agreement to protect the creditors.

Individuals. A sinking fund computation may be made for the purpose of meeting a balloon mortgage payment on a piece of property.

185 Systematic-Sampling Formula

DEFINITION. Systematic sampling consists of sequencing all items of the population. Sampling units are put in order (e.g., numerically). Systematic sampling may be employed for both statistical and nonstatistical sampling.

HOW IS IT COMPUTED?

$$\text{Selection interval} = \frac{\text{population size } (N)}{\text{sample size } (n)}$$

The population is divided into n intervals of equal size based on the number of sampling units that must be chosen for the sample (n). A sampling unit from each of the derived intervals is then chosen.

Example An auditor is examining 1,000 sales invoices from a population of 20,000 invoices. One random starting point is employed. Each twentieth invoice is chosen. To select 1,000 invoices, the auditor will move up or down from the random starting point. If a random starting point of invoice number 100 is selected, invoice number 80 (100 – 20) and number 60 (100 – 40) are included in the sample, as well as every twentieth invoice number after 100 (120, 140, 160, etc.). If the auditor selects 10 random starting points, 100 invoices (1,000/10) will be selected for audit. Thus, the auditor will select every two-hundredth invoice number (20,000/100) before and after each random beginning point.

HOW IS IT USED AND BY WHOM?

Internal and External Auditors. Systematic sampling is an approach used in auditing to test the population for accuracy. Auditors want assurance that the accounting and financial records are correct.

When a population is not in numerical sequence, it is easier to choose a systematic random sample instead of a pure random sample. If documents or transactions are unnumbered, there is no need to number them physically with this approach, as would be the case with random-number-table selection. Instead, with systematic sampling the auditor counts off the sampling interval to choose the documents.

186 Take-Home Pay to Debt-Service Charges

DEFINITION. The ratio of take-home pay to debt-service charges looks at one's net wages as a basis on which to pay monthly payments of principal and interest on debt (e.g., credit card balances, loans).

HOW IS IT COMPUTED?

$$\frac{\text{Take-home pay}}{\text{Debt-service charges}}$$

Example Your take-home pay is $40,000, and you must make payments of $10,000 on loans. The ratio is 4, meaning there is $4 in take-home pay for each $1 of necessary debt repayment.

HOW IS IT USED AND BY WHOM?

Individuals. In personal financial planning, a higher ratio is a better sign of debt-carrying ability. In general, the ratio should be at least 2.

187 Taxable Income

DEFINITION.   Taxable income is the amount on which tax is based.

HOW IS IT COMPUTED?   For an individual,

Taxable income = gross income − adjustments to gross income

= adjusted gross income − itemized deductions (or standard deduction)

− personal exemptions

For a corporation,

Taxable income = gross income − allowable business deductions

Example   A company's gross income for the year was $8,000,000, while its deductible business expenses were $5,200,000. Assuming a tax rate of 34 percent, taxable income and the related tax are:

Gross income	$8,000,000
Less: Allowable business deductions	5,200,000
Taxable income	$2,800,000
Tax (34% × $2,800,000)	$ 952,000

HOW IS IT USED AND BY WHOM?

Individuals.   Individuals use taxable income to determine the amount subject to tax when preparing a tax return. Tax-planning strategies may be implemented to lower taxes.

Corporate Financial Managers and Tax Preparers.   Corporate financial managers and tax preparers compute taxable income to determine how much of the company's income will go toward taxes. This computation is necessary for tax preparation and in deriving tax strategies to lower future taxes. The financial manager analyzes differing tax options to minimize the tax liability in current and future tax periods. Tax planning includes decisions as to when to receive income, when to pay expenditures, and how to obtain tax-free income.

188 Trading on the Equity (Real Estate)

DEFINITION.   In real estate, trading on the equity represents the amount of additional financing that can be obtained from the appreciated equity value of a real estate investment adjusted for the amount of any existing mortgage—that is, net appreciation. Trading on the equity is a form of real estate financing that is widely used to obtain second mortgages and equity loans for purposes including, but not limited to, household emergencies and other real estate investments. Indeed, some banks promote the concept of home equity loans for the purpose of taking a vacation.

HOW IS IT COMPUTED?

Trading on the equity = [new equity

– (original equity – existing mortgage)]

× amount eligible to be borrowed on new equity

Example Assume that a home was purchased in 1990 for $75,000. In 2000 it has 20 years remaining on a $40,000, 30-year mortgage. In 2000 the home has an appraised value of $200,000. How large a home equity loan can the new net equity qualify for, assuming that the bank will lend 80 percent of the new net equity?

Trading on the equity = [new equity – (original equity – existing mortgage)]

× amount eligible to be borrowed on new equity

= [$200,000 – ($75,000 – $40,000)] × 80%

= ($200,000 – $35,000) × 80% = $132,000

In this example, the bank would lend $132,000 on a home equity loan or second mortgage.

HOW IS IT USED AND APPLIED? In real estate, trading on the equity is used to obtain equity and second mortgage loans for secondary investment purposes. This form of real estate financing assumes that market appreciation will be stable for the period of the new loan; however, during the late 1980s and early 1990s, inflated real estate values collapsed in certain geographic areas of the country, causing many real estate investments to have higher financing than their market value. This resulted in foreclosures and numerous nonperforming loans for many banks, contributing to a national banking crisis.

In real estate, therefore, trading on the equity is inherently risky.

WHO USES IT AND WHEN?

Property Owners, Bank Mortgage Officers, and Home Equity Loan Underwriters. Trading on the equity is used for the purpose of obtaining or granting financing on a property's new net equity. The realized proceeds can be used for any purpose, including financing a child's college education.

189 Trend Equation

DEFINITION. The trend equation is a common method for forecasting sales or earnings. It involves a regression whereby a trend line is fitted to a time series of data.

HOW IS IT COMPUTED?

$$Y = a + bX$$

The formulas for the coefficients a and b are essentially the same as for simple regression; however, for regression purposes, a time period can be given a number so that $\Sigma X = 0$. When there is an odd number of periods, the period in the middle is assigned a zero value. If there is an even number, then -1 and $+1$ are assigned the two periods in the middle, so that again $\Sigma X = 0$.

With $\Sigma X = 0$, the formula for b and a reduces to:

$$b = \frac{n \sum XY}{n \sum X^2}$$

$$a = \frac{\sum Y}{n}$$

Example 1 This example demonstrates the use of trend equations in cases in which an even number and an odd number of periods occur.

Case 1 (odd number):

	19X1	19X2	19X3	19X4	19X5
$X =$	-2	-1	0	$+1$	$+2$

Case 2 (even number):

	19X1	19X2	19X3	19X4	19X5	19X6
$X =$	-3	-2	-1	$+1$	$+2$	$+3$

In each case, $\Sigma t = 0$.

Example 2 A company's historical earnings per share (EPS) are stated as:

Year	EPS
19X1	$1.00
19X2	1.20
19X3	1.30
19X4	1.60
19X5	1.70

Since the company has f years' data, which is an odd number, the year in the middle is assigned a zero value.

Year	X	EPS (Y)	XY	X^2
19X1	– 2	$1.00	– 2.00	4
19X2	– 1	1.20	– 1.20	1
19X3	0	1.30	0	0
19X4	+ 1	1.60	1.60	1
19X5	+ 2	1.70	3.40	4
	0	$6.80	1.80	10

$$b = \frac{(5)(1.80)}{(5)(10)} = \frac{9}{50} = \$0.18$$

$$a = \frac{\$6.80}{5} = \$1.36$$

Therefore, the estimated trend equation is

$$\hat{Y} = \$1.36 + \$0.18X$$

where $\hat{Y}$ = estimated EPS
    X = year index value

To project 19X6 sales, we assign + 3 to the X value for the year 19X6. Thus:

$$\hat{Y} = \$1.36 + \$0.18(+ 3)$$
$$= \$1.36 + \$0.54$$
$$= \$1.90$$

HOW IS IT USED AND BY WHOM?

Management. Managers use the trend equation for forecasting purposes, such as to project future revenue and costs.

190 Valuation of a Business

DEFINITION. A business may be valued based on a variety of factors, including earnings, cash flow, revenue, fair market value of net assets, and integration of methods. When earnings are used as the valuation base, they must be adjusted to arrive at a relevant figure. Valuation comparisons should be made between the company being valued and others in the same industry.

HOW IS IT COMPUTED? Eleven ways in which a company's value may be analyzed, including a combination of approaches, are as follows.

1. Adjustment of net income for business valuation purposes:

Net income
Adjustments: Add
Subtract
Restated net income (adjusted net income)

2. Adjusted average earnings for 5 years:

Adjusted average earnings for 5 years
 × Multiplier
Value of business

The multiplier depends on many factors, including risk, liquidity, growth potential, and economic conditions.

3. Capitalization of earnings valuation:

Weighted-average 5-year earnings
 × Multiplier
Value of business

4. Capitalization of excess earnings:

Weighted-average adjusted net income (5 years)
Less: Reasonable rate of return on weighted-average tangible net assets
Excess earnings
 × Multiplier
Value of intangibles
Add: Fair market value of net tangible assets
Value of business

5. Capitalization of cash flow:

Adjusted cash earnings
 × Multiplier

Capitalization of cash flow
Less: Liabilities assumed

Value of Business

---

6. Present value of future cash flows:

Present value (discounted) of future cash earnings
Add: Present value of expected selling price

Value of business

---

7. Tangible net worth:

Stockholders' equity
Less: Intangible assets

Value of business

---

8. Fair market value of net assets

9. Gross revenue multiplier:

Revenue
 × Gross revenue multiplier (common in industry)

Value of business

---

10. Price–earnings factor:

Earnings per share
× Price–Earnings Multiplier
Estimated market price per share
× Number of outstanding shares
P/E valuation of business

11. Combination of methods:

Weighted average of fair market value of net assets
Plus: Weighted average of capitalization of excess earnings
Value of business

Example 1 This example demonstrates a relatively simple calculation of business valuation.

Reported net income	$325,000
Adjustments:	
Personal expenses	50,000
Extraordinary or nonrecurring gain	(60,000)
Owner's fringe benefits	40,000
Excessive owner's salary relative to a reasonable salary	30,000
Interest expense	20,000
Dividend revenue	(10,000)
Low-cost rental payments relative to a fair rental charge	(5,000)
Excess depreciation from using an accelerated method	10,000
Restated net income	$400,000

Example 2 This example employs a combination of methods, using weighted averages to calculate valuation of a business.

Year	Net income	× Weight	=	Total
19X9	$120,000	× 5	=	$ 600,000
19X8	100,000	× 4	=	400,000

19X7	110,000	×	3	=	330,000
19X6	90,000	×	2	=	180,000
19X5	115,000	×	1	=	115,000
			15		$1,625,000

Weighted-average 5-year earnings ($1,625,000/15) $ 108,333

× Capitalization factor   × 5

Capitalization-of-earnings valuation $ 541,665

Example 3 In this example, valuation using weighted-average net tangible assets is computed.

Year	Amount	× Weight		=	Total	
19X1	$ 950,000	×	1	=	$	950,000
19X2	1,000,000	×	2	=		2,000,000
19X3	1,200,000	×	3	=		3,600,000
19X4	1,400,000	×	4	=		5,600,000
19X5	1,500,000	×	5	=		7,500,000
			15			$19,650,000

Weighted-average net tangible assets

($19,650,000/15)   = $1,310,000

Weighted-average adjusted net income (5 years)—

assumed $200,000

Reasonable rate of return on weighted-average tangible

net assets ($1,310,000 × 10%)   131,000

Excess earnings $69,000

Capitalization rate (20%)   × 5

Value of intangibles $345,000

Fair market value of net tangible assets   3,000,000

Capitalization-of-excess-earnings valuation $3,345,000

HOW IS IT USED AND BY WHOM?

Management.   Management may want to value its business to determine a potential selling price. Management may also want to value a targeted company to determine an offering price for the acquisition. In a lawsuit between parties, a business valuation is required as a basis on which to settle the claim. If a company wants to expand its credit line, the bank will likely require a business valuation. Valuations are required in some tax situations, such as to determine the taxability associated with a business liquidation.

Creditors.   Creditors may value a company to see if its worth exceeds the value of its obligations.

Tax Accountants and Attorneys.   The Internal Revenue Service will value a business in connection with tax matters.

Partners. Partners may want to value a partnership if there is an admission or withdrawal of a partner, a dispute between the parties requiring a settlement, or to establish a selling price.

Individuals. A business valuation may be needed in connection with a divorce action.

191 Value of Option (Call and Put)

DEFINITION. An *option* is the right (not the obligation) to either buy or sell a round lot (100) of a security at a predetermined price. The two types of options are calls and puts. The *call* option allows the holder to buy a stock at a set price for a predetermined period, while the *put* option allows the holder to sell the stock at a set price for a predetermined period.

Several important terms must be defined:

Exercise price: The fixed price at which a security can either be bought or sold with a call or put option, respectively. Options whose exercise price is close to the value of the underlying stock have a premium value. But the further the exercise price from the price of the underlying stock, the lower is the call option premium. This occurs because an "out of the money" option costs substantially more to purchase.

Expiration date: The date on which a call or put option expires.

Time premium: The greater the *time period* before the expiration date of the option, the more value the option has. This *time premium* exists because of the greater chance the underlying security can increase in value in the case of a call option, or decrease in value in the case of a put option.

HOW IS IT COMPUTED? The following discussion assumes no transaction costs. In reality, trading commissions would substantially alter the option valuations.

1. Absolute value of an option at maturity: The value of an option at expiration is equal to the price of the underlying security minus the exercise price:

   Value of a call option at maturity = stock price − exercise price

   Value of a put option at maturity = exercise price − stock price

2. The value of an option with time left before the expiration period:

   Value of a call option prior to maturity = stock price − exercise price

   Value of a put option prior to maturity = exercise price − stock price

3. The maximum value of an option:

   Maximum value of a call option = stock price

   Maximum value of a put option = exercise price

4. The minimum value of an option:

Minimum value of a call or put option = 0

Example 1: Value of Option at Exercise Date. *Call option:* The call option's exercise price is $45, the price of XYZ is $50 a share, and the option's expiration date is today. What is the value of the call option at expiration?

Value of a call option at maturity = stock price − exercise price

$$= \$50 - \$45 = \$5$$

Put option: The put option's exercise price is $50, the price of XYZ is $45 a share, and the put option's expiration date is today. What is the value of the put option at expiration?

Value of a put option at maturity = exercise price − stock price

$$= \$50 - \$45 = \$5$$

Example 2: Value of an Option with Time Remaining Prior to the Expiration Date. *Call option:* The call option's exercise price is $45, XYZ's stock price is $50, and the expiration date of the call option is in 6 months. What is the market price of the call option?

Value of a call option prior to maturity = stock price − exercise price

$$= \$50 - \$45 = \$5$$

Considering the 6-month time premium, the call option must exceed the $5 difference between the price of the stock and the exercise price of the call option.

Put option: The put option's exercise price is $50, XYZ's stock price is $45, and the expiration date of the put option is in 6 months. What is the market price of the put option?

Value of a put option prior to maturity = exercise price − stock price

$$= (\$50 - \$45) = \$5$$

Considering the 6-month time premium, the put option must exceed the $5 difference between the exercise price of the put option and the price of the stock.

Example 3: Maximum Value of an Option. *Call option:* The call option's exercise price is $0.01 and the XYZ stock price is $45 with 3 months left prior to expiration. How much is the call option worth?

Maximum value of a call option = stock price

$$= \$45$$

In this highly unlikely scenario, the call option must be worth at least, but not more than, the price of the stock, since the holder of the call option has the contractual right to buy the stock at $0.01. It should be pointed out, of course, that the exercise price of options are normally set at multiples of $5 increments consistent with recent market prices of the underlying security.

Put option: The put option's exercise price is $45 and the XYZ stock price is $0.01 with 3 months left prior to expiration. How much is the put option worth?

Maximum value of a put option = exercise price

$$= \$45$$

In this untypical scenario, the put option must be worth the value of the exercise price since the put option holder has the right to sell the underlying stock at the exercise price, $45.

Example 4: Minimum Value of an Option. If either a call or a put option expires without being exercised, what is it worth? An expired call or put option has no value:

$$\text{Minimum value of a call or put option} = 0$$

EFFECT OF STOCK PRICE VOLATILITY ON THE VALUE OF AN OPTION.

The major factors affecting the price of an option are the exercise price, the time premium, and the price of the underlying security; however, a less obvious factor that has a strong effect on the market price of the option is the variance over time of the price of the underlying security.

All things being equal, the greater the variance in the price of the underlying security, the greater will be the probability that the price of the underlying security will exceed the exercise price without decreasing the minimum value of the option, which is zero.

Exhibits 191.1 and 191.2 illustrate the effect of the variance on the value of an option. For the call option, the payoff for the high-variance stock is 233 percent higher than the payoff for the low-variance stock. For the put option, as with the call option, the payoff for the high-variance stock is 233 percent higher than the payoff for the low-variance stock.

HOW IS IT USED AND APPLIED?

An investor who feels that a stock may rise in value can buy a call option at a substantially lower price than the price of the stock with substantially higher leverage, risking only the cost of the call. Conversely, if the investor believes the stock will fall in price, a put option can be purchased for a fraction of the cost of the stock and the investor can profit when the stock declines in value with similar leverage.

Another strategy that can be employed is to buy a stock and then sell, or "short," a call option on the stock. This is known as "writing a call." The call premium strategy helps to offset the price of the stock and to hedge any losses down to the value of the option at the time it was sold:

Effects of a Call Option Writing Strategy on Stock XYZ

Cost of 100 shares of XYZ	Proceeds from a $45 call	Net cost of XYZ stock
$4500	$450	$4050

Exhibit 191.1 Effect of higher security variance on call option X's value.

Price of security	Proba-bility	Low-variance stock price	Payoff if X = $55	High-variance stock price	Payoff if X = $55
Up	.2	$50	$ 0	$20	$ 0
Unmoved	.6	60	5	60	5
Down	.2	70	15	90	35

Exhibit 191.2 Effect of higher security variance on put option Y's value.

Price of security	Proba- bility	Low- variance stock price	Payoff if X = $55	High- variance stock price	Payoff if X = $55
Down	.2	$70	$15	$90	$35
Unmoved	.6	60	5	60	5
Up	.2	50	0	20	0

If the stock closes at less than $45 per share at the time of the expiration of the call, the option will expire worthless and the seller may sell (write) another call option on the stock. If the stock is exercised, the seller will receive the original purchase price òf the stock while retaining the proceeds from the original call option sale.

A perfectly hedged transaction would be to purchase a stock, sell (write) a call option, and buy a put at the same exercise price as the call. Exhibit 191.3 illustrates a perfectly hedged transaction where 100 shares of XYZ are purchased at a cost of $4500, a call option with a $45 exercise price is sold for $450, and a put option with a $45 exercise price is purchased for $450. While this hedging strategy will protect the capital of the investment in the stock, in reality the commission costs for the stock and option transactions will impose a sizable loss on the exchange.

Another option strategy for an investor is to purchase a put option to protect an unrealized capital gain on a stock. Should the stock decline in value after the put option is purchased, the increase in the value of the put option will offset the capital loss on the stock. This could be done to defer capital gain taxes for another year without risking a capital loss.

WHO USES IT AND WHEN?

Investors and Portfolio Managers. Option strategies can be used for the purposes of increasing leverage, hedging risk, and improving the rate of return. This is accomplished by utilizing a call option writing strategy. Portfolio managers normally have relatively large amounts of assets under their management, which allows them to qualify for volume commission discounts that give option transactions even greater leverage.

Exhibit 191.3 A perfectly hedged transaction.

Price of stock XYZ	Value of 100 shares of XYZ	Value of $45 call option	Value of $45 put option	Net value
$35.00	$3500	0	$1000	$4500
45.00	4500	$ 450	450	4500
55.00	5500	1000	0	4500

Call option writing strategies are also a very conservative method of investing, since the premium from the call options provides a substantial hedge for a portfolio for downward price movements.

The purchase of calls and puts gives the investor tremendous financial leverage with limited downside risk. The buying of puts can be used as a strategy for protecting unrealized capital gains.

192 Value of Stock Rights

DEFINITION. Stock rights are preemptive rights giving current holders of common stock the right or option to purchase additional issues of common stock at a specified price during a given time period. In this event, the firm must present a rights offering to present stockholders when issuing new shares of stock. The offering is contained on a certificate termed a right. One right is issued for each share of stock owned by the stockholders.

A rights offering is important to current stockholders since it confers on them the right of maintaining equivalent financial control over a company despite a new stock offering, as well as offering them the ability to protect against dilution of the value of the shares during a new stock offering. Further, the rights offering may allow the purchase of stock at a discount below the current market price per share. Additionally, brokerage commissions may be saved.

For example, if Company XYZ issued 1,000,000 shares of stock with a market price of $50 per share, a new 500,000-share stock offering at $30 per share could considerably dilute the value of the currently held shares.

Rights On. During the rights offering period, the common shares of the company are trading with the value of the stock right *attached*—that is, if the stock is traded during this period, the value of the stock right goes to the new holder of record. The period during which this can occur is determined by the establishment of a holder of record date by the issuing company.

Ex Rights. During the period in which the stock is trading after the record date of the rights offering has expired, but prior to the actual issuance of the stock right, the stock right has gone *ex rights*, and the former owner of the common stock will receive the stock right. For example, assume that Company XYZ announces the terms of a new stock rights offering on April 15. XYZ has established a holder-of-record date of May 15. The company states that stock rights will be mailed out on June 1 to all holders of record as of the close of business on May 15. After May 15 and prior to June 1, the stock will be trading *ex rights*, and the new holders of record during this trading period will not be entitled to the stock right. The stock right will accrue to the former owner.

HOW IS IT COMPUTED? When a company is deciding on using a stock rights offering to raise equity capital, many computations must be made. The following cover the major management decision areas for reaching a conclusion regarding a stock rights issue:

1. Number of new shares needed to be issued:

$$\text{Number of new shares} = \frac{\text{funds to be raised}}{\text{stock offering price}}$$

2. Number of rights needed to buy a share of stock:

$$\text{Number of rights needed to buy a share of stock} = \frac{\text{old shares}}{\text{new shares}}$$

3. Value of one right: A stock right gives the holder the right to purchase a stock at a fixed price below the current market price by a certain period of time. Stock rights, therefore, have their own market value. The formula to determine the value of one right needed to buy a share of stock has to be adjusted for the *rights on* and *ex rights* conditions:

Rights on: Value of one right

$$= \frac{\text{market value of stock, rights on} - \text{subscription price}}{\text{number of rights required to purchase one share} + 1}$$

Ex rights: Value of one right

$$= \frac{\text{market value of stock, ex rights} - \text{subscription price}}{\text{number of rights required to purchase one share}}$$

Example 1: Number of New Shares Needed to Be Issued. Company XYZ is seeking $15 million in new equity funding and seeks to sell its stock at $30 per share. How many shares need to be sold to achieve its equity funding target?

$$\text{Number of new shares} = \frac{\text{funds to be raised}}{\text{stock offering price}}$$

$$= \frac{\$15,000,000}{30} = 500,000$$

Example 2: Number of Rights Needed to Buy a Share of Stock. In order to determine the number of rights needed to subscribe to one share of stock, divide the number of new shares to be offered through the rights offering into the previously outstanding shares. For Company XYZ of Example 1,

$$\text{Number of rights needed to buy a share of stock} = \frac{\text{old shares}}{\text{new shares}}$$

$$= \frac{1,000,000}{500,000} = 2$$

The stockholder must surrender two rights plus pay $30 to receive one of the newly issued shares through the rights offering. Should the number of new shares exceed the number of old shares, then the number of rights required to subscribe to each new share would be a fraction of 1. If, for example, the number of shares outstanding were 1,500,000 and 2,000,000 shares were offered, then 1,500,000/2,000,000 = 0.75 right would be required to subscribe to each new share of stock.

Example 3: Value of a Right. *Rights on:* When the stock is selling *ex rights*, what is the value of the right assuming its market value theoretically reflects the new funds raised in the stock rights issue? Using the example of the XYZ rights offering, its value can be determined as:

$$\text{Value of one right} = \frac{\text{market value of stock, rights on} - \text{subscription price}}{\text{number of rights required to purchase one share} + 1}$$

$$= \frac{\$50 - \$30}{2 + 1} = \frac{\$20}{3} = \$6.67$$

Ex rights: What would be the value of the stock right after the rights offering record date has expired, assuming its market theoretically reflects the new funds raised in the stock rights issue?

Again using the example of the XYZ rights offering, its value can be determined as:

$$\text{Value of one right} = \frac{\text{market value of stock, ex rights} - \text{subscription price}}{\text{number of rights required to purchase one share}}$$

$$= \frac{\$43.33 - \$30}{2} = \frac{\$13.33}{2} = \$6.67$$

A secondary market exists for those stockholders who do not wish to exercise their right to purchase additional stock, and wish, instead, to sell the stock right. Normally the market price of a right exceeds its theoretical value, as it is not unusual for investors to "bid up" the price of the stock in anticipation of future performance. Since rights do offer excellent leverage, investors can earn higher returns purchasing rights rather than the stock. As the expiration date of the stock right approaches, its premium market value corresponds more closely to its theoretical value.

Example 4: To Exercise Rights or Not to Exercise, That Is the Question. There is no net gain to shareholders to either exercise the stock rights and purchase the stock or to sell the right at the theoretical formula price. Using our previous example of XYZ Corporation, if two rights are required to buy one share of stock, an investor owning 100 shares of stock may purchase 50 shares. What would be the market value if the investor exercises the rights and buys 50 additional shares at $30 or sells the rights at $6.67 per right?:

Exercise 50 shares (100 shares/2 rights) @ $30 per share:

Stockholder market value = market value of stock rights on

+ market value of exercised stock − cost of exercising stock rights

$$= (100 \times \$50) + (50 \times \$30) - (50 \times \$30)$$

$$= (\$5000) + (\$1500) - (\$1500)$$

$$= \$5000$$

Sale of 100 rights @ $6.67 per right:

Stockholder market value = market value of stock ex rights

+ market value of ex rights

$$= (100 \times \$43.33) + (100 \times \$6.67)$$

$$= \$5000$$

Whether or not the stockholder exercises the stock rights and buys 50 additional shares or simply sells the 100 stock rights, the stockholder market value is $5000.

HOW IS IT USED AND APPLIED?

The use of rights allows shareholders to preserve their pro-rata share in the earnings and ownership of the company. Rights offerings are also beneficial to a firm, since it can be assumed they will have a more favorable reception with current stockholders than a public offering per se. One would have to assume that current stockholders are familiar with the company and view it favorably.

A secondary advantage is that issuing subscription stock rights to investors avoids the use of underwriters and higher related costs. In addition, the underpricing of the rights offering can have the effect of a stock split, reducing the market price of the stock and creating a more affordable investment choice.

On the whole, rights offerings have been received favorably by investors and the investment market. They have proved to be a cost-effective way of achieving additional equity financing.

An interesting aspect of stock rights issues is that a small percentage of stockholders, normally about 1½ percent, will not exercise or sell their rights. There are reasons for this, but the net result is that these stockholders lose substantial sums of money by not exercising or selling their stock rights.

WHO USES IT AND WHEN?

Stockholders and Financial Management. Management has the primary responsibility for determining the terms of a stock rights offering. The primary advantages of a stock rights offering are that it reduces or eliminates underwriting expenses, lowers the unit price of the stock offering, has a high certainty of raising the expected equity capital, and helps to increase stockholder loyalty.

On the other hand, since a stock rights offering usually has a lower market price than a public issuance of stock, more rights have to be issued in order to meet the desired equity capital target as compared to a traditional public stock offering. Yet stock rights offerings are popular with stockholders, and are a well-received method of raising equity capital.

193 Variable Costs to Fixed Costs

DEFINITION. Variable costs to fixed costs measures the relationship between costs that change with volume and costs that do not change. When there is idle capacity, additional volume may be produced but total fixed cost remains the same. However, fixed cost per unit decreases because total fixed cost is spread over more units. Total variable costs increase as more units are manufactured, but the variable cost per unit remains the same.

HOW IS IT COMPUTED?

$$\frac{\text{Total variable costs}}{\text{Total fixed costs}}$$

Examples of variable costs that change are direct material and direct labor going into a product. Examples of fixed costs that remain constant are rent, insurance, and property taxes.

Example A company reports total variable costs of $800,000 and total fixed costs of $8,000,000. The ratio is 0.10. This is unfavorable, because it is difficult to reduce fixed costs in the short run when business falls off.

HOW IS IT USED AND BY WHOM?

Management. The cost structure of the business indicates what costs may be cut if needed such as in a recessionary environment (e.g., the early 1990s). Management can more readily control and adjust variable costs than fixed costs.

194 Vertical (Common-Size) Analysis

DEFINITION. In vertical analysis of financial statements, an item is used as a base value and all other accounts in the financial statement are compared to this base value.

HOW IS IT COMPUTED? On the balance sheet, total assets equal 100 percent. In vertical analysis, each asset is stated as a percentage of total assets. Similarly, total liabilities and stockholders' equity are assigned 100 percent, with a given liability or equity account stated as a percentage of total liabilities and stockholders' equity.

On the income statement, 100 percent is assigned to net sales, with all revenue and expense accounts then related to it.

The following two examples illustrate vertical analysis of financial statement data.

Example 1

Net sales	$300,000	100%
Less: Cost of sales	60,000	20
Gross profit	$240,000	80%
Less: Operating expenses	150,000	50
Net income	$ 90,000	30%

Example 2

Current assets	$200,000	25%
Noncurrent assets	600,000	75
Total assets	$800,000	100%

HOW IS IT USED AND BY WHOM?

Financial Analysts, Investors, and Management. Common-size percentages can be compared from one period to another to identify areas that require improvements in performance.

Vertical analysis tends to exhibit the internal structure of the enterprise, indicating the relative amount of each income statement account to revenue. It shows clearly the mix of assets that produces the income and the mix of the sources of capital, regardless of whether they are provided by current or long-term liabilities, or by equity funding.

The vertical percentages of a particular company should be compared to competing companies or to industry percentages so that the firm's relative position may be ascertained.

As in horizontal analysis, vertical analysis is not a process that is an end in itself. The analyst or manager must be prepared to probe deeper into the areas that the analysis indicates may have possible problems.

195 Volume (Denominator) Variance

DEFINITION. In overhead variance analysis, the volume variance considers the utilization of plant facilities.

HOW IS IT COMPUTED?

Volume (denominator) variance = standard overhead versus budget
adjusted to standard hours

Standard overhead = standard hours × standard overhead rate

Budget adjusted to standard hours = fixed overhead
(denominator hours × standard fixed overhead rate) + variable overhead
(standard hours × standard variable overhead rate)

Example The standards for overhead in a particular company are:

Variable overhead: 2 hours @ $6 = $12 per unit
Fixed overhead: 2 hours @ $20 = $40 per unit

The related level of activity is:

Production: 9,500 units
Denominator activity: 10,000 units

The volume (production) variance is calculated as:

Standard overhead		$494,000
(9,500 × 2 = 19,000 × $26)		
Budget adjusted to standard hours		
Fixed overhead	$400,000	
(10,000 × 2 = 20,000 × $20)		
Variable overhead (19,000 × $6)	114,000	514,000
Variance		$ 20,000 U

A consistently unfavorable volume variance may be the result of having purchased a plant of incorrect size. An unfavorable volume variance may arise from controllable factors such as poor scheduling, lack of orders, shortages or defectiveness in raw materials, inadequate tooling, lack of employees, machine breakdowns, long operating times, and/or incompetent workers. Uncontrollable factors for the overhead volume variance are decreases in customer demand, excess plant capacity, and calendar fluctuations.

HOW IS IT USED AND BY WHOM?

Top Management and Plant Heads. The volume variance reveals information about plant utilization. Overhead capacity variances can bring the existence of slack resources to management's attention. Idle capacity may imply long-run operating planning deficiencies.

Responsibility for the factory overhead volume variance rests with those responsible for generating volume. In some cases, marketing managers, rather than manufacturing managers, bear this responsibility.

The volume of activity is often determined outside the factory, based on customer orders. If this is the case, volume variances may not be controllable by the department head or even by the plant manager. Volume variances should still be reported to plant managers to help in explaining the total overhead variance to higher management.

196 Warehouse Cost Variances

DEFINITION. Warehouse cost variances compare actual costs and standard costs to reveal the efficiency with which warehousing is being performed.

HOW IS IT COMPUTED? Variances in warehousing costs can be calculated by looking at the cost per unit to store the merchandise and the number of orders anticipated. Calculations include:

1. Total warehousing cost variance = total actual cost versus total standard cost

2. Variance in orders = (actual orders versus standard orders) × standard unit cost

3. Variance in cost = (actual cost per unit versus standard cost per unit) × actual orders

Example Assume that a company supplies the following information regarding a product and warehouse costs:

Standard cost	$12,100
Standard orders	5,500
Standard unit cost	$2.20
Actual cost	$14,030
Actual orders	6,100
Actual unit cost	$2.30

Total warehousing cost variance is:

Actual cost	$14,030
Standard cost	12,100
	$ 1,930 U

For the analysis, the total variance is segregated into the variance in orders and the variance in cost:

Variance in orders = (actual orders versus standard orders) × standard unit cost: (6100 versus 5500) × $2.20	$1320 U
Variance in cost = (actual cost per unit versus standard cost per unit) × actual orders: ($2.30 versus $2.20) × 6100	$ 610 U

HOW IS IT USED AND BY WHOM?

Production Management. Variances in warehousing costs are used by warehouse management to determine whether the warehousing function is being performed properly. Analysis of warehousing costs are made to identify possible problems and take necessary cost-saving measures.

197 Weighted Average (Mean)

DEFINITION. Weighted average (mean) is an average of observations having different degrees of importance or frequency.

HOW IS IT COMPUTED? The formula for a weighted average is:

$$\text{Weighted average} = \sum w_i x_i$$

where x_i = the data values and w_i = relative weight assigned to each observation, expressed as a percentage or relative frequency.

Example 1   The KJ Company uses three grades of labor to produce a finished product as follows:

Grade of labor	Labor hours per unit of labor	Hourly wages (X)
Skilled	6	$10.00
Semiskilled	3	8.00
Unskilled	1	6.00

The arithmetic average (mean) labor cost per hour for this product can be computed as:

$$\text{Arithmetic mean} = \frac{\$10.00 + \$8.00 + \$6.00}{3} = \$8.00 \text{ per hour}$$

This computation implies that each grade of labor was used in equal amounts, however, which is not the case. To calculate the average cost of labor per hour correctly, the weighted average should be computed as:

$$\text{Weighted average} = \$10.00\left(\frac{6}{10}\right) + \$8.00\left(\frac{3}{10}\right) + \$6.00\left(\frac{1}{10}\right)$$

$$= \$9.00 \text{ per hour}$$

where the weights used equal the proportion of the total labor required to manufacture the product.

Example 2   A prospective acquirer wants to determine the price to offer for a targeted business. It is decided that the business valuation should be based on two times the weighted-average earnings over the last 3 years. The most current year is always given the greatest weight.

Year	Net income	Weight	Weighted net income
19X1	$300,000	1	$ 300,000
19X2	260,000	2	520,000
19X3	350,000	3	1,050,000
		6	$1,870,000

$$\text{Weighted-average earnings} = \frac{\$1,870,000}{6} = \$311,667$$

$$\text{Business valuation} = \$311,667 \times 2 = \$623,334$$

HOW IS IT USED AND APPLIED?   Any time each value has a different degree of importance or frequency, the weighted-average formula must be used. An arithmetic average can be used only when the values are equally weighted. Expected value is basically a weighted average, the weights being the probabilities of occurrence.

WHO USES IT AND WHEN?

Management and Managerial Accountants. Managers of all functional areas of business must have an understanding of the difference between the arithmetic mean and the weighted mean in order to calculate the correct average.

In the case of multiproduct lines, it is necessary to predetermine the sales mix and then compute a weighted-average contribution margin (CM) in order to perform breakeven and cost–volume–profit (CVP) analysis. The weights used here are sales-mix ratios (see No. 170, Sales-Mix Analysis).

Investors. Investors are particularly interested in increasing the expected return on an investment, which is nothing more than the weighted-average return, the weights being the probabilities of different states of nature (such as different conditions of the economy).

Financial Managers and Treasurers. Financial officers need to know the weighted-average cost of capital in order to decide whether or not to accept a project. (See also No. 41, Cost of Capital.)

198 Wilcox's Gambler's-Ruin Prediction Formula

DEFINITION. Wilcox's gambler's-ruin prediction formula is used to obtain a company's liquidation value.

HOW IS IT COMPUTED?

Liquidation value equals:
   Cash + marketable securities at market value
   Plus: (Inventory, accounts receivable, and prepaid expenses) at 70% of book value
   Plus: Other assets at 50% of book value
   Minus: Current liabilities
   Minus: Long-term liabilities

Example A company reports the following balance sheet information: cash, $400,000; marketable securities (market value, $260,000), $250,000; accounts receivable, $700,000; inventory, $1,000,000; prepaid expenses, $300,000; other assets, $800,000; current liabilities, $900,000; and long-term liabilities, $1,200,000.

Using the above formula, the liquidation value of this company is calculated as follows:

Cash	$ 400,000
Marketable securities	260,000
Accounts receivable ($700,000 × 70%)	490,000
Inventory ($1,000,000 × 70%)	700,000
Prepaid expenses ($300,000 × 70%)	210,000
Other assets ($800,000 × 50%)	400,000
Current liabilities	(900,000)
Long-term liabilities	(1,200,000)
Liquidation value	$ 360,000

HOW IS IT USED AND BY WHOM?

Financial Management. The liquidation value is useful in gauging a company's solvency.

Creditors and Investors. The liquidation value indicates a company's net worth in a forced-sale situation. The liquidation value reveals the degree to which a residual balance will be left to meet creditor claims.

199 Working Capital

DEFINITION. Working capital compares current assets to current liabilities, and serves as the liquid reserve available to satisfy contingencies and uncertainties. A high working capital balance is mandated if the entity is unable to borrow on short notice. Working capital must be related to other financial statement elements, such as sales and total assets.

HOW IS IT COMPUTED? Working capital, along with several types of related ratios and analytical tools, is computed as follows:

1. Working capital = current assets − current liabilities

2. $\dfrac{\text{Working capital}}{\text{Sales}}$

3. $\dfrac{\text{Working capital}}{\text{Total assets}}$

4. Working capital provided from operations:

Net Income
Plus: Nonworking capital expenses (e.g., depreciation)
Minus: Nonworking capital revenue (e.g., amortization of deferred revenue)
Equals: Working capital provided from operations

5. $\dfrac{\text{Working capital provided from operations}}{\text{Net income}}$

6. $\dfrac{\text{Working capital provided from operations}}{\text{Total liabilities}}$

Example A company reports the following information on its financial statement:

Working capital provided from operations	$100,000
Net income	300,000
Current assets	900,000
Current liabilities	500,000
Noncurrent liabilities	600,000

The industry averages are:

Working capital provided from operations to total liabilities	30.5%
Working capital to net income	50.0%
Working capital	$1,100,000

The relevant ratios for the company follow:

Working capital	$400,000
Working capital provided from operations to total liabilities	9.1%
Working capital provided from operations to net income	33.3%

The analysis shows that working capital generated from operations is insufficient to meet total debt—an outcome that indicates poor liquidity. Further, the company has less earnings backed up by liquid funds than other companies in its industry. Overall, the company's working capital is shown to be deficient relative to the industry norms.

HOW IS IT USED AND BY WHOM?

Financial Management and Short-Term Creditors (such as Suppliers). Management may have to monitor the level of working capital closely, since loan agreements and bond indentures often contain stipulations regarding the maintenance of minimum working capital levels.

To spot changes in the composition of working capital, the creditor should determine the trend in the percentage of each current asset to total current assets. A shift from cash to inventory, for instance, implies less liquidity.

The working capital-to-sales ratio tells whether the entity is using its liquid balance optimally. A low ratio indicates the company's ability to generate revenue from liquid funds.

A high ratio of working capital provided by operations to net income is desirable, since a liquidity rating is higher when earnings are backed up by liquid funds.

The ratio of working capital provided from operations to total liabilities indicates the degree to which internally generated working capital flow is available to satisfy obligations.

200 Yield on Preferred Stock

DEFINITION. The yield on preferred stock is the preferred stockholders' expected return. The value of preferred stock is the present worth of a series of equal cash flow streams (dividends), continuing indefinitely. Since the dividends in each period are equal for preferred stock, the valuation model can be reduced to the following relationship:

$$V = \frac{D}{r}$$

where V = present value of a preferred stock
D = annual dividend
r = the investor's required rate of return

HOW IS IT COMPUTED? In computing the preferred stockholder's expected rate of return, the valuation equation is used as presented above. Solving for r,

$$r = \frac{D}{V}$$

which indicates that the expected rate of return of a preferred stock equals the dividend yield (annual dividend/market price).

Example A preferred stock paying $5.00 a year in dividends and having a market price of $25 would have a current yield r computed as follows:

$$r = \frac{D}{V} = \frac{\$5}{\$25} = 20\%$$

HOW IS IT USED AND APPLIED? Investors compare this rate with those of other fixed-income securities such as corporate bonds and government bonds to see which is more attractive. They have to exercise caution in comparing yields of different fixed-income instruments, since these instruments involve different degrees of risk. They should check the ratings provided by *Moody's*, *Fitch's*, and *Standard and Poor's*.

Investors and Fund Managers. Yields are major yardsticks for investment selection, along with quality ratings, maturity, and tax status. Yields are comparable only when other factors are deemed equal.

201 *Z*-Score Model: Forecasting Business Failures

DEFINITION. The *Z*-score model is a quantitative model developed in 1968 by Edward Altman to predict bankruptcy (financial distress) of a business, using a blend of the traditional financial ratios and a statistical method known as *multiple discriminant analysis* (MDA).

The *Z* score is known to be about 90 percent accurate in forecasting business failure one year into the future and about 80 percent accurate in forecasting it two years into the future.

HOW IS IT COMPUTED?

$$Z = 1.2^*X_1 + 1.4^*X_2 + 3.3^*X_3 + 0.6^*X_4 + 0.999^*X_5$$

where X_1 = working capital/total assets
X_2 = retained earnings/total assets
X_3 = earnings before interest and taxes (EBIT)/total assets
X_4 = market value of equity/book value of debt
X_5 = sales/total assets

Altman also established the following guidelines for classifying firms:

Z score	Probability of failure
1.8 or less	Very high
1.81–2.99	Not sure
3.0 or higher	Unlikely

Example The following financial data has been selected from the financial statements of ABC Company:

Total assets = $2000.
Retained earnings = $750.
EBIT = $266.
Sales = $3000.
Market value of common and preferred stock = $1425.
Book value of debt = $1100.

The calculation of ABC's Z scores is shown below:

$$
\begin{aligned}
X_1 &= 400/2000 \times 1.2 & &= 0.240 \\
X_2 &= 750/2000 \times 1.4 & &= 0.525 \\
X_3 &= 266/2000 \times 3.3 & &= 0.439 \\
X_4 &= 1425/1100 \times 0.6 & &= 0.777 \\
X_5 &= 3000/2000 \times 0.999 & &= \underline{1.499} \\
& & Z &= \overline{3.480}
\end{aligned}
$$

Since ABC's Z score of 3.480 is well into the "unlikely" zone, there is virtually no chance that ABC will go bankrupt within the next two years.

HOW IS IT USED AND APPLIED?   The MDA may be used for one company or a group of companies. The recessionary environment of the early 1990s witnessed an increasing trend in bankruptcies. The Z score model could be used to determine if an employer was on the verge of bankruptcy or if some other entity would go bankrupt. A major customer? An important supplier? A borrower?

If it can be predicted with reasonable accuracy that a company in which one is a participant is in increasing financial distress, protection measures and corrective actions can be taken. Some steps might be to curtail capital expansion, cut back on dividends, or engage in refinancing.

WHO USES IT AND WHEN?

Financial Managers and Analysts.   Financial managers and analysts apply the Z score in numerous ways, including the following.

Financial management analysis: The score can indicate whether capital expansion and dividends should be curtailed to keep needed funds within the business.

Merger analysis: The Z score can help identify potential problems with a merger candidate.

Loan and credit analysis: Bankers and lenders can use the Z score to determine if they should extend a loan. Other creditors, such as vendors, can use it to determine whether to extend credit.

Investment analysis: The Z score can help an investor in selecting stocks of potentially troubled companies.

Appendix

TABLE 1 The Future Value of $1.00

(Compounded Amount of $1.00)

$(1 + i)^n = \text{FVIF } (i,n)$

Periods	4%	6%	8%	10%	12%	14%	20%
1	1.040	1.060	1.080	1.100	1.120	1.140	1.200
2	1.082	1.124	1.166	1.210	1.254	1.300	1.440
3	1.125	1.191	1.260	1.331	1.405	1.482	1.728
4	1.170	1.263	1.361	1.464	1.574	1.689	2.074
5	1.217	1.338	1.469	1.611	1.762	1.925	2.488
6	1.265	1.419	1.587	1.772	1.974	2.195	2.986
7	1.316	1.504	1.714	1.949	2.211	2.502	3.583
8	1.369	1.594	1.851	2.144	2.476	2.853	4.300
9	1.423	1.690	1.999	2.359	2.773	3.252	5.160
10	1.480	1.791	2.159	2.594	3.106	3.707	6.192
11	1.540	1.898	2.332	2.853	3.479	4.226	7.430
12	1.601	2.012	2.518	3.139	3.896	4.818	8.916
13	1.665	2.133	2.720	3.452	4.364	5.492	10.699
14	1.732	2.261	2.937	3.798	4.887	6.261	12.839
15	1.801	2.397	3.172	4.177	5.474	7.138	15.407
16	1.873	2.540	3.426	4.595	6.130	8.137	18.488
17	1.948	2.693	3.700	5.055	6.866	9.277	22.186
18	2.026	2.854	3.996	5.560	7.690	10.575	26.623
19	2.107	3.026	4.316	6.116	8.613	12.056	31.948
20	2.191	3.207	4.661	6.728	9.646	13.743	38.338
30	3.243	5.744	10.063	17.450	29.960	50.950	237.380
40	4.801	10.286	21.725	45.260	93.051	188.880	1469.800

TABLE 2 The Future Value of an Annuity of $1.00[a]
(Compounded Amount of an Annuity of $1.00)

$$\frac{(1 + i)^n - 1}{i} = \text{FVIFA}(i,n)$$

Periods	4%	6%	8%	10%	12%	14%	20%
1	1.000	1.000	1.000	1.000	1.000	1.000	1.000
2	2.040	2.060	2.080	2.100	2.120	2.140	2.200
3	3.122	3.184	3.246	3.310	3.374	3.440	3.640
4	4.247	4.375	4.506	4.641	4.779	4.921	5.368
5	5.416	5.637	5.867	6.105	6.353	6.610	7.442
6	6.633	6.975	7.336	7.716	8.115	8.536	9.930
7	7.898	8.394	8.923	9.487	10.089	10.730	12.916
8	9.214	9.898	10.637	11.436	12.300	13.233	16.499
9	10.583	11.491	12.488	13.580	14.776	16.085	20.799
10	12.006	13.181	14.487	15.938	17.549	19.337	25.959
11	13.486	14.972	16.646	18.531	20.655	23.045	32.150
12	15.026	16.870	18.977	21.385	24.133	27.271	39.580
13	16.627	18.882	21.495	24.523	28.029	32.089	48.497
14	18.292	21.015	24.215	27.976	32.393	37.581	59.196
15	20.024	23.276	27.152	31.773	37.280	43.842	72.035
16	21.825	25.673	30.324	35.950	42.753	50.980	87.442
17	23.698	28.213	33.750	40.546	48.884	59.118	105.930
18	25.645	30.906	37.450	45.600	55.750	68.394	128.120
19	27.671	33.760	41.446	51.160	63.440	78.969	154.740
20	29.778	36.778	45.762	57.276	75.052	91.025	186.690
30	56.085	79.058	113.283	164.496	241.330	356.790	1181.900
40	95.026	154.762	259.057	442.597	767.090	1342.000	7343.900

[a]Payments (or receipts) at the *end* of each period.

TABLE 3 Present Value of $1

PVIF (i,n)

Periods	4%	5%	6%	8%	10%	12%	14%	16%	18%	20%	22%	24%	26%	28%	30%	40%
1	0.962	0.952	0.943	0.926	0.909	0.893	0.877	0.862	0.847	0.833	0.820	0.806	0.794	0.781	0.769	0.714
2	0.925	0.907	0.890	0.857	0.826	0.797	0.769	0.743	0.718	0.694	0.672	0.650	0.630	0.610	0.592	0.510
3	0.889	0.864	0.840	0.794	0.751	0.712	0.675	0.641	0.609	0.579	0.551	0.524	0.500	0.477	0.455	0.364
4	0.855	0.823	0.792	0.735	0.683	0.636	0.592	0.552	0.516	0.482	0.451	0.423	0.397	0.373	0.350	0.260
5	0.822	0.784	0.747	0.681	0.621	0.567	0.519	0.476	0.437	0.402	0.370	0.341	0.315	0.291	0.269	0.186
6	0.790	0.746	0.705	0.630	0.564	0.507	0.456	0.410	0.370	0.335	0.303	0.275	0.250	0.227	0.207	0.133
7	0.760	0.711	0.665	0.583	0.513	0.452	0.400	0.354	0.314	0.279	0.249	0.222	0.198	0.178	0.159	0.095
8	0.731	0.677	0.627	0.540	0.467	0.404	0.351	0.305	0.266	0.233	0.204	0.179	0.157	0.139	0.123	0.068
9	0.703	0.645	0.592	0.500	0.424	0.361	0.308	0.263	0.225	0.194	0.167	0.144	0.125	0.108	0.094	0.048
10	0.676	0.614	0.558	0.463	0.386	0.322	0.270	0.227	0.191	0.162	0.137	0.116	0.099	0.085	0.073	0.035
11	0.650	0.585	0.527	0.429	0.350	0.287	0.237	0.195	0.162	0.135	0.112	0.094	0.079	0.066	0.056	0.025
12	0.625	0.557	0.497	0.397	0.319	0.257	0.208	0.168	0.137	0.112	0.092	0.076	0.062	0.052	0.043	0.018
13	0.601	0.530	0.469	0.368	0.290	0.229	0.182	0.145	0.116	0.093	0.075	0.061	0.050	0.040	0.033	0.013
14	0.577	0.505	0.442	0.340	0.263	0.205	0.160	0.125	0.099	0.078	0.062	0.049	0.039	0.032	0.025	0.009
15	0.555	0.481	0.417	0.315	0.239	0.183	0.140	0.108	0.084	0.065	0.051	0.040	0.031	0.025	0.020	0.006
16	0.534	0.458	0.394	0.292	0.218	0.163	0.123	0.093	0.071	0.054	0.042	0.032	0.025	0.019	0.015	0.005
17	0.513	0.436	0.371	0.270	0.198	0.146	0.108	0.080	0.060	0.045	0.034	0.026	0.020	0.015	0.012	0.003
18	0.494	0.416	0.350	0.250	0.180	0.130	0.095	0.069	0.051	0.038	0.028	0.021	0.016	0.012	0.009	0.002
19	0.475	0.396	0.331	0.232	0.164	0.116	0.083	0.060	0.043	0.031	0.023	0.017	0.012	0.009	0.007	0.002
20	0.456	0.377	0.312	0.215	0.149	0.104	0.073	0.051	0.037	0.026	0.019	0.014	0.010	0.007	0.005	0.001
21	0.439	0.359	0.294	0.199	0.135	0.093	0.064	0.044	0.031	0.022	0.015	0.011	0.008	0.006	0.004	0.001
22	0.422	0.342	0.278	0.184	0.123	0.083	0.056	0.038	0.026	0.018	0.013	0.009	0.006	0.004	0.003	0.001
23	0.406	0.326	0.262	0.170	0.112	0.074	0.049	0.033	0.022	0.015	0.010	0.007	0.005	0.003	0.002	
24	0.390	0.310	0.247	0.158	0.102	0.066	0.043	0.028	0.019	0.013	0.008	0.006	0.004	0.003	0.002	
25	0.375	0.295	0.233	0.146	0.092	0.059	0.038	0.024	0.016	0.010	0.007	0.005	0.004	0.003	0.002	
26	0.361	0.281	0.220	0.135	0.084	0.053	0.033	0.021	0.014	0.009	0.006	0.004	0.003	0.002	0.001	
27	0.347	0.268	0.207	0.125	0.076	0.047	0.029	0.018	0.011	0.007	0.005	0.003	0.002	0.002	0.001	
28	0.333	0.255	0.196	0.116	0.069	0.042	0.026	0.016	0.010	0.006	0.004	0.002	0.002	0.001	0.001	
29	0.321	0.243	0.185	0.107	0.063	0.037	0.022	0.014	0.008	0.005	0.003	0.002	0.001	0.001	0.001	
30	0.308	0.231	0.174	0.099	0.057	0.033	0.020	0.012	0.007	0.004	0.003	0.002	0.001	0.001	0.001	
40	0.208	0.142	0.097	0.046	0.022	0.011	0.005	0.003	0.001	0.001						

TABLE 4 Present Value of Annuity of $1

PVIFA (i,n)

Periods	4%	5%	6%	8%	10%	12%	14%	16%	18%	20%	22%	24%	26%	28%	30%	40%
1	0.962	0.952	0.943	0.926	0.909	0.893	0.877	0.862	0.847	0.833	0.820	0.806	0.794	0.781	0.769	0.714
2	1.886	1.859	1.833	1.783	1.736	1.690	1.647	1.605	1.566	1.528	1.492	1.457	1.424	1.392	1.361	1.224
3	2.775	2.723	2.673	2.577	2.487	2.402	2.322	2.246	2.174	2.106	2.042	1.981	1.868	1.816	1.816	1.589
4	3.630	3.546	3.465	3.312	3.170	3.037	2.914	2.798	2.690	2.589	2.494	2.404	2.320	2.241	2.166	1.879
5	4.452	4.330	4.212	3.993	3.791	3.605	3.433	3.274	3.127	2.991	2.864	2.745	2.635	2.532	2.436	2.035
6	5.242	5.076	4.917	4.623	4.355	4.111	3.889	3.685	3.498	3.326	3.167	3.020	2.885	2.759	2.643	2.168
7	6.002	5.786	5.582	5.206	4.868	4.564	4.288	4.039	3.812	3.605	3.416	3.242	3.083	2.937	2.802	2.263
8	6.733	6.463	6.210	5.747	5.335	4.968	4.639	4.344	4.078	3.837	3.619	3.421	3.241	3.076	2.925	2.331
9	7.435	7.108	6.802	6.247	5.759	5.328	4.946	4.607	4.303	4.031	3.786	3.566	3.366	3.184	3.019	2.379
10	8.111	7.722	7.360	6.710	6.145	5.650	5.216	4.833	4.494	4.192	3.923	3.682	3.465	3.269	3.092	2.414
11	8.760	8.306	7.887	7.139	6.495	5.988	5.453	5.029	4.656	4.327	4.035	3.776	3.544	3.335	3.147	2.438
12	9.385	8.863	8.384	7.536	6.814	6.194	5.660	5.197	4.793	4.439	4.127	3.851	3.606	3.387	3.190	2.456
13	9.986	9.394	8.853	7.904	7.103	6.424	5.842	5.342	4.910	4.533	4.203	3.912	3.656	3.427	3.223	2.468
14	10.563	9.899	9.295	8.244	7.367	6.628	6.002	5.468	5.008	4.611	4.265	3.962	3.695	3.459	3.249	2.477
15	11.118	10.380	9.712	8.559	7.606	6.811	6.142	5.575	5.092	4.675	4.315	4.001	3.726	3.483	3.268	2.484
16	11.652	10.838	10.106	8.851	7.824	6.974	6.265	5.669	5.162	4.730	4.357	4.033	3.751	3.503	3.283	2.489
17	12.166	11.274	10.477	9.122	8.022	7.120	6.373	5.749	5.222	4.775	4.391	4.059	3.771	3.518	3.295	2.492
18	12.659	11.690	10.828	9.372	8.201	7.250	6.467	5.818	5.273	4.812	4.419	4.080	3.786	3.529	3.304	2.494
19	13.134	12.085	11.158	9.604	8.365	7.366	6.550	5.877	5.316	4.844	4.442	4.097	3.799	3.539	3.311	2.496
20	13.590	12.462	11.470	9.818	8.514	7.469	6.623	5.929	5.353	4.870	4.460	4.110	3.808	3.546	3.316	2.497
21	14.029	12.821	11.764	10.017	8.649	7.562	6.687	5.973	5.384	4.891	4.476	4.121	3.816	3.551	3.320	2.498
22	14.451	13.163	12.042	10.201	8.772	7.645	6.743	6.011	5.410	4.909	4.488	4.130	3.822	3.556	3.323	2.498
23	14.857	13.489	12.303	10.371	8.883	7.718	6.792	6.044	5.432	4.925	4.499	4.137	3.827	3.559	3.325	2.499
24	15.247	13.799	12.550	10.529	8.985	7.784	6.835	6.073	5.451	4.937	4.507	4.143	3.831	3.562	3.327	2.499
25	15.622	14.094	12.783	10.675	9.077	7.843	6.873	6.097	5.467	4.948	4.514	4.147	3.834	3.564	3.329	2.499
26	15.983	14.375	13.003	10.810	9.161	7.896	6.906	6.118	5.480	4.956	4.520	4.151	3.837	3.566	3.330	2.500
27	16.330	14.643	13.211	10.935	9.237	7.943	6.935	6.136	5.492	4.964	4.525	4.154	3.839	3.567	3.331	2.500
28	16.663	14.898	13.406	11.051	9.307	7.984	6.961	6.152	5.502	4.970	4.528	4.157	3.840	3.568	3.331	2.500
29	16.984	15.141	13.591	11.158	9.370	8.022	6.983	6.166	5.510	4.975	4.531	4.159	3.841	3.569	3.332	2.500
30	17.292	15.373	13.765	11.258	9.427	8.055	7.003	6.177	5.517	4.979	4.534	4.160	3.842	3.569	3.332	2.500
40	19.793	17.159	15.046	11.925	9.779	8.244	7.105	6.234	5.548	4.997	4.544	4.166	3.846	3.571	3.333	2.500

TABLE 5 Monthly Installment Loan Payments (to Repay a $1000, Simple-Interest Loan)

Rate of interest	Loan term						
	6 Months	12 Months	18 Months	24 Months	36 Months	48 Months	60 Months
7½%	$170.33	$86.76	$58.92	$45.00	$31.11	$24.18	$20.05
8	170.58	86.99	59.15	45.23	31.34	24.42	20.28
8½	170.82	87.22	59.37	45.46	31.57	24.65	20.52
9	171.07	87.46	59.60	45.69	31.80	24.89	20.76
9½	171.32	87.69	59.83	45.92	32.04	25.13	21.01
10	171.56	87.92	60.06	46.15	32.27	25.37	21.25
10½	171.81	88.15	60.29	46.38	32.51	25.61	21.50
11	172.05	88.50	60.64	46.73	32.86	25.97	21.87
11½	172.30	88.62	60.76	46.85	32.98	26.09	22.00
12	172.55	88.85	60.99	47.08	33.22	26.34	22.25
12½	172.80	89.09	61.22	47.31	33.46	26.58	22.50
13	173.04	89.32	61.45	47.55	33.70	26.83	22.76
14	173.54	89.79	61.92	48.02	34.18	27.33	23.27
15	174.03	90.26	62.39	48.49	34.67	27.84	23.79
16	174.53	90.74	62.86	48.97	35.16	28.35	24.32
17	175.03	91.21	63.34	49.45	35.66	28.86	24.86
18	175.53	91.68	63.81	49.93	36.16	29.38	25.40

TABLE 6   Normal Distribution Table

Areas under the normal curve

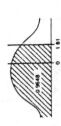

z	0	1	2	3	4	5	6	7	8	9
0.0	0.5000	0.5040	0.5080	0.5120	0.5160	0.5199	0.5239	0.5279	0.5319	0.5359
0.1	0.5398	0.5438	0.5478	0.5517	0.5557	0.5596	0.5636	0.5675	0.5714	0.5753
0.2	0.5793	0.5832	0.5871	0.5910	0.5948	0.5987	0.6026	0.6064	0.6103	0.6141
0.3	0.6179	0.6217	0.6255	0.6293	0.6331	0.6368	0.6406	0.6443	0.6480	0.6517
0.4	0.6554	0.6591	0.6628	0.6664	0.6700	0.6736	0.6772	0.6808	0.6844	0.6879
0.5	0.6915	0.6950	0.6985	0.7019	0.7054	0.7088	0.7123	0.7157	0.7190	0.7224
0.6	0.7257	0.7291	0.7324	0.7357	0.7389	0.7422	0.7454	0.7486	0.7517	0.7549
0.7	0.7580	0.7611	0.7642	0.7673	0.7703	0.7734	0.7764	0.7794	0.7823	0.7852
0.8	0.7881	0.7910	0.7939	0.7967	0.7995	0.8023	0.8051	0.8078	0.8106	0.8133
0.9	0.8159	0.8186	0.8212	0.8238	0.8264	0.8289	0.8315	0.8340	0.8365	0.8389
1.0	0.8413	0.8438	0.8461	0.8485	0.8508	0.8531	0.8554	0.8577	0.8599	0.8621
1.1	0.8643	0.8665	0.8686	0.8708	0.8729	0.8749	0.8770	0.8790	0.8810	0.8830
1.2	0.8849	0.8869	0.8888	0.8907	0.8925	0.8944	0.8962	0.8980	0.8997	0.9015
1.3	0.9032	0.9049	0.9066	0.9082	0.9099	0.9115	0.9131	0.9147	0.9162	0.9177
1.4	0.9192	0.9207	0.9222	0.9236	0.9251	0.9265	0.9278	0.9292	0.9306	0.9319
1.5	0.9332	0.9345	0.9357	0.9370	0.9382	0.9394	0.9406	0.9418	0.9430	0.9441
1.6	0.9452	0.9463	0.9474	0.9484	0.9495	0.9505	0.9515	0.9525	0.9535	0.9545
1.7	0.9554	0.9564	0.9573	0.9582	0.9591	0.9599	0.9608	0.9616	0.9625	0.9633
1.8	0.9641	0.9648	0.9656	0.9664	0.9671	0.9678	0.9686	0.9693	0.9700	0.9706
1.9	0.9713	0.9719	0.9726	0.9732	0.9738	0.9744	0.9750	0.9756	0.9762	0.9767
2.0	0.9772	0.9778	0.9783	0.9788	0.9793	0.9798	0.9803	0.9808	0.9812	0.9817
2.1	0.9821	0.9826	0.9830	0.9834	0.9838	0.9842	0.9846	0.9850	0.9854	0.9857
2.2	0.9861	0.9864	0.9868	0.9871	0.9874	0.9878	0.9881	0.9884	0.9887	0.9890
2.3	0.9893	0.9896	0.9898	0.9901	0.9904	0.9906	0.9909	0.9911	0.9913	0.9916
2.4	0.9918	0.9920	0.9922	0.9925	0.9927	0.9929	0.9931	0.9932	0.9934	0.9936
2.5	0.9938	0.9940	0.9941	0.9943	0.9945	0.9946	0.9948	0.9949	0.9951	0.9952
2.6	0.9953	0.9955	0.9956	0.9957	0.9959	0.9960	0.9961	0.9962	0.9963	0.9964
2.7	0.9965	0.9966	0.9967	0.9968	0.9969	0.9970	0.9971	0.9972	0.9973	0.9974
2.8	0.9974	0.9975	0.9976	0.9977	0.9977	0.9978	0.9979	0.9979	0.9980	0.9981
2.9	0.9981	0.9982	0.9982	0.9983	0.9984	0.9984	0.9985	0.9985	0.9986	0.9986
3.0	0.9987	0.9990	0.9993	0.9995	0.9997	0.9998	0.9998	0.9999	0.9999	1.0000

TABLE 7   *t*-Distribution Table

Values of *t*

d.f.	$t0.100$	$t0.050$	$t0.025$	$t0.010$	$t0.005$	d.f.
1	3.078	6.314	12.706	31.821	63.657	1
2	1.886	2.920	4.303	6.965	9.925	2
3	1.638	2.353	3.182	4.541	5.841	3
4	1.533	2.132	2.776	3.747	4.604	4
5	1.476	2.015	2.571	3.365	4.032	5
6	1.440	1.943	2.447	3.143	3.707	6
7	1.415	1.895	2.365	2.998	3.499	7
8	1.397	1.860	2.306	2.896	3.355	8
9	1.383	1.833	2.262	2.821	3.250	9
10	1.372	1.812	2.228	2.764	3.169	10
11	1.363	1.796	2.201	2.718	3.106	11
12	1.356	1.782	2.179	2.681	3.055	12
13	1.350	1.771	2.160	2.650	3.012	13
14	1.345	1.761	2.145	2.624	2.977	14
15	1.341	1.753	2.131	2.602	2.947	15
16	1.337	1.746	2.120	2.583	2.921	16
17	1.333	1.740	2.110	2.567	2.898	17
18	1.330	1.734	2.101	2.552	2.878	18
19	1.328	1.729	2.093	2.539	2.861	19
20	1.325	1.725	2.086	2.528	2.845	20
21	1.323	1.721	2.080	2.518	2.831	21
22	1.321	1.717	2.074	2.508	2.819	22
23	1.319	1.714	2.069	2.500	2.807	23
24	1.318	1.711	2.064	2.492	2.797	24
25	1.316	1.708	2.060	2.485	2.787	25
26	1.315	1.706	2.056	2.479	2.779	26
27	1.314	1.703	2.052	2.473	2.771	27
28	1.313	1.701	2.048	2.467	2.763	28
29	1.311	1.699	2.045	2.462	2.756	29
Inf.	1.282	1.645	1.960	2.326	2.576	Inf.

The *t*-value describes the sampling distribution of a deviation from a population value divided by the standard error.

Degrees of freedom (d.f.) are in the first column. The probabilities indicated as subvalues of *t* in the heading refer to the sum of a one-tailed area under the curve that lies outside the point *t*.

For example, in the distribution of the means of samples of size $n = 10$, d.f. $= n - 2 = 8$; then 0.025 of the area under the curve falls in one tail outside the interval $t \pm 2.306$.

TABLE 8 Area in the Right Tail of a Chi-Square (χ^2) Distribution

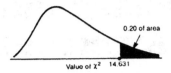

Example: In a chi-square distribution with 11 degrees of freedom, find the appropriate chi-square value for 0.20 of the area under the curve (the shaded area in the right tail), look under the 0.20 column in the table and proceed down to the 11 degrees of freedom row; the appropriate chi-square value there is 14.631

Degrees of freedom	Area in right tail				
	0.99	0.975	0.95	0.90	0.800
1	0.00016	0.00098	0.00398	0.0158	0.0642
2	0.0201	0.0506	0.103	0.211	0.446
3	0.115	0.216	0.352	0.584	1.005
4	0.297	0.484	0.711	1.064	1.649
5	0.554	0.831	1.145	1.610	2.343
6	0.872	1.237	1.635	2.204	3.070
7	1.239	1.690	2.167	2.833	3.822
8	1.646	2.180	2.733	3.490	4.594
9	2.088	2.700	3.325	4.168	5.380
10	2.558	3.247	3.940	4.865	6.179
11	3.053	3.816	4.575	5.578	6.989
12	3.571	4.404	5.226	6.304	7.807
13	4.107	5.009	5.892	7.042	8.634
14	4.660	5.629	6.571	7.790	9.467
15	5.229	6.262	7.261	8.547	10.307
16	5.812	6.908	7.962	9.312	11.152
17	6.408	7.564	8.672	10.085	12.002
18	7.015	8.231	9.390	10.865	12.857
19	7.633	8.907	10.117	11.651	13.716
20	8.260	9.591	10.851	12.443	14.578
21	8.897	10.283	11.591	13.240	15.445
22	9.542	10.982	12.338	14.041	16.314
23	10.196	11.689	13.091	14.848	17.187
24	10.856	12.401	13.848	15.658	18.062
25	11.524	13.120	14.611	16.473	18.940
26	12.198	13.844	15.379	17.292	19.820
27	12.879	14.573	16.151	18.114	20.703
28	13.565	15.308	16.928	18.939	21.588
29	14.256	16.047	17.708	19.768	22.475
30	14.953	16.791	18.493	20.599	23.364

TABLE 9 Values of *F* for *F* Distributions with 0.05 of the Area in the Right Tail

Example: For a test at a significance level of 0.05 where there are 15 degrees of freedom for the numerator and 6 degrees of freedom for the denominator, the appropriate *F* value is found by looking under the 15 degrees of freedom column and proceeding down to the 6 degrees of freedom row; there one finds the appropriate *F* value to be 3.94.

0.05 of area

3.94

d.f. for denom-inator	\multicolumn{19}{c}{Degrees of freedom for numerator}
	1	2	3	4	5	6	7	8	9	10	12	15	20	24	30	40	60	120	∞
1	161	200	216	225	230	234	237	239	241	242	244	246	248	249	250	251	252	253	254
2	18.5	19.0	19.2	19.2	19.3	19.3	19.4	19.4	19.4	19.4	19.4	19.4	19.4	19.5	19.5	19.5	19.5	19.5	19.5
3	10.1	9.55	9.28	9.12	9.01	8.94	8.89	8.85	8.81	8.79	8.74	8.70	8.66	8.64	8.62	8.59	8.57	8.55	8.53
4	7.71	6.94	6.59	6.39	6.26	6.16	6.09	6.04	6.00	5.96	5.91	5.86	5.80	5.77	5.75	5.72	5.69	5.66	5.63
5	6.61	5.79	5.41	5.19	5.05	4.95	4.88	4.82	4.77	4.74	4.68	4.62	4.56	4.53	4.50	4.46	4.43	4.40	4.37
6	5.99	5.14	4.76	4.53	4.39	4.28	4.21	4.15	4.10	4.06	4.00	3.94	3.87	3.84	3.81	3.77	3.74	3.70	3.67
7	5.59	4.74	4.35	4.12	3.97	3.87	3.79	3.73	3.68	3.64	3.57	3.51	3.44	3.41	3.38	3.34	3.30	3.27	3.23
8	5.32	4.46	4.07	3.84	3.69	3.58	3.50	3.44	3.39	3.35	3.28	3.22	3.15	3.12	3.08	3.04	3.01	2.97	2.93
9	5.12	4.26	3.86	3.63	3.48	3.37	3.29	3.23	3.18	3.14	3.07	3.01	2.94	2.90	2.86	2.83	2.79	2.75	2.71
10	4.96	4.10	3.71	3.48	3.33	3.22	3.14	3.07	3.02	2.98	2.91	2.85	2.77	2.74	2.70	2.66	2.62	2.58	2.54
11	4.84	3.98	3.59	3.36	3.20	3.09	3.01	2.95	2.90	2.85	2.79	2.72	2.65	2.61	2.57	2.53	2.49	2.45	2.40
12	4.75	3.89	3.49	3.26	3.11	3.00	2.91	2.85	2.80	2.75	2.69	2.62	2.54	2.51	2.47	2.43	2.38	2.34	2.30
13	4.67	3.81	3.41	3.18	3.03	2.92	2.83	2.77	2.71	2.67	2.60	2.53	2.46	2.42	2.38	2.34	2.30	2.25	2.21
14	4.60	3.74	3.34	3.11	2.96	2.85	2.76	2.70	2.65	2.60	2.53	2.46	2.39	2.35	2.31	2.27	2.22	2.18	2.13
15	4.54	3.68	3.29	3.06	2.90	2.79	2.71	2.64	2.59	2.54	2.48	2.40	2.33	2.29	2.25	2.20	2.16	2.11	2.07
16	4.49	3.63	3.24	3.01	2.85	2.74	2.66	2.59	2.54	2.49	2.42	2.35	2.28	2.24	2.19	2.15	2.11	2.06	2.01
17	4.45	3.59	3.20	2.96	2.81	2.70	2.61	2.55	2.49	2.45	2.38	2.31	2.23	2.19	2.15	2.10	2.06	2.01	1.96
18	4.41	3.55	3.16	2.93	2.77	2.66	2.58	2.51	2.46	2.41	2.34	2.27	2.19	2.15	2.11	2.06	2.02	1.97	1.92
19	4.38	3.52	3.13	2.90	2.74	2.63	2.54	2.48	2.42	2.38	2.31	2.23	2.16	2.11	2.07	2.03	1.98	1.93	1.88
20	4.35	3.49	3.10	2.87	2.71	2.60	2.51	2.45	2.39	2.35	2.28	2.20	2.12	2.08	2.04	1.99	1.95	1.90	1.84
21	4.32	3.47	3.07	2.84	2.68	2.57	2.49	2.42	2.37	2.32	2.25	2.18	2.10	2.05	2.01	1.96	1.92	1.87	1.81
22	4.30	3.44	3.05	2.82	2.66	2.55	2.46	2.40	2.34	2.30	2.23	2.15	2.07	2.03	1.98	1.94	1.89	1.84	1.78
23	4.28	3.42	3.03	2.80	2.64	2.53	2.44	2.37	2.32	2.27	2.20	2.13	2.05	2.01	1.96	1.91	1.86	1.81	1.76
24	4.26	3.40	3.01	2.78	2.62	2.51	2.42	2.36	2.30	2.25	2.18	2.11	2.03	1.98	1.94	1.89	1.84	1.79	1.73
25	4.24	3.39	2.99	2.76	2.60	2.49	2.40	2.34	2.28	2.24	2.16	2.09	2.01	1.96	1.92	1.87	1.82	1.77	1.71
30	4.17	3.32	2.92	2.69	2.53	2.42	2.33	2.27	2.21	2.16	2.09	2.01	1.93	1.89	1.84	1.79	1.74	1.68	1.62
40	4.08	3.23	2.84	2.61	2.45	2.34	2.25	2.18	2.12	2.08	2.00	1.92	1.84	1.79	1.74	1.69	1.64	1.58	1.51
60	4.00	3.15	2.76	2.53	2.37	2.25	2.17	2.10	2.04	1.99	1.92	1.84	1.75	1.70	1.65	1.59	1.53	1.47	1.39
120	3.92	3.07	2.68	2.45	2.29	2.18	2.09	2.02	1.96	1.91	1.83	1.75	1.66	1.61	1.55	1.50	1.43	1.35	1.25
∞	3.84	3.00	2.60	2.37	2.21	2.10	2.01	1.94	1.88	1.83	1.75	1.67	1.57	1.52	1.46	1.39	1.32	1.22	1.00

TABLE 9 (Continued) Values of *F* for *F* Distributions with 0.01 of the Area in the Right Tail

Example: For a test at a significance level of 0.01 where there are 7 degrees of freedom for the numerator and 5 degrees of freedom for the denominator, the appropriate *F* value is found by looking under the 7 degrees of freedom column and proceeding down to the 5 degrees of freedom row; there one finds the appropriate *F* value to be 10.5.

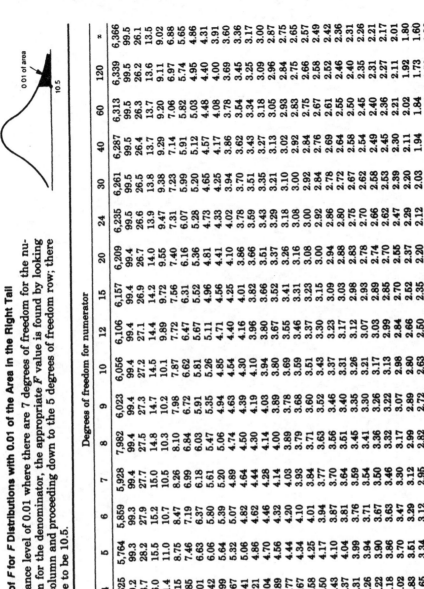

0.01 of area

10.5

d.f. for denominator	Degrees of freedom for numerator																		
	1	2	3	4	5	6	7	8	9	10	12	15	20	24	30	40	60	120	∞
1	4,052	5,000	5,403	5,625	5,764	5,859	5,928	5,982	6,023	6,056	6,106	6,157	6,209	6,235	6,261	6,287	6,313	6,339	6,366
2	98.5	99.0	99.2	99.2	99.3	99.3	99.4	99.4	99.4	99.4	99.4	99.4	99.4	99.5	99.5	99.5	99.5	99.5	99.5
3	34.1	30.8	29.5	28.7	28.2	27.9	27.7	27.5	27.3	27.2	27.1	26.9	26.7	26.6	26.5	26.4	26.3	26.2	26.1
4	21.2	18.0	16.7	16.0	15.5	15.2	15.0	14.8	14.7	14.5	14.4	14.2	14.0	13.9	13.8	13.7	13.7	13.6	13.5
5	16.3	13.3	12.1	11.4	11.0	10.7	10.5	10.3	10.2	10.1	9.89	9.72	9.55	9.47	9.38	9.29	9.20	9.11	9.02
6	13.7	10.9	9.78	9.15	8.75	8.47	8.26	8.10	7.98	7.87	7.72	7.56	7.40	7.31	7.23	7.14	7.06	6.97	6.88
7	12.2	9.55	8.45	7.85	7.46	7.19	6.99	6.84	6.72	6.62	6.47	6.31	6.16	6.07	5.99	5.91	5.82	5.74	5.65
8	11.3	8.65	7.59	7.01	6.63	6.37	6.18	6.03	5.91	5.81	5.67	5.52	5.36	5.28	5.20	5.12	5.03	4.95	4.86
9	10.6	8.02	6.99	6.42	6.06	5.80	5.61	5.47	5.35	5.26	5.11	4.96	4.81	4.73	4.65	4.57	4.48	4.40	4.31
10	10.0	7.56	6.55	5.99	5.64	5.39	5.20	5.06	4.94	4.85	4.71	4.56	4.41	4.33	4.25	4.17	4.08	4.00	3.91
11	9.65	7.21	6.22	5.67	5.32	5.07	4.89	4.74	4.63	4.54	4.40	4.25	4.10	4.02	3.94	3.86	3.78	3.69	3.60
12	9.33	6.93	5.95	5.41	5.06	4.82	4.64	4.50	4.39	4.30	4.16	4.01	3.86	3.78	3.70	3.62	3.54	3.45	3.36
13	9.07	6.70	5.74	5.21	4.86	4.62	4.44	4.30	4.19	4.10	3.96	3.82	3.66	3.59	3.51	3.43	3.34	3.25	3.17
14	8.86	6.51	5.56	5.04	4.70	4.46	4.28	4.14	4.03	3.94	3.80	3.66	3.51	3.43	3.35	3.27	3.18	3.09	3.00
15	8.68	6.36	5.42	4.89	4.56	4.32	4.14	4.00	3.89	3.80	3.67	3.52	3.37	3.29	3.21	3.13	3.05	2.96	2.87
16	8.53	6.23	5.29	4.77	4.44	4.20	4.03	3.89	3.78	3.69	3.55	3.41	3.26	3.18	3.10	3.02	2.93	2.84	2.75
17	8.40	6.11	5.19	4.67	4.34	4.10	3.93	3.79	3.68	3.59	3.46	3.31	3.16	3.08	3.00	2.92	2.83	2.75	2.65
18	8.29	6.01	5.09	4.58	4.25	4.01	3.84	3.71	3.60	3.51	3.37	3.23	3.08	3.00	2.92	2.84	2.75	2.66	2.57
19	8.19	5.93	5.01	4.50	4.17	3.94	3.77	3.63	3.52	3.43	3.30	3.15	3.00	2.92	2.84	2.76	2.67	2.58	2.49
20	8.10	5.85	4.94	4.43	4.10	3.87	3.70	3.56	3.46	3.37	3.23	3.09	2.94	2.86	2.78	2.69	2.61	2.52	2.42
21	8.02	5.78	4.87	4.37	4.04	3.81	3.64	3.51	3.40	3.31	3.17	3.03	2.88	2.80	2.72	2.64	2.55	2.46	2.36
22	7.95	5.72	4.82	4.31	3.99	3.76	3.59	3.45	3.35	3.26	3.12	2.98	2.83	2.75	2.67	2.58	2.50	2.40	2.31
23	7.88	5.66	4.76	4.26	3.94	3.71	3.54	3.41	3.30	3.21	3.07	2.93	2.78	2.70	2.62	2.54	2.45	2.35	2.26
24	7.82	5.61	4.72	4.22	3.90	3.67	3.50	3.36	3.26	3.17	3.03	2.89	2.74	2.66	2.58	2.49	2.40	2.31	2.21
25	7.77	5.57	4.68	4.18	3.86	3.63	3.46	3.32	3.22	3.13	2.99	2.85	2.70	2.62	2.53	2.45	2.36	2.27	2.17
30	7.56	5.39	4.51	4.02	3.70	3.47	3.30	3.17	3.07	2.98	2.84	2.70	2.55	2.47	2.39	2.30	2.21	2.11	2.01
40	7.31	5.18	4.31	3.83	3.51	3.29	3.12	2.99	2.89	2.80	2.66	2.52	2.37	2.29	2.20	2.11	2.02	1.92	1.80
60	7.08	4.98	4.13	3.65	3.34	3.12	2.95	2.82	2.72	2.63	2.50	2.35	2.20	2.12	2.03	1.94	1.84	1.73	1.60
120	6.85	4.79	3.95	3.48	3.17	2.96	2.79	2.66	2.56	2.47	2.34	2.19	2.03	1.95	1.86	1.76	1.66	1.53	1.38
∞	6.63	4.61	3.78	3.32	3.02	2.80	2.64	2.51	2.41	2.32	2.18	2.04	1.88	1.79	1.70	1.59	1.47	1.32	1.00

Index